PRINCIPLES OF MARKETING

PRINCIPLES OF **MARKETING**
A VALUE–BASED APPROACH

Edited by

Ayantunji Gbadamosi
Senior Lecturer, University of East London

Ian K. Bathgate
Principal Lecturer, University of East London

Sonny Nwankwo
Professor of Marketing, University of East London

First published 2013 by
PALGRAVE MACMILLAN

Palgrave Macmillan in the UK is an imprint of Macmillan Publishers Limited,
registered in England, company number 785998, of Houndmills, Basingstoke,
Hampshire RG21 6XS.

Palgrave Macmillan in the US is a division of St Martin's Press LLC,
175 Fifth Avenue, New York, NY 10010.

Palgrave Macmillan is the global academic imprint of the above companies
and has companies and representatives throughout the world.

Palgrave® and Macmillan® are registered trademarks in the United States,
the United Kingdom, Europe and other countries

ISBN: 978-0-230-39270-0 paperback

This book is printed on paper suitable for recycling and made from fully
managed and sustained forest sources. Logging, pulping and manufacturing
processes are expected to conform to the environmental regulations of the
country of origin.

A catalogue record for this book is available from the British Library.

A catalog record for this book is available from the Library of Congress.

SHORT CONTENTS

Ayantunji Gbadamosi, Ian K. Bathgate & Sonny Nwankwo (*University of East London*)

Peter Gruenwald Taylor (*Amity University in London*)

Hina Khan (*Northumbria University*)

Ayantunji Gbadamosi (*University of East London*) & Kaushik V. Pandya
(*Sheffield Hallam University*)

CONTENTS

1 THE PURPOSE OF MARKETING 1

Ayantunji Gbadamosi, Ian K. Bathgate & Sonny Nwankwo (*University of East London*)

2 UNDERSTANDING THE MARKETING ENVIRONMENT 25

Peter Gruenwald Taylor (*Amity University in London*)

3   CONSUMER BUYING BEHAVIOUR 71

Hina Khan (*Northumbria University*)

4   MANAGING MARKETING INFORMATION FOR VALUE CREATION 103

Ayantunji Gbadamosi (*University of East London*) & **Kaushik V. Pandya**
(*Sheffield Hallam University*)

5   MARKETING STRATEGY: SEGMENTATION, TARGETING AND POSITIONING 139

Uzoamaka Anozie (*Bournemouth University*)

6 THE PRODUCT AS A POINT OF VALUE 165

Maktoba Omar & Collins Osei (*Edinburgh Napier University*), Robert L. Williams Jr., (*Saint Mary's College, Notre Dame*) & Helena A. Williams (*Mar-Kadam Marketing Associates, Baltimore*)

7 PRICING STRATEGIES 201

Emmanuel Ohohe (*London Metropolitan University*)

8 VALUE−ADDED DISTRIBUTION STRATEGIES 231

Dulekha Kasturiratne & Hugh D. Conway (*University of Plymouth*)

9 MARKETING COMMUNICATIONS STRATEGIES 255

Linda Phillips & Sue Clews (*Staffordshsire University*)

LIST OF FIGURES

5   MARKETING STRATEGY: SEGMENTATION, TARGETING AND POSITIONING

6   THE PRODUCT AS A POINT OF VALUE

7   PRICING STRATEGIES

8   VALUE-ADDED DISTRIBUTION STRATEGIES

9   MARKETING COMMUNICATIONS STRATEGIES

10   SERVICES MARKETING

11   MARKETING PLANNING FOR VALUE DELIVERY

12   MARKETING IN A GLOBAL CONTEXT

13   SOCIAL MEDIA MARKETING

LIST OF TABLES

11 MARKETING PLANNING FOR VALUE DELIVERY

12 MARKETING IN A GLOBAL CONTEXT

EDITORS' ACKNOWLEDGEMENTS

For quite some time, concerns have been expressed about how marketing knowledge is produced, taught and disseminated by marketing academics. Such concerns reflect fundamental epistemological and pedagogical issues, some of which have to do with how teaching resources are prepared and presented in order to effectively engage students in their own learning. Increasingly, the transaction-oriented and '4Ps-centric' approaches are being debated, resulting in a broad-based acknowledgement that more innovative approaches need to be employed in order to scale up learner/practitioner capabilities in the face of the dynamically changing contours of modern marketing. To this end, there has been strong advocacy within the marketing profession for a value orientation, both in the teaching and practice of marketing.

The book puts together, in a pedagogical manner, contributions and student-focused resources aimed at illuminating the field of marketing and, very importantly, charting new directions for teaching the subject. Essentially, it is hoped that the book will:

● help students develop a coherent understanding of the basic underpinnings of marketing, with value composition, creation, delivery and maintenance as central tenets; and
● provide students with a basic understanding of how marketing principles can be applied in practical settings to create superior value for both customers and organisations.

Each chapter has been written by subject specialists who also teach and research marketing in various higher education institutions. As editors, we are greatly indebted to these colleagues – the book would not have been possible without the strong commitment and enthusiasm they have demonstrated during every stage of its preparation. They are, indeed, great scholars to work with and we congratulate each and every one of them on their valuable contributions.

We also acknowledge, with gratitude, the assistance afforded by our working partners at Palgrave Macmillan, especially Martin Drewe and Ceri Griffiths – their support has been immeasurable and it has been a pleasure working with them.

Finally, and most importantly, we acknowledge our students, who are always very keen to discuss marketing issues with us and thereby ensure teaching the subject remains interesting and rewarding. We dedicate this book to them and hope they will find it stimulating.

Dr Ayantunji Gbadamosi
Ian K. Bathgate
Professor Sonny Nwankwo
University of East London

PUBLISHER'S ACKNOWLEDGEMENTS

The author and publishers would like to thank the following for permission to reproduce copyright material:

Elsevier for Figure 1.1 from Lindgreen, A., Hingley, M., Grant, D. and Morgan, R. (2012) 'Value in Business and Industrial Marketing: Past, Present and Future', *Industrial Marketing Management*, 41, pp. 207–14, Figure 3.6 from Ajzen, I. (1991) 'The Theory of Planned Behavior', *Organizational Behavior and Human Decision Processes*, 50, pp. 179–211 and Figure 11.4 from Freytag, P. V. and Clarke, A. H. (2001) 'Business to Business Market Segmentation', *Industrial Marketing Management*, 30 (6) pp. 473–86

Tribune Media Services International for Figure 1.2 from Day, G. (2003) *Creating a Superior Customer-relating Capability*. Marketing Science Institute, MSI, Working Paper No. 03–001

Taylor and Francis for Figure 1.6 from Gbadamosi, A. (2011) 'Entrepreneurship Marketing Environment', in S. Nwankwo and A. Gbadamosi (eds) *'Entrepreneurship Marketing: Principles and Practice of SME Marketing'*. (Oxfordshire: Routledge) and Table 11.9 from Ambler, T., Kokkinaki, F., and Puntoni, S. (2004) 'Assessing Marketing Performance: Reasons for Metrics Selection', *Journal of Marketing Management*, 20, pp. 475–98

Marks and Spencer for the screenshot in Box 1.3

Academy of Management for Figure 2.5 from Carroll, A. (2004) 'Managing ethically with global stakeholders: A present and future challenge', *Academy of Management Perspectives*, 18 (2), pp. 114-120

Philosophy Documentation Centre for Figure 2.6 from Schwartz, M. and Carroll, A. (2003) 'Corporate Social Responsibility: A Three Domain Approach', *Business Ethics Quarterly*, 1 (4), pp. 503–30

John Wiley and Sons for Figure 2.8 from Belz, F-M. and Peattie, K. (2009) *Sustainability Marketing*. (Oxford: Wiley), Figure 4.9 from Aaker, D., Kumar, V., Day, G. and Leone, R. (2010) *Marketing Research 10th edition* (New Jersey: Wiley) and Table 6.1 from Aaker, D. A., Kumar, V. and Day, G. S. (1995) *Marketing Research 5th edition* (Chichester: John Wiley and Sons)

Pearson Education for Figure 3.1 and Figure 3.3 from Kotler, P. and Keller, K. L. (2007) *A Framework for Marketing Management*. (New York, NY: Pearson Prentice Hall) and Figure 9.8 from Kotler, P. and Keller, K. (2006) *Marketing Management 9th edition* (Upper Saddle River, NJ: Pearson Prentice Hall)

University of East London for image of page 90

Adidas for the logo on page 104

Ramsey Moore for the image in Example 4.1

VDM Publishing Group for Table 4.2 and Figure 4.8 from Gbadamosi, A. (2010) *Low-income Consumer Behaviour: A Contextual Focus on Women and Low-involvement Grocery Products*. (Saarbrücken: Lambert Academic Publishing)

Debenhams for the image on page 134

Morrisons for the logo on page 169

Samsung for the logo on page 197

Cengage for Figure 7.1 and Table 7.4 from Dibb, S., Simkin, I., Pride, W. and Ferrell, O. C. (2012) *Marketing Concepts and Strategies 6th edition* (Andover: Cengage Learning), Figure 9.2 from McDaniel, C., Lamb, C. W. and Hair, J. F. (2013) *Introduction to Marketing International 12th edition* (Independence, KY: Cengage Learning) and Table 9.3 from Semenik, R. J., Allen, C. T., O'Guinn, T. C. and Kaufmann, H. R. (2012) *Advertising and Promotions: An Integrated Brand Approach 6th edition* (Andover: Southwestern Cengage Learning)

J. Sainsbury Plc for the image on page 232

Innocent Drinks for the images on page 256

Katharine House Hospice for the logo on page 278

Zappos.com for the screenshot on page 284

DIY Doctor for the logo in example 10.2

Daily Telegraph for the text in example 11.2 from Pook, S. (2001) 'Sex Shop is Fined because its Videos are "Too Tame"', Daily Telegraph

Harvard Business Publishing for Figure 11.6 from Treacy, M. and Wiersema, F. (1993) 'Customer Intimacy and Other Value Disciplines', Harvard Business Review, January–February, pp. 84–93

IBM for Table 11.8 from IBM (2011) From Stretched to Strengthened: Insights from the IBM Global CMO Study, www.ibm.com/cmostudy2011

Turkish Airlines for the image in Example 12.3

Twitter for the screenshot in Example 13.1 and the image on page 372

IEEE for Figure 13.1 from Aggarwal, A., Singan, A. R., Kumaraguru, P. (2012) 'PhishAri: Automatic Realtime Phishing Detection on Twitters'. IEEE, 1 (1), pp. 1–12

Internet World Stats for Figure 13.3 and 13.5

LinkedIn for the screenshot on page 375

Facebook for the screenshot on page 379

TfL for the logo on page 383

The tables on page 119 the image on page 166 are reproduced under terms of the Open Government Licence v1.0

The image on page 364 is reproduced under a Creative Commons Attribution 3.0 License.

Every effort has been made to contact all copyright-holders, but if any have been inadvertently omitted the publishers will be pleased to make the necessary arrangements at the earliest opportunity.

ABOUT THE EDITORS

Dr Ayantunji Gbadamosi, BSc (Hons), MSc, PhD, MCIM, FHEA, is the Chair of the Research and Knowledge Exchange Committee at the Royal Docks Business School (RDBS) of the University of East London, UK. He is a Senior Lecturer in Marketing and the Programme Leader for the MSc in International Marketing Management. Prior to academia, he worked as an assistant executive officer in charge of sales of pharmaceutical and electrical products for companies in Lagos, Nigeria. Dr Gbadamosi received his PhD in Marketing from the University of Salford, UK, and has taught marketing courses at various institutions, including the University of Lagos, the University of Salford, Manchester Metropolitan University and Liverpool Hope University. His papers have been published in several refereed journals, including the *International Journal of Market Research*, *International Journal of Retail and Distribution Management*, *Marketing Intelligence and Planning*, *Social Marketing Quarterly*, *International Journal of Consumer Studies*, *Journal of Fashion Marketing and Management*, *Society and Business Review*, *International Journal of Small Business and Enterprise Development*, *Entrepreneurship and Regional Development*, *Place Branding and Public Diplomacy*, *Nutrition and Food Science*, *International Journal of Customer Relationship Marketing and Management* and *Thunderbird International Business Review*. He is the author of the book *Low-income Consumer Behaviour* and has contributed chapters to several edited books, as well as co-editing *Entrepreneurship Marketing: Principles and Practice of SME Marketing*. Dr Gbadamosi has supervised several undergraduate and postgraduate students, including PhD students, to successful completion and served as an examiner for several doctorate degree examinations. He is listed in *Who's Who in the World*. His research interests are in the areas of consumer behaviour, marketing to children, SME marketing, and marketing communications.

Ian K. Bathgate is the Head of Marketing and Entrepreneurship at the Royal Docks Business School of the University of East London, UK, and specializes

in marketing, lecturing across a broad range of postgraduate programmes within the School. His research interests lie in the area of buyer behaviour, with particular interest in online behavioural patterns and media convergence, as well as marketing and communication planning for organizations (including SMEs). Ian has extensive practical experience in the advertizing/media industry and has operated as consultant to a number of European organizations. He is also a consultant with the University, delivering programmes and consultancy projects to corporate and not-for-profit organizations.

Professor Sonny Nwankwo developed his research in marketing, specializing in consumerism under

conditions of market failure. Through his current research, he seeks to extend the normative boundaries of marketing by focusing on diverse and often culture-specific challenges of economic behaviour, and the power of individuals to create value and make choices in the marketplace, both as consumers and entrepreneurs. Thus, from the broader field of consumer behaviour and its role in shaping identities and interactions, he extends his attention to the dynamics of entrepreneurship among the British ethnic minority population, particularly the entrepreneurial processes of Africans in the UK. His research in this area examines the relations between entrepreneurial identity and individual life histories in the context of everyday interactions. Among his several roles, Professor Nwankwo is Director of the Noon Centre for Equality and Diversity in Business at the University of East London, and a Fellow of the Chartered Institute of Marketing.

ABOUT THE CONTRIBUTORS

Dr Uzoamaka Anozie is a Lecturer in Entrepreneurship and Marketing. She trained as a barrister and was called to the Nigerian Bar. Subsequently she received a master's degree in International Business and Management from the University of Westminster and a PhD in Enterprise and Marketing from the University of Hertfordshire. She has also received a Postgraduate Certificate in Higher Education (PGCHE) from the University of Hertfordshire and a Certificate on Doctoral Supervision from Bournemouth University. Her research interests, consulting activities and publications are mainly in the areas of small business management and development, strategic entrepreneurship and marketing, particularly in emerging economies. Dr Anozie has experience in both the private, public and third sectors in the UK and overseas and has been involved in consultancy work in the UK as well as overseas. She is a fellow of the Higher Education Academy (HEA) and currently serves as the CIM Coordinator for Undergraduate programmes at Bournemouth University, in addition to being a PhD supervisor.

Tao Chang works as a Lecturer and a Programme Leader at Manchester Metropolitan University, UK. He taught both undergraduate and postgraduate modules for a number of years at the University of Salford before he joined MMU. Currently he is the Programme Leader managing the International Consumer Marketing programme and is a Unit Leader for a number of marketing units, as well as supervising undergraduate and postgraduate dissertations. Tao has responsibility for promoting MMU courses in mainland China, Hong Kong and Taiwan – a role which involves managing existing partnerships, developing new links, training agents and giving public seminars organized by the British Council. Tao's research interests include customer acquisition and customer retention, international marketing, higher education marketing, relationship marketing, psychic distance and cross-cultural business relationship development, foreign-language competence and international business. Prior to his academic career he worked as a market researcher promoting public services on behalf of different local councils in the Greater Manchester area.

Sue Clews is a Senior Lecturer in the Faculty of Business, Education and Law at Staffordshire University. She acts as Programme Advisor in Crete for the Business School. Teaching a range of marketing subjects over the last 20 years has led to specialisms in marketing communication and marketing research, with interests in e-marketing and entrepreneurial marketing. She has a wide experience of teaching undergraduate and postgraduate programmes, the latter to both 'traditional' young adult students as well as to mature students, and has managed and developed the undergraduate part-time award portfolio within the Business School. Sue's marketing research expertise is founded on a number of years' professional practice in this area, namely with Ciba Geigy UK, J. Wedgwood and then as a senior research associate at the Strategic Renewal Group. Close links with local industry and the growing number of SMEs supported by Staffordshire University are maintained through continued involvement in research projects and consulting assignments.

Hugh D. Conway, MA, MCIM, FHEA, Lecturer in Marketing, is Programme Manager for the MSc in Marketing Management & Strategy within the Plymouth University Graduate School of Management. He is also a module leader on marketing modules teaching for final year and postgraduate students. He became an academic in 2008, having spent the previous 36 years in the commercial world, mainly with advertizing agencies. His teaching focuses on strategic marketing and marketing planning, wherein his special interests are the development of customer-centric networks. In the last year Hugh has been working with a range of organizations, including the Ellen MacArthur Foundation, to bring to the Plymouth Business School a greater involvement in teaching sustainable business. His profound belief is that it is business that will drive the sustainability programme forward and that the role of major organizations is pivotal to the well-being of global society in the future. Prior to joining the Business School he was a consultant to University of Plymouth Colleges, retained to develop the syllabus for a foundation degree in Airside Operations Management. He has been a company director of a yacht brokerage, Managing Director of Conway Clark Advertising, and an account director at various advertizing agencies: Carrington Caunter Associates, Rex Stewart Group and Hall Harrison Cowley. Clients for whom Hugh has worked include: Disneyland Paris, Jewson, Shell UK Oil, UBM, Vauxhall, Rosemount, Carrefour, and the National Motor Museum. He is married with 4 children and 3 grandchildren, and lives near the transition town of Totnes, close to the river Dart where he keeps his yacht.

Dr Chris Imafidon is an 'intellectual icon, and scholar who has taught at world leading universities, and consultant to governments', according to leading media outlets. He is currently a consultant to presidents, monarchs and governments of various nations, including Britain, America, and other European and African countries. He is the Director of Research (Honorary) and Chair of the Board of the Excellence in Education Programme. Chris Imafidon is one of the 'world's foremost scholars on leveraging informatics for learning and exceptional achievement (genius)', according to the BBC, CNN and *USA-Today*. He was described by *TIME* magazine as an 'intellectual icon'. Leading Harvard- and Oxford University-educated professors have described him as 'the patriarch of modern education and informatics'. Chris is a multi-award winning researcher and scientific pioneer. He is a member of the Information Age Executive Round-table forum, which is made up of the top 15 IT experts, decision-makers, CIOs and executives in the UK. He is a consultant to governments and industry leaders worldwide. As a former university lecturer based in Cambridge, he also has been a guest lecturer at the University of Oxford (Keble College) and a visiting professor at various American universities, including Harvard, Cornell, Columbia, SUNY, Georgetown, Miami and LSU, and has collaborated with scientists at Yale University. He continues to mentor, supervise and examine both internal and external PhD, postgraduate and undergraduate students at Imperial College, Cambridge, UCL and Queen Mary University of London, where he was formerly Head of the Management Technology Unit. Chris served on the Board of Governors at Woodford County High School (one of the nation's most successful schools) and he currently serves on the board of the Excellence in Education programme (www.ExcellenceinEducation.org.uk).

Dr Dulekha Kasturiratne is an Associate Professor in Marketing, and lectures in both undergraduate and postgraduate modules in Marketing and Consumer Behaviour. She was an examiner for the Chartered Institute of Marketing (CIM), and the Programme Manager for BA Marketing at Plymouth University Business School. She has co-authored course material for the MBA programme of Royal Holloway (University of London) and worked as a consultant tutor for Distance Learning on various programmes at Imperial College London and the School of Oriental and African Studies, both of the University of London. Dr Kasturiratne completed her PhD at Imperial College, London, and her PhD thesis won the Emerald/EFMD International Award for the Most Outstanding Doctoral Thesis in Marketing Strategy. She has worked as a consultant for the Food and Agriculture Organization (FAO) of the United Nations (UN) and the FORD Foundation on a number of projects using cases from the Sri Lankan tea industry and dairy sectors. She has published in top international journals and is an advocate of research-informed teaching. She brings her experience back to the classroom to benefit the student and add value to their learning experience.

Dr Hina Khan is a Senior Lecturer in International Marketing and Marketing Research and a programme leader for Business Creation at the Newcastle Business School, University of Northumbria, UK. As a Principal Supervisor, she has successfully supervised one DBA candidate from start to completion and is currently supervising one PhD and interviewing two potential PhD candidates. She has also examined one DBA thesis from the University of Newcastle, Australia. She is also on the editorial board of the *Journal of Small Business and Enterprise Development* and reviews papers for the *Academy of Marketing Science, International Marketing Review*, and *Journal of Services Marketing*. She has published in refereed international journals, written two book chapters, and chairs sessions and presents papers at international conferences regularly. Due to her expertise in both quantitative and qualitative research methods, she was appointed to an Advisory Panel at Knowledge Base Ltd. She was responsible for advising the team on data analysis and research methodologies. Two of her articles have been selected for the Emerald Reading ListAssist – the list is available to all the subscribers worldwide –an honour for her. She was Chief External Examiner at Birmingham City Business School (2009–2012), and Visiting Professor at Corvinus University, Budapest, Hungary. Her research focuses on consumer buying behaviour and small- and medium-size-enterprise development, challenges and impact of globalization on SMEs. She is also a leading researcher in country-of-origin effect on consumers' buying behaviour. She was one of the three finalists for Lloyds TSB Jewel Award in 2007.

Shuyu Lin is a Senior Lecturer in International Fashion Business at Manchester Metropolitan University. She joined MMU in 2010 and teaches on the fashion business and related subjects across various programmes. She has also served as Unit Leader for the Fashion Buying and Retail unit of the BSc Fashion Buying and Merchandising programme. Following a BA in Journalism, she entered the fashion industry as a PR account executive. She later took up the position of fashion editor at *Marie Claire* magazine. After a few years' experience in the industry, she continued her education, earning a master's degree in Management with Marketing at the University of Bath. Shuyu is an active researcher and contributes to international conferences and publications. She is presently completing a PhD on the subject of innovation management in the UK designer fashion sector. Her main research interests are in the area of strategic innovation management. Specifically, she is interested in the innovation process from product ideation to commercialization, particularly in the creative sector. After completing her MSc dissertation, focusing on relationship marketing of independent fashion boutiques, Shuyu pursued her interest in SME new product development of independent designer fashion labels. Her current research focuses on extending the application of new product development theory in the context of design-driven, network-based innovation. This includes a cross-disciplinary exploration through the integration of business (organizational behaviour, strategy, operations and marketing) and design management (creativity, product development and sustainability) in the creative industries.

Emmanuel Ohohe is a Senior Lecturer in Marketing and the Course Leader for BA Marketing at the Business School of London Metropolitan University. He holds an MComm in Marketing from Strathclyde Business School and a Postgraduate Diploma in Management Studies from Sheffield Hallam University. He started his academic career as a research assistant in the Local Enterprise Development Unit at the University of North London. He worked in private consultancy, then rejoined London Metropolitan University as a Lecturer in Marketing. He has been active in teaching undergraduate and postgraduate marketing modules, doing research and course administration. Emmanuel currently teaches Principles and Practice in Marketing, Design and Creativity in Marketing, Essentials of Marketing and Consumer Buying Behaviour, and supervises undergraduate marketing projects and master's dissertations. He is a member of the Chartered Institute of Marketing, the Institute of Learning and Teaching in Higher Education and the Royal African Society. His research interests are in the areas of SME development and entrepreneurship, particularly among black and ethnic minority groups, consumer buying behaviour, and teaching and learning.

Dr Maktoba Omar completed a PhD at the University of Leeds entitled 'Contextual Determinants of Standardisation and Entry Strategies in Internationalisation', which examined aspects of marketing, international marketing, business strategy, and management strategy. Currently she is a Reader in Marketing at Edinburgh Napier University. Maktoba is a member of a range of professional organizations, including the Academy of Marketing, the Academy of International Business and the Institute of Learning and Teaching in Higher Education. Maktoba has published and acted as editor and referee for a number of academic journals, and has performed as track chair, presenter and member of vetting panels for a number of national and international conferences. Maktoba is also Director of Studies and supervisor for a number of PhD and DBA students in the UK, Europe and elsewhere. Currently her main research focus is the study of the impact of branding, emerging markets and foreign direct investment in relation to UK companies operating overseas.

Collins Osei, BA (Hons), MBA, was a tutor and Senior Research Assistant at the University of Cape Coast in Ghana. He has taught and assessed students at various levels, and also contributed to the delivery of academic administrative functions, both in the UK and overseas. He is currently studying for a PhD at Edinburgh Napier University. His doctoral research focuses on attracting and retaining foreign direct investment in Africa. His other research interests include international marketing strategy, emerging markets, implications of foreign direct investment on host economies, and the branding of products, services, education institutions and nations. He has published in refereed journals and presented research papers at conferences.

Dr Kaushik V. Pandya is a senior academic at Sheffield Hallam University, UK. He has been researching and teaching in higher education since 1986 and has supervised research students at various levels. His research areas include: operations management, knowledge management, e-business, management of sustainable sources and related areas. He has worked as an academic at various higher education institutions in the UK.

Linda Phillips is Academic Group Leader, Enterprise Marketing & Services, and Principal Lecturer at Staffordshire University Faculty of Business, Education & Law. She is also Programme Advisor for programmes delivered in Kosovo for Staffordshire University, UK. Linda began her working career in industry, with the BBC in London, the Australian Government in Canberra, and for GEC in the Midlands, where latterly she worked as Senior Marketing Executive and Head of Marketing. She then moved to academic life as a Senior Lecturer in Marketing at Staffordshire University Business School, where she has expanded her horizons into award leadership and overseas work, and has played a major role in establishing the tourism and events disciplines within the School. Linda has taught on a range of programmes at undergraduate, post-graduate and professional level. She specializes in marketing, tourism and events, and has industry experience of marketing and corporate events. Linda has presented papers at conferences and published in academic journals and books. She is currently an external examiner for tourism and events and for business management, and is a chartered marketer and a member of the Academy of Marketing, the Chartered Institute of Marketing and the Association of Event Management Educators.

Dr Sanjit Kumar Roy is a Lecturer in Marketing at Coventry University, UK. His articles have appeared in the *Journal of Strategic Marketing* (forthcoming), *Journal of Services Marketing, Journal of Brand Management* (forthcoming), *Managing Service Quality, International Journal of Bank Marketing, Marketing Management Journal, Computers in Human Behaviour, Journal of Global Marketing, South Asian Journal of Management,* and *Case Studies in Business, Industry and Government Statistics.* He was previously a Visiting Research Scholar at Bentley University, USA. He serves on the Editorial Review Board of the *International Journal of Bank Marketing, Journal of Indian Business Research* and *South Asian Journal of Management.* He has recently guest-edited a special issue on India for the *International Journal of Bank Marketing.* He has attended and presented his research at several prestigious conferences on marketing, and has conducted a number of faculty development programmes on Structural Equation Modelling. His research and teaching interests include services marketing, consumer–brand relationships, principles of marketing management, customer relationship management and marketing research.

Zubin Sethna's PhD thesis examined the entrepreneurial marketing activities within ethnic firms in the UK, and his research interests lie at the interface of 'entrepreneurship and marketing'. Summer 2013 sees the publication of his book (with Rosalind Jones and Paul Harrigan) entitled *Entrepreneurial Marketing: Global Perspectives,* which is set to become the leading text in the field. As Principal Lecturer in Marketing at the University of Bedfordshire's Business School, Zubin oversees the postgraduate portfolio. Zubin has successfully launched five businesses (one of which won a National Award), and in his capacity as Managing Consultant with Baresman Consulting, he has integrated marketing strategy/communications with management consultancy and training for numerous organizations both in the UK and internationally, and across a variety of industry sectors (including healthcare, professional services, music, travel, manufacturing, retail, IT and education). His 22 years of industry experience allow him to take a practice-based approach to teaching whenever he is in the classroom. Zubin previously taught Innovation and Entrepreneurship on the AMBA accredited MBA programme at the University of Westminster, and prior to that ran an immensely popular and successful business start-up programme for creative industry graduates from the University of the Arts, London. Zubin is currently Co-Chair of the Academy of Marketing's Special Interest Group on Entrepreneurial and Small Business Marketing, and has been invited to conduct keynote lectures in the UK, the EU, China and India, and regularly speaks at South East Asia's leading business school, the Indian Institute of Management, Ahmadabad (IIMA). Zubin also serves as an Editorial Board member for the *Journal of Research in Marketing and Entrepreneurship* and the *Journal of Urban Regeneration and Renewal.* In addition to this, Zubin has also previously been instrumental in attracting funding in excess of £350k for academic projects from leading public and private bodies such as the Department for Education and Skills (DfES), the Learning and Skills Council (LSC) and Harrods!

Peter Gruenwald Taylor, PhD, a Canadian, spent the first part of his career in retailing, import/export and packaging. Academically, he became Professor of Marketing at Humber College, University of Guelph, Canada. Peter later joined the Marketing Department at the University of East London. Peter's degrees come from the University of Windsor, Canada, and his doctorate from UEL. In 2009, Peter became the Principal and Director of Amity University in London. Peter's research interests include tourism collaborations, sustainable marketing, and music in consumer behaviour.

Dr Robert L. Williams, Jr. is an Assistant Professor of Marketing at Saint Mary's College, Notre Dame, Indiana, USA. He has published in peer-reviewed journals such as the *Journal of Product and Brand Management* (Emerald Literati 2008 Award for Excellence winner), *Journal of Brand Management*, *Journal of Marketing for Higher Education* and *Journal of Technology Management and Innovation*. He has co-authored a textbook chapter on management of innovation in SMEs, and has presented at international conferences and workshops. After 20 years as a practitioner in Fortune 50/500 companies, his current academic research interests focus on competitive advantage, branding, innovation, higher education and market entry strategies.

Helena A. Williams, MPSSc, is a Partner and Co-founder at Mar-Kadam Associates, a firm that specializes in branding, rebranding and renaming in service industries and entrepreneurial ventures. Her research interests include economic development through entrepreneurship, emerging market entrepreneurship, gastro-tourism, education and social services. Previous experience includes 20 years of entrepreneurial management as president of a state-wide educational training and event-/conference-planning firm in Pennsylvania, and being the owner and executive chef of Baltimore's first gastro-café and gallery. Her current academic work includes curriculum development and teaching entrepreneurship courses, and consultation with small business and local venture capital networks.

Dr Hsiao-Pei (Sophie) Yang is Senior Lecturer in Marketing and Advertizing at Coventry University Business School. Sophie completed her PhD at Bournemouth University in 2008, and prior to her career in academia she held marketing posts in the direct marketing and private educational sectors. Her research interests include the marketing of higher education and consumer behaviour in services. Her previous research focused on business-to-business relationships between UK universities and their Chinese educational agents, and international students' use of online discussion forums to reduce perceived risks in selecting overseas universities. One of her current projects is on the internationalization of UK universities through their collaboration with overseas academic partners, focusing on business-to-business relationships, and power and dependency relations. She teaches on services and retail marketing, contemporary issues in marketing and principles of marketing, at both undergraduate and postgraduate level.

TOUR OF THE BOOK

LEARNING OUTCOMES

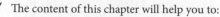

The content of this chapter will help you to:

- Understand the relevance of value and how this underpins what marketing is about
- Explain the key concepts associated with marketing
- Define marketing from the perspective of value creation and delivery
- Discuss evolutionary trends in marketing to map out changing value orientations
- Explain marketing as a philosophy and function of business

Learning Outcomes

A set of learning outcomes is identified at the start of each chapter. After you have studied the chapter, completed the activities and answered the review questions, you should be able to achieve each of the stated objectives.

Marketing in action
Nokia: fighting back on customer-based value

NOKIA WAS ONCE A 'GLOBAL SUPERSTAR' AND world market leader in mobile phones. It sold more smartphones than any of its competitors during the past decade but its market share had progressively declined in recent years. With both Samsung and Apple overtaking Nokia in smartphone sales, many people are beginning to forget that Nokia was actually the first company to introduce the smartphone device during the 1990s. However, Nokia is beginning to fight back to regain market share by focusing customer-based value through the use of price-competitive products and social media to reposition in the market. It is a matter of returning to the basics of what made the company popular in the early years – that is, its ability to tap into and connect with consumer values in relation to economy, versatility and affordability of products.

Several years ago, the company unveiled a new range of cheap products such as E7, C7 and C6 (now all discontinued) which it intended to use as weapons for fighting the smartphone wars. During an event that was appropriately termed 'Nokia World', the company's then Executive Vice President (Markets), Niklas Savander, declared to delegates that: 'We are not going to apologise for the fact that that we're not Apple or Google or anybody else. We're Nokia and we're unique.' By this strategy, the company aims to regain market attraction through its wide assortment of apps-loaded and price-competitive smartphones to appeal to a broad range of users. It has also teamed up with Microsoft to introduce the Lumia range, phones compatible with an emerging standard for wireless charging and in some cases also coupling in the necessary hardware and apps to enable users to pay for store purchases by simply tapping the phone on electronic payment card terminals. Recognising the growing potential of social media in mass marketing strategy, the company has introduced major improvements that would make it more lucrative and easier to introduce new apps. In all these, the organization wants to be seen as a company that makes great mobile products to satisfy a huge bundle of customer-based value needs.

Marketing in Action

Each chapter begins with an example of its main topic in practice. The aim here is to highlight how you can apply the theories and concepts in the chapter to marketing in the real world.

Example 1.3:
Societal marketing concept at Marks and Spencer (M&S)

Marks and Spencer, a British retailing organization, has been proactive in its social consciousness strategies. Essentially, its business consists of 51 per cent food and 49 per cent clothing and homeware products. The Group's revenue for 2012 was £9.9 billion, which represents an increase of 2 per cent on the figure recorded for the previous year – an indication of customers' appreciation of what the company is doing.

M&S is the UK market leader for womenswear, lingerie and menswear, but something else that significantly contributes to its success and popularity among its customers is the company's green credentials. It has shown commitments to improving the environment and healthier living conditions. For example, through its Plan A programme, the company demonstrates clearly to all its stakeholders, including customers, its intention to become the world's most sustainable retailer. Its eco and ethical programme is at the heart of how it practises its marketing activities. Through this plan, which was launched in January 2007, the organization is now working with customers and suppliers to combat climate change, use sustainable raw materials, reduce waste, trade ethically and help customers to maintain a healthier lifestyle. There were 100 Plan A targets when the programme was launched and that number has now increased to 180 to be achieved by 2015. So far, it has successfully achieved 138 targets and is making significant efforts to improve this record in the years to come. The organization makes the point clearly that marketing is not just about providing products or services and making profits, but also about ensuring a responsible approach that embraces environmental sustainability.

Examples

These short case studies feature throughout every chapter, and provide the opportunity for you to link the material covered to a real-life situation.

Case study
Apple: an epitome of value creation

Few people could doubt the popularity of Apple as a strong firm of global standard. Although many will attribute this to the innovative ability of the team in the organization, arguably the key success factor lies in Apple's ability to create and deliver value to its disparate customers all over the world. While it has had a number of challenges since its inception in 1976, it was clear from the early years that the company was on the way to making a remarkable impact on the world of computers and other electronic products. For instance, the introduction of Apple II in 1977, which followed Apple 1 introduced a year earlier, created a unique space for the organization in the competitive market. It being the first computer introduced in a plastic case and with colour graphics, consumers quickly realized that the product stood out among others and could meet their needs effectively. Hence, they responded positively. Similarly, the instant success of the first generation of the PowerBook in late 1991 is noteworthy and also shows that Apple is keenly determined to satisfy its customers in all ramifications and ensure value creation and delivery.

The company demonstrates that creating value revolves around all the elements of the marketing mix. Apart from the products designed to meet the needs of its various consumer groups, Apple announced on 10 November 1997 that it would sell computers directly over the phone and on the Internet, thereby strengthening how it provides time, place and possession utilities. Its pricing and communication strategies are strategically designed to be of good fit for its customers. It has a very strong presence in social media such as Facebook and Twitter through which it communicates with its customers. All of these are symptomatic of Apple's value-driven philosophy.

Apple's case clearly shows that good marketing practice revolves around the exchange of something of value. The more the company works at giving customers products that satisfy them, the more successful it becomes in the industry. Its market share increases, customers become increasingly loyal to the brand and the sales and profit figures increase considerably. Another classic example is the release of iTunes for Windows in October 2003, which led to the sale of more than 70 million songs in the first year. Indeed, the step captured the interest of music lovers. The subsequent improvement in sales figures is another pointer to the fact that customers have an affinity with Apple's offerings and are convinced of the value they derive from the transactions.

It is evident all around us that Apple has introduced many products since the inception of its business several decades ago. However, the impact of the iPhone and iPad in society has been highly remarkable in recent times. When the iPhone was introduced in 2007, the positive response of the market showed that Apple fully embraces the marketing orientation because it ensures that the new offering addresses what the market really needs. Hence this emphasizes that the key focus of the firm is about creating and delivering value. But the company is not complacent about its success level. It modifies the product to accommodate changes in consumers' tastes and developments in the market environment to suit the dynamic needs of the target market. For instance, the iPhone 5, which was released in September 2012, has been described as having the fastest chip and ultra-fast wireless technology, as being the thinnest and lightest iPhone ever. In the design of the headphones, as the Apple website says, 'Instead of starting with the speaker, we started with

Case Study

Each chapter ends with an extended case study. Companies included vary from large MNC's such as Apple to small, independent businesses. Questions are posed at the end of each case, which can be answered either in class or as part of an assignment.

Review questions

1 What is market segmentation?
2 Discuss the main bases for the segmentation of customer, business and international markets.
3 Describe how organizations might evaluate the attractiveness of a market segment.
4 Discuss the various market-targeting strategies available to businesses. Use suitable examples to illustrate your points.
5 Explain the concept of positioning.
6 If you were the marketing manager of a five-star hotel, what factors would you consider as crucial to position your organization successfully?
7 When you decide to shop for clothes, what shops do you initially consider? Why do you include these shops as alternatives? Do any of the shops get eliminated along the way and, if so, why? What could those in charge of marketing at the eliminated shops do to keep themselves under consideration?

Review Questions

These questions can be used as class exercises, or for self-testing and evaluating your knowledge and understanding about the chapter topic.

Group task

Construct a basic perceptual map based on your knowledge of ten different universities. Choose two distinguishing attributes or variables for the map's axes. Bear in mind that there is no right or wrong answer because a perceptual map is designed to visualize consumer perceptions of products. Afterwards, compare your map with those of others and discuss the following:

1 Why do you think the attributes chosen are important? Would you have chosen a different set of variables?
2 Do you think the map shows a significant difference between your perceptions of these universities?
3 How does your map differ from the maps of other students? Why do you think this difference exists?

Group Task

These exercises can be completed in class or as part of an assignment.

Glossary/Key terms

Market segment: A group of customers whose needs are distinct from the needs of other groups in relation to a particular product
Perceptual map: Graphs that help to show the relationship between competitors and the criteria that their consumers use when making purchase decisions

Glossary/Key Terms

Each chapter contains a list of important words, phrases and concepts that you need to know in order to understand basic marketing, its theoretical basis and its related areas.

Further reading

S. S. Hassan and S. Craft (2012) 'Examining World Market Segmentation and Brand Positioning Strategies', *Journal of Consumer Marketing*, Vol. 29, No. 5, pp. 344–56
This paper identifies a link between global brand positioning and segmentation factors.
T. K. Bose (2012) 'Market Segmentation and Customer Focus Strategies and their Contribution towards Effective Value Chain Management', *International Journal of Marketing Studies*, Vol. 4, No. 3, pp. 113–21
The paper suggests that market segmentation immensely assists in delivering diversified and customized products and services to customers.

Further Reading

Each chapter contains a list of important words, phrases and concepts that you need to know in order to understand basic marketing, its theoretical basis and its related areas.

ESL Vocab Checklist

Throughout each chapter words are highlighted which may be problematic for ESL students. Full definitions of all these words can be found on the book's companion website.

Most SM platforms provide users with modern, user-friendly functionalities to share news, opinions and information. Ironically, some online user-generated contents have been proven to be more viral. That is, a message or file self-propagates to everyone, even those who have not requested the message. Therefore, in this section of this work, the key elements affecting the viral propensity of some SM contents are reviewed, using a comparative analysis of the traditional mass media (TV, radio, newspapers) versus modern mass media (mobile devices, SNSs, internet), with a combination of well known case studies that aim to demystify proven hypotheses concerning some viral catalysts of a few online SM contents.

Companion Website

The book's companion website at www.palgrave.com/business/gbadamosi offers a number of resources for both lecturers and students, including PowerPoint slides, multiple choice question, a searchable glossary, ESL vocab definitions and much more.

1 THE PURPOSE OF MARKETING

AYANTUNJI GBADAMOSI, IAN K. BATHGATE & SONNY NWANKWO

UNIVERSITY OF EAST LONDON

CHAPTER CONTENTS

LEARNING OUTCOMES

The content of this chapter will help you to:

- Understand the relevance of value and how this underpins what marketing is about
- Explain the key concepts associated with marketing
- Define marketing from the perspective of value creation and delivery
- Discuss evolutionary trends in marketing to map out changing value orientations
- Explain marketing as a philosophy and function of business

Marketing in action
Nokia: fighting back on customer-based value

NOKIA WAS ONCE A 'GLOBAL SUPERSTAR' AND world market leader in mobile phones. It sold more smartphones than any of its competitors during the past decade but its market share had progressively declined in recent years. With both Samsung and Apple overtaking Nokia in smartphone sales, many people are beginning to forget that Nokia was actually the first company to introduce the smartphone device during the 1990s. However, Nokia is beginning to fight back to regain market share by focusing customer-based value through the use of price-competitive products and social media to reposition in the market. It is a matter of returning to the basics of what made the company popular in the early years – that is, its ability to tap into and connect with consumer values in relation to economy, versatility and affordability of products.

Several years ago, the company unveiled a new range of cheap products such as E7, C7 and C6 (now all discontinued) which it intended to use as weapons for fighting the smartphone wars. During an event that was appropriately termed 'Nokia World', the company's then Executive Vice President (Markets), Niklas Savander, declared to delegates that: 'We are not going to apologise for the fact that that we're not Apple or Google or anybody else. We're Nokia and we're unique.' By this strategy, the company aims to regain market attraction through its wide assortment of apps-loaded and price-competitive smartphones to appeal to a broad range of users. It has also teamed up with Microsoft to introduce the Lumia range, phones compatible with an emerging standard for wireless charging and in some cases also coupling in the necessary hardware and apps to enable users to pay for store purchases by simply tapping the phone on electronic payment card terminals. Recognising the growing potential of social media in mass marketing strategy, the company has introduced major improvements that would make it more lucrative and easier to introduce new apps. In all these, the organization wants to be seen as a company that makes great mobile products to satisfy a huge bundle of customer-based value needs.

INTRODUCTION

For quite some time, marketing analysts have been trying to answer some fundamental questions about the relevance and purpose of marketing in business organizations. Some of the questions include wondering why some companies out-perform others in any given sector? Is it because they:

- Provide 'better' products (if we can understand how 'a better product' should be defined)?
- Have better resources and access to the market?
- Are stronger or larger than the competition?
- Can sell more products or have more customers than the competition?

There are no clear-cut answers to these questions. However, a synthesis of the literature suggests that companies with sustained records of out-performing their competitors usually have a strong *value orientation*. It is this value orientation that really accounts for the *distinctive capability* of a successful company. This is illustrated by a quotation from a famous marketing scholar: 'Show me a success story and I will uncover a distinctive capability' (Day, 2003, p. 23). It is now widely accepted that a distinctive capability underlies how companies might differ competitively and embodies a company's value configuration.

1

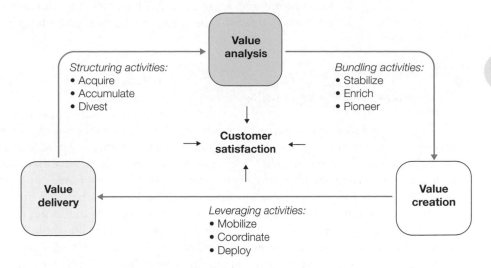

Figure 1.1: Value orchestration in business – managerial priorities
Source: Adapted from Lindgreen et al., 2012, p. 212

As shown in Figure 1.1, customer satisfaction is closely linked to, and a desired outcome of, how value is orchestrated in a company. The process reflects the interconnections between different activities that give force to a firm's ability to offer a superior bundle of value to customers.

Value configuration represents the processes through which a firm anticipates, creates, delivers and monitors what the customer values. Effective marketing is grounded in valid and insightful monitoring and enhancement of the sources of customer value. For a success-oriented company, sources of value might be evident in spheres such as technological leadership, product innovativeness, environmental sensitivity and quality of customer relationship processes. Therefore, the role of marketing is to illuminate the **manifestation** of superior customer value and use this as a source of competitive advantage in terms of improved customer satisfaction, customer loyalty, market share and profitability (see Figure 1.2).

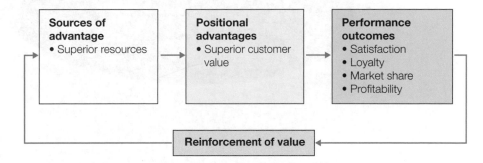

Figure 1.2: Value configuration
Source: Adapted from Day, 2003, p. 3

Effective value configuration is a solid foundation of successful marketing and, indeed, an enduring source of advantage. Essentially, the ability to create and deliver superior value is paramount to any company's long-term growth and sustainability. In fact, a company's long-term success hinges on offering customers the '*best value*'. What may be considered best value by customers is dynamic and changes with time and circumstances. Therefore, value needs to be constantly created, nurtured, implemented and appreciated. Without this, the company will become competitively disadvantaged, resulting in an erosion of profitability and shareholder wealth.

Example 1.1:
Value-oriented marketing at Kellogg's

Kellogg's, a world-leading producer of cereals, is widely known for creating and delivering value to its customers over ten decades. The success recorded by this company over the years is a sure proof of how it has continued to reinvent and reposition in consumer value maps.

The firm is passionate about delighting its customers. Its commitment to ensuring that customers have a great and delicious start to the day, with a Kellogg's brand of breakfast cereal, is demonstrated in how it positions its products to delight consumers. Kellogg's business revolves around processing grains into various end-products for specific consumer targets. Its choice of business line is greatly linked to the benefits of grains, which (as stated on its website) include being rich in carbohydrates and low in fat. The effort of this organization in ensuring that its customers have value has prompted its introduction of various forms of offerings such as cereals, biscuits, crisps, bars and fruit-flavoured snacks.

Its sales figures in 2011 were over $13 billion and it acquired the iconic Pringles business in May 2012 as a means of expanding further towards targeting and satisfying more customers. It is therefore not surprising that it is acknowledged in 2013 as one of the 'world's most reputable companies' by Forbes and one of the 'world's most admired companies' by Fortune.

istock © szokrika

DEFINING MARKETING FROM A VALUE PERPSPECTIVE

Marketing is a living subject mainly because it is dynamically evolving. This is what makes it hugely difficult to define precisely. The principal difficulty lies in the fact that the aspirations or expectations of primary marketing stakeholders (such as consumers, producers, suppliers, distributors, society) are in a **perpetual** state of **flux** and susceptible to dynamically continuous change. As the underlying aspirations or expectations change, so also does the understanding of what marketing means. To disentangle the complexity surrounding the definition of marketing, it is important first to outline its core concepts.

CORE CONCEPTS IN MARKETING

Figure 1.3 highlights the core concepts of marketing. An understanding of these concepts affords significant insights into how customer value might be conceived, created and delivered by a company. These core concepts include needs, wants, demand, market offering, exchange, satisfaction and profits. A brief discussion of these concepts follows.

Figure 1.3: Marketing value creation and delivery

Needs: Put simply, a need can be described as the difference between a person's *current state* and their *desired state*. We often hear people say 'I need a car'. This simply means that the individual feels there is a discrepancy between his/her current state of not having a car (which may be a constraint to travelling around) and the desired state of acquiring one to ease travel constraints. At a most basic level, marketing is about meeting consumers' needs. So, it resolves consumers' state of felt deprivation (unmet needs). Consumer needs may be categorized on two levels: primary needs (such as food and clothing) and secondary needs (for example, luxury goods such as cars, designer shoes and perfume).

A popular theory of motivation, the hierarchy of needs, proposed by Abraham Maslow, can be very helpful here. He suggests that human needs can be arranged in a hierarchical order, ranging from basic-order to high-order needs: **physiological** needs, safety and security, love and belongingness, esteem needs and self-actualization (see Figure 1.4).

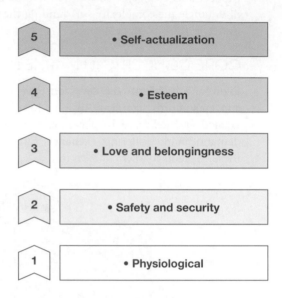

5	• Self-actualization
4	• Esteem
3	• Love and belongingness
2	• Safety and security
1	• Physiological

Figure 1.4: Hierarchy of needs

So, it is possible for consumers to be operating at different levels on the needs hierarchy. Each consumer's position on the ladder will influence the type of product or service s/he buys in order to satisfy his/her needs.

Wants: These are desires for particular offerings that will satisfy the felt or identified deprivation. It is important to state that consumers' wants are influenced by a number of factors such as personality, lifestyles, life history, learning and culture. For instance, it is possible that two friends may have a need for food at the same time. However, while one might prefer to buy chicken and chips, based on her lifestyle, the

istock © icetocker

other may decide to consume crispy noodles with mixed vegetables, not only because she is a vegetarian but also based on her doctor's advice. What differentiates wants from needs is the diversity in the offerings used to satisfy the basic need. These two friends both need food but each of them wants a different type of food.

Demand: This represents effective consumption-driven action, aimed at fulfilling wants and satisfaction of needs. Essentially, demand could be explained as consumers' wants for an offering coupled with purchasing power. A good number of people may desire a particular product or brand but this can only become an effective demand when the desires are backed up by purchasing power.

Market offering: Market offerings are '*something of value*' – **tangible** or intangible products that a firm puts out to the customer in the hope that such will satisfy their needs. Market offerings are the bases upon which value can be measured. They can take several forms such as physical products, services, ideas, people, places, information and organization. As an example, while consumers pay to buy physical electronic products from companies such as Sony and Apple in value-creation and value-delivery transactions, they will also pay for services such as those provided by British Airways and Barclays Bank. This further emphasizes that the key focus in marketing transactions is value.

Exchange: This involves swapping something considered to be of value between two or more parties, usually the producer (marketer) and the consumer. See Figure 1.5. Although we have explained the importance of needs, wants, demands and market offerings, they are brought together in marketing in a reasoned form through the notion of exchange. Some decades ago, a detailed explanation of exchange was provided by Bagozzi (1975), who explains that there are three forms – '*restricted exchange*', '*generalized exchange*' and '*complex exchange*'. The restricted exchange is a two-party **reciprocal** relationship which may be described in the form of A↔B, meaning that A gives to B and receives from B. The generalized exchange refers to a system of univocal, reciprocal relationships among at least three factors in the exchange system. In a univocal reciprocity situation, the three or more parties do not benefit from each other directly but do so indirectly. This generalized exchange situation can be diagrammatically represented as A→B→C→A. Unlike the other two exchange forms, the complex exchange is a system of at least three actors with mutual relationships. The relationship can thus be described as A↔B↔C. So, it is logical and very important for us to state at this stage that a marketing exchange will involve at least two parties. For example, recall the last time you bought a loaf of bread. You paid an amount of money that you considered right for the bread while the seller collected the money in return for the bread released to you. Without this exchange, marketing cannot be deemed to have taken place.

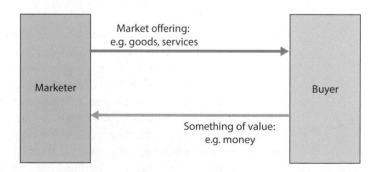

Figure 1.5: Exchange and marketing

Satisfaction: Since marketing is partly about the exchange of something of value between transacting parties, a relationship is bound to exist between the parties involved. This relationship could take several forms just like the relationships we keep with different people. Some can be more intimate than others. Some started well but stopped for certain reasons, while some are enduring. Marketers stand to benefit from developing and maintaining a very good relationship with their various customers. One of the key factors and arguably the most important reason why buyers remain in a relationship with marketers is the satisfaction they derive from their transactions with the firm. Usually, satisfaction is closely linked to customers' expectation and actual experience of the product or service involved. For the customer to be satisfied, marketers will need to ensure that the products or services offered match or exceed customers' expectation. Conversely, if the customers' experience falls short of their expectation, then dissatisfaction is deemed to have occurred.

Customers that are satisfied are most likely to engage in repeat purchases and subsequently become loyal. Conversely, the dissatisfied customer will not only stop buying but will most likely tell friends, family and neighbours not to buy the product. So, it is important for marketers to ensure that every activity involved in serving customers is geared towards satisfying them in order to maintain the relationship.

Example 1.2:
The market offerings of Virgin

The Virgin Group, originally founded by Richard Branson, has grown to become a formidable force in many market sectors. The organization has a number of market offerings which include mobile phone services, air travel, rail travel, credit cards, cosmetics, holidays, music and a host of others. But something common to all the product lines is that they are all in the unique, value-oriented positioning of the company which make the organization a globally respected brand.

In all, Virgin communicates that it stands for innovation, value for money, quality, fun and a sense of competitive advantage. Thus, the organization enjoys high customer patronage and loyalty in many of its business areas. The lesson from Virgin is that successful organizations often approach their markets from the perspective of customer value. The organization demonstrates an understanding that repeat purchases, brand loyalty and positive word of mouth by customers are important ingredients of success. To remain on top of the game in the marketplace, whether a company provides only one market offering or very many, as in the case of Virgin, its key focus should be on ensuring the delivery of customer value that is superior to that of its competitors.

Profits: A salient factor in the explanation of marketing thrusts is profit. For a marketing relationship to continue smoothly, it is important for both parties to derive benefits. Profit is a key benefit derived by the marketer from the marketing relationship while the customer gets the satisfaction from the product or service paid for. A company cannot survive for long without profits. But this is a complex issue because of lack of agreement on how profit might be measured. Further complications are added by the presence of non-profit-making organizations that are now embracing and integrating marketing principles in their operations. For such not-for-profit organizations, the core focus in business is not about profit-making because their survival is mainly ensured through donors' financial support. Nevertheless, they are also increasingly under pressure to satisfy their stakeholders through meeting their needs and value expectations.

TYPES OF MARKET

1

If the practice of marketing is based on the key concepts of value creation, exchange, satisfaction and relationships, then the term 'market' can be seen to cover a variety of situations. Different people have different views as to what constitutes a 'market'. For example, there is the stock market, the labour market, the tech market, the supermarket and so on. To view this on a very simplistic level, each individual is unique in terms of their background, culture, religion, language, household composition, consumption patterns, interests, aspirations and goals. A market is therefore an attempt to define a discrete set of actual or potential buyers of a product or service who possess common needs or wants coupled with a willingness, authority and purchasing power to buy that product or service. A market can also comprise individual consumers or organizations. In order to achieve some understanding of the types of market that organizations compete in, we can look briefly at common types of market below.

Consumer markets: These comprise consumers of goods and services. Consumers are the end-users of the marketed product and are normally the target of marketing activities generated by business. Examples of consumer goods include 'brown' goods (such as televisions), 'white' goods (such as dishwashers), common household items and foodstuffs (such as baked beans).

istock © swilmor

Business or industrial markets: These markets are characterized by goods and services that are generated by business for the exclusive use of business. These could include products and services that are used in the manufacture of other goods and services, either for the consumer market or for further resale in the business-to-business market.

Product markets: These can be split into tangible product markets (such as washing machines) or intangible markets, which are normally characterized by services (such as insurance and banking). The important point to remember here is that the end-user normally buys a 'package' of both goods and services. For example, when a buyer purchases a washing machine (tangible) there is also included a guarantee, a maintenance scheme, the brand name and so on (see Chapter 6). The customer can be seen in some circumstances to consume both tangible and intangible goods and services in one purchase package.

Not-for-profit markets: As the name suggests, this market consists of organizations for which an operating profit is not the primary business strategy. Examples will include museums, galleries, charities (sometimes called 'third sector'), universities, churches and hospitals. Such organizations normally have an emphasis on donations and focus on what is called 'donor marketing'.

Government markets: These markets normally comprise government agencies and can include defence, public health, transport and so on. The nature of the markets is that contracts are tightly monitored and result from a tendering process. These markets should be seen at a 'macro' level and are invariably concerned with services or industries that are government controlled or have national significance.

Public sector markets: These are very similar to the government markets but are on a local scale. Again, the tendering process for contracts is typical of this sector, which looks for best value.

Global markets: We live in an age of globalization where companies compete across the global stage. This can be business to business or business to consumer. The characteristic of these markets is the ability of an organization to take advantage of lower cost bases available around the world while also localizing their product in the market. This is termed an '*Act global, think local*' or 'glocal' strategy.

We can see that there are many other ways to define a market and this sometimes involves segmenting the generic market. For example, the white goods market could be segmented into refrigerators, deep freezes, dishwashers and washing machines, all of which could have their own distinct characteristics or drivers. It is up to the marketer to define the market properly in order to develop suitable marketing strategies and tactics to compete in that market.

istock © Milkos

MARKETING SYSTEM AND VALUE DELIVERY

The marketing system explains the interrelationship of the actors and elements that influence how organizations fulfil their value-creation and value-delivery goals for their target markets. The key components are the suppliers, marketers, channel members, customers and various value-seeking participants in the marketing system.

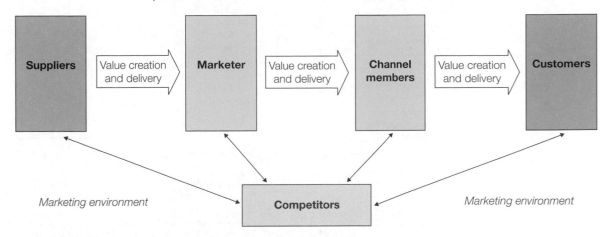

Figure 1.6: The marketing system as anchored by value creation and delivery
Source: Adapted from Gbadamosi, 2011, p. 66

Figure 1.6 demonstrates how the key elements in the system are anchored on the notion of value creation and delivery. This process begins with the suppliers of the relevant raw materials, whose activities make it possible for the marketers to produce the outputs needed by consumers in the right form. Channel members are responsible for providing time, place and possession utilities. They play significant roles in ensuring that customers derive value from the transactions. As the figure shows, the activities of competitors relate to all the elements in the system including the customers.

TOWARDS A VALUE–BASED UNDERSTANDING OF MARKETING

'Value is the perceived benefits minus the perceived costs in terms of time, money, or emotions.'

(Solomon et al., 2009, p. 29)

The starting point is the concept of '*more for less*'. The underlying assumption is that the '*average customer*' is a '*utility maximizer*' – striving to maximize benefits from market interactions (however defined) and minimize their outputs for acquiring those benefits. This suggests that consumers would want more (delivered value) for less cost (monetary cost, time cost, energy cost, psychic cost and so on). For this reason, consumers are strongly attracted to companies that they perceive to offer the highest value. In a way, just as companies desire to make profits, so also do consumers. According to this concept of more for less, when a customer believes that value received from a transaction outweighs the cost, then she or he has made a profit.

As shown in Figure 1.7, customer net value (CNV) tends toward maximization when total customer value (TCV) increases in an inverse proportion to total customer cost (TCC). That is, CNV will increase if TCV increases at a faster rate than TCC. This can be represented as follows: CNV = TCV − TCC.

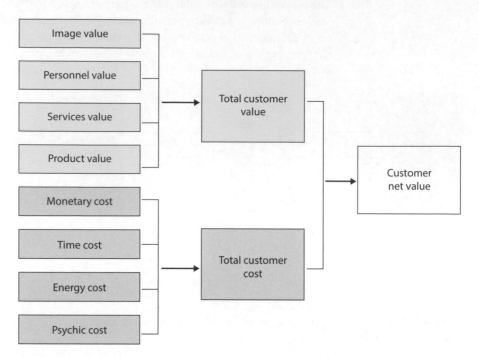

Figure 1.7: Customer value

It needs to be pointed out that the concept of value is multidimensional and can be interpreted differently by different stakeholder groups in the marketing system (see Figure 1.8). For example, shareholders may be inwardly more interested in profit maximization but this can only be achieved if profit-creating customers are attracted to what the company offers.

THE CONCEPT OF VALUE EMBODIED IN THE PURPOSE OF MARKETING

So far, we have deliberately avoided a one-size-fits-all, universalistic definition of marketing. This is because the values that drive marketing activities are continually changing and, as a result, profoundly expanding the frontiers of the marketing paradigm. Achrol and Kotler (2012) emphasize the point that there has always been an evident dynamic shift in marketing ethos since the origin of the discipline.

One of the more recent and equally rigorous attempts at constructing a definition of marketing was offered by Voss and Gilliam (2012), who argue that a definition process needs to integrate different dimensions of the *purpose of marketing*, not just one dimension. This means that, to gain a thorough understanding of marketing, there also needs to be deep reflection on the issues of the *purpose*, *process*, *contents*, *outcome/benefits* and *consequences*. Much earlier, almost working from this philosophical base, Keith Blois suggested that the meaning of marketing can be understood in 'five simple questions' (Blois, 1989).

Think and discuss

What is your understanding of 'value'? Consider Figure 1.8. Try to map out the value of each stakeholder and explain their interrelationships.

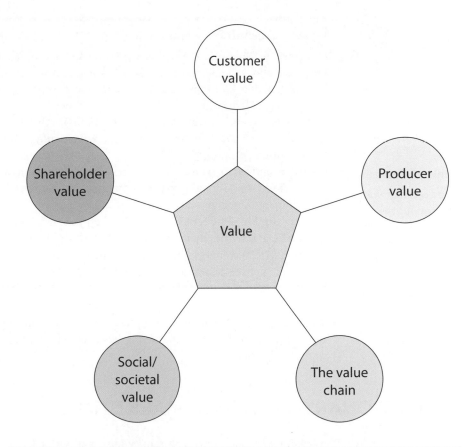

Figure 1.8: Typology of value

Marketing in five 'simple' questions

- Who are the customers?
- What does the customer want?
- Why does the customer make a purchase?
- Why should the customer make a purchase from my company?
- Why does my firm wish to supply the customer?

Underpinning the questions, either individually or collectively, is the concept of value. This concept is materially and symbolically crucial because it strategically lies at the heart of how marketers:

- Define their activities (that is, which market to serve, how and with what product)
- Understand what customers really want (needs and wants as a source of value composition)
- Design and deliver value propositions to the customer
- Differentiate their companies from the competition through, for example, a strong brand or corporate equity
- Generate added value for the business (that is, through profitability, stronger market share and market positioning or other measures that embed a firm's market and competitive strength)

> **General definitions of marketing**
>
> **American Marketing Association (AMA):** 'Marketing is the activity, set of institutions, and processes for creating, communicating, delivering, and exchanging offerings that have value for customers, clients, partners, and society at large.' (2007)
>
> **The Chartered Institute of Marketing (CIM):** 'Marketing is the management process responsible for identifying, anticipating, and satisfying customer requirements profitably.' (2001)
>
> **Kotler and Armstrong:** 'The process by which companies create value for customers and build strong customer relationships in order to capture value from customers in return.' (2014, p. 27)
>
> **Dibb, Simkin, Pride and Ferrell:** 'Marketing consists of individual and organizational activities that facilitate and expedite satisfying exchange relationships in a dynamic environment through the creation, distribution, promotion and pricing of goods, services and ideas.' (2012, p. 8)

Think and discuss

Based on what you know about the concept of 'value', how would you define marketing? Provide your own (albeit interim) definition of marketing.

To gain a sense of dynamic movements and value/philosophical shifts in marketing, we next consider how marketing has evolved and, importantly, the values that underlie the evolution.

EVOLUTIONARY TRENDS IN MARKETING

Marketing scholars have come up with a variety of frameworks to describe how marketing has evolved, though this should not be confused with the *history of marketing* (that is, the evolution of marketing thought), which is a topic of interest at an advanced stage in the study of the subject. A very popular framework that chronicles the evolution of marketing (see also Figure 1.9) outlines the stages that encompass the following:

- Production concept era
- Product concept era
- Selling concept era
- Marketing concept era
- Societal marketing concept era

Production concept: Approaching marketing from this perspective involves concentrating effort on attaining efficiency in production and ensuring wide distribution of the offering. The assumption is that the key factors that define value for the customers are *product availability and affordability*. Accordingly, the role of marketing was to ensure low-price value, usually in the form of mass production and intensive distribution.

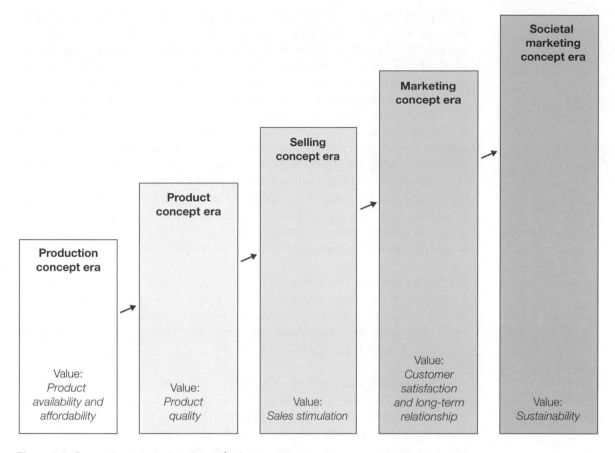

Production concept era

Value:
Product availability and affordability

Product concept era

Value:
Product quality

Selling concept era

Value:
Sales stimulation

Marketing concept era

Value:
Customer satisfaction and long-term relationship

Societal marketing concept era

Value:
Sustainability

Figure 1.9: Competing orientations in marketing

Product concept: In this phase, the key focus is on product quality. It assumes consumer value to be inherently linked to the availability of products of highest quality and performance. Hence, the marketing role was to offer products that the company determined to be of 'best value' to the consumer. A classic example was

istock © Peter Mah

Ford's Model T, where the company was severally cited to have said that customers could have any colour 'so long as it's black'. The focus is on the product and not on the customer. Nonetheless, consumers' perception of quality varies and may be different from the firm's. This is the main difficulty associated with this orientation to marketing.

Selling concept: The key factor emphasized in the selling orientation is *sales stimulation*. You may have heard people argue that 'a good product sells itself'. Those holding this view speak from the perspective of consumer satisfaction associated with a good offering, which often leads to repeat purchase, and possibly loyalty. However, if explored superficially, the expression could mislead by suggesting a marketing operation with no marketing communications budget. On the contrary, this is what the selling concept challenges. The belief of firms that practise the selling orientation is that the success of the organization is a product of various forceful promotional strategies aimed at convincing consumers to select the firm's product or brand over competitors' offerings. Hence, however good a product may be, consumers will not be in a position to consider buying it if they are not made aware of it. If considered very deeply, it will become clear that this approach is not about customer satisfaction or engendering a good and long-term relationship with the customer. It is about giving the firm the opportunity to make as many sales (and possibly as much profit) as possible from the transactions. That is the major downside of this approach.

Marketing concept: This emphasizes *customer satisfaction and long-term relationship*. Logically, for target customers to be satisfied, it is imperative that the firm should identify their needs and wants, and design the marketing mix elements to meet those needs and wants more efficiently and effectively than competitors do. This is the focus of marketing orientation.

Societal marketing concept: Much as the marketing concept seems good for both customers and the firm, it is short of perfect if it fails to incorporate the preservation of societal welfare into the scheme of things. The factor that primarily constitutes the value in this orientation to marketing is *sustainability*. Nowadays, consumers are more informed and are increasingly challenging firms to be more responsible to society. So, it is not surprising that, in addition to providing products or services in the exact form that consumers will love, using appropriate pricing, distribution and promotion strategies, most firms now emphasize their degree of environmental friendliness in order to woo customers. This takes a myriad of forms such as encouraging the recycling of packaging, promoting healthy consumption, safe disposal of by-products and many more.

MARKETING AS A FUNCTION AND PHILOSOPHY OF BUSINESS

Marketing has been recognized as a relatively new subject area that borrows freely from other disciplines such as economics, psychology and the behavioural sciences. Is marketing then an art or a science? The answer is that it is both! If we take a positivist view, then marketing exhibits objectivity (it takes a detached viewpoint of a particular situation), is measurable (it measures sales, brand recall, profit and so on) and is similar to a scientific process in that we can draw conclusions from the interaction of force A on force B to give a known outcome. However, it also exhibits a post-positivist view in that it is unlike the natural sciences, being based on the premise that the true meaning of phenomena is best discovered through qualitative

1

Example 1.3:
Societal marketing concept at Marks and Spencer (M&S)

Marks and Spencer, a British retailing organization, has been proactive in its social consciousness strategies. Essentially, its business consists of 51 per cent food and 49 per cent clothing and homeware products. The Group's revenue for 2012 was £9.9 billion, which represents an increase of 2 per cent on the figure recorded for the previous year – an indication of customers' appreciation of what the company is doing.

M&S is the UK market leader for womenswear, lingerie and menswear, but something else that significantly contributes to its success and popularity among its customers is the company's green credentials. It has shown commitments to improving the environment and healthier living conditions. For example, through its Plan A programme, the

company demonstrates clearly to all its stakeholders, including customers, its intention to become the world's most sustainable retailer. Its eco and ethical programme is at the heart of how it practises its marketing activities. Through this plan, which was launched in January 2007, the organization is now working with customers and suppliers to combat climate change, use sustainable raw materials, reduce waste, trade ethically and help customers to maintain a healthier lifestyle. There were 100 Plan A targets when the programme was launched and that number has now increased to 180 to be achieved by 2015. So far, it has successfully achieved 138 targets and is making significant efforts to improve this record in the years to come. The organization makes the point clearly that marketing is not just about providing products or services and making profits, but also about ensuring a responsible approach that embraces environmental sustainability.

approaches. Marketers should adopt both perspectives as befits a discipline that borrows from both the natural sciences and the social sciences.

The discipline, as has been seen above, has not always been the dominant business paradigm. It has evolved over the years from a production conceptual base to a societal one. Marketing will always be an important business paradigm. In this situation, the way that a company develops and delivers greater value to its target customers in relation to its competitors will invariably be the dominant success factor. This customer-centric approach is the foundation on which a business is built. Marketing then becomes a business philosophy of putting the customer first. In this situation, every company employee or department is involved in marketing – from the reception staff or those staff involved in direct customer interface through to the production department. Marketing and hence value creation then becomes the 'glue' between the internal functions of an organization and the interface with customers and external stakeholders (see Figure 1.10). Marketing is also a function of business, involving a series of techniques such as advertising and market research. However, these techniques will fail if no marketing philosophy is adopted.

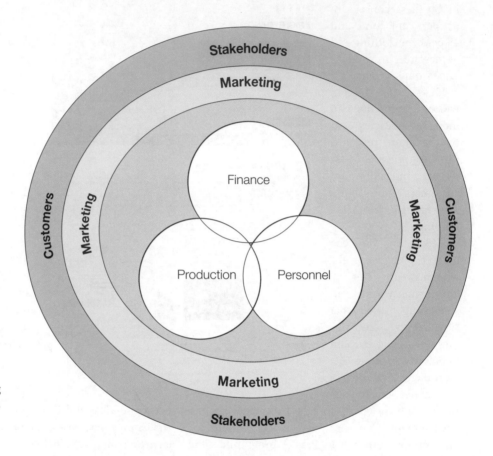

Figure 1.10: Marketing as an interface between the organization and society

As Figure 1.10 shows, marketing thus becomes the interface between an organization and its customers and external stakeholders

What is the difference, then, between marketing as a business approach and marketing management? As has been shown, marketing is both a business function and also a set of processes that creates and delivers value to customers. If marketing in the societal market era has a role in managing relationships between customers and the organization/stakeholders that benefit all parties, then marketing management is the *art and science* of choosing target markets and getting, keeping and growing customers through creating, delivering and communicating superior customer value.

It is evident that marketing has evolved from a transaction base – that is to say, occurring at the point of sale or where the transaction between buyers and sellers takes place. Marketing in the 21st century has evolved beyond this and can now be said to have a relational base. The differences between transactional and relational marketing are presented in Table 1.1 (Payne, 1994).

Table 1.1: From transactional to relational marketing

	Transactional marketing	**Relational marketing**
Focus on	Obtaining new customers	Customer retention
Orientation to	Service features	Customer benefits
Timescale	Short	Long
Customer service	Little emphasis	High emphasis
Customer commitment	Limited	High
Customer contact	Limited	High
Quality	Primarily operations concerns	The concern of all

THE MARKETING MIX AND VALUE CREATION

The aim of relational marketing is not just to gain new customers but to retain them over a long period of time through value-adding activities and superior benefits. The emphasis here is on customer service and high customer contact that generates higher levels of commitment either through repeat sales or increased word of mouth (oral or electronic via social networks). The basic premise is that everybody in the organization is in marketing. As Peter Drucker once said, marketing is too important to be delegated to the Marketing Department. Its fundamental purpose for any organization is to identify value points and create, deliver and maintain, on a continuous basis, consumer value aspirations.

This superior, customer-focused value is mainly delivered to target market segments through the marketing mix. This is the collection of tools that a particular marketer uses to target and satisfy their customers in value-oriented marketing. Traditionally, this was known as the '4 Ps' (product, price, place, promotion). However, the number of 'Ps' has grown to include three additional 'service' tools of *people*, *processes* and *physical evidence* as well as a number of allied tools such as packaging and positioning. For ease of use, the '7 Ps' framework in Figure 1.11 is generally the base from which an organization delivers value. The mix ensures that the right product is promoted to the right target market, and delivered at the right place and time and at the right price. The three service Ps ensure that the *people* who deliver the service/product, the *process* by which the product/services are delivered and the *physical* 'cues' (such as company livery, premises and signage) all add to the perceived and actual value delivered to the consumer. It could be stated that marketing is the conduit between the inputs/outputs of an organization and the utility derived from the consumption of those outputs by the end-user, the consumer. Therefore, the purpose of marketing, for an organization, is to create and deliver better comparative value than its competitors and thus achieve repeat business and build brand equity.

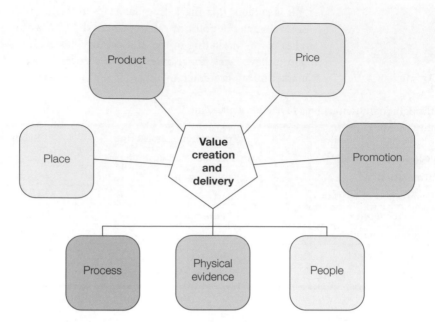

Figure 1.11: The marketing mix elements and value creation

CONCLUSION

Marketing is basically about creating and delivering value to customers, and the notion of value-orientation is becoming increasingly important for achieving success in the marketplace. This is because consumers now have innumerable choices and are therefore more selective about which products they buy to satisfy their needs. So having a strong value-orientation in business is a key reason why some companies out-perform others.

To be able to deliver value to customers, it is important to have a good appreciation of the links between the core concepts of marketing. These concepts include needs, wants, demand, exchange, market, satisfaction, market offering and profit. For example, a key factor in delivering value to customers is having the ability to move them from a state where they are deprived of certain products or services to their 'desired' state, where these products or services are provided. Meeting a need can be done in a variety of ways, but the one emphasized in marketing is that achieved through exchange; if a need is thus satisfied, customers can become loyal to a company or brands, and an organization becomes profitable and sustainable. It follows from this that while marketing may seem to be solely a function of an organization, success in the marketplace is achieved when its core concepts, listed above, are considered as a business philosophy wherein delivering value to the customers is the focus of all members of an organization.

Review questions

1 Using an appropriate example, discuss the concept of value and show how it is embedded in the marketing activities of a named company.
2 In what ways are consumer value and producer value likely to be similar?
3 How might society's marketplace value differ from that of the consumer?

Case study
Apple: an epitome of value creation

FEW PEOPLE COULD DOUBT THE POPULARITY OF Apple as a strong firm of global standard. Although many will attribute this to the innovative ability of the team in the organization, arguably the key success factor lies in Apple's ability to create and deliver value to its disparate customers all over the world. While it has had a number of challenges since its inception in 1976, it was clear from the early years that the company was on the way to making a remarkable impact on the world of computers and other electronic products. For instance, the introduction of Apple II in 1977, which followed Apple I introduced a year earlier, created a unique space for the organization in the competitive market. It being the first computer introduced in a plastic case

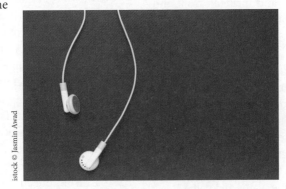

istock © Jasmin Awad

and with colour graphics, consumers quickly realized that the product stood out among others and could meet their needs effectively. Hence, they responded positively. Similarly, the instant success of the first generation of the PowerBook in late 1991 is noteworthy and also shows that Apple is keenly determined to satisfy its customers in all ramifications and ensure value creation and delivery.

The company demonstrates that creating value revolves around all the elements of the marketing mix. Apart from the products designed to meet the needs of its various consumer groups, Apple announced on 10 November 1997 that it would sell computers directly over the phone and on the Internet, thereby strengthening how it provides time, place and possession utilities. Its pricing and communication strategies are strategically designed to be of good fit for its customers. It has a very strong presence in social media such as Facebook and Twitter through which it communicates with its customers. All of these are symptomatic of Apple's value-driven philosophy.

Apple's case clearly shows that good marketing practice revolves around the exchange of something of value. The more the company works at giving customers products that satisfy them, the more successful it becomes in the industry. Its market share increases, customers become increasingly loyal to the brand and the sales and profit figures increase considerably. Another classic example is the release of iTunes for Windows in October 2003, which led to the sale of more than 70 million songs in the first year. Indeed, the step captured the interest of music lovers. The subsequent improvement in sales figures is another pointer to the fact that customers have an affinity with Apple's offerings and are convinced of the value they derive from the transactions.

It is evident all around us that Apple has introduced many products since the inception of its business several decades ago. However, the impact of the iPhone and iPad in society has been hailed as remarkable in recent times. When the iPhone was introduced in 2007, the positive response of the market showed that Apple fully embraces the marketing orientation because it ensures that the new offering addresses what the market really needs. Hence this emphasizes that the key focus of the firm is about creating and delivering value. But the company is not complacent about its success level. It modifies the product to accommodate changes in consumers' tastes and developments in the market environment to suit the dynamic needs of the target market. For instance, the iPhone 5, which was released in September 2012, has been described as having the fastest chip and ultra-fast wireless technology, and as being the thinnest and lightest iPhone ever. In the design of the headphones, as the Apple website says, 'Instead of starting with the speaker, we started with

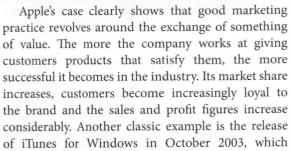

the ear.' The key focus in this approach was to make the headphone more comfortable for customers. In fact, Apple engineers asked a number of people to test more than 100 iterations of the Apple EarPods. The research shows that the product offers stronger protection in relation to sweat and water and is strikingly stable in the ear.

The same pattern of customer-oriented philosophy drives Apple's introduction of a series of tablet computers, branded iPad. The first generation of iPad was successful among various groups of consumers, as is evident in the sales figures, but the company ensured that the iPad 2, which was introduced in 2011, had a better processor and included front and back cameras and many other new features. Still keeping ahead of the game, Apple introduced what it calls The New iPad early in 2012. The unique selling point (USP) of this additional offering is highlighted by the company as the retina display. Ultimately, customers are becoming increasingly loyal to the organization and are eagerly looking forward to seeing and buying new offerings from Apple. The rationale for this is crystal clear. To be successful in marketing, the focus must be on the creation and delivery of three things – value, value and value.

Sources

http://apple-history.com/h1 (Retrieved 9 October 2012)

http://apple-history.com/h8 (Retrieved 9 October 2012)

J. Edward (2012) 'Apple's Biggest Marketing Secret Was Revealed in Federal Court', Business Insider, 5 August 2012, www.businessinsider.com/apples-biggest-marketing-secret-just-got-revealed-in-federal-court-2012-8 (Retrieved 10 June 2013)

www.apple.com/uk/iphone/ (Retrieved 24 October 2012)

www.apple.com/uk/ipad/ (Retrieved 9 October 2012)

www.apple.com/uk/iphone/features/ (Retrieved 24 October 2012)

Questions

1 Why do you think Apple has been so successful despite the complexity of the global marketing environment? Do you think the success can be sustained in view of the increasing volatility of the marketing environment?

2 It is stated that Apple consulted a number of people in the target market to test the suitability of EarPods. Which of the marketing management orientations does this approach represent? Justify your claim with relevant explanations. How would this have been handled if the production and selling orientations had been used?

3 Apart from the customer, which other parties could be significant to Apple's success in its marketing activities, and how?

4 What advice would you give Apple to increase its market share by 10 per cent in the next quarter?

Group task

Identify two companies operating in the same sector (for example, high street retailing). Your task is to analyse these companies and answer the following questions:

1 Which of the companies do you consider more successful?
2 Why is one company more successful than the other?
3 What are the sources of the company's success?

Glossary/Key terms

Customer-centric: A predominant focus on the customer

Superior customer value: Value advantages as perceived by customers

Unmet need: A consumer need that is insufficiently addressed or not addressed at all by companies

Value: The perceived benefits that consumers derive in consumption situations less the perceived costs (e.g. time, money or emotions) involved

Value configuration: Process of integrating the disparate activities to add value to what a firm offers

Value orientation: The principles or philosophy underlying how firms approach the task of value creation and delivery

Vocab check list for ESL students

Configuration	Myriad	Physiological	Synthesis
Flux	Paradigm	Reciprocal	Tangible
Manifestation	Perpetual	Salient	Universalistic

Definitions for these terms can be found in the 'Vocab Zone' of the companion website, which provides free access to the Macmillan English Dictionary online at www.palgrave.com/business/Gbadamosi

Further reading

B. Comstock, R. Gulati and S. Liguori (2010), 'Unleashing the Power of Marketing', *Harvard Business Review*, Vol. 88, No. 10, pp. 90–98
This article stresses that marketing is an engine for growth in organizations.

John C. Groth (1994) 'The Exclusive Value Principle: A Concept for Marketing', *Journal of Product and Brand Management*, Vol. 3, No. 3, pp. 8–18
This paper explains and links psychic needs to price, margin risk, customer satisfaction and value.

P. Kotler (1972) 'A Generic Concept of Marketing', *Journal of Marketing*, Vol. 36, No. 2, pp. 46–54
The key focus in this paper is the widening scope of marketing. It explains how marketing covers all transactions between an organization and all its publics.

T. Levitt (1960) 'Marketing Myopia', *Harvard Business Review*, July–August, pp. 45–56
In this article, the author argues that marketers will do better to focus on satisfying the needs of their customers than to be preoccupied with their products.

L. J. Ryals and S. Knox (2005) 'Measuring Risk-adjusted Customer Lifetime Value and its Impact on Relationship Marketing Strategies and Shareholder Value', *European Journal of Marketing*, Vol. 39, No. 5/6, pp. 456–72
This article shows why selecting customers for retention based on lifetime analysis could be very useful for relationship marketing strategies.

References

Achrol, R. and Kotler, P. (2012) 'Frontiers of the Marketing Paradigm in the Third Millennium', *Journal of the Academy of Marketing Science*, 40, pp. 35–52

AMA (2007) 'Definition of Marketing' http://www.marketingpower.com/aboutama/pages/definitionofmarketing.aspx (Accessed on 23rd July, 2013)

Bagozzi, R. P. (1975) 'Marketing as Exchange', *Journal of Marketing*, 39 (4), October, pp. 32–39

Blois, K. (1989) 'Marketing in Five "Simple" Questions', *Journal of Marketing Management*, 5 (2), pp. 113–21

CIM (2001) 'Official Definition of Marketing' http://www.cim.co.uk/Resources/JargonBuster.aspx (Accessed on 24th July, 2013)

Day, G. (2003) *Creating a Superior Customer-relating Capability*. Marketing Science Institute, MSI, Working Paper No. 03–001

Dibb, S., Simkin, L., Pride, W. M. and Ferrel, O. C. (2012) Marketing: Concepts and Strategies (6th edn). London: Cengage Learning

Gbadamosi, A. (2011) 'Entrepreneurship Marketing Environment', in S. Nwankwo and A. Gbadamosi (eds) *Entrepreneurship Marketing: Principles and Practice of SME Marketing*. Oxfordshire: Routledge, pp. 55–78

Kotler, P. and Armstrong, G. (2014) *Principles of Marketing* (15th edn). Harlow: Pearson Education

Lindgreen, A., Hingley, M., Grant, D. and Morgan, R. (2012) 'Value in Business and Industrial Marketing: Past, Present and Future', *Industrial Marketing Management*, 41, pp. 207–14

Payne, A. (1994) 'Relationship Marketing: Making the Customer Count', *Managing Service Quality*, 4 (6), pp. 29–31

Solomon, M. R., Marshall, G. W., Stuart, E. W., Barnes, B. R. and Mitchell, V.W. (2009) *Marketing: Real People, Real Decisions*, Harlow: Pearson Education

Voss, K. and Gilliam, D. (2012) 'A Proposed Procedure for Construct Definition in Marketing', *European Journal of Marketing*, 47 (1), pp. 5–26

2 UNDERSTANDING THE MARKETING ENVIRONMENT

PETER GRUENWALD TAYLOR

AMITY UNIVERSITY IN LONDON

CHAPTER CONTENTS

LEARNING OUTCOMES

The content of this chapter will help you to:

- Understand the nature of the marketing environment
- Analyse the changing environment, using appropriate techniques
- Explain how the changing environment impacts customer value
- Discuss present-day value systems such as corporate social responsibility and sustainability and their impacts on marketplace behaviours

Marketing in action
January blues ... those were very cold, not cool

IN JANUARY 2012, AFTER 123 YEARS OF SUCCESSFUL business, Kodak filed for bankruptcy protection. Similarly, after 78 years and with 187 shops, Jessops Cameras went into administration in January 2013.

Who could have **prophesied** that the promising mass market for digital cameras, forecast and anticipated to allow an industry transition from film cameras, would be made redundant by the integration of photo features in mobile phones? Jessops Cameras witnessed a slow shrinking of its camera market as its customers gradually migrated to computer stores, online retailers, department stores and even grocery stores. After 78 years, only the brand name was purchased to become solely an online retailer.

The radical changes in digital technologies negatively impacted on these two well-established and previously successful companies. As a desert is often characterized by skeletons of unfortunate animals that could not cope with the environment, so too are businesses which often succumb to changes in their operating environments.

istock © scanrail

INTRODUCTION

This chapter is focused on explaining the dimensions of the marketing environment, interconnections with serious events and their **ramifications**, which we **holistically** refer to as the 'business environment'. It is an arena that shapes how marketing is practised and how consumer values drive many of the dynamic changes that have become a prominent feature of the marketing environment. This arena in which business is conducted, with its radical changes, could easily turn out to be just as terminal, with slow **incremental** changes that gradually shrink a firm to closure.

So many small and large businesses across all industries and services have failed to recognize, or were incapable of responding to, the changing values, needs and demands of consumers even just to survive. Ask your parents if they remember Singer sewing machines and Costa's and Starbucks' famous grandparent, Lyons Corner Houses.

Changes in the business environment are hard to predict but consider a few that are still unravelling in many sectors (add further examples of your own):

- Fashion: such as man bags and skirts
- Tastes: such as bubble tea with crispy insects
- Technologies: such as 4G (we still expect to have 5 and probably 6G)
- New markets: new consumer segments such as new upper-class Chinese who enjoy beef and some red wine
- New competition: new products and new investors such as Haier, Tata, Canadian oil sheikhs

The marketing environment consists of the combination of actors and forces that directly or indirectly affect the ability of marketing decision makers to build and maintain successful relationships with their target markets.

Example 2.1:
The 3D world

A relatively new technology is 3D printing or additive manufacturing, which produces items by building layers of material to make objects. Most simplistically, picture thin layers of toothpaste piled layer upon layer until an object is produced. The current application is the new ability to make low volumes and bespoke products more efficiently. However the development is rapidly moving to enable greater production speeds and thereby starting to move into the traditional domain of mass production. With greater speed and lower cost, could this technology lead to the demise of inventorying spare parts (for automotive use and home appliances) – as, with one 'sample', a part could be efficiently made to order. This has the potential to wipe out the need for immensely costly inventories and inventory management systems. Smaller new companies could wrestle the spares/parts supply business from the domain of the currently generally large companies and original equipment manufacturers (OEMs). Similarly, this could mean that for 3D printing technology, due to the virtual absence of transportation costs and the new efficiency of short production, a significant portion of manufacturing might shift back from low-cost mass producers to numerous networks of small suppliers not just based in Asia but across the globe.

From this 3D printing scenario, you should appreciate that change is an opportunity but also that there are inherent ripple effects of change. These changes can positively or negatively impact a range of related markets, products, services, intermediaries and logistics, and provide a platform for yet further changes.

PERSPECTIVES ON THE MARKETING ENVIRONMENT: MACRO AND MICRO FEATURES

We have up to now been talking about 'change' and the 'environment'. Now let us look at the elements or components of the environment and consider some analysis of how different elements/events might actually affect business. The business environment is most often divided into macro-environmental factors and micro-environmental factors and/or the competitive environment. We will learn about the macro environment first and then look at the micro environment and some thought-provoking and useful models.

MACRO–ENVIRONMENTAL FACTORS

The macro environment includes a comprehensive view of the major significant changes that can impact the firm's decision making, performance and strategies. These changes are beyond the control of the firm domestically and, usually, internationally. Acronyms are commonly used to express these 'components'/impacting variable factors depending both on how researchers define the words and their **perimeters**, and on the factors they think are most or least inclusive. Hence STEEP stands for: **S**ocio-cultural and demographics, **T**echnology, **E**conomic conditions, **E**cology and physical environment and **P**olitical and legal. The two most-used acronyms of macro-environmental components/variables and their analysis are PEST and PESTEL.

Macro-environmental impacting variables

PEST (political, economic, social and technological factors) and PESTEL are schemas of individual identification and analysis, which can provide the profiling to determine and understand the context of the firm's environment (see Figure 2.1). The idea is that each variable (political, legal and so on) represents the potential for a significant impact on a firm or sector in both the short and the longer term. And as we stated earlier, by anticipating, knowing and understanding the possible implications of the changes, the firm can plan the best way to react in terms of defence or take advantage and exploit the change as a new opportunity.

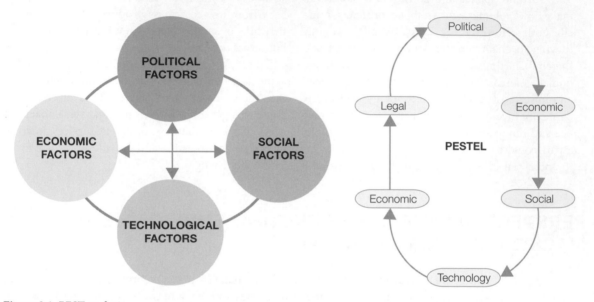

Figure 2.1: PEST analysis

Immediately you look at the 'variables', you should see that most changes in one variable impact, or have potential to impact, the other variables.

Both PEST and PESTEL models begin with 'political' but PEST normally includes 'legal' while with PESTEL it is a separate factor. To actually use this in business, we synthesize various data sources/sets for essential thoughtful and innovative analysis. As we go through, you should think of some examples of your own. By doing so, you will start to gain actual personal decision-making and analytical skills.

Political variables

It can be argued that much environmental change comes from changes at various levels of government, which can have an impact on both domestic and international conditions. Common political issues that emerge in challenging economic times include: levels of government spending, immigration concerns and protecting domestic industry. In challenging times, a political party which has a Keynesian economic policy will, for example, spend public money on public buildings and houses, schools, roads and so on. Arguably, one would expect the impact of such priorities and related government expenditure to increase demand for everything related to the construction industry, from architects and interior designers to builders and suppliers (intermediaries), and importers and manufacturers of building materials and equipment (from kitchen sinks, taps, and bathrooms to floor coverings and door bells).

It is challenging if not impossible to separate political and legal change. Political groups have their own priorities and express them in legal change. Legal change can come from expressed or perceived values of the electorate. Increasing legal restrictions on the marketing of cigarettes in the UK, for example, has led to punitive pricing (tax increases), sales restrictions, virtually no forms of advertising, severe restrictions on point of purchase, warnings required on packaging and expansion of no-smoking areas, and may indeed lead to essentially only plain packaging.

Legal dictate can set minimum prices on units of alcohol and require more consumer-friendly information about food and beverage ingredients. New legislation can govern the specifications for an external door, in terms of the length of time it can withstand fire, minimum sizes and materials of toys, and even whether you should pay 20 per cent VAT (UK) on a warm but not a hot Cornish pasty.

istock © monkeybusinessimages

International view: On a wider scale, international political forces can cross over diverse areas through exchange rates (which can have a significant impact on a country's exports and imports). They can close old markets or open new ones, affect the cost of raw materials, and offer new sources and new substitutes. Think about the legal and political dimensions of the energy industry – the impact of existing and new pipelines spanning the globe, various biofuels and their impact on global food production costs, 'fracking', seabed mining, wind, tidal and solar energy systems and the impact of shifting costs of energy on an individual market's competitiveness.

Economic variables

Slow economic times (or, more importantly, perceptions of slow economic times), the risk of being unemployed and lack of confidence in economic growth all contort spending. People delay major purchases. First hit usually are the discretionary items (where we can choose to delay, such as new cars, white goods, electronics, furnishings and floor coverings). With lower sales, firms seek lower operating costs (including cutting staff) and lower their inventories, which has a chain reaction so that all firms in the supply chain cut back – even those supplying raw materials. Firms pull back from hiring new staff and borrowing money for further investments, and business growth stagnates. At the dinner table, families may switch to cheaper food and private label products and become more cost conscious. Still at the dinner table, there are indications that people entertain at home instead of dining out and there are new markets for 'gourmet' prepared or semi-prepared foods. There is an old saying that in good times men buy suits but in bad times men only buy ties.

The essential point is that economic times drive different and dynamic consumer values and priorities which can certainly affect firms. A final small point is that firms with higher fixed costs are obviously more vulnerable in slower economic times but climb back faster in good economic times.

On a practical level, by knowing and understanding the economic environment, a firm may, for example, shift from emphasizing new windows and doors as enhancing the home's appearance or increasing its value to emphasizing them as being a cost-saving investment that enables lower heating costs. Curtains can be sold on the basis that they represent an energy-saving feature versus essentially a fashion decoration. Similarly, as an economy or perception of economy becomes more positive, then a firm must realize the change and adjust its position to survive and hopefully thrive.

International view: The global context of economic factors is both pervasive and significant. It is common for there to be fluctuations in trade sectors and markets. In 2011, the UK had a trade deficit with the other EU-27 members of £45.6 billion but had a trade surplus of £25 billion with non-EU trading partners (Allen, 2013). Certainly all member states are impacted to varying degrees by the economies of other member states as well as non-EU trading partners. Economic slowdown in the US affects China and other economies. To varying degrees, the world is interlocked and the US and China affect the world economy. In Canada, with 70 per cent of exports to the US, they say that if the US gets a cold, Canada gets a cough. There is both anecdotal and empirical evidence that China may be losing its competitive edge due to salary increases of up to 35 per cent in 2012. Think of the impact on global and regional competition and possibly even former export markets. Who knows – in the future, maybe a firm can make a T-shirt competitively in Europe! Finally, we should note that in many industries, including automotive, the focus is on global economies of scale.

Think and discuss

Most governments make efforts to produce a national plan and annual budgets. What are your views on these activities? Comment on their usefulness. In what ways might a national annual budget influence marketing activities in a particular country?

Social variables

The social element commonly includes significant shifts in cultural as well as consumer VALs (that is, values, attitudes and lifestyles). Obvious examples can be observed in the increasing consumer preference for 'organic' and 'natural' products, which are clearly here to stay. 'Natural products' with an awareness of chemical additives are now part of our attitude and values, as is the growing trend towards recycling. Can you throw a tin into the waste bin without feeling guilty?

Many large domestic and international consumer panels such as the Kantar World Panel and Neilsen Consumer Panel track purchase and usage behaviour in 250,000 households in 25 countries. These longitudinal studies are also augmented with 'special' on- and offline research such as Redshift Research's Crowdology. The research tracks movements and shifts in diverse areas. These include, for example, the current trends to or away from 'low fat' and 'natural' ingredients; the rise or decline in product

Example 2.2:
KFC

Changes in attitudes and values affect so many areas in comprehensive ways. In May 2012, Kentucky Fried Chicken (KFC) was accused of using takeaway boxes in the UK, Indonesia and China made from fibres of tropical hardwood, harvested from forests that formed the habitat of an endangered species of tiger. The charges were denied by the company. There was a clear concern by KFC that perhaps some consumers may decide not to buy KFC products on the basis of the allegation (Efstathiou and Patton, 2012). The congruence of concern for the environment and recycling, and the importance of 'responsible' business management gives some idea of the range and depth of feelings that flow from the 'tipping point' type of changes.

categories from frozen fish to frozen fish entrees; the relative importance of style or functionality of items; consumer adoption rates for everything from the new LED (light-emitting diode) light bulbs to robotic vacuum cleaners and lawn mowers. Obviously, the same techniques are used by political parties to gauge (reflect or ignore) public sentiment, with research by companies such as ICM, ComRes, Ipsos Mori and YouGov.

Think and discuss

What do you understand by 'globalization of business'? Give five examples of the impact of globalization, based on what you see around you.

International view: Globalization has led to unprecedented movements of people across the globe, such as students and economic migrants. This has led to transporting differing cultural values and, it may be argued, creating a new level of global consciousness.

Technological variables

Technological changes are constantly evolving. It is argued that there is a link between attitudes, values and technology. Some technologies – digital, biometrics, voice recognition and applications, touch-screen and cloud technology – are readily accepted and have been comfortably taken into use. In other areas, technology is impacted by values and attitudes in the form of feelings ranging from concern to absolute fear – for example in the case of stem cell research, and plant and animal to human genetic crossovers at any level. These technologies attract a dissenting public voice. Genetically modified (GM) food has its strong detractors and strong supporters and it is difficult to segregate 'science will not fail us' from 'we don't know what we're getting into'. Alternatively, the main idea is *to reduce the need for chemicals or that it is an attempt to get a stranglehold by large corporations so that they have a near-monopoly on farming*. It is important to recognize the impact of an individual's values and attitudes entering the technology fray and the difficulty of accurately assessing the environment.

It is common to differentiate between technological changes that are incremental and those that are often referred to as 'disruptive technologies'. Further, there is a differentiation between high- and low-end disruptive technologies. Low-end disruptive technologies are where the new offering gives little of real use to the user and/or the new market technologies actually fail to meet unfulfilled needs (Christensen, 2003).

Example 2.3:
The music revolution

An example of a disruptive technology would be digital music. It represents a paradigm shift in the industry (a totally new approach and technology), in everything from alternative totally new supply chains (such as iTunes and Amazon) and bands marketing themselves (such as through Pure Volume, iLike.com, OurWave and MP3.com) to selling individual songs and 'renting' music on a monthly or yearly basis (such as through Spotify). The music stores that have survived have had to significantly widen their product ranges to include games and electronic accessories.

istock © ambrits

It should be noted that disruptive technologies lead to many new applications. Consider all the applications of wireless technologies from remote printers to portable speakers, all of which could amount to just scratching the surface of the home entertainment product category.

Incremental improvements are solidly rooted in the Japanese concept of 'kaizen'. The interpretations of kaizen vary, with '*kai*' being 'continuous' or 'change' and '*zen*' meaning 'correct' or 'good', and it is part of a wider philosophy of seeking constant improvements in work and personal life. Kaizen could be viewed as a philosophical mindset for embedding change. An essential part of it is to reduce costs and improve quality by workers constantly refining their work and the production processes, using flexible work teams and candid feedback. To the marketers, kaizen may translate into constant small improvements with each new model of a product (i.e continuous product improvement).

Just a few reservations

We started by stating that in identifying and analysing each of the elements in the PEST variables, a firm should be in a better position to anticipate, or at least have some idea, what environmental changes might affect its business. Based on this knowledge of the market and our knowledge of our own capabilities and competencies, we can best prepare our business and hopefully take advantage of what these changes may bring. Examples have been given for possible and actual ramifications of these impacting variables and you should think them through yourself so that they make sense to you.

However, this is not quite as simple as could be inferred. One key problem is that changes do not have a constant or consistent pace. Some changes move very quickly and then rapidly slow down, or move very slowly and then suddenly reach the tipping point. It is alleged that 15 per cent of all waste comes from toilet paper. People increasingly express concerns about the environment, and yet sales of toilet tissue made from recycled paper are less than 3.5 per cent of the UK market. Similarly, the eBook had a presence earlier but was named and got its initial public awareness in 1985. Sony's Reader was joined by Google's initial entry, Kindle, in 2007 and sales of the category started gathering momentum to 2010. However, by 2012, there were major indications and concerns that the market was using the format on tablets rather than on dedicated readers (Greenfield, 2012).

Think and discuss

Make a list of products or services affected by political or legal change. Take the position of a member of the supply chain.

- What would be possible impacts on your business?

- What can you do to lessen or stop the impact?

- Suggest 'response strategies' to make the change into an opportunity.

The two previous examples could be contrasted with the crushing of competition in the smartphone and tablet market. In just two years from introduction, Apple sold more than 60 million iPhones and the brand was almost synonymous with smartphones. However, by 2012 iPhone and iPad were battling it out with Android-powered Samsung. Sales dominance moved between product launches – Galaxy 3, iPhone 5, then Galaxy S4 and so on. Certainly, competition will grow in the technology sectors but the adoption of these products from introduction to setting the benchmark in terms of features is astonishing.

istock © UmbertoPantalone

Market volatility: Irrespective of the available data, and computing data synthesis abilities (technological) and competencies, the expression 'volatile' is ever present regarding today's business environment. This is arguably the result of a combination of rapidly developing and competing technologies, shortening life cycles, rapid diffusion of information through, for example, opinion from social media, massive mergers and acquisitions, and actual unforeseen events.

Taleb (2007), in a somewhat controversial book, *The Black Swan*, suggests that we grossly understate the high level of uncertainty and randomness of events and are satisfied with erroneous retrospective explanations. Essentially, he suggests that so many events and changes are simply not predictable or based on any extrapolation of data. Taleb suggests that firms focus more on identifying vulnerabilities and planning defence and/or exploitation. Evocatively and memorably, Taleb is quoted as saying 'to bankrupt a fool, give him information'.

MICRO–ENVIRONMENTAL FACTORS

You note that 'competitors' are not included in the macro-environmental factors but of course they can have a significant impact on the firm. Some researchers refer to the 'competitive environment', which includes customers and the direct and indirect competitors. Porter (2002, p. 3) notes that 'wealth is actually created at the micro-economic level – in the ability of firms to create valuable goods and services using efficient methods'.

The micro-economic environment refers to the forces of change imposed on a firm by its various stakeholders (groups or individuals that have interests in or concerns with the firm). Other academics suggest they are factors 'close to the firm' and most directly affect the firm's activities.

In Figure 2.2, the relationship between the firm, its micro environment and the macro environment (in the sequence of PESTEL) are indicated.

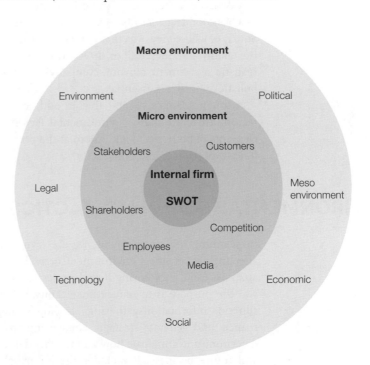

Figure 2.2: Relationship between firm and micro- and macro-environmental factors

Micro-environmental stakeholders and conflicts

As you would expect, the various micro-environmental stakeholders will have varying priorities and conflicts do arise as each of the groups think and push for their own values and best interests.

An obvious conflict might be the employees' salaries (including pensions), expectations and requirements and those of management and shareholders. Management is assessed and rewarded generally on the basis of achieved profitability delivered to the shareholders. Profits in the form of dividends are only part of the assessment as often the actual share prices are also dependent on profitability or other fiscal measures such as return on capital employed. Hence, there is a high potential for conflict.

Other conflicts could include excessive, unsustainable pressure on suppliers on price, which may enhance a firm's profit but destroy the suppliers and result in unemployment. This puts pressure on government through a decline in collected taxes, a rise in benefit costs and lower sales for businesses that cater for consumers.

A final example would be conflicts with those concerned about the environment in the local community – for example, concerning the creation, disposal or storage of potential waste by-products. These people are possibly in conflict with the cost implications to the firm and possibly a number of levels of government.

Some theorists hold the view that the micro environment includes all the competencies and assets with which the firm can respond to challenges and opportunities. These could include the relative competitiveness of its hard assets such as facilities (including their location) and equipment and its soft assets such as proprietary knowledge and competencies – holistically as a company, but also those of its various individuals, special relationships with various stakeholders from customers and other interest groups.

Taking both the macro- and micro-environmental factors together, their analysis as a basis for decisions fits very well with the teachings of the famous Chinese general Sun Tzu, whose view was that to be successful (in war as in business) one must know the enemy and oneself (Tzu, 1994). Knowing oneself in business is having a candid, realistic assessment of your company's potential strengths and weaknesses. This holistic approach is essential.

A few academics suggest that in addition to micro- and macro-environmental factors, there are meso-environmental factors. These are factors that may include elements of both macro and micro at the point of their interfacing on a creative and fluid level (Dopfer and Potts, 2009).

ENVIRONMENTAL SCANNING: TACTICS AND TECHNIQUES

In scanning the environment, we are trying to discern change. What is actually affecting our business environment or will do so ahead? Scanning includes trend analysis, trend monitoring, trend projection and scenario development and analysis. The purpose is to reduce uncertainty, achieve competitive advantages through superior information gathering, develop strategies that improve financial performance, and generate strategic change. Environmental scanning (ES) attempts to determine and anticipate how and to what degree a change could impact our current and future business. It includes the 'futuring' (what 'futurists' do) of actions by competitors, customers and suppliers, and macro factors ranging from economic to social change.

Choo (1999, p. 13) gives a good formal definition of environmental scanning as: 'the acquisition and use of information about events, trends and relationships in an organization's external environment, the knowledge of which would assist management in planning the organization's future course of action.'

It involves seeking information that must be both 'read' and 'interpreted' and that has the potential for an impact on the firm. There are some inherent limitations, such as in the case of a check on the environment specially relating to legal stock market information. By the time most people know or recognize what is happening, the real opportunities have often already been taken. It is not just about finding the signs, but also about the analysis and transformation of potential to opportunity. Environmental scanning involves gathering, understanding and evaluating information generally from outside the firm and to a lesser degree from inside the firm.

TYPES OF SCANNING

As you would expect of a topic that has such market-erasing and market-creating potential ramifications, scanning has attracted much discussion by practitioners and academic researchers. Generally, marketers are interested in mastering the tool for scanning the environment. For this purpose, there are those mostly interested in the exploitation and utilization of scanning technologies and those who focus on the cognitive and behavioural aspects (i.e. how and/or why decisions are affected by personal mindset and perceptions of industry risk). These perspectives also include general aspects of what is referred to as a bounded rationality in consumer behaviour.

Bounded rationality, expressed in its most compressed form, means that decision makers have to make decisions based on incomplete and/or inaccurate information within excessive time constraints. The result is often called 'satisficing' (from 'satisfy' and 'suffice') – that is, acceptable but not optimal decision making (Solomon et al., 2010).

One school of thought places emphasis on the actual application and results of scanning. The differentiation within this group is the main basis or objective of the scanning. Most commonly, it is divided into: 'business', 'competitor' and 'competitive intelligence' – all of which seek information and knowledge in order to plan for action that will change or pre-empt the vicissitudes of the environment.

Business intelligence

Business intelligence (BI) subsumes previous terms such as decision support systems, executive information systems and management information systems. Data warehousing (a 'place' to store disparate information from disparate sources) is at the core of BI. Related activities are 'data cleaning', which basically refers to the constant removal of irrelevant, dated or erroneous data, and 'data mining', which refers to technology and mathematical modelling to organize and classify information that can be accessed by various parties to flexibly create logical correlations with varying levels of probabilities. More succinctly, Negash (2004, p. 177) suggests that 'BI combines operation data (actual activities, sales by categories, etc.) with analytic tools to present complex and competitive information to planners and decision makers'. It has also been suggested that BI includes analysis of potential acquisitions and mergers and risk assessments for present and future country markets.

Competitiveness intelligence

Competitive scanning has a different focus but may have similar technologies and processes. Competitiveness intelligence (CI) is characterized by:

- The use of internal company data integrated with salient intelligence on market information
- An emphasis on assessing a firm's competitive position, often using benchmarking techniques
- Indicating the difference between information and its analysis to produce intelligence
- A specific focus on providing a platform for upper management decision making

The suggestion that different levels of management scan more broadly and that there is therefore a need for more 'bespoke' information is a popular view in the literature.

Competitor intelligence: Competitiveness versus competitor intelligence

Competitor intelligence (CI) is more specific and different from *competitive intelligence* in that it has a narrower focus. Rather than looking at general competitiveness, this technique concentrates on in-depth study, analysis and assessment of specific, significant, present and potential competitors – their product and service features and relative quality, pricing structures, distribution channel development, logistics infrastructure, growth and expansionary information, research and development and/or intended acquisitions.

Within the unrelenting expansion and importance of the Internet, competitive intelligence also includes competitor website analysis (that is, the study of links, keyword terms, adwords (UK) and meta key word tags, and the nature and extent of any search enhancement activities).

Though it should not, scanning could include illegal (perhaps even criminal) activities that are generally referred to as 'industrial espionage', where spies are placed within competing firms, particularly in the research and development department. A contentious or grey area that has caused law suits and charges in the past comes from the situation where an individual (especially in a senior position) moves to a competing firm. Allegations are often made that they took secret information with them which, unfairly or illegally, may bring some advantage to the new employer.

This constant watching and analysing of what is happening is part of environmental scanning. Even better, scanning includes forecasting, predicting and making educated guesses about the future. More formally and comprehensively, it is the process of gathering information about events and relationships in a company's external environment. The knowledge obtained could profoundly assist top management in the difficult task of charting the company's future course of action. The emphasis is on analysing and interpreting wide-ranging information about the environment which might impact how a company 'does business'.

In summary, environmental scanning helps to reduce an unfavourable impact of environmental changes and reveals possibilities for acquiring or preserving competitive advantage. While they are outside the marketing frame, it should be noted that appropriate response strategies can only be successful if they are complemented and energized by management and employee commitment and an appropriate organizational culture, structure and systems.

SCENARIO PLANNING: BACK INTO THE FUTURE

Before we delve into detailed analysis of methods for assessing the current environment, we will take a brief look at a perhaps more conjectural basis of planning for change. It has validity in that there is a high degree of unpredictability of the future based on the present. In fact, at least one author even suggests that there is really no predictability of the future based on the present (Taleb, 2007).

Scenario planning entails developing a list of different possible changes or events that could affect the firm in a kind of 'what if?' process. The firm then plans for appropriate responses to these possible occurrences. Alternatively, firms can *backcast*, which means starting from some assumed future state and then filling in the sequence of developments that could lead there.

Here are some possible events that would evoke scenario planning by firms:

- What if a laser treatment became commonly available to remove facial hair? What might Gillette's response be?
- What if floor-cleaning, vacuuming and lawn-cutting robots were now in the 'innovator' stage of diffusion? What response might there be from firms that are currently in the sector, and also from electronics firms?

You are probably already familiar with less futurist or more realistic versions of scenario planning in the form of environmental impact studies that use the technique, with levels of probability, as the basis for recommendations. These focus semi-exclusively on ecosystem components, usually assessing the various possible environmental consequences of the development of a new rail line, new airport in the middle of a river or new gas or oil pipelines or the location of wind turbine farms.

SWOT ANALYSIS

An analysis of a firm's existing strengths and weaknesses and possible opportunities and threats is referred to by its acronym, 'SWOT'. It is as basic and commonly used in marketing strategy as liquidity ratios are in finance (see Figure 2.3).

	HELPFUL TO OBJECTIVE	HARMFUL TO OBJECTIVE
INTERNAL (COMPANY)	STRENGTHS	WEAKNESSES
EXTERNAL (ENVIRONMENT)	OPPORTUNITIES	THREATS

Figure 2.3: The SWOT framework

Business cards on the go

With changes in technology, quality printing is readily available without the services of a commercial printer. Software and printer quality renders custom graphics fairly simple and of acceptable quality for a firm to print its own letterheads, compliments slips, price lists, business cards and even some brochures.

However, there are growing opportunities in online custom graphic work for firms that print their own material but require higher quality. Commercial printers have graphic departments that provide expertise and hence there is a possible opportunity to capitalize on these competencies. Similarly, some large printers can change their business model to online low-cost printing.

Think and discuss

Do a SWOT analysis of yourself. What are your personal strengths and weaknesses? What are the opportunities and threats in the present business market? Given the opportunities and threats, what should you do in terms of your strengths and weaknesses?

Essentially, a firm is doing a self-assessment, with as much accuracy and candour as possible, to determine what are its strengths and what are its weaknesses. Simplistically, our strengths could be that our products are most competitive in terms of features and price and there is a knowledgeable salesforce with good service support. However, our weaknesses could be that we have a narrower product range than competitors, and limited financial resources, which restrict marketing communications and levels of inventory. As you note in the diagram, these factors are internal to the firm. These are the reality of what the firm has to work with to succeed.

The attempt is to match strengths with the identified opportunities such as new markets and/or to try to use our strengths to lessen the impact of our weaknesses.

SWOT analysis has been criticized as being too simplistic and too broad. The analysis may lead to strategic errors if there is an insufficiently detailed analysis. Similarly, a SWOT analysis is a static tool in a dynamic environment, which means, perhaps, that it is only valid on the first day of preparation and all of the variables may change (Pickton and Wright, 1998). A case in point would be that having a large number of bank branches with wide coverage used to be considered a strength. In today's market, branches may be seen as a weakness because of their operating cost and the migration to online banking.

Part of the problem is in accurately assessing the firm's strengths and weaknesses. What management may think is a strength may actually be a weakness; some strengths of the firm may just be assumed and not recognized. Another difficulty is that the assessment of each variable is not the same through different levels of the company. Something may be a strength at a managerial level, but this may not be the case as we assess people or departments in lower levels of the firm. The various problems cited may lead to a view that the technique does not sufficiently define the firm's competence.

Despite the possible limitations, SWOT analysis is generally known to have a high level of user awareness (estimated at about 90–95 per cent) and at least 50 per cent active users. It is a valuable analytic tool.

PORTER'S FIVE FORCES OF COMPETITION

This model has been used in business schools and business across the globe for many years and applies to an industry rather than to an individual firm. However, it is very much within the context of the business environment. It essentially facilitates the evaluation and analysis of an industry as to its relative attractiveness or unattractiveness for investment. Relative attractiveness means relative profitability, if not **propensity** (tendency) for profitability (Grundy, 2006).

We assess, analyse and evaluate each threat to the industry.

New entrants

The potential for new entrants adds competition (unattractiveness) to the industry as new entrants will take at least some market share and hence probably put downward pressure on price. Arguably, the major factor affecting new entrants is entry costs. The costs of starting the business – such as high initial investment costs and the large volumes needed in order to achieve competitive economies of scale and hence price – are major potentially negative factors.

Ease of market entry is also affected by relative differentiation. If there is little difference between the offerings of products or services (including weak branding), other firms will find it potentially easy to create a unique value. In other markets there may be segments that have not been competitively serviced. For example, most recently in the UK, short-term money lenders offering smaller, shorter, less documented but expensive loans to individuals and small firms have created a new market in the undifferentiated banking industry.

Substitutes

The evolution and development of technologies can cause increased competition in an industry as it has 'new competition' for its existing customers. Wireless keyboards, mice and printers are becoming the norm. Certainly, the market for coffee pods or individual unit capsules presents growing competitive substitution on the basis of taste, convenience and more competitive pricing. Nespresso (Nestlé, with $3.82 billion sales in 2011), Lavazza Blue, Tassimo (Kraft Foods) and Kenco (Cadbury) add to pressure on traditional ground and instant coffee. It could be argued that as a result of added convenience and improved taste, the product may encroach on tea and other hot beverages. It could become similar to the major shift from loose tea to tea bags.

Still, as regards substitutes, some people use the example of Pepsi and Coca-Cola. The thinking is that if the price of Pepsi were higher than that of Coke, people would buy Coke and vice versa (this is 'elasticity' to economics fans). The **caveat** is that this assumes the two products have the same value and are seen as being acceptable substitutes. As marketers, we cannot simply accept that. There will be a point where elasticity will in fact click in – we just do not know at what price this will occur.

One element of substitution is called 'switching cost'. At its most simplistic level, if a person wishes to change to Wilkinson Sword from Gillette blades, they will have to buy a new razor in order to use the blades, which is a financial cost. There is also a non-financial element of switching costs which involves a sense of risk (such as switching insurance companies) or psychological and emotional costs.

Bargaining power of buyers

In an industry where there are few buyers, the industry would be attractive for buyers as they can demand lower prices and better value from the sellers. The sellers have too few alternative people to sell to, hence a 'buyer's market' means lower prices for sellers.

Few buyers often reflects a 'concentrated market' – that is, when a few buyers control the majority of the business in that industry. Producers of food products from milk to cereals have to deal with relatively few buyers in the UK. In the first quarter of 2012, the top four supermarkets (Tesco, Asda, Sainsbury's and Morrisons) had 76.1 per cent of the total food market in the UK. The power comes from the level of market share, the fact that there are few major buyers and the quantities they purchase relative to the rest of the market.

Bargaining power of suppliers

As with the power of the buyer, the power of the supplier comes from concentration, from having relatively few suppliers who do the majority of the business. Additionally, power is enhanced when the products are deemed to be actually differentiated, very often by branding.

Just as with buyers, if suppliers have sufficient volumes and marketing capability, they may decide to sell directly to the final customers. This could mean clothing, glasses and tyre manufacturers opening their own retail stores and controlling the prices, selection, merchandising and promotion. Examples include Levi, Sony and Bose, which operate their own retail outlets.

Existing market rivalry

An industry with intense rivalry has some significant characteristics. It has been argued that 'intense rivalry drives down prices or elevates cost of marketing, R & D, or customer service, reducing margin' (Porter, 2008, p. 29).

Key intensity-provoking factors would be if there are many firms and if they are similar in size so that one or two firms do not have a substantive advantage in products or services. It is this competition that Porter is saying leads to discounting price and the requirement for other costly defensive activities. He refers to an intense rivalry market as being a 'zero-sum competition – one firm's gain is often another's loss' (Porter, 1998, p. 33).

High fixed costs by way of the process, required inventory and/or other asset investment levels force firms to keep competing as the cost of exit would be high and a most unattractive alternative. Similarly, if the industry is in low growth, this also exacerbates the problems of high costs and lower prices because of the high costs of fighting for market share.

All the factors and their analysis collectively contribute to the assessment of the relative attractiveness or unattractiveness of an industry as a basis for decisions about investment and divestment, and should reflect a critical analysis of the environment.

Some reservations

As with SWOT analysis, the five-forces model has attracted some criticism from various researchers. It has been noted that the model has proved more popular academically than in actual business (Grundy, 2006). Alleged weaknesses include the view that the various 'categories of forces' fit with the language of micro-economic theory rather than that of the business community. Similarly, the categories are abstract and not adaptable to strategic business decisions being made incrementally.

CONTEMPORARY ISSUES IN THE MARKETING ENVIRONMENT

The key steps in the evolution of marketing's development to our present perspectives and priorities were explained in Chapter 1.

It can be argued that the societal marketing orientation era (introduced in Chapter 1) was the seminal point at which marketing moved to a wider context of values. The view emerged that how a company was perceived in terms of its relative adherence to wider responsibilities (more than just legal compliance) and societal problems had a positive, holistic impact and hence exploitative potential (Kotler et al., 2014). It was believed that an enhanced corporate image can 'impact on brand strength and equity' (Lichtenstein et al., 2000, p. 4). Further, being seen as what we would now call a good corporate citizen was 'a way of differentiation with consumers by building an emotional, even spiritual, bond with the consumer' (Meyer, 1999, p. 29). The idea was that part of meeting the needs, wants and demands of customers in terms of product offering and value was also to promote society's well-being.

Just as relationship marketing (also cited in Chapter 1) led to the development of customer relationship management, so the focus on corporate image and responsibilities was the catalyst for cause-related marketing. Most essentially, it was the beginning of the now well-established practice of firms linking themselves and/or their products to a social cause and thereby contributing to a positive image. Indeed, Dawar and Pillutla (2000) suggest that an essential reason for relationship marketing is to build a 'reservoir' of goodwill to help protect against negative publicity.

There is a good case to be made that the basic premises of societal marketing, relationship marketing and cause-related marketing all contributed to the changes in the contemporary environment most often termed the 'era of corporate social responsibility' and 'sustainable marketing' or 'green marketing'.

CORPORATE SOCIAL RESPONSIBILITY

Those Victorians: Not just great moustaches

As stated previously, changes in the environment are often incremental and evolutionary rather than revolutionary. While essentially based on more recent developments, it can be argued that the origins of corporate social responsibility (CSR) can be traced back to the Victorian era. At that time, some family businesses were concerned about their employees' standards of living and quality of life in local communities.

It took until the latter half of the 20th century for the values to re-emerge. The sense of responsibility flowed from the awareness of consumers' needs and wants and concentrated profitability on the best alignment of the firm's organization

Cadbury's pioneering role in corporate and social responsibility

In the first half of the 19th century, John Cadbury (of chocolate fame) held the belief that business had significant social obligations in addition to its commercial interests. As well as striving to prevent cruelty to animals, he pioneered Saturday half-day closing and closing on Bank Holidays. He instituted employee councils, one for men and one for women, with secret ballots to deal with working conditions, health and safety, education and social life. The company encouraged staff to attend night school and staff were allowed to leave work an hour early twice a week to attend. This was all at a time when child labour was still practised and employee rights were a non-issue, and was years before women had a vote.

Similarly, in 1852, Jeremiah Colman (of mustard fame) did pioneering work in social welfare by opening a school for employees' children and employing a nurse to help sick members of staff. However, both Cadbury and Colman were quite unique individuals and companies for many years to follow.

and resources to suit the consumer. As we discussed earlier, there was a gradual and emerging awareness of the importance of a company's 'image'. It was felt that consumers increasingly based their opinions of a business on factors such as treatment of employees, community involvement and environmental issues, instead of just the traditional factors such as product quality, value for money and financial performance.

From this evolution of awareness and appreciation of a firm's behaviour as part of the consumer's evaluation and consideration in purchasing decisions, the term corporate social responsibility (CSR) entered our business vocabulary.

A formal definition of CSR would be: 'a concept whereby companies integrate social and environmental concerns in their business operations and in their interaction with stakeholders on a voluntary basis' (Belz and Peattie, 2009, p. 34). Please note the word 'voluntary' and that strictly speaking there remains no legally binding code of conduct for companies to comply with CSR.

Most generally, CSR activities include: 'a firm's commitment to contribute to sustainable economic development, working with employees, their families, local communities and society at large to improve the general quality of life' (Holmes and Watts, 2000, p. 10). Lantos (2001, p. 620) includes 'employee morale, corporate image, reputation, goodwill and popular opinion'. With the passage of time and enhanced interest, some distinctions within the term 'CSR' emerged. Carroll, for example, introduced the term 'corporate social performance (CSP). This term basically describes the execution of CSR and thus has the meaning of putting theoretical concepts of social responsibility into practice. Hence, CSR and CSP differ only in the way in which they describe the practical application, but the ideas behind both terms are the same.

I have a problem with you not having the correct opinion

While there appears to be general agreement on various activities included under CSR, there remain significant differences of opinion as to its ultimate intent and purpose, relative importance, impact, priorities, choice of activities and levels of commitment.

There are two fundamentally differing values for CSR. Some argue that the motivation behind CSR should be to 'do the right thing' and act 'morally', meeting obligations to the welfare of society as a whole. The essential and obvious missing point is the absence of profit making as the main goal (Gossling and Vocht, 2007).

The contrary but commonly cited view is that the only social responsibility of a business is to increase its profits (Friedman, 1970). Indeed Friedman is quoted as going further to suggest that it is not legitimate for a firm to act in a way that is detrimental to shareholders' returns. Duties to the owners must 'take preference over the duties to other parties'. Often partially portrayed as a variant of the Gekko character of the film *Wall Street* ('greed, for lack of a better word, is good'), Friedman actually said, 'the fundamental responsibility of any business in a free-enterprise system is to make a profit while conforming to the basic rules of society, both those embodied in the law and those embodied in ethical customs' (Carroll, 1998, p. 2). Arguably, he was actually edging towards CSR.

Okay, but 'show me the money'

Staying within the opinion that profits should be the only ultimate goal, various associated or corollary views have developed. One view is that CSR should be adopted not on the basis of social merit but rather in order for a firm to be perceived to be responsible and a good citizen, which in turn will increase its profitability and therefore be a good strategy. This is the perception of societal marketing we discussed earlier. While not endorsing insincerity, Michael Porter suggested that CSR could provide a basis for a competitive advantage (Belz and Peattie, 2009, p. 36). Indeed, some theorists suggest that CSR could be a first-mover advantage (the first firm to enter a new market may gain advantages over its actual and potential rivals) and therefore may compel competing firms to use CSR.

Irrespective of various *profit-focused* CSR-practising firms, there remains much debate and disagreement as to whether CSR is actually profitable. Some hold the view that the cost of CSR has no effect on profitability, that the costs outweigh the benefits to the company (Kolstad, 2007) or that it can actually have a negative impact on profit.

Yet another opinion is that CSR is profitable, but the returns are very long term and therefore such investments should be considered 'strategic' (important and long term). Hence, a firm should act/select accordingly (McWilliams et al., 2006, p. 4).

As with the question of profitability, as you would expect, there are differing opinions as to how and whether it is possible actually to determine the financial return of CSR 'investments'. Much of the evaluation of relative profitability (as opposed to being essentially a good corporate citizen) is that the measurement and analysis of return is complex (McWilliams and Siegel, 2000). In addition to the 'investment' being long term by nature, how can a firm determine and measure the actual impacts of an improved or enhanced image? To what extent was the image enhanced and how many extra sales or profits can be attributed to that enhancement?

Belz and Peattie (2009, p. 36) suggest that the difficulty of establishing benefits and returns is that generally firms do not treat CSR expenditure as an integrated part of the business. It is regarded more like traditional charitable donations than an ongoing strategic investment. Porter and Kramer go further on this point and suggest that if companies did treat the costs as an integrated part of the business, 'they would discover that CSR can be much more than obligation, a cost or constraint; it can in fact be an opportunity for innovation and competitive advantage' (Belz and Peattie, 2009, p. 36).

The various concerns around relative profitability and its determination have resulted in views such as that CSR financial return analysis should be 'interpreted with care' (Darnall et al., 2004) or 'are clearly ambiguous' (Wood and Jones, 1995 p. 261).

Annual social responsibility reports

Giving additional clarity to concealment or achievement?

Given the importance (irrespective of motive) and increasing levels of funding CSR (Moir, 2001), it has become standard practice for firms to publish annually a CSR report. The report sets out the company's efforts and activities as regards CSR. These reports should be viewed in the context that different companies have different views on what their role in society should be and this influences their involvement in social issues (Moir, 2001).

The communication is formally intended for shareholders but is also for wider stakeholder consumption. The reports are: 'to communicate to society that they care about issues like well-being of their environment, their employees and/or society in general' (Gossling and Vocht, 2007, p. 365).

The nature of some reports has attracted negative comments such as: 'Many CSR activities and reports are cosmetic, with emphasis on their public relations value' (Belz and Peattie, 2009, p. 36). Again, on the less positive side, there is the complaint that since the reports are within a marketing context, the information leads to confusion and cynicism. The most severe critics have said that social responsibility reports are 'meaningless and should never be termed responsible' (Emery, 2012, p. 13). Bakan (2004) cynically goes as far as to suggest that not only are such reports and policies basically insincere, but also CSR should only be used if it is in fact insincere, so as to promote shareholder interest!

These negative assertions should be framed by the fact that differences of opinion are to be expected in such a pluralist audience of stakeholders. Equally, the information to shareholders (including financial) is presented in a way that is 'user friendly', and should not be. Certainly, as with our next topic, sustainable marketing, there is a high degree of scepticism as to the honesty and intent of commitments, with impressions being more important than reality.

It may be argued that more recently CSR has evolved and developed a new legitimacy. Most large companies have entire departments whose remit is CSR conscious-

Example 2.6:

A view of corporate social responsibility from HP

The statement below is indicative of the current attitude towards CSR as given by the then CEO of HP, Carly Fiorina.

'I honestly believe that the winning companies of this century will be those who prove with their actions that they can be profitable and increase social value – companies that do well and do good ... Increasingly, shareholders, customers, partners and employees are going to vote with their feet – rewarding those companies that fuel social change through business. This is simply the new reality of business – one that we should and must embrace' (http://www8.hp.com/us/en/hp-information/global-citizenship/index.html).

ness, evaluation and implementation. CSR reports are now thought to be 'less flaky' and 'more than empty phrases'. In the past, companies have: 'bowed to anti-business activists and made "amends" through good work. Today's CSR is less self-abasing and more constructive' (Schumpeter, 2012, p. 66).

In addition to annual social responsibility reports, there are other prominent 'indicators' of CSR commitment. These include the Dow Jones Sustainability Index (USA) and the London Stock Exchange FTSE4Good, based on the stated premise that business can make a profit while helping both the environment and society. They allegedly measure the performance of companies objectively in terms of their environmental and social responsibility (attainment and progression). The level of diffusion and accepted importance of CSR is also reflected in the fact that the International Labour Organization has written a set of ethical rules on the companies' treatment of employees. The EU has presented a Green Paper on encouraging companies to act responsibly, and the UN has formulated a Global Compact that contains ten principles for human rights, the environment, anti-corruption and so on.

1. Leadership, vision and values
Purpose, values and vision (to include CSR)
Policies and procedures
Putting it into practice
Ethical leadership (including involving relevant stakeholders)

2. Marketplace activities
Responsible customer relations
Product responsibility (includes production that respects human rights)
CSR product labelling (accurate and not misleading)
Ethical competition (listening and responding to customer complaints)

3. Workforce activities
Employee communication and representation
Ensuring employability and skills development
Diversity and equality (race, gender, disabilities)
Responsible/fair remuneration
Work/life balance
Health, safety and well-being

4. Supply chain activities
Being a fair customer (fair pricing, fair terms, timely payment)
Driving standards (suppliers' compliance with CSR values)
Promoting social and economic inclusion

5. Stakeholder engagement
Stakeholder consultation
Responding and managing (employee consultation, feedback)
Reporting and communication (open and transparent channels)

6. Community activities
Donations (cash, sponsorships, loans)
Giving employees time (to do charitable work)
Giving gifts
Being a good neighbour (liaising with community)

7. Environmental activities
Resource and energy use (awareness initiatives)
Pollution and waste management (includes improvement initiatives)
Environmental product responsibility (levels of recycling and so on)
Transport planning (reduced mileage: products and employees)

Figure 2.4: Corporate social responsibilities

The scope of CSR activities

The activities in which firms have their main focus are to a degree specific to them and to their industry (Moir, 2001). However, in Figure 2.4, seven major groups of CSR activities are cited. The list has been abridged and has short explanations and comments so that you can relate to companies or events of which you are aware.

Social responsibility models

Academics have a model for everything. Otherwise what can be on the test?

As a student, you would expect there to be various models that have been developed to try to analyse and understand CSR. It can be argued that at the core of theory in this area has been Archie Carroll, who developed, revised and updated theoretical models and is probably the most cited theorist in CSR. Carroll even worked with Schwartz on identifying possible shortcomings in his own model (Schwartz and Carroll, 2003).

We will start with the more popular of Carroll's models, the pyramid of corporate social responsibility. Artistic fans of Maslow's hierarchy of needs will feel especially comfortable here (see Figure 2.5).

Figure 2.5: Carroll's corporate social responsibility pyramid
Source: *Managing ethically with global stakeholders: A present and future challenge.* Archie B. Carroll, Academy of Management Perspectives, Academy of Management, May 1, 2004. Copyright © Academy of Management, 2004

As stated previously, Carroll (1998) believes that CSR responsibility must embrace the entire business's responsibilities and he argues that it constitutes four kinds of social responsibilities: economic, legal, ethical and philanthropic. The model shows each of those responsibilites in successive layers of the pyramid. Each 'builds' on the others and therefore no two elements are mutually exclusive. The 'size' and level of the layer indicates its relative importance, hence philanthropic is the last and smallest layer. Simplistically, a firm can continue without philanthropy but it cannot without a viable profit.

Economic responsibilities

Economic reponsibilties are the foundation and primary drivers for entrepreneurship. A firm's role is to provide goods and services to consumers and make a profit. Without acceptable profit, there is no need or reason to engage in any of the other responsibilites, hence the economic 'foundation'. Specific economic responsibilities include being committed to being as profitable as possible, and to maintaining a strong competitive position and a high level of operating efficiency (Korkchi and Rombaut, 2006).

Legal responsibilities

Legal responsibilities include adherence to the framework of regulations and compliance with all legal obligations. Legal adherence is an imperative to economic responsibilites (Carroll, 1991). However, you might be thinking how the nature of law and legal proceedings makes the 'line' of illegality and legality less than rigid.

Ethical responsibilities

A firm's compliance with ethical responsibilities shows concern for what is regarded by current norms, values and expectations as being fair and just – by consumers, employees, shareholders, the community and other stakeholders. Ethical responsibilities go further than economic and legal ones and are intertwined with the latter. They push for more legislation and heightened stakeholder expectations (Carroll, 1991).

Branco and Rodrigues (2006, p. 114) suggest that ethical responsibilities include 'unwritten standards, norms and values implicitly derived from society'. Certainly, you can think of public cases or events where some activities were in the strictest sense legal but really unethical. Korkchi and Rombaut (2006), interpreting Carroll, suggest that ethical responsibilities translate into: performing in a manner consistent with expectations of societal mores and ethical norms and preventing ethical norms from being compromised in order to achieve corporate goals. They stress that corporate integrity and ethical behaviour go beyond mere legal compliance.

Philanthropic responsibilities

Originally called 'discretionary' (Carroll, 1983, p. 604), philanthropic responsibilities are those diverse activities that help to define the firm as being a good corporate citizen. They include engaging in programmes for human welfare or education, charitable activities, support for cultural activities and 'venture philanthropy', where firms provide funding and technical advice to community-based organizations. Kosminsky refers to these ventures as 'laboratories of the streets' (Kosminsky, 1997, p. 28). Philanthropic responsibilities obviously go beyond the ethical and are 'icing on the cake' (Carroll, 1991), while voluntary donations enhance the quality of life in society (Crane et al., 2007, p. 66). Carroll (1991) notes, however, that a firm's not being philanthropic does not mean that it is viewed as being unethical.

Relative value of the model

Carroll states that the model is intended primarily to help academics to identify and understand the 'distinctions among definitions of social responsibility that have appeared in the literature' (Carroll, 1979, p. 502). The model is arguably the most commonly cited CSR model in academic literature. For business managers, Carroll suggests that his model sets out the interrelationship between economic performance and social responsibility (Carroll, 1979). The general opinion is that the model meets the stated intentions to a significant degree (Korkchi and Rombaut, 2006).

The model has been subject to many revisions by Carroll since its introduction. In 2003 Carroll suggested that philanthropy may not be justifiable as being within the remit of social responsibility (Schwartz and Carroll, 2003).

Some academics have both praised and criticized the model for being simple. It has been praised because it is easy to understand and to appreciate the concepts and relationships. It has been criticized because it provides no recognition of the role of the macro environment. Similarly, it has been criticized for its implicit assumption that today's problems have known and agreed solutions as the model implies.

Three-domain model

Candid evaluation of one's own opinion is both difficult and unusual. However, in 2003 Carroll co-wrote an article with Schwartz in which they addressed what they felt were areas of further clarification, required emphasis and more closely reflected the integrative nature of CSR. From this, a three-domain model of CSR was proposed. See Figure 2.6.

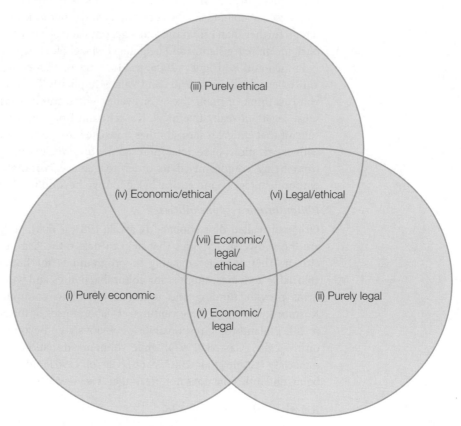

Figure 2.6: Three-domain model of corporate social responsibility
Source: Schwartz and Carroll, 2003, p. 509

As with the pyramid model, the core CSR responsibilities (economic, legal and ethical) remain. However 'philanthropic' has been omitted on the basis that it is by definition purely discretionary and is therefore outside what should be considered 'responsibilities' (Schwartz and Carroll, 2003).

When you look at the Venn diagram, it becomes clear that there are not only the three main and 'pure' domains, but also four overlapping sectors which in total result in seven categories for companies to 'conceptualize, analyze and illustrate their CSR actions' (Schwartz and Carroll, 2003, p. 513). As you see, the seven categories are: purely economic, purely legal, purely ethical, economic/ethical, economic/legal, legal/ethical, economic/legal/ethical.

The model draws attention to and emphasizes the fact that the core responsibilities are really not discrete but overlap each other. The suggestion is that each core responsibility is of equal importance but that no responsibility can exist without being impacted by other responsibilities. 'Pure', one of the three responsibilities by themselves, would be most unusual (Schwartz and Carroll, 2003). To be 'pure' would mean that the other responsibilities were not considered at all or just happened to be complied with (ibid.). An example would be a purely legal activity taking place mainly because of the legal system without considering potential economic benefits and ethical constraints. One could suggest that a specific example would be Napster's original peer-to-peer file-sharing format, essentially allowing people to share each other's music. The original company was bankrupted over copyright infringements. At the time, peer-to-peer file sharing brought no economic gain to its operators, and was not seen as unethical (the participants own the music individually but not collectively).

Nevertheless, the heart of the model suggests that all responsibilities have impacts and repercussions on other responsibilities. In fact the authors offer few examples of discrete responsibilities (Schwartz and Carroll, 2003). The model is intended to emphasize by identification the integrative symbiotic nature of social responsibilities.

Schwartz and Carroll (2003) suggest that companies should strive to operate in the economic/legal/ethical category whenever possible because it also fulfils all the requirements of the pure categories. Another alternative for corporations that are already passively complying with the law is to locate their actions in the economic/ethical category, since then they can generate economic benefits without running the risk of litigation (Vollmert, 2007, p. 13).

Look after our Earth; we may not have anywhere else to live

To tie together our various perspectives and thoughts about CSR, it would be beneficial to set out what are the possible benefits for a firm in today's environment, as shown in Example 2.7.

The corporate social responsibility platform

The introduction, evolution and development of CSR has changed and is changing the entire business environment significantly and pervasively. Profit alone is an insufficient and deficient motive for business enterprises. A commonly held view is that businesses have a wide range of responsibilities. Additionally, this view is held increasingly by both consumers and a wide range of shareholders. Many new terms and associated values have entered our vocabulary, such as corporate citizenship, strategic philanthropy, carbon ecological and water footprints, ecological overshoot, eco-entrepreneurship and so on (Emery, 2012, p. 44). However, most terms still lack uniformity of meaning (Murray and Vogel, 1997).

BUSINESS BENEFITS OF CORPORATE SOCIAL RESPONSIBILITY

1.   Offers economic benefit

A commonly cited benefit has been that a firm's honest and trustworthy image can lead to sales growth and profitability. However, it is also probably true that: 'A socially responsible consumer would, therefore, avoid buying products from companies that harm society and actively seek out products from companies that help society' (Mohr et al., 2001, p. 47).

It is also contended that a firm perceived as socially responsible will attract increased customer loyalty, benefit from a positive corporate profile and is likely to be an influential player within financial circles or with potential investors. A strong CSR reputation can contribute to the longevity of the firm.

While there is no unanimity of opinion, it has been stated that good CSR can lead to the acceptance of premium pricing (Creyer and Ross, 1996) and to achieving superior performance and greater profits (Paine, 2004). Good CSR has in some studies been shown to have a positive impact on buying behaviour (Holmes and Kilbane, 1993). Likewise, perceived higher CSR activities have led to higher evaluation of the firm's products and, further, socially responsible behaviour can even overshadow price consideration in a purchase decision (Handelman and Arnold, 1999).

Finally, firms with a sound CSR record increasingly attract socially responsible investment funds (SRI) and individual investors, making it easier to raise capital as a result of the alleged correlation between social and financial performance (Gates et al., 2006).

2.   Can combat damaging effects of negative events

Telling the truth (which is seen by some as a unique idea) and being open and honest about the firm's mistakes or bad practice is part of a CSR response that can lead to stakeholders forgiving the firm. Further, consistent transparency as regards negatives can actually build goodwill (Howley, 2006). However, some unethical behaviour has been found to be 'unforgivable' and appears to stigmatize a firm and/or its products indelibly (Folkes and Kamins, 1999).

3.   Provides a source of competitive advantage

As mentioned in the opening discussion, Porter and Kramer believe that CSR can be 'an opportunity of innovation and competitive advantage' (Belz and Peattie, 2009, p. 36). A strong CSR image can serve to distinguish a firm from other firms (Smith, 2003) and can enhance the firm's reputation, build its brand and create trust with customers, suppliers and business partners (Paine, 1991). Additionally, the values encourage staff to greater cooperation, inspire commitment and increase their motivation (Korkchi and Rombaut, 2006).

4.   Is proactive to avoid excessive regulation

There is an arguable link between unethical behaviour and legislation. This is simplistic in the sense that activities that are on the nebulous line between unethical and illegal are what often cause problems. Nevertheless, following a series of immense losses of publicly traded companies in the US (Enron, WorldCom and so on), new legislation was introduced. Public furore over loss of investments and pensions drove the rapid introduction of the Sarbanes-Oxley (SOX) Act of 2002 (De George, 2008). It is beyond our interest here to examine the details of SOX except to say that the law set guidelines for financial disclosure, which still have an army of critics in 2012. They argue that this 'moment of anger' Act went too far (see http://www.ehow.com/sarbanes-oxley-act/).

Similarly, the still unfolding saga of Bernard Madoff, whose activities cost investors £34 billion and cost Madoff a lifetime jail sentence, will result in various changes in legislation – parts of which may possibly be illogical, unworkable and beyond the intended remit (see http://www.telegraph.co.uk/finance/financetopics/bernard-madoff/4277800/Bernard-Madoff-How-the-scandal-worked.html).

The examples, while extreme, illustrate another possible benefit of CSR. By active and high-profile acts of CSR, firms can offer their perspectives on a publicly raised issue. This hopefully either serves to diffuse the public pressure and avoid legislation, or at least gives the firm input into the nature and details of the resultant legislation, which would be less challenging in compliance. Stated definitively, 'Companies rely on CSR programmes as defences against problems such as consumer boycotts, public relations disasters, and increased government regulations' (Martin and Schouten, 2012, p. 30).

Davis offers a decidedly proactive position: 'if business delays dealing with social problems now, it may find itself constantly occupied with putting out social fires so that it has no time to accomplish its primary goal of producing goods and services' (Davis, 1973, p. 317). Ending on a more downbeat note, some business people feel that any intervention by government and legislation is not appropriate for business (Crook, 2005).

5. Aids the attraction and retention of staff
There is ample evidence that CSR can have a positive effect on attracting applications, work satisfaction and staff retention (Smith, 2003). Studies have found that: 'applicants are not only attracted to companies with high social responsibility but they are also more likely to go to a job interview with such a firm or to prefer a firm's job offer' (Greening and Turban, 2000, p. 276).

6. Can lead to a reduction in costs
There is growing evidence that CSR activities can lead to both risk and cost reductions. They can both enhance efficiencies and reduce operating costs. In a survey by PricewaterhouseCoopers, 73 per cent of respondents indicated that one of the top three reasons for becoming socially responsible was 'cost savings' (Berman et al., 1999).

Figure 2.7: Core business benefits of CSR

Example 2.7:
Environmental issues

Walkers Crisps (Pepsico) adopted a carbon footprint label for its product and reduced the carbon footprint by 7 per cent. Similarly, UPS provides a carbon calculator to track the carbon footprint on individual packages. Many air freshener and hairspray firms no longer use butane, but use air as a propellant. Deutsche Bank UK employees take children to the zoo for the day; Tesco donates computers to schools.

McDonald's restaurants, in addition to using cooking oils for fuel in their lorries, have a study looking at reducing the flatulent gas given off by cattle. The company uses 350,000 cattle a year for its burgers and the methane gas from livestock accounts for 4 per cent of the UK's total carbon emission. This is nothing to sniff about as methane is 23 times more powerful than carbon dioxide as a greenhouse agent.

Coffee with your burger? Starbucks has a global 'Shared Planet' initiative which includes ethical sourcing and environ-mental stewardship. Its goals include: 100 per cent of cups will be reusable or recyclable by 2015, and 50 per cent of the energy used in company-owned stores will be derived from renewable resources by 2012.

Think and discuss

1. In groups, prepare a list of five activities or events that are 'legal' but not 'ethical'. Why do you think they are unethical? Prepare arguments to substantiate your position. Each group presents its findings and substantiation.

2. As a class, select the two events that you all agree are the most significant in terms of impact on any stakeholders. Discuss what guidelines should be applied to make future similar events more ethical. Discuss the possible role of legislation, both its benefits and possible challenges.

We do not inherit the earth ... we borrow it from our children.

(North American Indian saying)

Applications and synthesis

Across businesses and functions including the supply chain, the social responsibility imperative has become a customary and expected feature. Various companies such as P&G and Walmart (Asda) use sustainability scorecards to encourage their suppliers to use less water, manage waste better and reduce emissions of greenhouse gases. Nike has a materials sustainability index that provides designers with the potential environmental impact of the products they design (Kosminsky, 1997).

It can be argued that some advertising may be seen as being more socially responsible. While also encountering criticism, Unilever's Dove brand slogan of 'women are ok at whatever size' encourages consumers to simply accept their appearance.

There is ample evidence that a sense of social responsibility is spreading. A study in the UK found that 63 per cent of UK employees believe that having paid time off during working hours to commit to charitable initiatives would significantly improve employee engagement (Wood, 2011). Similarly, Ottman (2011, p. 62) found that 52 per cent of consumers consider an eco-label in their purchase decision.

CSR, from its introduction as a set of additional values/responsibilities for organizations to adopt, has evolved to being an acknowledged, pervasive, embedded, constantly progressing business imperative.

SUSTAINABLE MARKETING

Sustainability is the pervading reality of the contemporary business environment. Sustainability is a substantial expansion of the precepts and context of CSR. Sustainable marketing (SM) has a wider spectrum of activities, perceptions and responsibilities, which have evolved from the CSR values platform and its expected levels of conduct and raised the profile of ethical and responsible behaviour for businesses to include the entire planet.

Let's start with the triple bottom line

The 'triple bottom line' is a term cited as part of CSR, but it can be used to illustrate the broad platform of values which have coalesced into sustainable marketing. Sustainability refers to social equity, and economic and environmental sustainability, and these three factors are now often called the *triple bottom line* (TBL), as opposed to just the 'bottom line' (profit) (Elkington, 2004). Obviously, triple bottom line theory proposes that profitability is not the sole objective of a company, but that companies must also have objectives of adding environmental and social value to society (Crane and Matten, 2007).

Social equity responsibilities may include labour practices (fair pay issues, living and working conditions), health and safety, community impacts, a range of human rights and product safety issues (Martin and Schouten, 2012). As you would expect, a firm's economic responsibilities include sales, profit, return on investment, taxes paid, monetary flows and jobs created (ibid.). The wide set of environmental responsibilities includes air and water quality, energy usage and waste produced (Savitz and Weber, 2006).

In turn, these wider responsibilities require credibility with accountability and transparency. Accountability is both taking responsibility and providing accurate information to stakeholders. Full transparency is reporting on all aspects of the business and its activities, including environmental and social, to the stakeholders (Henriques, 2004). The implication is that where the firm falls short of its obligations it has the imperative to address the issues (Adams et al., 2004).

Not so fast …

We discussed earlier in the chapter that much change takes place incrementally. There is a recognition that 'consumptive marketing' cannot continue indefinitely (such as where oil is made into a plastic bag, used to carry an item home and then discarded). Further, the answer is not simply finding more oil via different extraction processes or finding substitutes (Emery, 2012). Schmidheiny sums it up succinctly: 'products are produced, purchased, used and dumped with little regard for environmental efficiency or impact' (Schmidheiny, 1992, p. 109).

Certainly, consumers and businesses did not suddenly just change. For centuries we polluted our environment and depleted our natural resources. Records back to the 13th century in England note the problem. The River Thames in London may still not be safe to swim in, but for years it was where human waste, animal remains and chemicals from leather making were simply dumped. We will not talk about what was thrown from windows onto the streets below in case you are having a kebab. The Thames was

istock © dutourdumonde

a sewer. As late as 1952, pollutants from factories and home fireplaces mixed with air condensation killed at least 4,000 people in London over the course of several days. But over time we have slowly developed an appreciation and recognition of the environment and society's and our own personal responsibilities. Various messages, images, voiced opinions or perhaps a school project have over time gradually got us to where we feel guilty if we just throw away an empty can of Red Bull. Perhaps you buy only line-caught fish, Fairtrade bananas, tea and coffee, and energy-efficient gadgets. In short, we have reached the tipping point where concerns about the environment are now branded on the consumer's conscience.

Finally, need a definition?

Because sustainability has just so many implications and applications, many new terms have been created. The term 'sustainable marketing' is attributed to Sheth and Parvatiyar (1995) and was intended 'to address the reconciliation of economic and ecological factors utilizing product innovation and product supply chains' (Fuller, 1999, p. 3). Other terms for essentially the same value focus include *green marketing* (Ottman, 2011), *environmental marketing* (Coddington, 1993), *ecological marketing* (Henion, 1976) and *eco-marketing* (Fuller and Butler, 1994).

Belz (2006, p. 140) refers to sustainable marketing as 'building and maintaining sustainable relationships with customers, the social environment and the natural environment'. A more comprehensive definition is 'the process of planning, implementing, and controlling the development, pricing, promotion, and distribution of products in a manner that satisfies the following three criteria: (1) customer needs are met (2) organisational goals are attained and (3) the process is compatible with ecosystems' (Fuller, 1999, p. 4).

Figure 2.8 summarizes the core characteristics of sustainable marketing, using the acronym 'EVER'.

Figure 2.8: EVER acronym for sustainable marketing
Source: Abridged from Belz and Peattie, 2009, p. 18

Core characteristics of sustainable marketing: EVER

Ecologically oriented: Taking account of the ecological limits of the planet and seeking to satisfy our needs without compromising the health of ecosystems

Viable: Technically feasible and providing economic competitiveness

Ethical: Promoting social justice and equity

Relationship-based: Moving from 'economic exchanges' to relationships between businesses, their customers and other key stakeholders

Impact of sustainable marketing on specific marketing activities

Let us look at the possible implications for a marketing mix, using the simple but venerated and trustworthy '4 Ps'.

Product

Marketing sustainability requires reinventing marketing principles and practices towards greater sustainability and environmental consciousness. 'Product' is probably the most studied element of the marketing mix. This is likely to be because products and services are the basis for determining price, place and promotion.

You will soon recognize that sustainable or green marketing is relatively new and expanding rapidly into many areas, with differing emphases and perspectives. Therefore, there are many different interpretations of the same terms, duplicate or similar meanings and new terms entering the vocabulary. A few examples: green entrepreneurship, ecopreneurship, environmental entrepreneurship, enviropreneurship and sustainable entrepreneurship (Kraus and Melay, 2012, p. 1).

New look at product cycles

Product lifecycle design (PLD) has emerged as a key concept. PLD is not the same as product lifecycle (PLC), which models sales and costs, market and consumer characteristics and associated strategies from product introduction to demise. Rather, the concept of PLD encompasses all the activities (and environmental and ethical considerations) from raw materials extraction and sources, manufacturing or processing, to the final disposal of all the residuals (Keoleian and Menerey, 1994). More formally, sustainable products and services are defined as 'offerings that satisfy customer needs and significantly improve the social and environmental performance along with whole life cycle in comparison to conventional or competing offers' (Belz and Peattie, 2009, p. 154).

Think and discuss

Marketers must try to determine what is the best strategy to survive or capitalize on change, based on the realities of their resources and those of their competitors.

Sketch out what you consider to be the most pressing sustainability issues facing marketers.

Within sustainable 'product' considerations

Within this wide concept are related initiatives such as Design for Environment (DfE) and Design for Sustainability (D4S or DfS) (Spangenberg et al., 2010). With very similar meanings, both concepts are systematic approaches to embedding and integrating the consideration of ethical and environmental issues into all the activities associated with a product from initial sourcing to waste disposal.

D4S/DfS can be subdivided into product design (including materials) and product production. Product design can be pure innovation or redesigning an existing product to meet ecological and ethical goals while retaining its functionality (Crul and Diehl, 2006, p. 414).

Product design

We will look first at product design issues. This is arguably the area with the most activity and involves a high degree of technologically innovative applications, including intelligent materials and newly developed materials such as carbon fibres. Intelligent or smart materials can react and adapt to the environment (Zhang and Tao, 2001). You are familiar with Gore-Tex, a pioneering intelligent fabric that allows sweat to pass through from the inside out, but does not allow rain to enter from the outside. Other smart fabrics include a Wearable Motherboard shirt, which is only one of many applications where the garment has sensors that measure various body functions (Park and Jayaraman, 2002). Smart medicines can react to the conditions in which they find themselves by increasing or decreasing their potencies. Similarly, sensors can be swallowed with a patient's pill, which give an electrical signal to a skin patch, which in turn transmits the data to a smartphone. More futuristic are electrochromic paints, which change colour with electric inputs. These are being researched for both domestic and automotive applications.

As you can see from some of the examples above, the basis for design can be a radical and/or innovative strategy (new materials or new applications) which leads to breakthroughs by which a firm might get a competitive advantage. All of this is within the context of ecological, economic and ethical considerations. Another strategy is 'benchmarking', which in this application means comparing our firm's product or service (using sustainable criteria) with those of our competitors and then moving into the design phase (Crul and Diehl, 2006, p. 415)

Another part of product design would be 'design for remanufacturing', where embedded in the original design is a provision for 'disassembly, design for longer and more lifecycles, modular design and future product support' (Nasr and Thurston, 2006, p. 15). This also includes both waste avoidance and flexibility in recycling (Clark et al., 2009, p. 410).

Production

Production issues are part of and should be seen in the holistic context of the sources-to-waste-and-recycling model. Sustainability means that there is an integration of product design and its manufacture.

Production issues obviously include the various processes in the actual production, seeking general efficiencies (material, man hours, energy, water, chemicals) to reduce waste, and to have waste that is less harmful and that has the capacity to be used profitably.

A major developing field is 'cleaner production', sometimes just called just clean production (CP). It is a holistic concept that covers all processes and stakeholders in the production process, again from materials to end ancillary products. For definition lovers, CP is 'the continuous application of an integrated preventive environmental strategy to process end products to reduce risks to humans and the environment' (Nasr and Thurston, 2006, p. 13). More comprehensively, Thorpe states: 'Clean production is any practice which eliminates at source the use or formation of hazardous substances through the use of non-hazardous chemicals in production processes, or through product or process redesign, and thereby prevents releases of hazardous substances into the environment by all routes, directly or indirectly' (Thorpe, 2009, p. 1).

istock © dulezidar

These various points also lead to concentrating on lessening the amount of 'waste' from production, and modifying the nature of the waste to ensure the least possible impact on the environment. This area is also an important and a growing field and is generally referred to as end-of-pipe technology. In addition to developing technologies to prevent direct release of harmful substances into the environment (water, soil, air) noise pollution is also an important issue of concern.

Looking at waste as simply 'waste', just a cost, has become redundant. All the various and diverse innovative activities around CP have led to an explosion in interest, use and investment in waste as having income potential; often attributed to Berle, there are various versions of 'One man's garbage is another man's treasure' (1991). Loosely referred to by some as 'by-product synergy' (BPS), the idea is to use rather than discard. Malt, which is a by-product of beer production, is now routinely being sold as animal food and used as a source of energy. There are numerous programmes across the globe that collect methane from organic waste matter. Beef by-products may end up as jet engine lubricants. Potato scraps from potato crisps used to make vodka may be a more interesting scenario. The existence of the Chartered Institution of Wastes Management ('Setting professional standards in sustainable resource and waste management') is an indication of the importance of the sector.

On a more strategic level, and putting on our accounting hat, any revenue derived over cost, from what was before an expense, is a profit or at least a contribution to overheads. This means that if one firm gains income from waste and its competitor does not, or does so less successfully, the first firm has gained a competitive advantage. Think value chain. It has even been suggested that relative efficiency in waste management will be a major competitive area and affect existing firms and those considering entering the market (Hockerts and Wustenhagen, 2010).

The final area that we should mention is that of repairing, reconditioning and remanufacturing, recycling and reusing (Prakash, 2002, p. 286).

Within the EU there are various Directives that vary from encouragement to enforcement of manufactured goods handling, disposal and alternative treatments. The Waste Electrical and Electronic Equipment Directive (WEEE) is the core document. I think that if your toaster failed to deliver your morning crunch, you would not think of repairing it; you would be off to the shop to buy a replacement. There is empirical evidence that the cost of repairs has become prohibitive relative to a replacement. The assertion is that companies concentrate on design for cost reduction rather than design for easy repair. Reconditioning products (such as laptops) has not really gained high acceptance because of the perception of quality and the narrow price difference compared with buying new.

istock © surely

However, for higher-cost and more technical products remanufacturing (replacement of key parts, extensive refurbishment, upgrade and so on) has become more accepted with prices 60 per cent lower than for new (Bras and McIntosh, 1999). A good example would be Xerox, which has a highly successful global remanufacturing programme for its copiers (Kerr and Ryan, 2001).

Lastly we should mention reverse logistics, which generically could include the fading tradition of Coca-Cola collecting its empty bottles, and cleaning and refilling them. Germany's Green Dot programme essentially transfers the responsibility for and cost of waste management for categories of product from the general taxpayer to the individual manufacturers. They must make provision to collect, process and recycle 95 per cent of their product including packaging (Min and Galle, 1997).

Price

As the market environment moves to meet requirements related to more sustainable, responsible or ethical production, environmentally friendlier products and more responsible consumption, there are new issues concerning price and pricing. As Carroll (1991) has noted, the shift requires various legal initiatives and incentives. These can promote use, such as subsidizing alternative forms of energy from wind farms or solar panels on homes or having vegetable gardens in schools. They can ban the use of various substances and, on the ethical side, intercede and introduce laws that hopefully lessen unethical practices and promote positive ones. The latter might include the previously mentioned recycling requirements, the type of materials in packaging and placing responsibility for pollution on the polluter.

Demarketing

A commonly used term is demarketing, which is a method instituted by companies or governments to try to reduce over-consumption of products. It sounds rather contrary to traditional marketing goals. Generally it is a matter of government intervention or at least pressure. Demarketing is one way that companies could make responsible marketing decisions for the sake of sustainability. The goal of demarketing is to decrease over-consumption of a product by raising prices or reducing access or distribution. High-profile examples are the constant rise in prices, lack of point of purchase displays, and possibly only generic packaging for cigarettes. For alcohol, all companies have 'responsible drinking' campaigns, but there is also a push by government for a minimum unit price for alcohol.

The major pricing problem is that environmentally friendly and ethical products are premium priced. Fairtrade and organic products actually cost more due to the aggregation of higher wages and cost of raw materials, and various ethical and environmental compliances (Martin and Schouten, 2012, p. 61).

However, there is not a consensus as to whether consumers will pay more for sustainable products. Some research indicates that consumers will pay more and under certain circumstances even considerably more (Ottman, 2011, p. 41). However, other research indicates that the higher price is the major point of resistance to adoption of sustainable products (Beattie, 2005). There is also evidence that credibility and perceived incomplete information is part of the price resistance (Hawken, 1993). There is a view that if the consumer realized the full implication of the nature of the product, they would be more disposed to pay the premium (Martin and Schouten, 2012, p. 61). This idea fits well with the traditional concept of value meaning the combination of price and quality. Similarly it fits the '3 Cs' which form the basic influences on price decisions, namely unit cost structure, customer perception and competitive products and prices (Fuller, 1999). As with any consumer behaviour research, we do have a problem about the gap between expressed opinion and purchase behaviour. Consistently, more consumers say they will buy green products than actually do (McGuire, 1985).

Another essential question is the way that 'cost' is actually calculated. The argument states that products that are not environmentally friendly have 'hidden costs' which are in fact 'paid' by others. Charter states: 'traditional economics models have not included environmental and social costs as a portion of the total cost of a product or service' (Charter et al., 2002, p. 23). The total cost includes what are often referred to as eco-costs: 'depleted resources, pollution, loss of biodiversity, undesirable impacts on the developing world' (Green, 2002, p. 34). These costs are effectively passed on to a wide range of present and future stakeholders. Peattie (1995, p. 284) goes further and states that non-ecological products are effectively receiving a subsidy from society.

It has been argued that the lower volumes of sustainable product increase the price differential with non-green products. The research would indicate that it will be up to the marketer to demonstrate the real 'value', the full implications of green products, to overcome resistance to a higher price (Charter et al., 2002). Perhaps more pessimistically, Ottman goes as far as to suggest that people may not pay a premium for green products but will only buy at the same or similar price to 'non-eco' alternatives. She writes: 'environment attributes can act as a powerful tie-breaker and provide a source of differentiation and value added' (Ottman, 1993, p. 44).

Place

SM has a number of elements in terms of place. Place typically refers to where products or services are made available and to the associated channel architecture (producer–distributor–wholesaler–retailer, or producer–consumer, and so on), strategies (from selective to mass availability) and logistics (physical movement of goods).

The emphasis in terms of SM is towards localization of production and distribution systems for both environmental and economic benefit (Kotler, 2011, p. 133). By localizing as much as possible, the intention is to lessen the impact on the environment of moving goods, notably in terms of the carbon footprint but also in other areas. Localization effectively asks retailers, suppliers, manufacturers, transport companies and indeed all levels of the supply chain to improve upon energy efficiency, waste management and recycling efforts in order to reduce the impact on the environment (Charter et al., 2002, p. 25). All products and handling systems must be evaluated in comparison with the harm caused by comparable alternatives (Schaltegger and Wagner, 2003, p. 231).

In this context, retailers can support the demand for environmentally friendly products by requiring suppliers to provide such products and make them readily available to their consumers (Pesonen, 2008). Good examples of this are the increased popularity of local products (despite some supplier relationship problems) as reflected in major supermarkets including Asda, the Co-operative and Waitrose choosing to source locally instead of from countries such as Spain, Kenya and Peru. Local sourcing has witnessed a 50 per cent increase year on year (Wagner et al., 2005). It is interesting to note that CO_2 (carbon dioxide) emissions for ships are now restricted and some shipping companies, such as Maersk, have reduced the speed of their ships to reduce CO_2 emissions by 30 per cent. However, there remains no restriction on SO_2 (sulphur dioxide) and 16 large ships emit as much SO_2 as all the cars in the world (Pearce, 2010, p. 16). This is an example of eco-cost (or grey cost) as mentioned earlier. Localization provides a short supply chain, just-in-time delivery and lower transportation costs. Similarly there is evidence that the consumer appreciates the sense of supporting the community (Morrell, 2010).

Promotion

Promotion normally consists of various forms of sales promotion, personal selling, public relations and mass advertising. Marketing communications normally excludes personal selling but reflects the fact that all the tools of communication should be integrative and symbiotic.

We will focus on advertising and especially on the underpinning consumer behaviour elements. There is a common view that sustainable marketing needs greater emphasis on this area. Consumers want safe, environmentally friendly products. It is very much a problem of communicating this message to consumers and other stakeholders in a manner that raises their level of sensitivity to the concept.

Harrison describes sustainable communication as: 'a continuous, multilevel and consistent exchange between the organisation and its customer-publics … it draws upon and reinforces a cooperative green mentality … to constantly deal with the changing forces and channels involved in environmental performance and reputation' (Harrison, 1994, p. 8). Further, Belz and Peattie (2009, p. 180) suggest that: 'Firms communicate with customers about the sustainability solutions it provides through their products, and also communicate with customers and other stakeholders about the company as a whole … [they wish to] keep an open dialogue between the company and its customers and other stakeholders so that they could all understand and learn from each other.' The premise is that firms have to 'sell' the SM message of environmental and ethical consciousness actively (Belz, 2006).

There are arguably two fundamental parts to the communication problem. Firstly, it is a matter of a wider and deeper awareness of the significance of environmental and ethical problems. Fuller states that: 'the greening of marketing will not take place until consumers and producers recognize the imminent ecological crisis. When these groups change their behaviour and priorities, then new social institutions informed by ecological consciousness can evolve' (Fuller, 1999, p. 226). Effectively, if the consciousness and values are not present, no communication alluding to the values will have an impact on the consumer. The 'educating' of the consumer, according to Carroll (1991), must involve the 'silent hand' of governments. However, additionally, just as with the innovation diffusion/adoption curve (innovators, early adopters, early majority, later adopters, laggards), there is presently a momentum and growing acceptance of the importance of sustainability (Belz and Peattie, 2009).

The second problem remains credibility. 'Greenwashing' refers to making statements that are misleading in order to conceal negative information or to present a positive view. The term includes references to unsubstantiated claims (false or manipulating the truth, insincere) as well as irrelevant, vacuous 'distractions' evident in CSR reports, advertising claims and labelling (Futerra, 2008). One study found that 58 per cent of environmental ads sampled contained at least one misleading or deceptive claim (Kangun et al., 1991). It is not surprising that in another study only 8 per cent of consumers were very confident in environmental advertising information (Fuller, 1999, p. 226) and that consumers stated that advertising was the least credible source of environmental information.

The United Nations Environment Programme (UNEP) describes greenwashing as 'opaque and illegitimate communication practices in the form of misleading or deceitful advertising in order to minimize or conceal the social or environmental consequences of the main activities of companies' (UNEP, 2007). Unfortunately, there does not appear to be a decline in the use of greenwashing, which in turn makes credible and effective sustainable marketing advertising remain a major challenge (ASA, 2008).

Read the label

Arguably the most visible area of promotion is 'eco-labelling'. This has been an area which has contributed to the confusion and credibility problems associated with sustainable marketing communications (Emery, 2012).

The main problem appears to be that labels created by individual firms and labels created by third parties co-exist but conflict, with some greenwashing in the mix. There is empirical evidence that lack of credibility has led to a degree of negativity as regards eco-labels and products (Delmas, 2008). Some authors differentiate on the basis of self-labelling being *eco-labelling* and *eco-certification* being by a third party. The consumer is exposed to numerous voluntary environmental schemes for almost every type of product, including cut flowers, paper, paint, various organic labels (products and soil), Forestry Stewardship Council (FSC) labels for wood products, Carbon Trust carbon reduction labels and WRAP (Waste and Resources Action Programme), developed by the British Retail Consortium.

It is therefore no surprise that there are now more than 415 eco-label programmes, which adds to the confusion and credibility issues (ecolabels.com).

The most fundamental problem, of course, is that products look the same whatever the claim. The consumer cannot actually see any of the activities and processes and therefore is totally dependent on their perception of reliability and authenticity (Crespi and Marette, 2005). What if your takeaway coffee was not actually Fairtrade as claimed? A proposed benchmark for eco-labels is offered by Ibanez and Grolleau (2007), who suggest distinguishing characteristics by the way the standard underlying the eco-label is defined, the way the claim is verified and the way it is signalled to consumers. Labelling will continue to be a problem until it is a credible endorsement of the superiority in terms of environmental and ethical compliance (Crespi and Marette, 2005).

Promotion within the context of the new environment, as with traditional marketing, means that all the components of the four Ps are interrelated. Price probably impacts on choice of communicated message, media choice, distribution channels and so on. In the case of sustainable marketing, all the activities fit into whole lifecycle: product design, raw materials utilized, production, transportation, consumption and disposal. All the activities are related to each other and to the environmentally responsible infrastructure, often referred to as environmental management (Grundey and Zaharia, 2008).

As you munch on your Fairtrade chocolate bar, drinking your all-natural-ingredient beverage, while sitting on your FSC-certificate wooden chair, wearing your new bamboo natural cotton top, reading in your soon-to-be-recycled newspaper about some banks possibly being unethical (perhaps wearing your sunglasses which meet the new UV index rating), you should be well and truly aware of the new sustainable environment in which we must conduct business.

As you further develop the implications of environmentally and ethically aware markets, you should think of the various impacts these values have on products and services and possibly think of innovative ways to take advantage of these changes and associated opportunities.

CONCLUSION

You should now recognize that changes in the business environment can wipe out entire industries and /or reduce successful, market-dominating firms to bankruptcy. No business escapes being impacted by change in the business environment. To raise the heat a little further, virtually no business is entirely domestic in terms of immunity from international changes and their implications and ramifications.

An important point, however, is that change does not just disrupt, threaten survival or close businesses. Change can drive new opportunities. It is hopefully an acceptable stretch of an analogy to a forest fire. The heat pops open the cones on the burning trees and releases seeds, which shower down on the forest floor. Less than a month after the fire is out, a fraction of these seeds germinate and little green plumes flash the start of renewal.

Change clearly offers opportunities through both positive and negative ripple effects. The essential difficulty is in the identification, understanding, analysis and exploitive responses, together with flexible thinking and higher levels of innovation. From a marketing perspective, companies have to decide on markets they want to or can target. They must determine, in the light of competition and consumer market analysis, the most competitive marketing strategy given their total resources, and whether these lie with actual products and features, relative price competitiveness or distribution and marketing competencies.

The abiding assumption is that firms are aware of and sensitive to changes in the business environment. Accurate information remains difficult to collect and is usually incomplete. Firms spend considerable time and effort in collecting, analysing and speculating about business environment information.

Case study
Bubble but no squeak

IN THE 1980S A MR LIU HAN CHIEH STARTED selling a brew of cold green tea which contained bits of tapioca or 'pearls' or 'boba', with the name of 'bubble tea'.

Its popularity grew to the point where today there are some 8,000 'bubble tea' cafes in Taiwan alone. The idea spread to Japan, through Asia, the Middle East and Russia, and is now on offer in German and Austrian McDonald's McCafés. The new brew appears to have come ashore in the UK in the shape of the Bubbleology brand, its entry being first in London's Soho and then at Harvey Nichols in Knightsbridge.

With travel, time, local adaptations and creativity, the product has efflorescence with extensive variations and local names. Varieties now include different teas, including black, the inclusion of milk, fruit flavours including peach, mango and lychee, and other flavours including coffee, chocolate and ginger. There are also choices on offer of different flavours of the 'pearls' (floaty bits) while these retain their essential characteristic of a chewy rubber texture. As a final amendment and taste diffusion, it is now enjoyed as both a hot and a cold beverage.

At the time of printing there is no hard data on the number of bubble shops in the UK. However, there is ample anecdotal evidence that the product and its

istock © davewalkerphotography

category is a strong and potentially significant new contestant in the global beverage market.

Change and its latent and actual impact has been the focus of this chapter. In accordance with our wide discussions in this chapter, bubble tea is clearly a 'change' but there still remains a level of uncertainty as to the magnitude of its impact on the food service, hospitality, retail, home, office and pick-up beverage market.

Factors to consider, ponder even

The knock-on effects of bubble tea include a growth in various market intermediaries including importers of the ingredients and various wholesale suppliers such as for long, thick straws, longer plastic spoons, powders and confectionaries. The long straws apparently have a market as the tier supports for multiple-level cakes! For the eco-aware consumer, there are now stainless straws.

Finally, there are some who express the caveat/view that the 'pearls' may be carcinogenic and also, because of their texture, may be a potential health hazard if lodged in a child's respiratory tract.

Tea: The UK remains the nation with the largest per capita consumption of tea in the world, with 80 per cent of consumers enjoying their traditional refresher. We drink 165 million cups a day. Tea consumption in comparison with coffee consumption is like Lord Nelson versus a Trafalgar Square pigeon in stature with over 60 billion cups a year enjoyed versus an estimated 70 million cups of coffee.

It is important to note that the number of consumers of 'English breakfast' tea in the UK dropped 6 per cent from 2006 to 2010 and there is evidence to suggest that tea is being consumed by older people (over 65) while the appeal is slipping for the 16–24 age group. The exceptions to the low growth rate are the teas associated with health benefits such as herbal and various green teas. There is also a small but growing gourmet specialist tea market.

Coffee: While coffee is not a market leader, coffee consumption in the UK grew 7.5 per cent in 2012 and there are now 15,723 coffee shops. Branded coffee chains (Costa, Starbucks, Nero) with a combined market share of 54 per cent enjoyed a 10 per cent growth in 2012. There is anecdotal evidence that there is also expansion of 'non-specialist' stores such as EAT, Greggs, Pret A Manger, Tesco's Harris + Hoole and at McDonald's.

Another new frontier?

A possible change is also for 'tea' made from coffee leaves rather than the beans. This beverage has been cited as having more of the health properties of tea from tea leaves. The new brew has lower levels of caffeine and is not as strong or as bitter as its traditional cousins.

Questions

1 Prepare a SWOT analysis for one or more of the following topics:
  a The bubble tea market in the UK
  b The 'breakfast' or traditional tea market in the UK
  c The coffee market in the UK
  d The 'tastes like tea but is actually healthier coffee' market in the UK

2 Using macro-environmental factors, suggest the arguments that could be used to gain investors in a new 'My Chai' (tea in many languages) chain of tea shops selling a range of regular and speciality teas.

3 Based on an environmental scan of the retail food and hospitality food markets, suggest why Tesco (UK) would buy a 49 per cent investment in Harris + Hoole tea shops.

4 Suggest some appropriate environmental scans for the proposed investment. What could be the possible 'ripple effects' if speciality teas did match the prominence of the current branded coffee shops?

5 Study the 'adoption' curve with its consumer categories and identify which adoption group is the main market for (a) coffee shops – branded and otherwise, and (b) shops that sell bubble tea. Given the theoretical profile of the adoption group, offer suggestions as to expansion strategies.

6 From plant to cup, identify all the environmental considerations of tea or coffee. Suggest a brief guideline for good practice at each stage.

Review questions

1 What do you understand by the term 'marketing environment'?
2 Outline the basic features of the marketing environment and discuss the implications for marketing.
3 In what ways could an understanding of the marketing environment enhance value-creating activities of firms? Use appropriate examples to illustrate your answer.
4 Should marketers worry about 'sustainability issues'? Argue and justify your answer.

Group tasks

1 Working in groups of three to five, conduct a small amount of research, possibly online. Your role is to identify *good* and *not-so-good* practices in corporate social

responsibility (CSR) based on your research of two companies. Explain why you think that a particular approach is better than another by comparing the CSR practices of the two companies chosen.

2 Working in groups of four to five, identify or suggest three major potential innovation-led market expansions for any company or product based on some current evidence. For each of these possible innovations, propose response strategies for the existing firms. For each innovation, suggest other firms with different expertise that might enter the market. Some examples of innovation breakthroughs: you could look at new cooking technologies which are currently entering the market but in very early stages; the concept of shelf-stable foods and how this could develop; new technologies entering the market for maintaining freshness of produce while retaining flavour; etc. Each group presents its ideas and suggestions for discussion.

Glossary/Key terms

Demarketing: A strategy for reducing or discouraging the demand for a product, especially during periods of scarcity or overflowing demand levels that cannot be met by a company

Eco-certification: Vote of confidence given by a credible third party to attest that a product or company meets appropriate standards in relation to sustainability values

Ecology: The interaction between living organisms (such as human beings) and the environment

Environmentally friendly products: Products that do not cause harm to the environment, such as biodegradable or recyclable packages

Market volatility: Sometimes referred to as market dynamism – explains the rate of change (usually fast-paced) and unpredictability of elements of the marketing environment

STEEP: Represents socio-cultural and demographic, technological, economic, ecological and political/legal aspects of the marketing environment. It is the same as PESTEL or PEST

Sustainability marketing: 'The formulation and implementation of marketing strategies activities (such as production, distribution and promotion decisions) in ways that are sensitive and respectful of both the natural and social environments' (Nwankwo and Gbadamosi, 2011, p. 371)

Vocab check list for ESL students

Adherence	Differentiation	Holistically	Prophesied
Aggregation	Dissenting	Incremental	Ramifications
Caveat	Fiscal	Perimeters	Vacuous
Corollary	Gauge	Propensity	Vicissitudes

Definitions for these terms can be found in the 'Vocab Zone' of the companion website, which provides free access to the Macmillan English Dictionary online at www.palgrave.com/business/Gbadamosi

Further reading

A. Gbadamosi (2011) 'The Entrepreneurship Marketing Environment', in S. Nwankwo and A. Gbadamosi (eds), *Entrepreneurship Marketing: Principles and Practices of SME Marketing*, pp. 55–79. London: Routledge

This chapter provides a broad overview of the marketing environment (both principles and practices) but also relates the discussion to the conditions of marketing in small-to-medium-sized enterprises.

T. Levitt (1960) 'Marketing Myopia', *Harvard Business Review*, 38 (July–August), pp. 24–47

This is a classic paper which every marketing student should read. It is old but the issues it raises remain as valid today as they were when the paper was published. Prof. Levitt demonstrates clearly that the primary reason why many companies get into difficulty or even fail is inappropriate understanding of the marketing environment or poor alignment with it.

References

Adams, C., Frost, G. and Webber, W. (2004) 'Triple Bottom Line: A Review of the Literature' in A. Henriques and J. Richardson (eds) *The Triple Bottom Line: Does it All Add Up? Assessing the Sustainability of Business and CSR*. London: Earthscan, pp. 26–33

Ashridge (2005) *Report for the Danish Commerce and Companies Agency*. September, p. 29 www.ashridge.org.uk

Bakan, J. (2004) *The Corporation: The Pathological Pursuit of Profit and Power*. New York: Simon and Schuster

Beattie, A. (2005) 'Coffees with a conscience', *The Financial Times* (18 October), p. 13

Belz, F.-M. (2006) 'Marketing in the 21st Century', *Business Strategy and the Environment*, 15 (3), pp. 139–44

Belz, F-M. and Peattie, K. (2009) *Sustainability Marketing*. Oxford: Wiley

Berle, G. (1991) *The green entrepreneur: Business opportunities that can save the earth and make you money*. Blue Ridge, USA: Liberty Hall Press

Berman, S., Wicks, A., Kotha, S. and Jones, T. (1999) 'Does stakeholder orientation matter? The relationship between stakeholder management models and firm financial performance', *Academy of Management Journal*, 42 (5), pp. 488–506

Branco, M. and Rodrigues, L. (2006) 'Social Responsibility and Resource-Based Perspectives', *Journal of Business Ethics*, 69, pp. 111–32

Bras, B. and McIntosh, M. (1999) 'Product, process and organizational design for remanufacture – an overview of research', *Robotics Computer Integrated Mfg*, 15, pp. 167–78

Carroll, A. (1979) 'A three-dimensional conceptual model of corporate social performance', *Academy of Management Review*, 4, pp. 497–505

Carroll, A (1983) 'Corporate social responsibility: Will industry respond to cut-backs in social program funding?', *Vital Speeches of the Day*, 49, pp. 604–8

Carroll, A. (1991) 'The Pyramid of Corporate Social Responsibility: Towards the Moral Management of Organizational Stakeholders', *Business Horizons*, pp. 39–48

Carroll, A. (1998) 'The Four Faces of Corporate Citizenship', *Business and Society Review*, Fall, 100/101, pp. 1–7

Carroll, A. (1999) 'Corporate Social Responsibility Evolutions of a Definitional Construct', *Business and Society*, 38 (3), pp. 268–95

Charter, M., Peattie, K., Ottman, J. and Polonsky, M. (2002) 'Marketing and Sustainability', *Centre for Business Relationships, Accountability, Sustainability Society*, pp. 1–36

Christensen, Clayton M. (2003) *The Innovator's Solution: Creating and Sustaining Successful Growth*, Cambridge, MA: Harvard Business Press, pp. 23–45

Choo, C. W. (1999) 'The Art of Scanning the Environment', *Bulletin of the American Society for Information Science*, 23 (3), pp. 13–19

Clark, G., Kosoris, J., Hong, L.-N. and Crul, M. (2009) 'Design for Sustainability: Current Trends in Sustainable Product Design and Development', *Sustainability*, 1, pp. 409–24

Coddington, W. (1993) *Environmental Marketing*. New York: McGraw-Hill

Crane, A. and Matten, D. (2007) *Business Ethics* (2nd edn). Oxford University Press

Crespi, J. and Marette, S. (2005) 'Eco-labelling economics: Is public involvement necessary?' in S. Karup and C. Russell (eds) *Environment, Information and Consumer Behaviour*. Cheltenham: Edward Elgar Publishing, pp. 93–110

Creyer, E. and Ross, W. T. Jr. (1996) 'The Impact of Corporate Behaviour on Perceived Product Value', *Marketing Letters*, 7 (2), pp. 173–85

Crook C. (2005) 'The good company – A survey of corporate social responsibility', *The Economist*, January

Crul, M. and Diehl, J. (2006) *Design for Sustainability: A Practical Approach for Developing Economies*. Paris: UNEP&TU Delft

Darnall, N., Jolley, G., Ytterhus B. and Johnstone, N. (2004) 'Environmental Policy Tools and Firm-level Management Practices: Does Environmental Performance Predict a Facility's Financial Performance', OECD

Davis, K. (1973) 'The case for and against business assumption of social responsibilities', *Academy of Management Journal*, 16, pp. 312–22

Dawar, N. and Pillutla. M. (2000) 'Impact of Product-Harm Crises on Brand Equity: The Moderating Role of Consumer Expectations', *Journal of Marketing Research*, (May) 37, pp. 215–26

De George, R. (2008) 'An American Perspective on Corporate Social Responsibility and the Tenuous Relevance of Jacques Derrida', *Business Ethics*, 17 (1), 74–86

Delmas, M. (2008) *Perception of eco-labels: Organic and biodynamic wines*. Working paper. UCLA Institute of the Environment

Dopfer, K. and Potts, J. (2009) 'The General Theory of Economic Evolution', *Journal of Economic Literature*, 47 (1), March, pp. 173–74

Efstathion, J. and Patton, L. (2012) 'KFC Using Rain-Forest Wood in Boxes, Greenpeace Says', available at: http://www.bloomberg.com/news/2012-05-23/kfc-chicken-buckets-made-with-rain-forest-wood-greenpeace-finds.html. Accessed 20 July 2013

Elkington, J. (2004) 'Enter the Triple Bottom Line' in A. Henriques and J. Richardson (eds) *The Triple Bottom Line: Does it All Add Up?* London: Earthscan

Emery, B. (2012) *Sustainable Marketing*. Harlow: Pearson Education

Folkes, V. A. and Kamins, M. A. (1999) 'Effects of Information About Firms' Ethical and Unethical Actions on Consumers' Attitudes', *Journal of Consumer Psychology*, 8 (3), pp. 243–59

Friedman, M. (1970) 'The Social Responsibility of Business is to Increase its Profits', *New York Times Magazine*, September 13

Fuller, D. (1999) *Sustainable Marketing – Managerial-Ecological Issues*. USA: Sage Publications

Fuller, D. and Butler, D. (1994) 'Eco-Marketing: A Waste Management Perspective' in E. Wilson and W. Black (eds) *Developments in Marketing Science*, 17, p. 331 Proceedings of the Academy of Marketing Science

Futerra (2008) *The Greenwash Guide*, www.futerra.co.uk

Gates, Stephen, Lukomnik, Jon and Pitt-Watson, David (2006) *The New Capitalists: How Citizen Investors Are Reshaping The Business Agenda*. Harvard Business School Press

Gossling, T. and Vocht, C. (2007) 'Social Role Conceptions and CSR policy success', *Journal of Business Ethics*, 74 (4), Ethics in and of Global Organisations: The EBEN 19th Annual Conference in Vienna (September), pp. 363–72

Green, R. (2002) 'Changing production and consumption patterns: progress made and remaining challenges', Cleaner Production Seventh International High-level Seminar Prague, ISSN 0378-9993 in *Industry and Environment*, 25 (3–4) (July–December), pp. 33–35. A publication of the United Nations Environment Programme Division of Technology, Industry and Economics

Greenfield, J. (2012) *Consumers Increasingly Choose Tablets Over E-Readers, E-Book Sales to Suffer*. DBW Insights, posted 2 May, accessed 20 June 2012 http://www.digitalbookworld.com/2012/consumers-increasingly-choose-tablets-over-e-readers-e-book-sales-to-suffer/

Greening, D. W. and Turban, D. B. (2000) 'Corporate Social Performance as a Competitive Advantage in Attracting a Quality Workforce', *Business & Society*, 39 (3), pp. 254–80

Grundey, D. and Zaharia, R. (2008) 'Sustainable Incentives in Marketing and Strategic Greening: The Case of Lithuania and Romania', *Technological and Economic Development*, 14 (2), pp. 130–43

Grundy, T. (2006) 'Rethinking and reinventing Michael Porter's five forces model', *Strategic Change*, (August) 15 (5), pp. 213–29

Handelman, J. M. and Arnold, S. J. (1999) 'The Role of Marketing Actions with a Social Dimension: Appeals to the Institutional Environment', *Journal of Marketing*, 63 (July), pp. 33–38

Harrison, B. (1994) *Lean and Mean: The Changing Landscape of Corporate Power in the Age of Flexibility*. New York: Basic Books

Hawken, P. (1993) *The Ecology of Commerce: A Declaration of Sustainability*. New York: Harper-Collins

Henion, K. (1976) *Ecological Marketing*. Columbus, Ohio: Grid

Henriques, A. (2004). 'CSR, Sustainability and the Triple Bottom Line', in A. Henriques and J. Richardson (eds) *The Triple Bottom Line: Does it All Add Up? Assessing the Sustainability of Business and CSR*, London: Earthscan, pp. 26–33

Hockerts, K. and Wüstenhagen, R. (2010) 'Greening Goliaths versus emerging Davids – Theorizing about the role of incumbents and new entrants in sustainable entrepreneurship', *Journal of Business Venturing*, 25 (5), pp. 481–92

Holmes, J. H. and Kilbane, C. J. (1993). 'Cause-Related Marketing: Selected Effects of Price and Charitable Donations', *Journal of Nonprofit & Public Sector Marketing*, 1 (4), pp. 67–83

Holmes, L. and Watts, R. (2000) 'Corporate Social Responsibility: Making Good Business Sense', World Business Council for Sustainable Development, Geneva

Hooley, G., Piercy, N. and Nicoulaud, B. (2008) *Marketing Strategy and Competitive Positioning* (4th edn). Harlow: Pearson Education

Howley, K. (2006) Ireland Government Affairs & Europe CSR Manager, Intel Ireland (2006) 'From CSR aware to CSR active', *Ethical Corporation Conference*, Internal CSR Communications, Practical Tools to Communicate your Ethical Values to Employees, Brussels

Ibanez, L. and Grolleau, G. (2008) 'Can ecolabeling schemes preserve the environment?' *Environmental Resource Economics*, 40 (2), pp. 233–49

Kangun, N., Carlson, L. and Grove, S. (1991) 'Environmental Advertising Claims: A Preliminary Investigation', *Journal of Public Policy and Marketing*, 12 (Fall), pp. 47–58

Keoleian, G. and Menerey, D. (1994) 'Sustainable Development by Design: Review of Life Cycle Design and Related Approaches', *Journal of the Air and Waste Management Association*, 44 (5), pp. 645–68

Kerr, W. and Ryan, C. (2001) 'Eco-efficiency gains from remanufacturing. A case study of photocopier remanufacturing at Fuji Xerox Australia', *Journal of Cleaner Production*, 9, pp. 75–81

Kolstad, I. (2007) 'Why Firms Should Not Always Maximize Profits', *Journal of Business Ethics*, 76 (2), pp. 137–45

Korkchi, S. and Rombaut, N. (2006) 'Corporate Social Responsibility: A case study on private corporations in Sweden', BA thesis, South Stockholm University, 108 pages

Kosminsky, J. (1997) 'Venture Philanthropy: A New Model for Corporate Giving', *Fund Raising Management*, August (6), pp. 28–31

Kotler, P. (2011) 'Reinventing Marketing to Manage the Environmental Imperative', *Journal of Marketing*, 75, pp. 132–35

Kotler, P. and Keller, K. (2005) *Marketing Management* (12th edn). Prentice Hall.

Kotler, P. and Armstrong, G. (2014) *Principles of Marketing* (15th edn). Harlow: Pearson Education

Kraus, S. and Melay, I. (2012) 'Green entrepreneurship: definitions of related concepts', *International Journal of Strategic Management*, 12 (2) (Aug), p. 1

Lantos, G. (2001) 'The Boundaries of Strategic Corporate Social Responsibility', *Journal of Consumer Marketing*, 18 (7), pp. 595–630

Lichtenstein, D., Drumwright, M. and Braig, B. (2004) 'The Effect of Corporate Social Responsibility on Customer Donations to Corporate-supported Nonprofits', *Journal of Marketing*, (October) 68 (4), pp. 16–32

Martin, D. and Schouten, J. (2012) *Sustainable Marketing*. New Jersey, USA: Prentice Hall

McGuire, W. (1985) 'Attitudes and attitude change' in G. Lindzey, and E. Aronson (eds) *Handbook of Social Psychology*. N.Y.: Random House, pp. 233–346

McWilliams, A. and Siegal, D. (2000) 'Corporate Social Responsibility and Financial Correlation or Misspecification', *Strategic Management Journal*, 21 (5), pp. 603–9

McWilliams, A., Siegal, D. and Wright, P. (2006) 'Corporate Social Responsibility: Strategic Implications', *Journal of Management Studies*, 43 (1), pp. 1–18

Meyer, H. (1999) 'When the cause is right', *Journal of Business Strategy*, (November–December) 20, pp. 27–31

Min, W. and Galle, W. (1997) 'Green Purchasing Strategies: Trends and Implications', *Journal of Supply Chain Management*, June 33 (3), pp. 10–17

Mohr, L., Webb, D. and Harris, K. (2001) 'Do Consumers Expect Companies to be Socially Responsible? The Impact of Corporate Social Responsibility on Buying Behaviour', *The Journal of Consumer Affairs*, 35 (1), pp. 45–72

Moir, L. (2001) 'What Do We Mean by Corporate Social Responsibility?' *Corporate Governance*, 1 (2), pp. 16–22

Morrell, L. (2010) 'The benefits of local sourcing', *Retail Week* (February) http://www.retail-week.com/in-business/supply-chain/the-benefits-of-local-sourcing/5010688.article

Murray, K. B. and Vogel, C. M. (1997) 'Using a Hierarchy of Effects Approach to Gauge the Effectiveness of Corporate Social Responsibility to Generate Goodwill Toward the Firm: Financial versus Nonfinancial Impacts', *Journal of Business Research*, 38 (2), pp. 141–59

Nasr, N. and Thurston, M. (2006) 'Remanufacturing: A Key Enabler to Sustainable Product Systems', *International Conference on Life Cycle Engineering*, pp. 15–18 http://www.mech.kuleuven.be/lce2006/key4.pdf

Negash, S. (2004) 'Business Intelligence', *Communications of the Association for Information Systems*, 13, pp. 177–95

Nwankwo, S. and Gbadamosi, A. (2011) *Entrepreneurship Marketing: Principles and Practice of SME Marketing*. Abingdon: Routledge

Ottman, J. (1993) *Green Marketing: Challenges and Opportunities for the New Marketing Age*. Lincolnwood, IL: NTC Business Press

Ottman, J. (2013) *The New Rules of Green Marketing*. San Francisco: Berrett-Koehler

Paine, Lynn S. (1991) 'Review of *Good Intentions Aside* by L. Nash', *Human Resource Planning*, 14 (3), pp. 64–69

Paine, Lynn Sharp (2004) *Value Shift: Why Companies Must Merge Social and Financial Imperatives to Achieve Superior Performance*. New York: McGraw-Hill

Park, S. and Jayaraman, S. (2002) 'The Wearable Motherboard: the new class of adaptive and responsive textile structures', *International Interactive Textiles for the Warrior Conference*, 9–11 July http://www.wearable-electronics.de/intl/fotos_vorbereitungen.asp

Pearce, F. (2010) 'Polluting ships have been doing the climate a favour', *New Scientist*, (March), p. 16

Peattie, K. (1995) *Environmental Marketing Management*. London: Pitman

Pesonen, H.-L. (2008) 'Arvojen ja toiminnan välinen ristiriita kulutuksessa – teoriaa ja haasteita vastuullista kulutusta edistävälle ruuan markkinoinnille' *Futura* (translated into English)

Pickton, D. and Wright, S. (1998) 'What's SWOT in Strategic Analysis?' *Strategic Change*, (March/April) 7 (2), pp. 101–9

Porter, M. (2002) 'Building the Microeconomic Foundations of Prosperity: Findings from the Microeconomic Competitiveness Index', *Global Competitiveness Report*, Citeseer, p. 3

Porter, M. (2008) 'The Five Competitive Forces that shape strategy', *Harvard Business Review*, January, pp. 25–40

Prakash, A. (2002) 'Green Marketing, Public Policy and Managerial Strategies', *Business Strategy and the Environment*, 11, pp. 285–97. http://www.greeneconomics.net/GreenMarketing.pdf

Savitz, A. and Weber, K. (2006) *The Triple Bottom Line: How Today's Best-Run Companies are Achieving Economic, Social and Environmental Success – And How You Can Too*. New York: Wiley

Schaltegger, S. and Wagner, M. (2003) 'Managing and Measuring the Business Case for Sustainability' http://www.greenleaf-publishing.com/content/pdfs/bcsintro

Schmidheiny, S. (1992) *Changing Course: A Global Perspective in Development and the Environment*, MIT Press

Schumpeter (2012) 'Good business; nice beaches', *The Economist*, 19–25 May, p. 66

Schwartz, Mark and Carroll, Archie (2003) 'Corporate Social Responsibility: A Three Domain Approach', *Business Ethics Quarterly*, 1 (4) (October), pp. 503–30

Sheth, J. and Parvatiyar, A. (1995) 'Ecological Imperatives and the Role of Marketing' in M. J. Polonsky and A. T. Mintu-Wimsatt (eds) *Environmental Marketing: Strategies, Practice, Theory and Research*. Binghamton, N.Y.: Haworth Press, pp. 3–20

Smith, N. C. (2003) 'Corporate Social Responsibility: Whether or How?' *California Management Review*, 45 (4), pp. 52–76

Solomon, M., Bamossy, G., Askegaard, S. and Hogg, M. (2010) *Consumer Behaviour: A European Perspective* (4th edn). Harlow: Prentice-Hall

Spangenberg, J., Fuad-Luke, A. and Blincoe, K. (2010) 'Design for Sustainability (DfS): the interface of sustainable production and consumption', *Journal of Cleaner Production*, 18 (15) (November), pp. 1485–93

Taleb, N. (2007) *The Black Swan: The Impact of the Highly Improbable*. London: Random House

Thorpe, B. (2009) *Clean Production Strategies: What is Clean Production?* Posted June, http://www.cleanproduction.org accessed 5 July, 2012

Tzu, S. (1994) translation of *The Art of War*. Stanford: Oxford University Press

United Nations Environment Programme (2007) *Sustainability Communications: A Toolkit for Marketing and Advertising Courses*, UNEP, p. 77

Vollmert, M. (2007) 'Corporate Social Responsibility: Impact on applying and buying behaviour', Master's thesis, Maastricht University

Wagner, B., Fillis, I. and Johansson, U. (2005) 'An exploratory study of SME local sourcing and supplier development in the grocery retail sector', *International Journal of Retail & Distribution Management*, 33 (10), pp. 716–33

Wood, D. and Jones, R. (1995) 'Stakeholder Mis-matching: A Theoretical Problem in Empirical Research on Corporate Social Responsibility', *The International Journal of Organisational Analysis*, 3 (3), pp. 229–67

Zhang, X. and Tao, X. (2001) 'Smart textiles: Passive smart', *Textile Asia*, June, pp. 45–49

3 CONSUMER BUYING BEHAVIOUR

HINA KHAN

NORTHUMBRIA UNIVERSITY

CHAPTER CONTENTS

LEARNING OUTCOMES

The content of this chapter will help you to:

- Understand the importance of buying behaviour for providing a value-added buying experience
- Recognize the stages of the consumer and organizational buying decision processes
- Identify the factors that may affect consumer and organizational buying decisions

CREATING CUSTOMER VALUE IS A KEY TO ACHIEVING competitive advantage. Particularly in today's competitive marketplace, consumers are spoilt for choice and it is becoming more and more challenging for companies to keep their customers satisfied and loyal. Companies are therefore developing value-based marketing strategies to offer value-added attributes that enhance their products and services in order to satisfy customers' expectations.

For example, EasyJet has developed insurance cover for its customers when they inadvertently miss their flights because of alarm clock failure, bad weather, traffic jams, or delays due to security clearance or processing issues at the airport (Guardian, 2012).

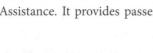
istock © bociek666

The policy is offered by a company called No Exclusions in association with the insurer Mondial Assistance. It provides passengers with a new ticket on the next available flight at no additional cost, or gives the option of a full refund. The missed departure cover will also pay passengers any extra expenses that may have been incurred due to the missed flight. However, passengers will not be able to claim the insurance if they did not leave their homes in good time to get to the airport.

The missed flight cover is offered on any EasyJet bookings, including those made online and via travel agents. Travellers are also allowed to swap airports with the EasyJet service. If you missed a flight from Gatwick, for example, but there was another flight going from Luton to the same destination, you could transfer to that flight. However, interconnecting travel costs such as train fares are not covered by the policy.

This is a prime example of how companies are striving to deliver extra value for their customers.

INTRODUCTION

In today's intensely competitive marketplace, learning about consumers' values and attitudes and what actually drives them to select a product and then purchase it, is crucial for a product or a brand to be successful. Companies aim to maximize their sales, which in turn maximizes their profits, and for most organizations this is the main objective. On the other hand, consumers are presented with a great range of products and services to choose from to satisfy their needs and wants. There are a number of factors that affect consumers' intentions to purchase a product or service. Consumers are concerned about the total value they can acquire from the consumption of products and services. Thus, it has become extremely important for an organization to understand consumers' buying behaviour, particularly why and how consumers seek to actualize value from their consumption experiences. Hence, a value-driven marketing strategy is extremely important to attract consumers, to keep up with changing consumer needs and wants and to achieve a competitive advantage. Against this background, this chapter aims to explore consumer buying behaviour, values, motivation and perceptions and to highlight patterns of behaviour that affect consumers' decision making when purchasing a product.

STIMULUS–RESPONSE MODEL OF CONSUMER BUYING BEHAVIOUR

The stimulus–response model, which is also known as the 'buyer's black box' (see Figure 3.1), provides a starting point to understand consumer buying behaviour.

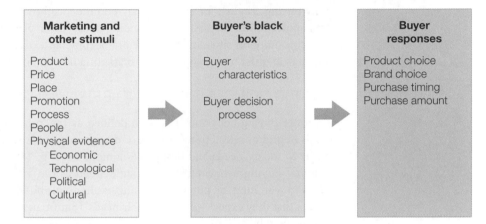

Figure 3.1: Stimulus–response model of consumer buying behaviour

Source: Adapted from Kotler and Keller, 2007

As shown in Figure 3.1, marketing stimuli comprise marketing mix elements and other external stimuli (such as economic, technological, political and cultural factors) that affect the consumer buying behaviour. All these factors, along with the combination of buyer psychological factors and characteristics (buyer's black box) influence the consumer buying decision process and thereby the final purchasing decision. Hence, it is extremely important for marketers to understand marketing stimuli and the relationship between these and consumers' characteristics as well as psychological factors that affect the ultimate purchasing decision (Kotler and Keller, 2007). These factors are discussed in detail later in this chapter.

CONSUMER BUYING ROLES

One of the key ways to understand consumer buying behaviour is to understand the different roles played by a consumer. In a standard buying situation, a consumer can be defined as the one who pays for and receives goods and services in return for the payment made. However, in most situations, consumer buying decisions tend to be complex. This is because a consumer may play different roles in a transaction process. Five key roles played by consumers in purchasing decisions are:

Initiator: Individuals who recognize a need to purchase

Influencer: Those who are interested in the purchase. These individuals may have experience of the product or service to be purchased

Users: Those who actually use the product or service

Decider: The individuals who make the ultimate decision to purchase

Purchaser: The person who pays for the product or service

These roles can be interlinked and hence can affect the consumer decision-making process in various ways. Furthermore, the role played by an individual within a family buying context, for example, may be influenced by buyer characteristics and social and cultural factors. Understanding these roles played by consumers in a given consumption situation has therefore become an extremely important task for marketers in order to develop effective marketing mix and communication strategies.

WHAT IS CONSUMER BUYING BEHAVIOUR?

Consumer buying behaviour has been defined as the 'process involved when individuals or groups select, purchase, use or dispose of products, services, ideas or experiences to satisfy needs and desires' (Solomon, 2004, p. 189). In a similar manner, consumer buying behaviour can also be defined as the 'behaviour that consumers display in searching for, purchasing, using, evaluating, and disposing of products and services that they expect will satisfy their needs' (Shiffman and Kanuk, 2010, p. 3).

Consumer behaviour was originally known as 'buyer behaviour', reflecting an emphasis on the interaction between consumers and retailers at the time of purchase. However, more recently, marketers have realized that consumer behaviour is an ongoing process, not merely what happens when the goods or service are purchased. Also relevant is the extent to which the purchase satisfied the consumer and how it was evaluated based on perceived benefits after the purchase.

The difference between a customer/buyer and a consumer

A *customer* is a person who buys the product but a *consumer* is a person who finally uses/consumes the product. A customer purchases and pays for a product or service. A consumer is the user of the product or service. The consumer may not have paid for the product or service. For example, a chocolate manufacturing company makes own-label chocolate bars for a major supermarket. So, in this case, the customer is the supermarket to which it supplies bars. The consumer is the individual who consumes the chocolate. In terms of its marketing effort, the manufacturing company needs to understand the needs and wants of both the customer and the consumer.

If you choose to purchase the chocolate and you eat

istock © Picsfive

it, you are the customer and consumer. If, though, your child chooses and eats the chocolate but you pay for it, your child is the consumer and you are the customer. Consumers and customers may not demonstrate the same beliefs, values and attitudes. Marketers often try to influence the consumers (in this case, children) and exploit the power they have over the customers (in this case, parents). For instance, they may advertise tempting toys or food items during breaks in children's television programmes or place sweets within reach of small children in supermarkets. They are attempting to use children to persuade parents to purchase their product. As a result, these types of marketing activities are criticized for addressing the wants of children without much consideration for the expectations of their parents, the customers.

3

CONSUMER DECISION-MAKING PROCESS

A consumer goes through five key stages when making a purchase decision: problem recognition, information search, alternative evaluation, purchase decision and post-purchase evaluation.

The following sections of the chapter will briefly explain these key stages.

Need recognition: Need arousal or recognition factors are the starting point for any purchase decision and occur when an individual discovers a change in what he or she perceives to be an ideal state versus their actual (current) state and is both externally and internally influenced. Need recognition can be marketer generated. A need could be aroused by a display, a special offer in the supermarket or an advertisement while shopping. It is important to understand what drives or connects the customer to the product class or brand as well as what makes the customer feel that purchasing a product or brand could satisfy the need or drive in the first place.

For example, in the car industry, the creation of a new model intrudes on the consumer's environmental and social needs to make them feel inadequate by owning an inferior, older model. Furthermore, internal generation can come from a change in circumstances, such as the arrival of a child so that a bigger car is required, or the current car becoming unreliable. Understanding how this process is generated can help to give a deeper insight into further decision-making attributes. The model also drives the marketer to take into account the whole buying process rather than just considering the purchasing decisions – for example, how and when to influence a purchasing decision or a choice.

Problem recognition: The first stage, problem recognition, is where the consumer realizes that they want to purchase a product – for example, a bottle of wine.

Information search: The second stage, information search, involves the consumer looking along the shelf at the different styles of wine available. At the information search stage, the consumer is looking to build information on the product they are intending to buy to aid the purchase decision. At this stage, the consumer may alternatively use the Internet to search for product information even if they do not intend to buy online. The same goes for using the high street to search for a product and the consumer may return home to gather further information regarding that product. Information such as price and where to buy will be gathered. The consumer will collect information to enable them to purchase the product wherever it is most convenient and wherever has the best price and carries the least risk. For example, a consumer looking to buy a decent bottle of wine may start to look for information about types of wine available in the market through brands, price level, country of origin and taste in order to maximize value and minimize perceived risk.

Perceived risk refers to the consumer's uncertainty or anxiety about the outcome of a purchase decision, particularly in the case of an expensive or a high-involvement product such as a car or a complex item like a computer. Consumers seek to reduce their anxiety by collecting more information and by seeking the recommendations of a peer group such as friends or family members or a sales person. The perceived risk the product carries is identified at this stage of the process and will also have an effect on where the product is purchased. If the risk of a product is high, the product choice is visible to others and the consumer runs the risk of embarrassment, the decision may be made to purchase the product online, where they are not visible.

In terms of the consumer's decision-making process, the reasons people make purchases over the Internet are convenience, lower prices and a wider choice of goods. These factors will be taken into consideration at the information search stage.

The information search is an important stage as it will equip the consumer with the information they need to decide whether to shop online or not. This decision very much depends upon the product being bought, the perceived risk and what would be most beneficial to the consumer. This stage of the process has become increasingly important with the boom of the Internet, where so much information is available. If retailers target consumers effectively, they can turn an online search into a purchase, as can an effective offline campaign. Alternatively, marketers can use both online and offline methods where the purchasers can use online methods only for information search and offline methods to make the purchase.

Evaluation of alternatives: At the third stage, alternative evaluation, the consumer evaluates the intrinsic attributes (ingredients, taste, colour) and extrinsic attributes (brand quality, country of origin, price) of available alternative products. This evaluation will depend on individual characteristics and the reason for purchase. For instance, consumers may be willing to pay a higher price for a product that has a positive or a popular country of origin when purchasing a gift for a family member or a friend. Thus, consumers' evaluation of alternatives may be more rigorous when purchasing a product for a special occasion compared with purchasing a product for utilitarian purposes. For example, a consumer who may wish to purchase a bottle of wine may evaluate the colour, brand name, country of origin and price of different wines available in a store before making their purchase decision.

Purchase decision: The fourth stage, the purchase decision, will be based on the evaluations made in the previous stage. At this stage, the attitudes of other people and other situational factors will also influence the final purchase decision. In line with the previous example, this is where the consumer will agree upon a wine through an informed decision and make the final purchase.

Post-purchase evaluation – cognitive dissonance: The final stage is the post-purchase evaluation of the decision. In this stage, the consumer will evaluate the purchase they have made according to their expectations. This will allow them to see whether their uncertainty or anxiety about the outcome of a purchase decision helped them to make an informed decision. If the decision process went well, a possible repeat purchase will be made. However, if the decision was not satisfactory, when the need for that particular product arises, the purchase decision process will start again. In the case of an unsatisfactory purchase, consumers are more likely to switch to another brand.

istock © diego_cervo

For example, after the wine has been purchased, the consumer tastes the wine. If it is in line with their expectations, the consumer may be satisfied. Otherwise, it may lead to 'cognitive dissonance' where the consumer experiences concerns and dissatisfaction after making a purchase decision. The customer, having bought a product, may feel that an alternative would have been preferable. In these circumstances, the customer will not repurchase immediately and is likely to switch brands next time.

To manage the post-purchase stage, it is the job of the marketing team to persuade the potential customer that the product will satisfy their needs. Then, after having made a purchase, the customer should be encouraged to believe that he or she has made the right decision. So, companies must deliver what they promise to customers as failure to do so would have serious consequences for the company's reputation and the customer's loyalty (Schiffman and Kanuk, 2010).

Example 3.1:

Did you know that the majority of consumer brands are owned by ten multinational companies?

Have you ever wondered where most of your products and brands come from or who owns them? For instance, it may be obvious that Corn Flakes and Frosted Flakes are both made by Kellogg's, but did you know that Hot Pockets and L'Oréal share a parent company in Nestlé?

The consumer goods industry has become consolidated. Enormous numbers of brands are produced by just ten major companies: Kraft, Coca-Cola, Pepsico, General Mills, Kellogg's, Mars, Unilever, Johnson & Johnson, P&G and Nestlé.

HIGH-INVOLVEMENT VS. LOW-INVOLVEMENT PURCHASING DECISIONS

There are several versions of the consumer decision process model. Most agree that the consumer goes through a cognitive decision-making process as demonstrated in Figure 3.2. The cognitive types of model emphasize that consumers' decision making differs according to the level of involvement and product type – that is, whether the products are high involvement or low involvement.

HIGH-INVOLVEMENT PURCHASING DECISIONS

In **high-involvement decisions**, the marketer needs to provide a good deal of information about the positive outcomes of buying

High-involvement purchases tend to be expensive and include those involving personal risk. High-involvement/emotional purchases can include jewellery, a wedding dress and holiday travel. On the other hand, high-involvement/rational purchases include buying a house, a car or major electronic appliances or making financial investments. In high-involvement decisions, the marketer needs to provide a good deal of information about the positive outcomes of buying (O'Cass, 2000). The sales force may need to stress the important attributes of the product and the advantages compared with the competition and may even encourage a 'trial' or 'sampling' of the product in the hope of securing the sale – for example, test driving a car or taking part in a wine-tasting event.

LOW-INVOLVEMENT PURCHASING DECISIONS

When consumers are purchasing **low-involvement products**, the purchase decisions are less risky so they require little information or support. This decision-making process is referred to as **limited problem solving** (LPS)

A low-involvement purchase tends to be inexpensive or represents habitual buying. So, the decision-making process differs from that in a high-involvement purchase, as demonstrated in Figure 3.2. Low-involvement/rational purchases include most of the things you put in your shopping basket, such as over-the-counter medicine, shampoo and toothpaste, breakfast cereal and chocolate. They include the things we buy without much thought and involve very simple evaluation processes. Low-involvement/emotional purchases invoke the gratification we get from these products, which does not last a long time. We do not spend a lot of time thinking about these purchases, such as going to the movies or buying a 'gossip' magazine or a birthday card.

Figure 3.2: Extended problem-solving and limited problem-solving processes.
Source: Based on Foxall (1990)

Extended problem solving	Limited problem solving
• Extensive information search	• Short internal information search
• Attitude/intention	• Trial/experimentation
• Trial/experimentation	• Attitude/future intention
• Long-term behaviour	• Long-term behaviour

Example 3.2:
Wilkinson: Growing with students

Developing appropriate strategies to deliver a value-added service to consumers is key to achieving a sustainable competitive advantage. Wilkinson, one of the major retailers of food, home, garden and health and beauty products, is a classic example of how customer value is added via responding to changing consumer needs effectively.

Wilkinson was founded by JK Wilkinson in 1930. Today it is among the top 30 retailers in the UK. Recently, Wilkinson has experienced tremendous competition from supermarkets in the UK and has therefore carried out extensive marketing research with a view to developing new growth avenues. This has led Wilkinson to develop a marketing strategy to target the student segment.

Growing with students

With the aim of encouraging students to shop at Wilkinson, the company conducted marketing research in 60 universities in the UK. The research was designed to assess students' awareness of the Wilkinson brand and to determine reasons for not shopping at Wilkinson shops regularly. The findings of the research provided Wilkinson with a significant insight into the factors that would motivate students to purchase products from Wilkinson. Being cheaper than competitors and easily accessible was cited by students as the main reason for shopping at Wilkinson. Moreover, distance from the university was mentioned as the main reason for not shopping there regularly. All this data helped Wilkinson to identify motivation factors associated with the student audience that would encourage students to shop with the company. Hence, Wilkinson integrated the information it had gathered into its future campaigns.

Targeting students

Integrating the findings of the research, Wilkinson launched a marketing campaign that included a range of product tactics to attract university students to shop at Wilkinson.

These included:

- Free 'goody bags' given to students at freshers' fairs
- Direct mail flyers sent to homes and student halls, prior to students arriving
- Advertisements with fun teams
- Gift vouchers
- Free wall planners
- Web banners

Outcomes

The results of the campaigns revealed that the level of awareness of the Wilkinson brand had increased from 77 per cent to 95 per cent of those interviewed.

The post-campaign results showed that the campaign had made Wilkinson more appealing for 67 per cent of the students interviewed. The number of customers who shopped at Wilkinson at least once a month had increased from 13 per cent to 33 per cent.

Conclusion

With the fierce competition faced from supermarkets, Wilkinson aimed to grow and increase its stores across the UK. The company conducted marketing research among students across the UK to identify customer views of the Wilkinson brand and what motivates consumers to shop at Wilkinson. Integrating the data gathered, a marketing campaign was launched which included product tactics targeted at students. The post-campaign results indicated that it increased the level of brand awareness among the target group and increased repeat visits.

Source: Times 100, 2013

Think and discuss

Think of any two high-involvement products you or your close relations bought recently. Identify the various sources consulted during the search for information stage. Do you think these sources will be different if you are buying low-involvement products? Discuss the reasons for your opinion with other members of the group.

EXTENDED PROBLEM SOLVING FOR HIGH–INVOLVEMENT PRODUCTS

When consumers are making a decision to buy an expensive or high-involvement product, they usually engage in an extensive information search before making a purchasing decision. This process is referred to as extended problem solving (EPS). Consumers would move through the process demonstrated in Figure 3.3.

A consumer looks for essential information and their attitude is developed before an intention to purchase or trial is determined. Consumers tend to explore different sources such as mass media, word of mouth, point of sale display and communications. After evaluation of the information about the key attributes and alternatives, an understanding or 'belief' is formed which may then lead to a trial of a product. If the perceived quality of the product is satisfactory and comes up to the consumer's expectations, a long-term behaviour is determined. EPS also takes place at the introductory stage of the product lifecycle, when consumers are exposed to a new product or a brand.

LIMITED PROBLEM SOLVING FOR LOW–INVOLVEMENT PRODUCTS

When consumers are making a low-involvement product choice, such as for frequently purchased and low-cost products, the need to search for information is low. The purchase decisions are less risky so consumers require little information or support. This decision-making process is referred to as limited problem solving (LPS). Consumers tend to move through the process as demonstrated in Figure 3.3.

Purchasing a lotion or chocolate bar, for example, usually requires simple decision making. These types of purchasing decisions tend to evoke mild curiosity. After conducting a quick mental search, a decision to purchase or trial is made. After trying the product, if the consumer is satisfied with the quality and perceived benefits, there is potential for a long-term behaviour, which may result in a repeat purchase. This type of consumer decision making also takes place at the growth stage of a product lifecycle as consumers become familiar with and more knowledgeable about the product or brand. So, when there are more brands or products to choose from, the risks associated with the purchase decline.

ORGANIZATIONAL BUYING BEHAVIOUR

As discussed above, consumer buying behaviour refers to the buying behaviour of individuals or families that purchase products or services for their own use. By contrast, organizational buying behaviour relates to the purchase of goods and services in order to provide goods and services to the final customer. The following sections of this chapter will provide an overview of organizational buying behaviour to enable you to compare and contrast the similarities and differences between consumer buying behaviour and organizational buying behaviour.

STAGES COMPRISING AN ORGANIZATIONAL BUYING DECISION–MAKING PROCESS

In many ways, organizational buying behaviour is similar to that of consumers. Both processes start with need recognition and go through similar stages such as an information search, evaluation, selection and post-purchase evaluation. The phases involved in organizational buying are presented in Figure 3.3. Each of the stages is discussed below and you will be able to see how organizational buying behaviour differs from consumer buying behaviour.

3

Figure 3.3: Stages in organizational buying decision-making process
Source: Based on Kotler & Keller, 2007

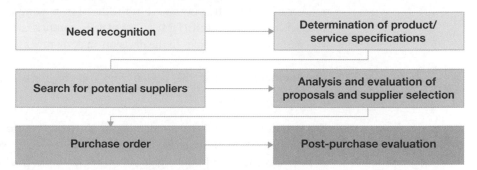

Need recognition

A need for a purchase could result from an internal or external factor. For example, an organization using old machinery may decide to buy new machinery to enhance its production efficiency.

Determination of product/service specifications

In this phase, an organization may decide what is specifically required to be purchased. Here, the members involved in decision making will determine the type of purchase and the quantity, and the models associated with the required product. For example, an organization may determine that it requires 12 new production machines made in Japan under Model B.

Search for potential suppliers

Having specified the product requirements, the organization will then look for potential suppliers. During this stage, an organization may search for suppliers in a variety of sources such as trade directories and supplier databases. They may also advertise for tenders or seek advice from experts or presentations from sales representatives.

Analysis and evaluation of proposals and supplier selection

After gathering information on potential suppliers, the next task involves the analysis of supplier tender/quotations. Here, factors such as supplier reputation and technical expertise will be considered. Thereafter, each tender/offer will be evaluated against the organization's needs and other requirements and the best supplier will be selected for the purchase order.

Purchase order

Once the supplier is selected, the purchase order will be placed by the organization.

Post-purchase evaluation

After completing the purchase, post-purchase evaluations will be conducted to determine to what extent the purchase satisfied the organization's requirements. These can be conducted by formal investigation of user satisfaction, through informal conversations with the user or by monitoring production efficiency.

Members involved in organizational buying decision-making unit

One of the key differences between consumer and organizational buying is that the latter involves group decision making. A typical organizational purchase involves a number of people who play a part in the decision-making process. They are termed the decision-making unit (DMU). This DMU comprises the following individuals who perform different roles in the decision-making process.

The purchaser: This is the person who has the formal authority to make the purchase.

The initiator: The person who identifies the need to buy goods and services for an organization. Thus an initiator could be a member of staff, a senior manager or even an external consultant to the organization. For example, this could be an IT manager who sees the need to purchase new computers for staff.

The influencer: The influencer may be a person who will be affected by the purchase and may have a positive or negative influence on the purchase decision. For example, an influencer could be a technician who provides product specifications or a finance officer who imposes financial constraints on the purchase decision.

The user: Users are the people in the organization who would actually use the product. For example, they may be computer operators who would be using the computers in a department.

The decision maker: This is the person who makes the buying decision. It could be the head of the department or the managing director of the company who approves the purchase decision.

The gatekeeper: This may be an individual who controls the flow of information to and from the buying group. For example, a gatekeeper could be the secretarial team that is responsible for dealing with the approvals and correspondence.

FACTORS INFLUENCING ORGANIZATIONAL BUYING DECISIONS

As with consumer buying behaviour, there are factors that can affect organizational buying decisions. These factors can be categorized as internal and external. Internal factors are those within the control of an organization such as the culture, structure and policies of the organization that may have a positive or negative influence on organizational buying decisions. External factors are those outside an organization that cannot be controlled. These could include political, legal, economic and socio-cultural factors that have a positive or negative impact on organizational buying decisions. These factors are shown in Figure 3.4.

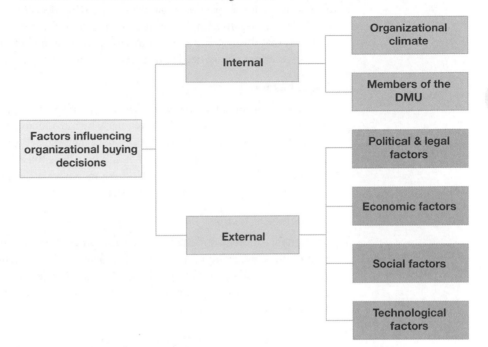

Figure 3.4: Factors influencing organizational buying decisions

INTERNAL FACTORS

Organizational climate

The culture, structure, systems and procedures within the organization may have a significant influence on organizational buying decisions. For example, an organization with a centralized structure may have a different approach to decision making from an organization with a decentralized structure.

Members of the DMU

The knowledge, expertise and decision-making styles of the DMU of an organization may also have a significant impact on organizational buying decisions. Different members of the DMU may evaluate buying decisions on the basis of different criteria and individual beliefs. Thus, it is essential to have a good communication between each member of the DMU to make effective buying decisions.

EXTERNAL FACTORS

Political and legal factors

The changes in the political and legal environment may cause a significant impact on organizational buying decisions. For example, a change in corporate taxation or accounting and financial policies may have a significant impact on the organizational purchase decisions and procedures (Cheeseman & Jones, 2005).

Economic factors

Economic factors such as inflation or change in demand and supply conditions may have a significant impact on organizational buying decisions. For example, inflation would have a negative impact on the organization if it increased the cost of the raw materials that the organization requires in order to manufacture products. New product specifications would need to be drawn, requiring changes in buying decisions.

Social factors

Changes in consumer demand and taste with respect to products will require an organization to update its products regularly by introducing new models and ranges. Thus, an organization may have to buy new materials or production facilities that require a significant level of investment and may have to seek new suppliers or make changes to product specifications. All these may have a significant positive or negative impact on organizational buying decisions.

Technological factors

Changing technology and the increase in automated systems and online buying have significantly changed the way an organization can buy raw materials, take orders and supply goods and services to consumers. These changes also significantly influence the organizational buying decision-making process, requiring new systems installations for communications and placing orders.

TYPES OF ORGANIZATIONAL BUYING

In terms of its complexity, organizational buying can be categorized into three groups, namely straight rebuys, modified rebuys and new tasks. These three types are described below.

Straight rebuy

This involves routine buying of items required by an organization. For instance, the buyer places the order without making any changes to the product specification. This is very similar to repeat buying by consumers. Examples of straight rebuys include purchases of stationery or lubricants that are required by the organization on a day-to-day basis. The purchase will be made from existing suppliers following a standard, routine procedure. Thus very little new information is required.

istock © Sashimw

Modified rebuy

In a modified rebuy situation, an organization may change the product specification. This could reflect external factors such as inflation or technological changes. For a modified rebuy, an organization may therefore need to gather additional information and may require a change in suppliers or renegotiation with existing suppliers.

New task

New task buying involves the purchase of products or services for the first time. This is more complex and takes more time and effort than the other two buying situations. In a new task buying scenario, the organization may have little or no previous experience regarding the purchase. Thus, the members of the DMU may require a lot of information prior to making the purchase decision.

FACTORS INFLUENCING CONSUMER PURCHASING DECISIONS

The following section examines a comprehensive range of factors that may influence consumers' decision-making process.

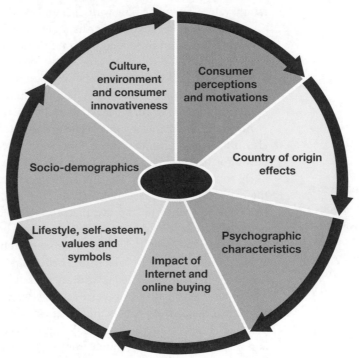

Figure 3.5: Factors influencing consumer purchasing decisions

SOCIO–CULTURAL AND ENVIRONMENTAL INFLUENCES

A variety of factors affect consumers as individuals and as members of society, determining how they live and how they purchase and consume goods. External influences such as culture, ethnicity and social class influence how consumers make purchasing decisions and help explain how groups of consumers behave the way they do. Thus, culture and environmental factors play a vital role in consumers' purchasing decisions. Socio-cultural and environmental factors comprise all aspects of a society such as its religion, knowledge, language, laws, customs, traditions, music, art, technology, work patterns, products, politics and economic situation. All these socio-cultural and environmental factors influence consumers and it is therefore critical for companies to understand the impact of these factors on consumer purchase decisions (Haugtvedt et al., 2008).

Culture can be defined as 'the sum total of learned beliefs, values and customs that influence behaviour of all members of that society'. It can be defined as a pattern of behaviour or a set of traditional ideas, and in particular the values which are attached to these ideas. Thus, culture comprises a set of learned beliefs, values, attitudes, habits and forms of behaviour that are shared by a society and are transmitted from generation to generation within that society (Blythe, 2008).

Culture also determines what is acceptable when advertising to the target market. Companies must understand what kind of language, images and even colours are acceptable or not acceptable in a particular market.

Culture influences the pattern of living, consumption and decision-making by individuals. For example, cultural values in Eastern and Western societies are very different. Eastern consumers often have strong religious and cultural beliefs and family values. Spending time with the family and respect for elders are considered an essential part of life. On the other hand, in the West, time for family is an increasing problem because of the economic conditions. Both men and women are working long hours so 'food to go' or 'take aways' seem to be more tempting options than preparing a meal for oneself or a family. Culture forms boundaries within which an individual thinks and acts. When one thinks and acts beyond these boundaries, one is adopting a cross-cultural behaviour and there are cross-cultural influences as well.

Advances in technology and exposure to satellite communication systems have also influenced consumers' behaviour a great deal. Technology provides access to new information and culture and new ways of life. Young consumers are particularly likely to adopt clothing styles and fashions and mobile phones, and we have seen the expansion of the Facebook website. These changes in behavioural pattern give marketers a chance to improve the product, packaging and offering to meet the needs of the target market regardless of national boundaries.

Norms are the boundaries that culture sets on behaviour. Norms are derived from cultural values, which are widely told beliefs that specify what is desirable and what is not (Haugtvedt et al., 2008). Culture also outlines many business norms, family norms and behaviour norms, such as how we greet people, how close one should stand to others while conducting business, the clothes one wears and any other patterns of behaviour (Blythe, 2008). Culture keeps changing slowly over time and is not static. Changes may result from rapid technological development. In case of emergency, war or natural calamities, companies must gain insights into the existing culture as well as the changing culture of their target market. Nowadays, companies are quick to adapt to the culture of their target market. Most of the international companies give cross-cultural training to their employees. By making cross-cultural mistakes, many companies have struggled to capture a place in the consumer's heart and mind. For example, McDonald's withdrew its beefburger from the Indian market

Culture can be defined as 'the sum total of learned beliefs, values, and customs that influence behaviour of all members of that society'

(Blythe, 2008, p. 62)

Think and discuss

There are various family buying roles. Discuss the extent to which culture could change this structure. For example, do you think the roles of the children, wife and husband will remain the same for a particular product if the purchase is made by families from different cultural contexts?

because the majority of the population is Hindu and does not eat beef, as cows are considered sacred.

Values

Values are the basic beliefs that direct or motivate behaviour and decision making. A person's set of values plays an important role in their consumption activities because many people purchase products and services that they believe will help them to attain a value-related goal. For example, consumers may purchase luxury goods because they feel they can achieve more through what they regard as a luxury brand than through an inferior brand.

Self-esteem

Self-esteem refers to the degree of positivity of a person's self-concept. Others often relate self-esteem to acceptance. Cultural symbols such as clothing fashion brands and the act of appearance management can function to express one's self-esteem. That is to say, when people feel good about themselves, they may pay a great amount of attention to their appearance. On the other hand, people with a low self-esteem may ignore their appearance or overcompensate by being obsessive about it. This is known as 'adaptive functioning' as more people use clothing brands as a means of gaining social approval. Purchasing luxury brands can be used as a way for consumers to hide their low self-esteem as they feel people will not so much look at them as look at the clothes they are wearing. Consumers who relate to this are likely to see the image and message portrayed by a luxury product as more important and fulfilling. They feel that owning such a brand would enhance their image and prestige. It is not necessarily what the brand is but what people see the brand as that matters the most.

CONSUMER PERCEPTION

How consumers perceive a brand has a big impact on any organization. In a world where image is everything, marketers should rightly worry about how their brands are perceived by consumers. Image and reputation build strong brands and drive sales.

While perceived value occurs at various stages of the purchase process, including the pre-purchase stage, satisfaction is universally agreed to be a post-purchase and post-use evaluation. As a result, consumer perceptions can be created without the product or service being bought or used, while satisfaction depends on experience of having used the product or service.

For luxury clothing, this is an important concept as many people see luxury as something they desire; therefore, there may be a distinct difference in the consumer perception of those who have bought a luxury item and those who have not. The value of the brands an organization carries is a major asset for the retailer in its battle for increased customer loyalty and associated higher profits. Successful retailers deliver genuine value to customers through their commitment to the products sold as well as their retailing concept. Such retail strategies enhance store-merchandising authenticity by acknowledging and blending the various dimensions of consumer-perceived product value into their market positions. Price helps the analysis of perception as consumers could believe that a higher price might suggest high quality and demonstrate their ability to purchase expensive products and help enhance their status in society. Other factors include enjoyment or pleasure derived from the product (emotional value) and the social consequences of what the product communicates to others (social value).

MOTIVATIONAL FACTORS

Consumers' **motivation** behind purchasing **utilitarian** and **hedonic** products differs greatly

Motivation refers to the processes that cause people to behave as they do. Motivation in buying results when consumers' needs are stimulated and so need to be satisfied. One way to look at the needs consumers have is the typology of utilitarian versus hedonic. Utilitarian needs are the desires to have something practical such as comfort or protection; consumers will emphasize the objective and tangible attributes of the product. Hedonic needs influence consumers' intentions to purchase a product. Consumers are likely to rely on the product to meet their needs for excitement, self-confidence, fantasy and so on. Exclusive goods are seen by many consumers as meeting hedonic needs because of the luxurious image they portray.

A basic need can be satisfied in a number of ways. The specific path a person chooses is individual to that person, based on their personality, culture and values. The particular form of consumption used to satisfy a need is a want. 'Wants are manifestations of needs' (Solomon, 2004). Once the goal is attained, tension is reduced and the motivation retreats. Motivation can be described in terms of how it lures a consumer and the particular way the consumer attempts to reduce the motivational tension. As a luxury product can be seen as a 'luxury' and not a 'necessity', the drive that is exerted on consumers to purchase luxury products is mainly about the want.

Thus, it is crucial to understand what motivates and drives a person to purchase a certain product or brand. Why do people purchase what they purchase? It could be to enhance their status, to be part of their peer group or to seek gratification.

PSYCHOGRAPHIC CHARACTERISTICS

Psychographic characteristics are defined as 'the classification of people according to their attitudes' (Concise Oxford English Dictionary, 2010). Attitudes refer to a person's feelings, convictions or beliefs with regard to an object, idea or individual and might be seen as precursors of behaviour. There is a difference between attitudes to the product itself (internal) and attitudes to the action of buying the product (external). For instance, it is often found that attitudes to a product are related to attitudes to its purchase, so the distinction must be made as external variables are not necessarily related to buying attitudes (Tarkiainen et al., 2009).

The purchasing of luxury brands can be seen as a motivational conflict, more specifically an approach-avoidance conflict. Lewin (1935) was the first psychologist to investigate conflict experimentally. He concentrated on three types: approach-approach, avoidance-avoidance and approach-avoidance. In an approach-avoidance conflict, a person experiences tension because they are simultaneously attracted to and repulsed by the same goal. This is primarily because many of the products and services consumers want have negative consequences attached to them as well. Consumers may feel guilty when buying a status-laden product such as a Gucci handbag. When consumers desire a goal but wish to avoid it at the same time, an approach-avoidance conflict exists. Luxury companies try to overcome this guilt by emphasizing the feel-good factor in their communication and advertising campaigns in order to make the consumer feel that they deserve the luxury.

DEMOGRAPHIC INFLUENCES

Socio-demographic profiles influence the purchasing decision. Consumer profiles are essential in marketing as they will act as a guide when segmenting the market and designing campaigns for the target markets.

Age

A consumer is considered to be the same as other consumers born around the same time. As consumers get older, their needs and preferences change; this is usually in unison with those of the same age. It is important for marketers to understand this and be able to communicate with members of an age group in their own language and tone.

Teens

Today's teens and young adults in their early twenties have been born and raised in an era of technology and media. As a result they have been categorized as 'shopaholics' and luxury fashion addicts. In the case of teenage girls, the main way they dispose of their income is fashion (Solomon, 2004). Tweens (pre-teens aged between eight and twelve) are beginning to show the same characteristics as teens as they seem to grow up faster than in previous years. Most teens are keen consumers of luxury brands and other brands that enhance their image and appearance. More and more luxury brands are targeting younger consumers and expanding their product range to include ranges for teenagers.

Middle-aged

The middle-aged consumer, aged 25–45, is likely to show characteristics of both the teens and the seniors. This is because they will have taken the values and morals from parents and older influencers in their life. However, they will also be influenced by the teens and so show characteristics of the generation below them.

Seniors

There is a lot of potential in the clothing brand industry for the over-45 market. The older generations regard luxury brands as comfortable. The majority lived through the Second World War and so experienced rationing, and are not firm believers in purchasing luxury goods. The senior perception of a luxury good is likely to constitute good fit, good fabrics, good styling and easy care. The concept of image and branding are not a priority for them (Solomon et al., 2006).

Gender

'In many societies, males are controlled by argentic goals, which stress self-assertion and mastery' (Solomon et al., 2010, p. 154). Females, on the other hand, are typically 'taught to value communal goals, such as affiliation and the fostering of harmonious relations' (ibid.), which implies that males prefer a product to show their success and dominance, and women are more nurturing and considerate. In a married household environment, however, males are often more susceptible to influence from their partner. Blythe (2008) remarks on how a husband will usually alter his own viewpoint to take into consideration his wife's needs and attitudes. However Schiffman and Kanuk (2010) report that men are less sensitive to the views and opinions of their friendship groups than women (Mitchell and Walsh, 2004,

p. 332). This suggests that males only consider primary stakeholders in the decision where financial risk and outcome are more likely to affect the relationship.

According to research by Blythe (2008) women make up around 80 to 95 per cent of compulsive buyers and often do not evaluate their purchases as thoroughly as expected by EPS product search, males being far more cautious when undertaking purchasing decisions. Within the context of the automotive market, this implies initially that females are often more led by their hearts into a decision than by their heads. Women tend to purchase items which are symbolic and self-expressive, concerned with appearance and emotional appeal. Websites for female car searching, though, suggest otherwise. The Evecars (2010) website has a search interface which selects the best options for a female, based on search criteria for deposit, monthly budget and other financial factors. This reinforces the theory of females having financial control in household situations, as well as disputing the notion that women do not go into decisions with their heads but with their hearts.

The focus here is on gender and traits that cause or engender in individuals a social awareness. A growing body of work on clothing brands has identified that consumers undertake and engage in differential behaviour depending on their gender. For example, women may be described as more excitable, indulgent and contemporary than men. In the context of luxury clothing brands, females could be significantly more involved than males, which implies that females use clothing more than males do to emphasize their status. As males and females appear to use products for different reasons and demonstrate different attitudes towards brands, it is even more crucial to understand and serve their needs and wants differently.

Education

Education affects consumers' attitudes and purchasing decisions. Overall, more positive attitudes towards organic food have been detected by consumers with a higher level of education as they seem to be better informed about its advantages.

Reproduced with permission of the University of East London

Social class

Different products and brands are perceived by consumers to be appropriate for certain social classes. Working-class consumers are likely to evaluate luxury brands in terms of comfort rather than image or style and would state that the factors include cost and distribution. They would regard luxury products as being expensive and exclusive. In contrast, more affluent people tend to be more concerned about their appearance so the purchase of luxury items would be based on branding, prestige, image and so on.

STATUS SYMBOLS

A major motivation for consumers to purchase and display luxury brands is not to enjoy them but rather to let people know that they can afford to own then. Therefore, these products act as status symbols. It is a way of showing people their financial status. This has been known as 'conspicuous labelling', where the clothing needs to be recognized by others as being expensive so as to convey status, and that can be accomplished by moving the brand name from the inside to the outside. Consumers who purchase luxury brands because of their labels are likely to measure luxury through brand name, symbolic values and cost as they do not look at the quality and function of a brand. They measure it on how it enhances their image and status amongst their peers and how other people see them wearing the luxury brand.

FAMILY AND REFERENCE GROUPS

A family is two or more persons residing together who are related by blood, adoption or marriage; a household is one or more persons sharing the same housing unit.

Example 3.3:
Expanding the consumer base abroad

With increased competition, development of new technologies and trade liberalization, companies are trying to expand their customer base by entering emerging markets such as China and India. However, it is not an easy task since companies need to consider a variety of factors such as differences in consumer perceptions, values and beliefs in a different market. In a world where image is considered as everything, marketers should rightly worry about how their brands are perceived by consumers in different countries. Thus, it is extremely important for companies to understand the differences in consumer perceptions and attitudes towards brands in different contexts.

Bottega Veneta, an Italian-based company, plans to invest in Europe and open new shops as part of a strategy to grow consumer confidence in emerging markets about their brands. This clearly shows that it is vital for companies to consider how their brands are perceived by consumers from different countries. Bottega Veneta believes that maintaining a positive brand image in developed countries is key to achieving success in emerging markets such as China (Bottega Veneta website).

Bottega Veneta, known for its woven leather totes starting at around €5,000 (£4,500), is the second-largest luxury brand behind Gucci in terms of sales. The company opened 26 shops in 2012 and runs 196 boutiques worldwide. It plans to increase the size of its retail network by 10–15 per cent annually.

Chief Executive Marco Bizzarri said: 'I am convinced that consumers from emerging markets will buy there [in emerging markets] if they see that the brand is well positioned in Europe.' Analysts say that the strategy makes sense. 'Chinese consumers find it reassuring if the brands they like are also strong in Europe,' and 'success in Europe also means to the Chinese they are buying "the real thing",' said Exane BNP Paribas analyst Luca Solca.

Since brands are perceived differently by different consumers, it is extremely important for companies to determine how their brands are positioned in the minds of consumers. Research indicates that consumers in emerging markets believe that brands from developed nations are high quality and reliable. Therefore, building a strong image in developed markets may enable companies to gain entry into emerging markets such as China, which consist of con-sumers with different cultural values, beliefs and perceptions.

A family makes many purchasing decisions and consumer behaviour varies over the family lifecycle (based on age, marital status, number and ages of children).

A *reference group* is a group of individuals that has a direct or indirect influence on a person's attitudes or behaviour. Consumers may also form stereotypes of the generalized user of the product and form product images, which will then serve to influence the consumer decision-making process.

The influence of reference groups and family on individual behaviour is often manifested in the types of products and brands purchased by them. There are two main types of reference groups. Parents, teachers and peers are representative of normative referents that provide the individual with norms, attitudes and values through direct interaction. Comparative referents, such as sporting heroes and celebrities, provide standards of achievement to which individuals aspire and are relatively further removed from the individual, who relates to them in a more observational manner.

The family and reference groups' influence on brand decisions is likely to be facilitated by the degree to which social interaction occurs or public observation of consumption behaviour occurs (Bearden and Etzel, 1982). Luxuries, unlike necessities, are not owned by everybody and thus tend to be relatively more conspicuous. In a purchase context, the degree to which they are observed in the consumption process should positively affect the degree of conspicuousness of the product. There is strong reference group influence in public consumption circumstances, or for luxuries, as these products are more conspicuous. As a result, the individual is able to observe the products and brands purchased by referents or interact with referents regarding the appropriate products and brands to buy. Conversely, for products that are not conspicuously consumed, the individual has little opportunity to interact with referents regarding the purchase of the product or the appropriate brand.

THE INFLUENCE OF THE INTERNET ON CONSUMER BUYING BEHAVIOUR

The tough economic climate on the high street has seen major players such as Woolworths closing their doors yet continuing to sell goods online as electronic retailers or 'e-tailers'. The convenience of shopping without having to leave the comfort of your own home is the attraction of online shopping for most consumers. It may not always be easy to go to the high street, so having the technology at home is a huge benefit to consumers.

The Internet is the retail sector's fastest growing sales channel and with this comes the challenge of marketing and influencing the key opinion formers online. Arcadia has used fashion bloggers, inviting them to preview collections in a move that follows in the footsteps of the fashion house Chanel and shows how important the Internet is in influencing sales. IMRG reports that 40 per cent of fashion sales are in some way influenced by the Internet (IMRG, 2009 and 2013).

The British Retail Consortium (BBC, 2008) published its first report on online shopping and the high street in 2008, showing that there was an increase of sales of 16 per cent online while high street sales had fallen. The statement that online sales only account for around 4 per cent of total retail sales indicates that the high street is most certainly not dead with 96 per cent of sales made offline.

'The growing interest in online transactions does not necessarily mean all companies are moving towards online retailing' (Doherty et al., 1999). The overall business strategy must be taken into account by the retailer, looking at their target market and whether it would be of benefit to have an online store.

'A website cannot replace the social experience of shopping' (BBC, 2008). This statement is true to an extent; consumers do want to touch and feel the products they are buying, be amongst other shoppers, go out, and have a day out. However, Internet shopping is creating its own social experience, with many websites very interactive and shopping forums allowing shoppers to talk and compare products. It is fast becoming a new social experience with different tools for social interaction rather than the traditional methods of face-to-face interaction.

'It is highly unlikely that conventional retail stores will be completely usurped by the Internet, because the majority of consumers prefer the social and physical interaction of "going to the shops".' (KPMG and OXIRM, 1996). It is true that the Internet cannot provide the social interaction that going to an actual store, meeting people and seeing the products can give. However, technology is improving so that e-tailers include podcasts, videos of products, voice instructions and photographs on their sites to make the e-tail experience as interactive as possible. Therefore, a new social experience is currently being developed and the statement by KPMG can be challenged.

ADVANTAGES AND DISADVANTAGES OF E-TAILING AND THE HIGH STREET

There are a number of benefits and downsides to the emerging e-tailing method compared with the traditional method of shopping on the high street, both for the retailer and for the consumer. The benefits of e-tailing to the consumer are that they can shop 24 hours a day: there are no opening hours when it comes to an online store unlike a store on the high street. The consumer can shop from the comfort of their own home instead of having to travel to their nearest high street. Therefore, no travel or parking costs are involved. Comparing prices can be done at the click of a button compared with having to go from store to store, which is more time consuming. Comparisons can be made all over the world not just on the local high street. Where there are a limited number of competitors, the price on the high street is usually not as good as on the Internet. This can save the consumer money. There is a greater choice of products available online at competitive prices. Delivery can be fast, with a choice from around the world. Consumers can purchase from stores that are not on the local high street and if the consumer is not geographically near to a high street they can still purchase. It is more efficient to shop online; consumers do not have to wait in queues.

The benefits to the retailer of e-tailing are that they can reach new international markets, as the Internet is accessible worldwide whereas a high street is only locally available. Compared with high street selling, e-tailing reduces the costs in terms of having personnel assistance in a shop. Moreover, less interactive skills are needed to manage e-tailing. E-tailing thus decreases the overall business costs to the retailer. More success is available to specialist retailers as the customer base can be worldwide rather than local.

The benefits to the retailer of **e-tailing** are that they can reach new international markets, as the Internet is accessible worldwide whereas a high street is only locally available

The disadvantages to the consumer are that they cannot touch, see or try the product before buying. The social experience of going to the actual store, seeing other shoppers and having help from shop assistants is limited. It can be expensive to have products posted and can take a long time for them to arrive, whereas on the high street consumers can take the product home with them straight away. It is also more costly and time consuming to send products back if they are faulty or not wanted. On the high street, it is generally easy to swap items for a different size but it is a longer process with purchasing online. Pictures may be deceptive and the consumer may not receive the product they were expecting, having relied heavily on the description. Although technology is constantly developing, there are still fears of fraud when purchasing online and giving confidential information. If the consumer does not have access to a computer or mobile device, it is impossible to shop online.

There are also a number of disadvantages of e-tailing for the retailer. It is difficult for retailers to stay competitive online and retain customer loyalty as there is so much choice available at competitive prices. It is important for retailers to offer more than a good price. With it being so easy for a consumer to click onto another website, e-tailers generally have one chance to impress the consumer before they click away. This puts pressures on the e-tailer to build an online environment that instantly attracts the consumer and keeps their interest (Solomon et al., 2006).

Innovativeness of the consumer

Consumer innovativeness, especially personal characteristics, usually influences new product adoption. Research by Citrin et al. (2000) identifies that the innovativeness of the Internet user will indicate whether they are likely to purchase online or not. They found that higher Internet usage resulted in the user being more likely to engage in e-commerce. Those with the Internet and who use it regularly are most likely to exploit the e-tailing boom. With this in mind, the increase in the uptake of households using the Internet suggests that online purchasing will continue to increase as consumers have easier access and increase their knowledge/skills in using the Internet. From an organizational perspective, the reasons for creating a website could include internal factors such as strategic vision and resource availability, and environmental factors such as competitive pressures, changing lifestyle and buying behaviour of consumers, who are increasingly seeking convenient and efficient shopping experience.

Another growing trend incorporates online and offline retailing, whereby retailers allow consumers to order products online and collect in-store (AdMap, 2009). Most of the major retailers on the high street, such as Next, John Lewis and M&S, offer this service. This trend identifies the link between the two methods of shopping and that they are both needed. Rather than e-tailing taking over from the high street, the two are used in conjunction and satisfy the needs of the consumer.

Country of origin effects on consumers' buying behaviour

The country of origin (COO) effect can be defined as the picture, the reputation and the stereotype that organizations and consumers attach to products according to their country of origin.

Products have extrinsic and intrinsic cues. Intrinsic cues are tangible or physical characteristics, such as design or colour, and extrinsic cues are intangible product characteristics, such as warranty or brand name. The COO effect has been described as an extrinsic cue that is used by the consumer to evaluate a product's quality. Accordingly, COO, acting as an extrinsic cue, has considerable effect on consumer attitudes and the likelihood of product purchase. The COO effect is also known as the 'made in' concept and has been described as the favourable or unfavourable influence a product's country of manufacture may have on consumers' attitudes and decision making.

'A developed country origin of a product is seen as an insurance on the product's quality and performance'

(Kaynak et al., 2000)

COO does influence the consumer's decision to purchase. For example, consumers from developed nations prefer products from developed nations. For these consumers, the preference may include homemade products as opposed to products from less developed nations. On the other hand, consumers from less developed nations prefer products from developed nations. For these consumers, the purchase preference is also likely to be for products from developed nations. For example, research demonstrated that Bangladeshi consumers were more willing to purchase products from developed nations than products from developing countries. 'A developed country origin of a product was seen as insurance on the product's quality and performance' (Kaynak et al., 2000, p. 88). Consumers were willing to pay a higher price for a Philips tape recorder made in Austria than for one made in India, even though it was manufactured by the same company and the quality of the product was identical.

COO serves as a cue from which consumers make inferences about products and product attributes. The COO cue triggers a global evaluation of quality, performance or specific product or service attributes. Consumers ascribe attributes to the product based on country stereotypes and experiences with products from that country (Erickson et al., 1984). Country image is defined as consumers' general perceptions of the quality of products made in a given country. The COO cue has 'become an important information cue for consumers who are exposed to a far more internationalised selection of products and multinational marketing than ever before' (Baker and Michie, 1995, p. 93).

Country images may influence product evaluations in a negative or positive way. In terms of the cognitive processes that lead to these evaluations, consumers use the COO cue symbolically, that is, as an associative link. For instance, Denmark means agriculture, France is associated with fashion and design, Germany symbolizes technology and engineering. There seem to be strong perceptual linkages between country stereotypes and product categories. Certain products are considered more 'ethnic', more typical of some countries than of others, and producers often attempt to benefit from these linkages by referring to their national origin in the marketing of their products. Hence, COO stereotypes tend to be product specific. Even though country stereotypes are often deep-rooted in the customer's mind, they could be reversed. Negative country images may be improved through advertising or national export promotion campaigns that seek to enhance both the general image of the country and its national product image.

ATTITUDE MODELS AND CONSUMER BUYING BEHAVIOUR

In this section, theories relating to attitudes and consumer behaviour are illustrated, such as the theory of planned behaviour, the expectancy–value model and social cognition theory.

THE THEORY OF PLANNED BEHAVIOUR

In simple terms, the theory of planned behaviour (TPB), developed by Ajzen (1991) and as shown in Figure 3.6, suggests that the consumer's behaviour can be determined through their intention to perform the behaviour. The intention to perform a particular behaviour is in turn a function of three components: the consumer's attitude toward the behaviour, subjective norms and their perceived behavioural control.

Here, the individual *attitude towards behaviour* (AtB) is defined as the positive or negative perception of a particular behaviour. Moreover, the AtB is determined through the beliefs about a particular behaviour, which are described as the subjective probability that the behaviour will produce a certain outcome. The AtB is a function of one's salient belief about performing the behaviour and an evaluation of the outcomes resulting from the behaviour. However, an individual AtB is normally varied according to the type of behaviour.

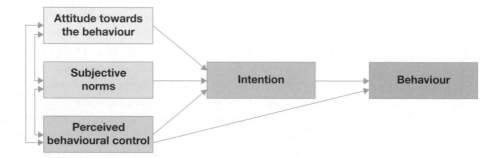

Figure 3.6: The theory of planned behaviour model
Source: Adapted from Ajzen, 1991

Subjective norms are defined as what other people who are important to an individual believe that the individual should do, or the normative belief (NB) about a particular behaviour. Therefore, subjective norms are based on the judgements of the people who are important to the individual, such as friends, spouse or family members. Subjective norms refer to a person's perception of the social pressures about performing the behaviour. More specifically, they refer to the social pressure that an individual experiences about whether to perform a particular behaviour or not. According to the TPB, the subjective norms are a function of an NB and a motivation to comply with referents. The normative belief refers to the perceived expectation that the referent thinks an individual should perform the behaviour.

Finally, *perceived behavioural control* (PBC) refers to an individual's perceived ease or difficulty in performing a particular behaviour. This is determined through the collective strength of an individual's beliefs about the presence of factors that can facilitate or impede the performance of particular behaviour. According to previous research on consumer behaviour, many factors can influence an individual's control over a particular behaviour. These factors could include the context of opportunity, the resources or action, and control.

EXPECTANCY–VALUE MODEL

According to the expectancy-value model, outlined in Figure 3.7, attitudes are based on the beliefs or knowledge consumers have about an object or action and their evaluation of these particular beliefs. For instance, if consumers do not believe they will suffer the bad effects of smoking, then the use of health issues to try to persuade them not to smoke will prove ineffective. It is important to understand what is most important to consumers in order to know how best to target them. Moreover, the issues shown in the anti-smoking adverts can determine what the audience will learn about the consequences of smoking. This could affect the audience's feelings, which should lead to a change in their future behaviour if this theory proves correct.

The **experiential hierarchy** insists that 'consumers act on the basis of their emotional reactions' (Solomon et al., 2006, p. 143) and so this model suggests that 'attitudes can be strongly influenced by intangible product attributes such as package design, and by consumers' reactions to accompanying stimuli such as advertising' (ibid.).

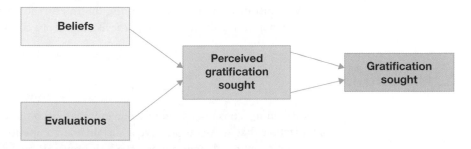

Figure 3.7: The expectancy-value theory
Source: Based on Solomon et al., 2006

ABC MODEL OF ATTITUDES

An attitude has three types of components: affective, behavioural and cognitive. The ABC model of attitudes, as shown in Figure 3.8, emphasizes the interrelationships between knowing, feeling and doing (Solomon et al., 2006). In this model, 'affective' refers to the consumer's feelings towards and evaluation of an object/product. 'Behavioural' refers to a person's intention to do something, to purchase a product or service or not, although intention does not always lead to actual purchase. 'Cognitive' refers to a person's belief, opinions and understanding of an object or product and relates, for example, to the extent to which a person would be satisfied with the actual purchase.

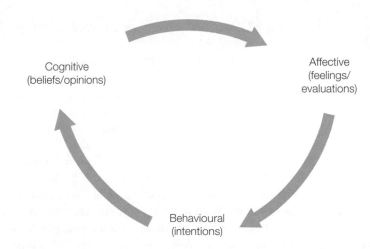

Figure 3.8: The ABC model of attitudes
Source: Adapted from Solomon et al., 2006

SOCIAL COGNITIVE THEORY

Social cognitive theory suggests that human behaviour is 'a continuous reciprocal causation among environmental factors and cognitive factors' (Meng et al., 2004, p. 766. This theory outlines that behaviour is not only influenced by environmental cognitive beliefs but also by outcome expectations and self-efficacy that influences consumers to continue using the Internet. Positive outcome expectations, such as finding bargains online and reducing product search and transaction costs, were the basis for this theory linked with e-tailing.

The theory outlines a belief that consumers are more likely to use the Internet if they feel they have the ability to use it effectively and if the outcome will be positive – that is, if they will get a product cheaper than on the high street. This theory does not suggest whether consumers are more likely to use the Internet for purchasing than the high street, but it indicates the reasoning for the likelihood of a consumer purchasing online.

CONCLUSION

Understanding consumer buying behaviour has become a critical factor for any organization that strives to achieve a sustainable competitive advantage. However, the changing external environment, the trend towards globalization, the emergence of new technology, consumers' preferences for local and global products, and changing consumer needs have made it a very complex task. Against this backdrop, this chapter provided an overview of consumer buying behaviour, focusing on key stages that a consumer goes through when making a purchase decision. The key internal and external factors influencing consumer buying decisions and the new products' adaptation process were also discussed. Finally, a few theories on consumer buying behaviour were identified and presented. Overall, it is vitally important to understand consumers' buying behaviour in order to meet their expectations and gain competitive advantage.

Case study
Time for Convenient-Books to change

CONVENIENT-BOOKS IS A HIGH STREET BOOKSELLER which opened in the 1980s. It sells its own published books as well as publications by a variety of publishers and authors covering a range of subjects for the mass market. Apart from the core product, it also sells stationery, magazines and newspapers to cater for the needs of the reading community and the public.

During the last few years, the company has experienced a decline in its profits and sales. The number of customers who visit the store has also been reducing. The emergence of new technology and the growth of the Internet have changed consumers' book-buying methods and reading habits. The growth of online

booksellers such as Amazon has provided consumers with an opportunity to shop for books at their convenience without physically visiting a bookstore. Therefore, consumers now have the ability to shop for books across the world in seconds. The 24/7 accessibility, ability to download e-books, availability of books from a range of publishers around the world and the facility to compare prices between sellers online have made buying online a more attractive channel to consumers. These advantages have attracted mainly younger consumers and those working professionals with a busy, 'cash rich, time poor' lifestyle. The advantages have encouraged them to buy more

istock © Nikada

online than through physically visiting a store.

On the other hand, consumers increasingly buy e-books rather than physical books, especially in the case of younger consumers. All this presents a substantial threat to traditional booksellers like Convenient-Books. To address these challenges, Convenient-Books is now planning to launch an online bookshop in the next year. It has hired you as a marketing assistant and asked you to carry out an assessment of the book-buying behaviour of its consumers.

Questions

1 Why is it important for Convenient-Books to address changes in consumer book-buying preferences (from traditional stores to online)?
2 What factors do you think may influence consumer book-buying decisions?
3 Outline the decision-making process that a consumer may go through when buying a book. How can Convenient-Books facilitate this process by launching an online bookstore?
4 From the Convenient-Books company perspective, what factors do you think the company needs to consider when developing its online bookstore?

Review questions

1 Explain why it is important to understand consumer buying behaviour and how such understanding can be utilized to achieve a competitive advantage?
2 Identify key roles played by consumers in making a decision to purchase a product or service.
3 Explain the 'buyer's black box' theory of consumer behaviour. Why is it important for marketers to understand the interactions between marketing stimuli and the buyer's black box?
4 Explain the key differences between consumer buying behaviour and organizational buying behaviour.
5 Explain the factors that affect consumer buying behaviour and organizational buying behaviour.
6 What are the roles played by each member of the decision-making unit of an organization?
7 Discuss how the emergence of the Internet has changed consumers' buying behaviour.
8 Explain how the product country of origin impacts consumer purchase decisions.

Group tasks

1 In a group, prepare a list of factors that influence your choice of university. Write out what you think will be the marketing implications of this for the management of the university.
2 Assume you are a member of the decision-making unit of your organization and are in a meeting to discuss the supplier of 500 new computers you are proposing to buy. Prepare what will be your criteria for the choice of the right supplier and why you think the factors are important for this purchase.

Glossary/Key terms

Attitudes: Attitudes refer to a person's feelings, convictions or beliefs about an object, idea or individual and might be seen as precursors of behaviour.

Buying roles: Buying roles include key roles played by consumers in purchasing decisions.

Cognitive dissonance: Dissatisfaction about the purchase decision.

Consumer: A consumer is the person who finally uses/consumes the product.

Consumer buying behaviour: The process involved when individuals or groups select, purchase, use or dispose of products, services, ideas or experiences to satisfy needs and desires.

Consumer decision-making process: The consumer decision-making process consists of five key stages that a consumer goes through when making a purchase decision.

Country of origin (COO) effects: Country of origin (COO) effects can be defined as the picture, perceptions, reputation and stereotype that businessmen and consumers associate with the products.

Culture: Culture refers to the sum total of learned beliefs, values and customs that influence the behaviour of all members of that society.

Customer: A customer is the person who buys the products.

Decider: The individual who makes the ultimate decision to purchase.

Expectancy-value model: The expectancy-value model suggests that attitudes are based on the beliefs or knowledge consumers have about an object or action and on consumers' evaluation of these particular beliefs.

Influencer: The person who is interested in the purchase. This individual may have prior experience of the product or service to be purchased.

Initiator: An individual who recognizes a need to purchase.

Modified rebuy situation: An organization may change the product specification in a modified rebuy situation.

New task buying: New task buying involves the purchase of products or services for the first time.

Organizational buying behaviour: Relates to the purchase of goods and services in order to provide goods and services to the final customer.

Perceived behaviour control (PBC): Perceived behaviour control (PBC) refers to an individual's perceived ease or difficulty in performing a particular behaviour.

Perceived risk: The consumer's uncertainty or anxiety about the outcome of a purchase decision.

Purchaser: The person who pays for the product or service.

Reference group: A reference group is a group of individuals that has a direct or indirect influence on a person's attitudes or behaviour.

Social cognitive theory: Social cognitive theory suggests that human behaviour is an interaction of environmental and cognitive factors.

Straight rebuy: Straight rebuy involves routine buying of items required by an organization.

Subjective norms: Subjective norms what other people who are important to an individual believe that the individual should do; also called normative beliefs (NB) about a particular behaviour.

Theory of planned behaviour (TPB): The theory of planned behaviour (TPB) suggests that the consumer's behaviour can be determined through their intention to perform the behaviour.

Users: Those who actually use a service.

Values: Values are the basic beliefs that direct or motivate behaviour and decision making.

Vocab check list for ESL students

Arousal	Experiential	Intrinsic	Stimuli
Attributes	Hedonic	Referent	Typology
Cognitive	Hierarchy	Self-efficacy	Utilitarian
Conspicuously			

Definitions for these terms can be found in the 'Vocab Zone' of the companion website, which provides free access to the Macmillan English Dictionary online at www.palgrave.com/business/Gbadamosi

Further reading

E. J. Arnould and C. J. Thomspson (2005) 'Consumer Culture Theory (CCT): Twenty Years of Research', *Journal of Consumer Research*, Vol. 31, No. 4, pp. 868–82
This article provides an eclectic view of two decades of consumer research as it revolves around the socio-cultural, experiential, symbolic and ideological aspects of consumption.

Charles Dennis, Bill Merrilees, Chanaka Jayawardhena and Len Tiu Wright (2009) 'E-consumer Behaviour', *European Journal of Marketing*, Vol. 43, No. 9/10, pp. 1121–39
In view of the increasing development in the world of technology, the main focus of this article is to present an integrated model of e-consumer behaviour.

A. Gbadamosi (2009) 'Cognitive Dissonance: The Implicit Explication in Low-income Consumers' Shopping Behaviour for 'Low-involvement' Grocery Products, *International Journal of Retail and Distribution Management*, Vol. 37, No. 12, pp. 1077–95
This paper explains the consumption behaviour of a consumer group (low income) in relation to low-involvement products.

Cheryl Leo, Rebekah Bennett and Charmine E. J. Härtel (2005) 'Cross-cultural Differences in Consumer Decision-making Styles', *Cross Cultural Management: An International Journal*, Vol. 12, No. 3, pp. 32–62
This article compares consumer decision-making styles between two nationalities, Singaporeans and Australians, and shows that cultural dimensions influence consumer decision-making styles.

References

AdMap Magazine (2009) 'The Future of the High Street: Two-tier Shopping' http://www.warc.com/admap (Accessed on 12 July 2012)

Ajzen, I. (1991) 'The Theory of Planned Behavior', *Organizational Behavior and Human Decision Processes*, 50, pp. 179–211

Baker, M. J. and Michie, J. (1995) 'Product Country Images: Perceptions of Asian Cars', Working Paper Series, Department of Marketing, University of Strathclyde, Glasgow, No. 95/3

BBC (2008) 'Will the Web Kill the High Street?' http://www.bbc.co.uk/blogs/technology/2008/11/will_the_web_kill_the_high_str.html (Accessed on 14 July 2012)

Bearden, William O. and Etzel, Michael J. (1982) 'Reference Group Influence on Product and Brand Purchase Decisions', *Journal of Consumer Research*, 9 (September), pp. 183–94

Blythe, J. (2008) *Consumer Behaviour*. London: Thompson Learning

Bottega Veneta website: http://www.bottegaveneta.com (Accessed on 23 July 2013)

Citrin, A. V., Spritt, D. E., Silverman, S. N. and Stem, D. E. (2000) 'Adoption of Internet shopping: The role of consumer innovativeness', *Industrial Management and Data Systems*, 100 (7), pp. 294–300

Cheeseman, A. and, Jones, M. (2005) *Customer Communications in Marketing*, 2004/2005 CIM Official Coursebook. London: Butterworth-Heinemann

Doherty, N. F., Ellis-Chadwick, F. and Hart, C. A. (1999) 'Cyber Retailing in the UK: The Potential of the Internet as a Retail Channel', *International Journal of Retail and Distribution Management*, 27 (1), pp. 22–36

Erickson G. M., Johansson J. K. and Chao P. (1984) 'Image variables in multi-attribute product evaluations: country-of-origin effects' *Journal of Consumer Research*, 11 (September), pp. 694–9

Evecars: http://www.evecars.com (Accessed on 1 August 2012)

Foxall, G. (1990) *Consumer Psychology in Behavioural Perspective*. London: Routledge

Guardian (2012) 'EasyJet' http://www.guardian.co.uk/money/2012/jul/12/missed-flight-insurance-cover-easyjet

Haugtvedt, P., Herr, M. and Kardes, F. R. (eds) (2008) *Handbook of Consumer Psychology*. New York: Psychology Press

Huffington Post (2012) http://www.huffingtonpost.com/2012/04/27/consumer-brands-owned-ten-companies-graphic_n_1458812.html

IMRG (2009 and 2013) http://www.imrg.org/ImrgWebsite/IndustryStatiscs.aspc

KPMG and OXIRM (1996) 'The Internet: Its Potential and Use by European Retailers', *A report by the Oxford Institute of Retail Management*, No. 5114

Kaynak, E., Kucukemiroglu, O. and Hyder, A. S. (2000) 'Consumers' country-of-origin (COO) perceptions of imported products in a homogeneous, less-developed country', *European Journal of Marketing*, 34 (9/10), pp. 1221–41

Kotler, P. and Keller, K. L. (2007) *A Framework for Marketing Management*. New York, NY: Pearson Prentice Hall

Meng, H. H., Chao, M. C. and Ju, T. L. (2004) 'Determinants of continued use of the WWW: an integration of two theoretical models', *Industrial Managememnt and Data Systems*, 104 (9), pp. 766–75

Mitchell, V. W. and Walsh, G. (2004) 'Gender differences in German consumer decision making styles', *Journal of Consumer Behavior*, 3 (4), pp. 331–46

Oxford Dictionaries (ed.) (2010) (11th edn). Oxford University Press

Schiffman, L. G. and Kanuk, L. L. (2010) *Consumer Behaviour* (10th edn). New Jersey: Pearson Prentice Hall

Solomon, M. (2004) *Consumer Behaviour in Fashion*. Harlow: Prentice Hall

Solomon, M. R., Bamossy, G., Askegaard, S. and Hogg, M. K. (2006) *Consumer Behaviour: A European Perspective* (3rd edn). New Jersey: Pearson Prentice Hall

Solomon, M. R., Bamossy, G., Askegaard, S. and Hogg, M. K. (2010) *Consumer Behaviour: A European Perspective*, (4th edn). New Jersey: Pearson Prentice Hall

Tarkiainen, A., Lee, N., Cadogan, J. W. and Sundqvist, S. (2009) 'The Managerial Determinants of Unethical Behavior in the Sales Force', *EMAC Annual Conference*, Nantes, France

Times 100 (2013) http://businesscasestudies.co.uk/wilkinson/#axzz2LrDYl0VF

4 MANAGING MARKETING INFORMATION FOR VALUE CREATION

AYANTUNJI GBADAMOSI
UNIVERSITY OF EAST LONDON

KAUSHIK V. PANDYA
SHEFFIELD HALLAM UNIVERSITY

CHAPTER CONTENTS

LEARNING OUTCOMES

The content of this chapter will help you to:

- Understand marketing information systems and the link to value creation
- Explain the scope of marketing research
- Discuss the steps in the marketing research process
- Explain the difference between primary and secondary research
- Understand various means of collecting primary and secondary data
- Discuss how to analyse data in marketing research for value creation
- Understand and discuss online marketing research
- Explain the ethical issues in marketing research

Marketing in action
Managing customer information for value creation at Adidas

WHILE THE IMPACT OF THE PREVAILING GLOBAL economic recession is evident in the number of firms folding up, a good number of organizations that constantly seek information about the needs and wants of their customers are still thriving in the marketing environment. One example is Adidas, a company registered in 1949, which now has over 40,000 employees with brands built on a passion for sports and a sporting lifestyle.

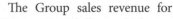

The Group sales revenue for 2012 was €14.9 billion, which represents a new record level and is a 6 per cent increase on the previous record on a currency neutral basis. This is the pattern for all regions of its operations – Western Europe, European Emerging Markets, North America, Greater China, Other Asian Markets and Latin America. The Group CEO Herbert Hainer's comments, shown on the organization's website sum it up: 'Our products and brands were again at the fore, not only being the most visible at the year's major sports events, but also enjoy-ing several important market share victories along the way. The resulting margin improvements and signifi-cant cash flow generation underpin the trajectory and value we are unlocking with our Route 2015 strategic plan.'

Something remarkable about this organization is its impressive use of marketing information systems. It combines internal data records with marketing intelligence and synthesizes them with the findings of its periodic marketing research. The market-ing decision makers in the organization have inputs from the macro and micro environment and the inter-nal data. This approach is adopted for all of its product lines including shoes, clothing and accessories, and various consumer segments. Adidas' successful record in sporting products confirms that customers are will-ing to favour organizations that are customer driven, up to date with relevant information about their needs and wants, and ultimately keen to create and deliver value to them in a timely manner.

INTRODUCTION

As we have established, marketing is essentially about creating and delivering value to the target market. It is becoming increasingly clear by the day that no organiz-ation, irrespective of its size, is guaranteed success if it is not customer driven. Having up-to-date information about the needs and wants of the target market, and provid-ing offerings that will satisfy it, are key steps to succeeding in the current competitive and **turbulent** marketing environment. Big organizations such as Tesco, Coca-Cola and McDonald's have realized that it is important to know what their customers need and want, how they buy it, where, how often, why and many other relevant issues that relate to their day-to-day transactions. This explains why they are able to create value for their customers and succeed in the present economic situation while many organizations are folding up. This brings in the relevance of the market-ing information system (MIS) and all of its elements, including marketing research. So, we can say that the analysis, implementation and control of the marketing plans greatly depends on the available relevant information and how it is managed. In this chapter we shall be looking at how this works. We will explore the approaches that marketers use to collect, analyse and manage this information, and other relevant issues that are associated with the use of marketing information.

MARKETING INFORMATION SYSTEMS

Perhaps a good way to start the discussion of MIS is to look at what 'system' means. In simple terms, a system is the combination of certain elements that form a whole. With this in mind, we can now look at the definition of MIS offered by the American Marketing Association. This body defines MIS as 'a set of procedures and methods for the regular, planned collection, analysis, and presentation of information for use in making marketing decisions'. This is a very useful definition in many ramifications. It emphasizes that a number of things are combined in the system, as we have established in our definition, and states that the interaction of these elements is on a regular basis. Meanwhile, Armstrong and Kotler (2013) offer another interesting definition that is noteworthy. They define MIS as the combination of people and procedures for assessing information needs, developing the needed information, and helping decision makers to use the information to generate and validate actionable customer and market insights. While this definition offers the same explanation as the first one given, it emphasizes the involvement of people in the process of collecting, managing and using the information in the system.

Essentially, this system ensures the integration of internal company data, marketing intelligence and marketing research in a continuous flow for marketing decision making that will deliver customer value. This interaction is illustrated in Figure 4.1. As shown in the diagram, information flows to and from the elements in the system and ultimately provides marketing managers with the timely and accurate information needed for marketing decision making towards creating value for the target customer.

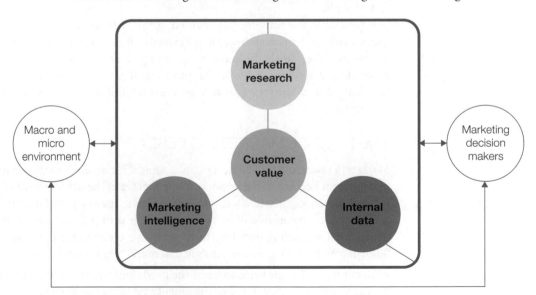

Figure 4.1: Interactions in a marketing information system

The elements of the marketing information system are:

- Internal records
- Marketing intelligence
- Marketing research

Internal records consist of information that marketers can obtain from sources within their organizations which can help them in the evaluation of opportunities and threats from the marketing environment. Very common examples of this category of data are the sales record and financial data. For instance, because their role involves mediating between the customer and the organization, salespeople can obtain valuable information from the market that will enrich the quality of decisions in the organization. Marketing intelligence refers to everyday information regarding the marketing environment in which the organization operates that aids managers' decisions about necessary changes to the marketing plans in place. There are a good number of sources of marketing intelligence for an organization. Examples of these are sales representatives, customers and firms that supply **syndicated** data. More often than not, information obtained from intelligence may not be adequate to solve the problem at hand; hence, marketers often use marketing research to provide the needed information. We'll look at marketing research in detail in the next section.

MARKETING RESEARCH

There are many definitions of marketing research given by many authors. In this case, we shall refer to the most recent definition provided by the American Marketing Association, which it sourced from the Marketing Accountability Standards Board (MASB). This definition states that: 'Marketing research is the **systematic** gathering, recording, and analysis of data about issues relating to marketing products and services.'

If we look at the activities highlighted in this definition, the following key issues about marketing research become noteworthy. It is a systematic issue and involves a process. Also, since the purpose of doing it is to facilitate the marketing of products and services and to make informed decisions in this context, it is logical for us to state that it revolves around creating and delivering value to the target customers.

THE ROLE OF MARKETING RESEARCH

Marketing research has become a popular topic for marketers in the current business environment because of the important role it plays in the achievement of the organizations' objectives. If we reflect on what we have discussed so far in the chapter, it is clear that the main role of marketing research is to provide information that will enhance the marketing decisions to ensure value creation for the target market. So, following on from this, we can also say that marketing research:

- Makes it possible for firms to know the needs and wants of the target market
- Reveals opportunities in the environment that firms can explore

Many others have explained these key roles differently. For example, Dillon et al. (1994) also outline that marketing research helps the marketing decision maker to learn customers' values, analyse customer purchase patterns, continually monitor customers and develop product strategy. In this context, marketing research could be seen as what can be used to measure consumer satisfaction which could also prevent investment into offerings that will not be customer oriented and might affect firms' profitability. So we can conclude that marketing research is used to carry out marketing management which covers analysis, planning, implementation and control, and above all the creation of value for the target market.

APPROACHES TO MARKETING RESEARCH

Marketers go about their research activities in different ways. The choice of an approach is based on a number of factors, which often include resources available for research, experience of marketing research already possessed and organizational policy. Although there can be as many approaches as the number of organizations in a particular marketing environment, we will examine the following arrangements that are commonly used.

In some relatively small organizations, marketing research is considered as an expense that is not worth the trouble. In this category, organizations that do marketing research may only engage in it on occasions when they are compelled to do so, such as for obtaining a loan from the bank (Gbadamosi, 2011). If we look at the roles of marketing research that we discussed earlier, these firms often pay dearly for this approach to marketing research. They fit the category of firms that Gbadamosi describes as *vulnerable* because they are not scanning the marketing environment and are not well positioned to meet the turbulence. At another level, small firms usually entrust their marketing research activities to an individual who gathers, examines and analyses the needed data for the organization. In some cases, the owner-manager of a small firm plays this role and ensures that the organization is managed on the basis of the data gathered.

In some other cases, the organization can have a marketing research department as part of the organization structure and the members of this unit will be mainly involved in marketing research activities. In this case, the marketing research department will work as a subsystem of the marketing department, which is usually regarded as the interface between the entire organization and the customers in a consumer-oriented organization where customer value creation is the key focus of operations.

You may have received a letter in the post from an organization representing your bank or supermarket, asking for information on how these organizations can serve you better. This approach is about engaging external consultants to conduct the research and make the findings available for decision making in the organization. You may be wondering why an organization should give such a task to an outsider. There are many reasons for this. It could be *lack of time*, *lack of marketing research experience and skills*, or *the desire to engage a neutral hand, which could look at things more objectively*. For example, Asda, one of the leading British supermarkets, engaged the services of Cambridge Market Research prior to the launch of its 'Chosen by You' range of products. This last method usually involves some formalities such as exchange of contracts, drafting of a marketing research brief and development of a research proposal. We look at issues about research briefs and proposals below. Meanwhile, it is important to point out that, in reality, most business organizations can combine some of these approaches. This is because marketers often see the approaches as complementary in terms of the benefits they yield. Proctor (2003) explains that handing over a complex study completely to an outside firm can be fraught with problems and that allowing internal personnel to have too much of an input may prevent new and useful insights from emerging. But ultimately the decision should be about obtaining the best information that will allow the organization to satisfy the customer and deliver value to them efficiently and effectively.

THE RESEARCH BRIEF AND PROPOSAL

RESEARCH BRIEF

This document is usually prepared by the client to begin the process of commissioning a marketing research project from consultants. It gives them information surrounding the proposed study. Essentially, the brief for the marketing research agency is expected to have:

- Background information
- A statement of the problem
- The research objective(s)
- The scale or scope of the project
- The timetable for the project

Background information is basically the data related to the company and the particular product or brand in question, and all the various events that have taken place since it was introduced. This part of the brief could address the following:

- Information available about the competing offerings
- Available information about customers' view about the product
- Information about the sales records and profitability of the offerings
- The market share of the product or brand

While this list is not exhaustive because the information provided will be based on the product or brand for which marketing research is commissioned, it is important to stress that the quality of information supplied here by the client will go a long way to equipping the marketing research agency to deliver the services effectively. We can liken this brief to the ones clients always give their lawyers. The more information provided, the clearer the case will be and the easier it might be to handle the case.

Stating the problem of the research clearly is an important task that should not be handled with levity. When you visit your doctor about an ailment, your input in stating your experience when the illness started and describing your feelings at each stage of the illness will be very helpful to the doctor's process for handling the treatment. We commonly hear the expression 'a well-defined problem is partly solved' and this also holds true for marketing research. It is also important that members of the organization who have the relevant information are allowed to contribute as much as they can at this stage. For instance, by virtue of their role and contacts with the customers, salespeople may have more information that will enhance the formulation of the research problem than top executives. It will be very beneficial to allow them to provide such useful information. Sometimes it may prove more helpful to organize brainstorming sessions where the problem will be discussed and collated. Apart from having well-stated research problems documented, listing the objectives to be achieved in the proposed study will also provide a sense of direction to the researchers.

istock © alphaspirit

Another relevant and equally essential task in the preparation of a marketing research brief is the specification of the scale of the project. While a small project will cost less and finish earlier than a large-scale project, the latter often involves extensive and thorough investigation, which would likely provide findings with wide-ranging applications. Moreover, as a guide to the marketing researcher, an approximate timetable is also expected to feature in the brief. This is very important because the organization might have some forms of in-house programmes to which the findings are expected to contribute. An example could be the scheduled introduction of a new product or a pending decision on a product at the decline stage of its product lifecycle. Nevertheless, it could be very useful if the client could be flexible about this where possible to avoid a situation where the quality of the research will be compromised.

RESEARCH PROPOSAL

As Figure 4.2 shows, a research proposal is the document prepared by the marketing research agency for the company. Although there can be some variations in what agencies include in the proposal submitted, it is very common for the following to feature in a good and well-prepared research proposal:

- Introduction and background to the study
- Statement of the research problem
- Research questions
- Research objectives
- Research methodology
- Timetable for the study
- Budget
- Terms of the contract

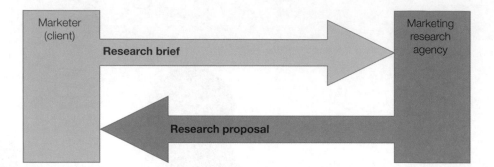

Figure 4.2: Research brief and proposal

The marketing research proposal often starts with an introduction and background. Apart from serving as an opening for the entire document, the inclusion of the background to the study in this segment of the proposal is a demonstration that the marketing research agency really understands what the client has detailed in the brief submitted.

As we have discussed earlier in relation to the research brief, stating the research problem and objectives of the study clearly is important. This is also applicable to the proposal. How articulately the problems and objectives of the study are written is a measure of how the marketing research agency understands the client's problems and objectives.

Another important part of a research proposal is the description of the intended methodological stance for the study. This covers the designated population of the study, the sampling plan (the sample size, how the sample will be drawn, where it will be drawn from) the data collection methods and of course the justification of the choice of methodological stance.

Although an idea of the timetable for the project may have been given in the marketing research brief, the marketing research agency is expected to present a most realistic version that takes into consideration the activities involved. The client will have presented a deadline for when it wants the findings of the project delivered but lack of relevant knowledge of the activities involved in the project means that this deadline may not be as realistic as the one submitted by the agency.

In addition to the contents listed for the proposal, it is of great importance for the agency to bring its terms and conditions of contract to the client's awareness from the outset in the proposal. They can then be considered along with other strategic issues in the course of examining the proposals submitted by various agencies. An example of these terms of contract is the payment arrangement. The following are some of the questions that should be considered, and the answers should be incorporated into the proposal:

Reproduced with permission of Ramsey Moore

Example 4.1:
Small-scale marketing research for Ramsey Moore

While big organizations such as British Airways and P&G will engage in extensive marketing research and spend heavily to know about better ways to deliver value to their customers, some small establishments use other approaches that suit their size and operations. Ramsey Moore is a good example in this regard. It is a small independent estate agency that offers property for sale and to let and provides mortgage advice to its customers. However, the partners of this firm, Mark Harris and Michael O'Brien, know that the key route to satisfying their customers and ensuring that they have value in their transactions is to engage in some form of marketing research. They also acknowledge that no fewer than ten other estate agents operate in Dagenham, East London, where their business is located. So, the battle is now for those who can go the extra mile to create value for the landlords, those looking to buy properties of their own, those interested in renting properties and other customers.

The directors approached the University of East London (UEL) in 2010 for marketing research intervention at a very low budget. Given the scope of their business operations, the team effort of a tutor and his students at UEL produced the report that meets the directors' needs. The turnaround of the business after implementing the findings is remarkable. It proves that marketing research can vary in terms of scale and in relation to the circumstances of the sponsor. But what is common to all the approaches is that they make it possible to collect information that can enable companies to solve specific marketing problems and to create and deliver superior value to their target markets.

- What percentage of the approved budget will be paid before the project commences?
- When will the balance be paid to the agency?
- Will there be changes to the approved budget in consideration of the rate of inflation or will the budget remain the same over the scheduled period of the project?
- What will be the arrangement about the copyright of the documents associated with the project?

If the firm has given the brief to more than one agency and accordingly invited proposals from them, the proposals submitted could constitute the major objective criterion for selecting the one which will be entrusted with the project.

THE SCOPE OF MARKETING RESEARCH

The scope of marketing research reflects the areas of marketing decisions and covers a wide range of issues. For the sake of clarity, we shall cover two key areas, which are environmental factors and the marketing mix elements. This is because each of the marketing mix elements contributes to the overall efforts of value creation in marketing transactions. So, we can rely on the claim that marketing research should involve having a thorough and detailed knowledge of issues that are likely to influence demand for specific products and services (Chisnall, 2005).

This also means that marketing research activities could be directed at any or a combination of macro- and micro-environmental factors and the marketing mix elements as explained in Figure 4.3. This is because they all have impacts on the demand for the offerings of the organization. For instance, it will be very beneficial for marketers to know how political, legal, social-cultural, economic and technological forces will affect the introduction of a new product, or a proposed sales promotion programme. Similarly, having information about competitors, intermediaries, suppliers, customers, pressure groups and their activities as related to the firm's planned marketing decisions will also be crucial to succeeding in the marketplace.

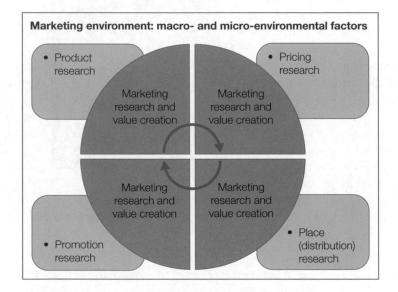

Figure 4.3: The scope of marketing research
Source: Adapted from Chisnall, 2005

STEPS IN THE MARKETING RESEARCH PROCESS

Different textbooks may show various patterns of the marketing research process and varying numbers of stages because in some cases activities are summed up while in other cases they are broken down into their components. Essentially, the process will involve the five stages presented in Figure 4.4. So, we shall look at the stages one after the other to explain the activities associated with them.

DEFINING THE RESEARCH PROBLEM AND OBJECTIVES

Defining the research problem often starts the marketing research process. Whether small scale or large scale in nature, all research is commissioned to solve particular problems. As we have discussed earlier in the scope of marketing research, the research problem could relate to any factor or a combination of factors in the

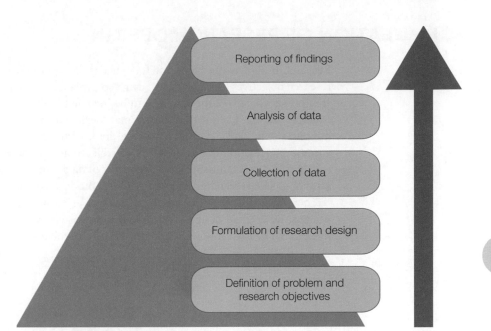

Figure 4.4: The marketing research process

environment, and could revolve around any specific element or a combination of the elements of the marketing mix. For example, changes to interest rates, unemployment rates and inflation rates could trigger problems relating to the products of an organization. Unexpected change in government regulations for particular products, changes in the demographic variables and shifts in the socio-cultural environment could also cause problems that might necessitate the commissioning of a marketing research project. The problem could also be internal such as loss of market share, sudden reduction in sales of particular product lines, consumers' negative perception of the company's brand, ineffective packaging, loss of committed salespeople to competing firms and ineffective marketing communication campaigns. Whatever the problem may be, it is very important that marketing researchers define it clearly.

When the research problems have been clearly defined, then they can be fine tuned to show the objectives of the research. The basic questions to bear in mind while formulating the research objectives are 'Why is this research necessary?' and 'What will this research deliver?' Examples of marketing research objectives are to:

- Determine consumers' perception of the effectiveness of a proposed new product in relation to consumers' needs
- Compare current and potential packaging of a product with regard to customer value
- Determine the best combination of marketing mix elements that will increase repeat purchase behaviour for a product
- Gauge customers' view of a proposed change to service process for value delivery
- Determine the appropriate distribution networks for certain products
- Assess the effectiveness of a specific marketing communication programme
- Determine the appropriate pricing of certain products

FORMULATION OF RESEARCH DESIGN

Research design is the blueprint for what is to be done to achieve the marketing research objectives formulated. We can also explain it as the framework that provides step-by-step details of the activities to be involved in the research. In our day-to-day example, we can liken it to a master plan designed for the building of a house. So, how it is done will determine the final look of the building. Basically, it provides specific information about methods of collecting and analysing the data. In other words, it sketches out issues such as sources of data, how the sources will be explored, sampling plan, research instruments and methods of contacting the informants.

There are three types of research designs as shown in Figure 4.5: exploratory designs, descriptive designs and **causal** designs. We will next look at how each of these could be used to solve marketing research problems.

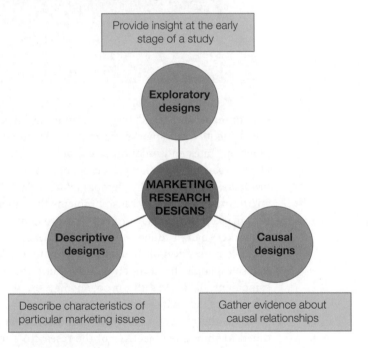

Figure 4.5: Types of marketing research designs

EXPLORATORY DESIGN

Exploratory design is usually adopted as the initial step in a marketing research enquiry. It often identifies the real nature of the research problem being investigated and provides insight into the proposed study before an extensive study is carried out. Marketing researchers will find this design useful for gaining background information, clarifying concepts, developing relevant **hypotheses** that will be tested later in the course of the study, and establishing research priorities. By its nature, this type of research tends to be qualitative rather than quantitative. The following are common methods of conducting exploratory research:

● Secondary data analysis
● Case analysis
● Focus groups

- In-depth interviews
- Other projective techniques

DESCRIPTIVE DESIGN

Descriptive marketing research design identifies characteristics of marketing issues such as answering questions about how many customers buy Brand X of the company's product, what quantity they buy and their perception of the product characteristics. It may also be undertaken to describe consumers' demographics (such as age, gender and income), beliefs, attitudes, preferences and behaviour. Basically, there are two types of descriptive research studies:

- Cross-sectional studies
- Longitudinal studies

The difference between the two is that cross-sectional studies take the sample of population under investigation for study at one single time whereas in longitudinal studies a fixed sample of population subjects is measured repeatedly.

CAUSAL RESEARCH

Causal research design is for gathering evidence regarding cause and effect relationships. So, it is concerned with addressing the question of whether one variable causes a change to occur in another. The factors that might cause other factors to change are usually called the 'independent variables', while the factors that change as a result of changes in the independent variables are called the 'dependent variables'. An example of causal research is the intention to know the effect of a 60 per cent reduction in price on sales of a particular product. Also, research could be used to find out the effect of a new marketing communication campaign on consumers' attitude to a particular product.

COLLECTION OF DATA

Basically, there are two main sources of data. These are primary sources and secondary sources and they produce primary data and secondary data, respectively, as Figure 4.6 shows. Primary data is new data that is gathered specifically to help solve the problem at hand whereas secondary data is collections of information that have been previously gathered and are considered relevant to the problem at hand.

SECONDARY DATA

Secondary sources of information can be broadly categorized into *internal sources* and *external sources*. Internal sources of secondary data are available within the organization and include:

- Sales records
- Stock levels
- Invoices
- Previous research reports

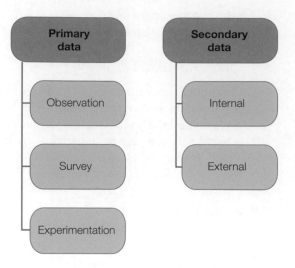

Figure 4.6: Sources of data

- Profit and loss statements
- The company's balance sheet

There are a good number of external sources of secondary data available to marketers, including the following:

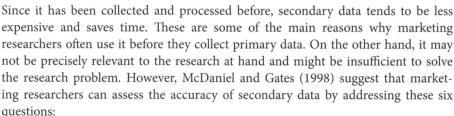

- Relevant publications from government agencies
- News media
- Trade publications
- Journals
- Publications from other non-governmental organizations

Since it has been collected and processed before, secondary data tends to be less expensive and saves time. These are some of the main reasons why marketing researchers often use it before they collect primary data. On the other hand, it may not be precisely relevant to the research at hand and might be insufficient to solve the research problem. However, McDaniel and Gates (1998) suggest that marketing researchers can assess the accuracy of secondary data by addressing these six questions:

- Who gathered the data?
- What was the purpose of the study?
- What information was collected?
- How was the information collected?
- When was the information collected?
- Is the information consistent with other information?

In this age of rapid development in the world of technology, the use of Internet search engines makes **secondary data** more readily available than it used to be

PRIMARY DATA

Now let us take another look at Figure 4.6 to see the methods for collecting primary data. The figure shows this can be done through observation, survey and experimentation. We will now discuss each of these methods.

Observation

As the name suggests, this method is about watching people, objects and occurrences for the purpose of knowing how they operate in the environment or circumstance of interest. This is often done without communicating with those being observed. In marketing research, this method is often used to know how consumers react to marketing stimuli in a natural setting. For instance, marketing researchers can visit retail environments such as supermarkets and pose as shoppers to know how consumers react to a new product on the shelf. Also, trained observers could be sent to watch how consumers will react to a particular menu in a restaurant. The basic interest is to learn about the behaviour of the consumers without controlling it.

Observational studies can take various forms. Table 4.1 shows the various commonly used observation methods in marketing research.

Table 4.1: Types of observation

Type of observation	Description
Participant observation	The researcher acts as a co-participant in the actions he or she is observing.
Non-participant observation	The researcher observes the people in a setting without taking part in the activities and events being observed.
Open observation	The people being observed are aware that they are being observed.
Disguised observation	The people under observation are not aware that they are being observed.
Structured observation	An already prepared questionnaire-like form is used to record the actions of those being observed.
Unstructured observation	The marketing researcher observing the people simply makes notes of things that happen at the setting being observed without having any particular format for it.
Equipment-based observation	This involves using equipment such as cameras and other audio-visual devices to record events at the setting being observed.

The main advantage of using observation as a source of primary data is that people's actions are really observed compared with relying on information they give regarding what they claim they do (McDaniel and Gates, 1998). However, the downside of using observation for research is that it might not be useful for revealing people's attitudes and motives for the behaviour they show openly. If not handled properly it could also be unethical. A major ethical requirement is that the consent of the subjects should be sought in relation to the study being conducted.

Survey

When marketing researchers are asking people about their knowledge, perception, attitudes, preferences and buying behaviour, they are using a survey method of collecting primary data. So, unlike disguised observation, the survey method is about communicating with the participants that have been chosen to represent the population of interest, with the aim of collecting relevant information. The main characteristic of a social survey is that the same information is collected from all cases in the sample and variation in the methods of collection allows variations between cases to be measured (Bloch, 2004). Surveys can be in several forms. Techniques used most often are:

- Self-administered questionnaires
- Person-administered questionnaires
- Interviews
  - Individual interviews
  - Group interviews (discussion)
  - Telephone interviews

Marketers can use various combinations of these methods. The decision about which and how many of the methods should be mixed for a particular marketing research project will depend on the following factors:

- Scale of the funds available for research (the budget)
- Time available for the study
- Level of diversity of the target respondents
- Sensitivity of the topic being studied

Experimentation

Hearing the word 'experiment', what will likely first come to your mind is experimentation in physical sciences where scientists work with materials such as test tubes and chemicals. However, this research method is also used in marketing research in many instances. As we explained in relation to causal research design, experimentation involves manipulating *independent variables* to know the effect changes will have on the *dependent variables*. We can also explain that it is done to evaluate the causal relationship between the two variables. For the purpose of explanation, let us assume that the independent variable is x and the dependent variable is y.

To demonstrate the existence of a causal relationship between variables, three major evidences are used:

- **Concomitant** variation
- Time order of occurrence
- The elimination of other possible causal factors

Showing concomitant variation means providing evidence of the extent to which (x) and (y) occur together in the predicted way. The time order of occurrence means that the marketing researcher should be able to demonstrate that (x) occurred before (y) or they occurred simultaneously. The third and key evidence of causality in experimental design is that other possible causal factors have been eliminated. Let us now use examples of the relationship between sales and advertising to illustrate these evidences. For the first condition, if advertising is to be considered to be the cause of an increase in sales, then there should not be any significant change in sales when advertising is not introduced. However, there should be a significant change in sales when the company advertises the product. For the second evidence, we can predict that an increase in sales is caused by advertising if the introduction of the advertising programme precedes or happens simultaneously with the rise in sales. However, we cannot attribute the increase in sales to advertising if the increase precedes the introduction of the advertising message.

The third evidence is the most difficult to provide in marketing. This is because most factors interplay to yield the result that marketers see. However, marketing researchers might hold other factors constant while manipulating the relevant variable(s). In the given example, to show that the increase in sales is caused by

Example 4.2:
Secondary data from the Office for National Statistics

There are many opportunities for collecting secondary data that could be useful to marketers. The tables below, obtained from the Office for National Statistics (ONS), show the pattern of commercial activities in retailing and the trend in Internet sales in the UK. Information like this can be used to gain initial insight into possible areas of investment and the possibility of success in the areas shown.

Specifically, the first table shows that the quantity of products bought in the retail sector as at February 2013 was 2.6 per cent greater than in February 2012. The second table indicates that there was an increase of 10.1 per cent in online sales between February 2012 and February 2013.

All retailing, February 2013 (seasonally adjusted percentage change)

	Most recent month on a year earlier	Most recent 3 months on a year earlier	Most recent month on previous month	Most recent 3 months on previous 3 months
Amount spent (value)	2.6	1.1	1.8	−0.1
Quantity bought (volume)	2.6	0.8	2.1	−0.2
Value excluding automotive fuel	3.4	2.2	1.4	0.2
Volume excluding automotive fuel	3.3	1.5	1.9	−0.1

Source: ONS, 2013

Summary of Internet sales performance, February 2013

Category	Weight	Year-on-year growth %	Contribution to year-on-year growth % points
All retailing	100	10.1	
All food	17.3	9.3	1.9
All non-food	41.4	1.0	0.5
Department stores	7.0	27.4	1.9
Textile, clothing and footwear stores	11.7	7.9	1.1
Household goods stores	8.2	−24.2	−2.0
Other stores	14.5	−4.3	−0.5
Non-store retailing	41.3	17.5	7.7

Source: ONS, 2013

advertising, other possible causal factors such as price reduction, the arrival of visitors during a major event such as the Olympics, unfavourable business performance of competitors and intensive distribution of the products should be eliminated in the experimental arrangement.

QUANTITATIVE AND QUALITATIVE DATA

Now that we have looked at various data collection methods, it is important for us to discuss them in terms of the nature of the data to be collected. So, the data to be collected could be qualitative or quantitative in nature and accordingly we use the terms qualitative research for studies based on qualitative data and quantitative research for studies based on quantitative data. The key difference between the two is that while qualitative research is often relatively flexible, focused on verbal data collected from small samples, quantitative research is relatively less flexible, focused on numerical data usually collected from large samples. From this explanation, most of the data collection methods, including mail questionnaires, telephone questionnaires and online questionnaires, fit the definition of quantitative methods of collecting marketing research data. We shall explain this point a little further under the data analysis section.

The commonly used methods of collecting qualitative data are:

- In-depth interviews
- Focus group interviews (discussion)
- Ethnography

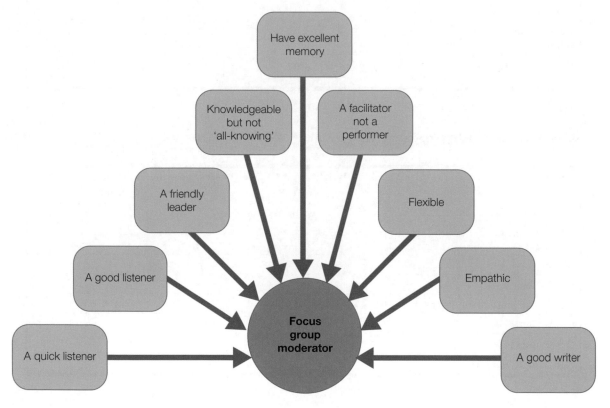

Figure 4.7: Attributes of a good focus group moderator
Source: Based on Churchill, 1996

A focus group is a group of people brought together in a suitable place to sit and talk to the sponsor of the research for about one to two hours in relation to some topics of interest. Usually, the participants are paid for participating and the event is moderated by a knowledgeable or well-trained moderator. The discussions of focus groups are usually audio-taped or sometimes video-taped while the moderator concentrates on studying the event and the interactions between the participants, and taking notes. Essentially, the goal of a focus group is to draw out ideas, themes, feelings and experiences about the issue being studied to illuminate further studies into the **phenomenon**. One of the key factors that differentiate it from the individual interview is that it is dependent upon interaction between participants (Cronin, 2003). This stance is also supported by Madriz (2003), who argues that focus group discussion allows access to research participants who may find one-to-one, face-to-face interaction 'scary' or 'intimidating'.

The opinion of authors varies on the number in a focus group setting, as Table 4.2 shows. But the key guide here is that the group should not be too large (because that may not be conducive to a natural discussion) or too small (because that does not generate the group dynamics necessary for a truly valuable session) (Burns and Bush, 1995; Bernard, 2000). It is very common for marketing researchers to use a group of 6–12 members.

Table 4.2: Different views on focus group composition
Source: Adapted from Gbadamosi, 2010

Suggested number of participants	Author/year of publication
2–12	Wilkinson, 2004
6–9	Denscombe, 1998
6–10	Zikmund, 1997; Tonkiss, 2004; Kotler and Armstrong, 2014
6–12	Bernard, 2000; Malhotra and Birks, 2003; Welman et al., 2005
7–10	Marshall and Rossman, 1999
8–12	Myers, 1986; Burns and Bush, 1995; May, 2001; Robson, 2002

Two major problems that are often associated with the use of focus group interviews are the possibility of having one or two people who are shy or reluctant to join in the discussion, and the possibility of having at least one who will try to dominate the conversation, thereby suppressing others' opinions (Cronin, 2003). These limitations can be overcome by ensuring that those observed to be shy are drawn into the discussion by directing questions at them, and those attempting to dominate the discussion are politely instructed to allow others to contribute.

In recent times, the development in the world of technology has made it possible to conduct focus group interviews online. This involves chatting about the subject under study on the Internet and collating and analysing the data later. This method is becoming increasingly popular these days and has been used successfully to address some challenging marketing problems (Brimelow et al., 2011).

IN-DEPTH INTERVIEW

An in-depth interview is a one-to-one interview conducted with the hope of gaining insight into the motivation, beliefs and attitudes of the respondents in respect of the topic being studied. This method of collecting data qualitatively is also sometimes called 'conversation with a purpose' (Seale, 2004). In an in-depth interview, the interviewer starts by building a rapport quickly and then proceeds into a set of questions about the subject at hand. The list of questions is usually prepared to act as a guide about the topic rather than the highly structured pattern we often see in a questionnaire. In other words, the questions and questioning are quite flexible. Essentially, in-depth interviewing is about probing and prompting. Prompting involves encouraging the interviewee to give an answer to the question raised, while probing entails asking for fuller responses and clarification. This may involve reframing the questions or asking questions such as 'Why is that so?', 'Can you tell me more on that point?' and 'Could you give other reasons why it is so?' Care should be taken by the interviewer not to ask suggestive questions such as 'Don't you think packaging is important when buying breakfast cereals?' There is a high tendency for respondents to give a 'yes' response to questions like this. Indeed, the process of in-depth interviewing is a skilled one in which the interviewer needs to listen carefully, field the right question at the right time and study the non-verbal cues and body language of the respondents.

One major limitation of or charge against the use of in-depth interviews is the possibility of interviewer bias, such as active commitment to a perspective during the interview (Fielding and Thomas, 2003). The effect of this limitation can be overcome or at least minimized if the interviewer does not influence the direction of the conversation with the interviewee, while encouraging him or her to talk freely.

ETHNOGRAPHY

This method is commonly used in anthropology to study people's culture and social systems but is now becoming increasingly used in marketing research. It involves having prolonged engagements with the group of people being studied in a particular cultural setting. With this method, the researcher will be living with the target group of people for several months, visiting them as necessary and observing their consumption pattern in order to provide answers to the research questions developed.

SAMPLING PLAN

A sample is a part of the population of study selected to represent the population as a whole. Researchers often resort to sampling for many reasons, among which are: the cost of studying the whole population is exorbitant; similarities in the characteristics of the members of the same population make it possible to use a sample as an approximate estimate of the whole population of interest; it saves time; sometimes it is unrealistic to study the entire population of interest.

There are two broad types of sampling: *probability sampling* and *non-probability sampling*. These are shown in Figure 4.8. In probability sampling, the marketing researcher has some notion of probability that the sample chosen to represent the population will be a representative cross-section of the conceivable elements that make up the population of interest. So, every individual element in the population is chosen at random and has a known and non-zero chance of being selected.

There are four common types of probability sampling; simple random sampling, systematic sampling, stratified random sampling and cluster or area sampling.

Think and discuss

To what extent do you think culture would have an impact on the findings of marketing research conducted into teenagers' purchasing behaviour for smartphones? Think and discuss this question in groups. Use examples of four countries to facilitate the discussion.

Major types of non-probability sampling methods commonly used are: convenience sampling, judgement (or purposive) sampling, quota sampling, snowballing and theoretical sampling.

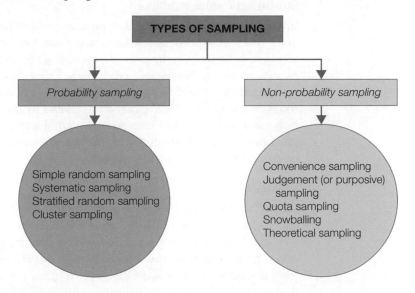

Figure 4.8: Types of sampling
Source: Adapted from Gbadamosi, 2010

PROBABILITY SAMPLING

Simple random sampling

In a simple random sample, each member of the population under study has a known and equal chance of being selected into the sample. The advantages of this sampling method are that it is simple and fulfils all the criteria of a probability sampling method. Nonetheless, it is infeasible in marketing research that involves large numbers of population and samples. This is because all population elements must be known and numbered for it to be amenable to random sampling. This process can also be time consuming and very expensive.

Systematic sampling

A systematic sampling method involves selecting every nth element of a numbered population. In other words, a fixed skip interval is maintained in the course of drawing the sample. Assume that 500 students are waiting to be served in a queue in a restaurant and are given serial numbers. If the marketing researcher is interested in giving questionnaires to only 100 of them using the systematic sampling methods, the skip interval can be calculated as follows:

$$\text{Skip interval:} \quad \frac{\text{Population sized}}{\text{Sample size}} \quad \frac{500}{100} = 5$$

So, while the marketing researcher may have started randomly, he or she will then give the questionnaire to every fifth student in the queue. Systematic sampling has been found to out-perform simple random sampling methods in terms of its economy, time saving and cost saving (McDaniel and Gates, 1998, p. 315). However, the main problem of using it is that the population arrangement may already have contained some hidden patterns which could put the randomness at risk.

Stratified random sampling

In stratified random sampling, the population is divided into separate identifiable units, which are known as strata, and a separate probability sampling is carried out within each stratum. For instance, if a marketing researcher is interested in consumer reactions to new packaging of a product and knows that sex and marital status could have significant implications for the consumption pattern of the product, then he could choose to use stratified random sampling to ensure that the right selection of males and females and all categories of marital status are included. This method is often found significantly useful in marketing research because it usually increases precision, though at an additional cost.

Cluster sampling

Cluster sampling involves dividing the population into mutually exclusive groups and a random sample of the groups is selected. Each of these groups is known as a cluster. If the marketing researchers collect data from all elements in the clusters selected, the procedure is known as *one-stage cluster sampling* but if they collect data from a sample of elements in the selected groups in some **probabilistic** manner, then it is called *two-stage sampling*. According to Zikmund (1997), the purpose of cluster sampling is to sample economically while retaining the characteristics of a probability sample. Given that both methods involve dividing the population into mutually exclusive groups, one may wonder what is really the difference between the stratified random sampling and cluster sampling. The basic difference between the two is that while elements are selected from each subset in a stratified sampling, a sample of subgroups (clusters) is taken in a cluster sampling (Churchill and Iacobucci, 2005, p. 349).

NON-PROBABILITY SAMPLING

As the name indicates, if we are to select elements to be in a sample in a non-probability sampling method, the process will not be based on probability. This means that we will not know the probability of any particular member being chosen to be in the sample. The selection of the sample in this method depends on human judgement without any statistical methods in contrast to probability sampling.

Convenience sampling

As the name suggests, the convenience sampling method involves using elements of the population that are most conveniently available for the study. There are very many examples of convenience sampling around us. Perhaps you have been approached by press people on the street for interview to comment on government policies, elections and other issues? In certain instances, radio and television stations ask volunteers to call in and contribute to ongoing discussions. These are examples of convenience sampling. When a marketing researcher decides to ask volunteers at a shopping mall to complete a prepared questionnaire for a study, s/he is deemed to be employing convenience sampling. While convenience sampling can be very cheap and easy to adopt and saves a lot of time, it lacks objec-

istock © timchen

tivity because the selection of the place and participants is subjective. In fact, it has been argued that it runs counter to the rigour of scientific research and suggests a lazy approach to the work. Its practice is not equated with good research (Denscombe, 2003). Despite this criticism, the growth of the convenience sampling method seems to be proliferating, especially for exploratory studies. This, of course, is because of its listed advantages, and sometimes marketing researchers use it at the preliminary stage of their research to generate ideas and insight into the phenomenon being investigated.

Judgement sampling

Judgement sampling, which is also known as purposive sampling, is a method in which an experienced researcher uses his or her judgement to select the sample which he or she believes will satisfy the specific purpose of the study or produce the most valuable data. It is also often used in exploratory studies such as focus groups where the objective is to generate ideas and insight into the problem at hand.

Quota sampling

In this method, marketing researchers select the sample in such a way that the demographical characteristics that they are interested in (such as age, sex or marital status) are represented in the sample according to their proportion in the population. The use of quota sampling is meant to ensure that the various subgroups in a population of interest are represented based on the relevance of the sample characteristics to the study at hand and the desire of the researcher. This is because it is relatively economical compared with probability sampling as relevant expenses such as travelling and times needed are far lower.

Snowballing

Snowballing, which is also called referral sampling, involves contacting a member of the population to be studied and asking him or her for additional respondents. When marketing researchers use this method, they usually start with a few participants, who are asked to nominate more people who have the qualities expected of the respondents, such as a particular age, sex, ethnicity, qualification and income. The new respondents would also be asked to nominate more people and the chain continues until a reasonable size of sample is achieved. The major strength of the method is that it vouches for the legitimacy of the researcher in that the researcher can use the nominator as a kind of personal reference or recommendation to enhance his or her credibility (Arber, 2003; Denscombe, 2003). Also, the cost and time expended will be minimal. On the other hand, the informant who is recommending another and the person who is introduced will likely be similar in certain characteristics. This might prevent there being a cross-section presentation of the population if required. Because it involves usually small numbers of respondents, snowballing is often used in industrial and organizational marketing research.

Theoretical sampling

Theoretical sampling involves gathering data for generating theory whereby the researcher jointly collects, codes and analyses his or her data and decides what data to collect next and where to find it, in order to develop a theory as it emerges (Glaser and Strauss, 1967; Seale, 2004). Hence, it can be stated that it involves selecting people according to how likely it is that their interview will contribute to the emerging theory (Byrne, 2004). In this approach, the researcher is guided by data and the study data being collected is driven by the evolving theory. It is also based on the concept of 'making comparisons' and its purpose is to go to places, people or events that will maximize the opportunity to discover variations among relevant concepts, events, incidents and happenings in terms of their properties and dimensions (Strauss and Corbin, 1998). Obviously, in theoretical sampling, the sampling is not predetermined before the commencement of the research but evolves during the process. The use of this method is also becoming more popular by the day in marketing research to extend understanding and create customer value.

RESEARCH INSTRUMENT

Just as a technician requires a set of tools to carry out his operations, marketing researchers also need instruments to collect their data. Kotler and Armstrong (2014) identify these instruments as falling into two types: *mechanical devices* and *questionnaires*.

Although the use of questionnaires for marketing research has been relatively popular over the years, the constant changes in the technological environment are increasing the usage of mechanical devices for marketing research. These are non-human devices for collecting data from people. One very common example of this is 'people meters', which are unique audience measurement systems that track what consumers listen to on the radio and what they are watching on the TV and the Internet. Another example is the tachistoscope, which marketing researchers use to find out how well people recall advertising messages they have been exposed to.

A questionnaire is a standardized document which consists of a set of questions presented to the chosen participants in a study in order to collect information needed for achieving predetermined research objectives. It ensures that every informant is asked the same question, with the same opportunities for response, in the same order (Barnes et al., 1998).

Usually, the questions contained in the questionnaire should emerge from the broad research questions and be set such that research objectives can be accomplished from the responses. So, it is important for target respondents to understand the questions, be able to provide the information and be willing to provide it so that the researchers are able to get a good response from a study (Jobber, 2004). Figure 4.9 shows the sequential stages to follow when designing a questionnaire and Table 4.3 gives various types of questions and their corresponding example.

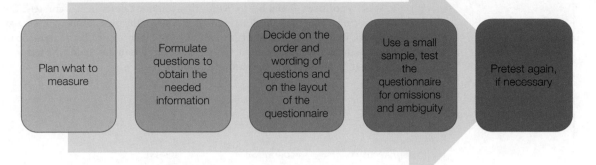

Figure 4.9: Stages involved in designing a questionnaire
Source: Adapted from Kumar et al., 2002

Table 4.3: Types of questions for questionnaires and other data collection methods

Question type	Examples/explanation
Dichotomous questions: offering a choice of two answers	Have you bought Brand X online within the past 7 days? (a) Yes (b) No
Multiple choice questions	Which factor encouraged you to buy Brand X on your last shopping trip? (a) Price (b) Spouse influence (c) Brand name (d) Advertisement (e) Other (please specify) _____
Likert scale	Point of purchase promotion (POP) has made me buy products I do not ordinarily plan to buy in the past one month Strongly disagree (1) Disagree (2) Uncertain (3) Agree (4) Strongly agree (5)
Semantic differential	After reading the book 'Low-income Consumer Behaviour', I find it: Entertaining 1 2 3 4 5 6 7 Boring Contemporary 1 2 3 4 5 6 7 Old-fashioned Educative 1 2 3 4 5 6 7 Uninformative
Rating items	How significant would you rate the following factors in influencing your purchase of soft drinks? <table><tr><td></td><td>Very significant</td><td></td><td></td><td></td><td>Not significant</td><td></td></tr><tr><td>Price</td><td>1</td><td>2</td><td>3</td><td>4</td><td>5</td><td>6 7</td></tr><tr><td>Children's influence</td><td>1</td><td>2</td><td>3</td><td>4</td><td>5</td><td>6 7</td></tr><tr><td>Spouse's influence</td><td>1</td><td>2</td><td>3</td><td>4</td><td>5</td><td>6 7</td></tr><tr><td>Brand name</td><td>1</td><td>2</td><td>3</td><td>4</td><td>5</td><td>6 7</td></tr><tr><td>Point of purchase promotion</td><td>1</td><td>2</td><td>3</td><td>4</td><td>5</td><td>6 7</td></tr></table>
Ranking scales	Rank the following factors that can influence your choice of soft drinks from the most important to the least important with 1 = most important, 2 = second important, 3 = third important, and 4 = least important. Low sugar level Availability Brand name Price

(continued overleaf)

Table 4.3 *continued*

Staple scales	With your experience of the use of Brand Y car, use the following scales to describe it. Select a positive (+) number for words that you think describe it accurately. The more accurate you think the description is, the larger the plus number you should choose. On the other hand, select a negative (-) number for words you think do not describe the car. The less accurate you think the word is in describing the feature, the larger the minus number you should choose. 5 5 5 4 4 4 3 3 3 2 2 2 1 1 1 Expensive Economical Safe −1 −1 −1 −2 −2 −2 −3 −3 −3 −4 −4 −4 −5 −5 −5
Unstructured questions	Why do you prefer the services of Bank Z to others that operate in the United Kingdom?
Sentence completion	The main reason why I buy Brand X body lotion is _____
Word association	Write the first word that comes to your mind when you hear the following words: Beverages _____ Tesco _____ Author _____ Supermarket _____
Story completion	Read the following passage and complete the story. 'I can remember vividly the second time I visited the supermarket to buy detergents _____ '
Lists	Examine the shopping list of Dr Miracle, Ms Favour and Mrs Joy and describe each of the people in the light of the products they have bought **Dr Miracle** **Mrs Favour** **Mrs Joy** Bread Crisps Cucumber Shoe polish Groundnut oil Carrot Toothpaste Canned drinks Olive oil
Thematic apperception test	A picture is presented to the subjects and they are then asked to tell or write a story about the picture and what they think is happening in it
Rorschach ink blot test	Subjects are shown ink blots and asked to say what they look like. As presented, the stimulus is incomplete in itself and as respondents attempt to make sense of the given scenario, they will be providing very useful information
Picture completion	Researchers present a picture showing the characters in it making statements. They then ask the subjects to respond to a statement shown to have been made by a character. In this method, the researcher could present cartoons and sketches of people talking in a given setting and ask the target participant to fill the empty balloon, which is meant to be a response to what one of the people in the picture has said

THE IMPORTANCE OF DATA COLLECTION

You will recall that, earlier, we described research design to be like a building plan that determines the final look of the structure. But we know that the plan cannot transform to the building if the activities detailed in it are not implemented. This is how important the stage of collection of data is. It is the stage at which most of the parts of the blueprint highlighted in the previous stage of research design are implemented. The marketing researcher or the research team set the ball in motion and contact informants through the methods which have been deemed appropriate. The success of this stage is partly related to how well the stage of research design has been handled. The series of activities involved at this stage often consumes most of the allocated budget. Hence, the research team is expected to be very effective in the way it handles the events in this stage.

ANALYSIS OF DATA

4

To understand the importance of the data analysis stage, you will need to imagine that you now have about 450 returned questionnaires on the desk in front of you after conducting a study. The piles of paper will tell you nothing that will assist you to make decisions about your research objectives. At best, they will occupy space on the table and can even disturb you from doing other meaningful activities. It is important to analyse the data into something useful. At the stage of data analysis, the data will be put into forms that are readily understood by people for the purpose for which they have been gathered. Hence, the data analysis stage is an important phase in the research process. It involves putting the data in tables appropriately, exploring significant relationships, interpretation and many other things.

QUANTITATIVE DATA ANALYSIS

Basically, data analysis can be done quantitatively or qualitatively, but the choice depends on the type of data collection method used for the study. The analysis of quantitative data has been made easier with the increased number of computer programs (software) that can be used for various types of analysis. A very common example is the Statistical Package for Social Sciences (SPSS). However, some preliminary activities are often required at the early stage of data analysis, which include:

- Editing
- Coding
- Data entry

Editing involves checking the questionnaires to ensure that they are properly filled in and that every question has been properly answered. If they have not, effort should be made to obtain the missing information from the informants where possible. Marketing researchers are expected to examine the questionnaires closely for consistency and accuracy of the responses given. If the research design has been done effectively, the effort at the editing stage will be greatly minimized.

Coding involves assigning numerical values to all response categories in order to make them amenable to computer processing. In essence, coding makes it possible to transfer the responses to numeric codes. Examples are assigning '1' to males and '2' to females, or '1' for strongly disagree, '2' for disagree, '3' for undecided, '4' for agree and '5' for strongly agree. In most instances, all possible answers would have been coded earlier in the design of the questionnaire to facilitate data processing. The basic rules that guide coding, as stated by Fielding and Thomas (2003), are:

- Codes must be mutually exclusive: any particular response must fit into one, and only one, category
- Codes must be exhaustive: all possible coding options must have been covered and be allowed for in the scheme
- Codes must be consistently applied throughout the analysis process

Having edited and coded the questionnaires, the researcher must enter the data into a computer software program such as Microsoft Excel or SPSS for the analysis. This stage usually involves having data-entry operators to 'load' or input the data into the software. There is a possibility of making some errors at this stage. For example '448' could be wrongly entered as '844', and '08' as '80'. This can have a significant impact on the findings and could affect the achievement of the objective of the research. Hence, it is important that the researcher makes provision for someone else to recheck what the data-entry operator has entered into the system.

Once the data is input into the computer and has been freed of errors, the marketing researcher can then proceed to the stage of analysis. The findings can be presented in several ways but it is very common to report findings in the form of tables and charts with an explanation of what they mean. What is reported at this stage will be what people can read and understand because all the technical details will be explained if they are included in the findings.

QUALITATIVE DATA ANALYSIS

The discussion about data analysis also relates to data collected through qualitative methods. Analysing qualitative studies involves coding, and in this context requires the breaking-down of the data into discrete chunks and assigning references to the chunks. Essentially, the first stage in the analysis of qualitative data is to transcribe the data from the tape recorder or field notes into a readable form, after which the coding will begin. Qualitative data can be coded line by line, sentence by sentence or even paragraph by paragraph. While the decision of what constitutes the unit of analysis is for the researcher to make, it is crucial that he or she does it in such a way that it will enhance the answering of research questions and ultimately the achievement of the research objectives.

Just as there are computer programs that facilitate analysis of quantitative data, some software packages for analysing qualitative data have also been developed. Examples are Non-numerical Unstructured Data Indexing Searching and Theorizing (NUD.IST) and NVivo. They assist researchers in bringing out the pattern in the data collected and performing further analysis on it. They are especially relevant when the volume of data to be processed is very large.

PRESENTATION OF FINDINGS

The last stage in the marketing research process is the presentation of the findings of the research to management. It is important for the researcher to use the appropriate language so that it will be understood by the audience for the report. For instance, not all managers will be interested in the 'sophisticated' statistical techniques in research reports. Some may find this boring. So, to ensure that the report is used, the researcher should consider the reader's background, experience and role in decision making. It is best to keep the report short and concise, and to follow a natural writing style, using ordinary language and avoiding jargon. The researcher should address the research objectives but avoid extraneous materials, ensure the accuracy of all statistical information presented and illustrate the report with charts, diagrams and tables, according more space to important items (Bradley, 1995). It has been suggested further that there may be a need to 'translate' the language of the report for different audiences or provide **verbatim** quotes from individual respondents to support and simplify the statistics (Czinkota and Kotabe, 2001). These efforts are necessary for the report to appeal to the audience.

The outline of the marketing research report takes the following order:

- Cover page
- Table of contents
- Background and objectives
- Executive summary
- Methodology
- Findings
- Recommendations
- Appendices

Although there may be variations in the layout and the content of marketing research reports presented by researchers and agencies, only slight differences will exist between the content of a good report and the outline above.

ONLINE MARKETING RESEARCH

All available evidence shows that online activities are on the increase. More purchases are now made online than used to be the case, and consumers interact with each other and with companies online. You will notice that either you or someone close to you will have made one transaction or another on the Internet within the last month or so. All these developments have brought people and businesses all over the world closer to one another. As it is commonly said, the world is becoming a global village as someone at one end of the world can easily communicate and interact with someone at the other end. Similarly, these advancements and improvements in technology have opened new opportunities for conducting marketing research. Several businesses now collect data from customers online in forms such as online surveys, online focus groups, blogs, online feedback and complaints from customers, and data from social media such as Facebook, Twitter and LinkedIn. Considering that they save time and cost less, it is not surprising that these marketing research methods are becoming increasingly popular.

British Airways is a well-known, full-service global airline. It celebrated 90 years of flying with pride on 25 August 2009. The success it has had over the past decades points to the favourable positioning of the organization in the transportation sector. Although its prices may not be the lowest when compared with budget airlines, the continuous **patronage** that the company enjoys from its customers emphasizes that it delivers value to its various customer groups. As expected, doing this efficiently has often involved collecting information from customers on their needs and working on this information. While it collects information from its customers in order to make informed decisions, BA does not ignore the issue of ethics. For example, it clearly states on its websites its privacy policy, which covers a number of important issues. It tells informants how it uses the data they supply, the countries that the data will pass through and the efforts it makes to keep the data secure – among many other measures it has in place to manage their data. This provides the openness that customers often crave. It is therefore not surprising that the organization continuously enjoys the support of the volunteers who provide this data. This further demonstrates that being ethical in data collection and data management could be related to customers' perception of the firm and may link to how successful the business will be in a competitive marketing environment.

As is the case in traditional marketing research approaches, data that customers provide online will be collated and carefully analysed such that the findings will serve as input to decisions that will be made in the organization to create value for the customers in their transactions.

ETHICAL ISSUES IN MARKETING RESEARCH

If marketing researchers are collecting data from people in any of the forms we have explained in this chapter, they need to be aware of the ethical issues associated with this activity. Bulmer (2003) explains the issues of ethics in research as a matter of principled sensitivity to the rights of others. These rights impinge upon all scientific research but do so particularly sharply in the case of human sciences, where people are studying other people. Some of the key questions that marketing research ethics address include the following:

- To what lengths can the marketing researchers go to get information from a person?
- How should they be treated in this situation?
- Can they refuse to participate without being made to feel bad about this decision?
- What will the researcher do to the information after they have finished using it for their research?
- Would the person's identity be protected or revealed as the source of this information?

We can summarize the key ethical practices in marketing research as shown in Figure 4.10.

Some regulatory and other relevant bodies that make efforts to ensure that marketing researchers conform to these practices have been working hard to ensure that these guidelines are followed. For instance, the Market Research Society (MRS), the world's leading research association, drives the development of quality standards both in the UK and internationally.

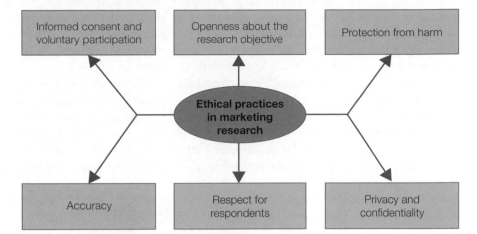

Figure 4.10: Key ethical practices in marketing research
Source: Adapted from Fontana and Frey, 1998, and Robson, 2002

4

CONCLUSION

Think and discuss

A British firm, which has successfully sold toys and childrenswear in the UK, is contemplating selling these products abroad. The company has approached you to conduct marketing research into how the needs of young consumers could be integrated with the firm's offerings. Discuss the ethical issues you are likely to be confronted with.

To create and deliver value to customers, firms need to have timely and up-to-date information about the needs and wants of their target market. Doing this effectively is clearly linked to having a solid marketing information system in place. This system comprises internal data, marketing intelligence and marketing research. The interaction of these elements helps marketers to obtain the right information about their consumers' needs and how to satisfy them. Although the approaches adopted could vary with the size, structure and policy of various organizations, the need to obtain marketing information as input to informed decisions is relevant to all organizations.

As we witness many changes in the technological environment, many different opportunities for collecting and analysing marketing information continue to emerge. For example, the conduct of online marketing research is now becoming popular. However, irrespective of the approach of the research, be it quantitative or qualitative, the need to be mindful of ethical issues pertaining to the study is becoming increasingly important and should be addressed. By and large, whether in terms of the process involved in the conduct of the marketing research or in terms of the use of the report, the key focus still ultimately remains to create and deliver value to a firm's various customer groups and ensure business sustainability.

Case study
Debenhams: Winning where many are losing

The fashion market today is very dynamic and competitive. Be it for social, cultural, functional or other purposes, people still buy fashion products and knowing their reasons, and how to influence consumers, is one of the key challenges facing fashion marketers these days. Some organizations have realized that the key to surviving in the ever changing marketing environment is to do it the customer way. Debenhams, a leading multinational multichannel fashion firm, is in this category. It competes with other major players such as Next, Marks & Spencer and House of Fraser. The competition becomes even fiercer and stiffer by the day, as supermarkets that previously dealt in groceries have now penetrated the fashion business and sell clothes, shoes and other basic fashion items. News of retailers folding up and going into administration constantly appears in the media.

However, Debenhams knows that for it to succeed where others are failing, the rules of the game must be followed. In marketing, this is about satisfying the customer in all areas and being conscious of their need to have value for the money they part with. As stated in its annual report, the organization is truly passionate about the products it sells and puts the customer at the heart of everything it does. In 2012, the profit before tax grew by 4.2 per cent when compared with the record of the previous year. Also, 2012 was another year of significant growth in terms of online sales for the company as the sales of the group grew by 39.8 per cent. On Friday 5 April 2013, Debenhams became the first high street retailer in the UK to promote its collections of the latest fashions by using diverse types of models who vary in terms of their looks, age and size.

It is clear that Debenhams' achievement involves having the right information about what consumers need and how the marketing mix elements work to deliver the value to them. Debenhams ensures that all this goes into its marketing research design and other stages involved in the way it does its research. As it is a multinational firm with about 240 stores in 28 countries, the use of online surveys can be a very efficient way to gather data from customers. This explains why Debenhams invites its customers to join its design team online by providing information about the type of offerings that will satisfy their needs. Since this programme was launched in 2008,

Reproduced with permission of Debenhams Retail plc

thousands of people have participated and the results have been remarkable. It has most importantly won customers over because they have been left in charge of the designs of the products they buy. Also, as they participate, they have the opportunity to be entered into prize draws to win exciting prizes such as company gift cards.

The openness in the way the organization handles issues is also reflected in its marketing research approaches. It knows that customers who provide information through the design team have the right to know what the information is used for, so this is clearly explained in the form of frequently asked questions. It is clearly stated that the responses will be analysed and results will be used for making key decisions about improving how the organization does its business. So, it is not surprising that Debenhams has won many awards including the Best Accessories Award at the Prima High Street Fashion Awards, the Best One-stop Shop in the Fabulous High Street Fashion Awards in 2011 and the Multichannel Retailer of the Oracle Retail Week Awards in 2012.

In an attempt to remain relevant in the fashion retail sector, Debenhams regularly keeps a close eye on all the factors in the macro environment and micro environment, and uses the information to enrich its managers' decisions. Maintaining good relationships with suppliers, which are in various countries including China, India, Bangladesh and Vietnam, is a key part of the company's strategy. This has helped to strengthen its 'right product, right country' sourcing strategy. It is also conscious of what competitors are doing without ignoring the impacts of other environmental factors. These efforts have kept the company on the winning side, and proved that succeeding while others are failing is about delivering value to customers. This greatly depends on having the right information about their needs and wants, and in a timely manner.

Questions

1 Explain the relevance of the marketing information system in Debenhams' success record and give specific evidence of this from the case study.

2 Assume that you have been approached by Debenhams to conduct marketing research that will give the firm the insight needed into the range of products that could be launched for low-income consumers. What will be the contents of your proposal to the firm?

3 Do you think Debenhams' decision to use an online survey is the right one? Mention two other methods that you think the company could use to collect information about their customers and explain why you have specifically suggested these.

4 Design a questionnaire that could be used by Debenhams to know the perception of its target market in relation to a proposed new product planned to be launched next summer.

5 In which circumstance do you think Debenhams would consider the use of cluster sampling?

Review questions

1 What is a marketing information system? Distinguish between marketing research and marketing information systems. Discuss the scope of marketing research and give examples to justify your claims.

2 Enumerate the components of a marketing research brief and a marketing research proposal. Apply these components to develop the two documents for any hypothetical marketing-related problem of your choice.

3 Why would you suggest the use of primary sources of data to your friend who is conducting a study into the effectiveness of the use of sales promotion for fast-moving consumer goods?

4 Why might a marketing researcher prefer to use an in-depth interview rather than a focus group to gather data concerning consumers' perceptions of newly introduced packaging for table salt? What kind of skill does the moderator need to use in a focus group discussion?

5 Design a questionnaire to address a marketing-related issue. It should contain 20 questions made up of five relating to respondents' characteristics, five Likert scale, five semantic differential and multiple choice, three dichotomous scale and two open-ended questions.

6 Explain the term 'experimental research design'. What are the major evidences needed to demonstrate the existence of a causal relationship between variables in an exploratory research design?

Group tasks

1 Develop a hypothetical marketing research problem, and write out what you think will be the marketing objectives that could emerge from it.

2 In a group of four, search the Internet for external sources of information about family consumption. Make this into a table containing the name of the sources, the web pages and the particular information each contains.

3 Conduct a focus group discussion to get an appropriate brand name for a new brand of body lotion to be developed for teenagers. While one person should act as the moderator, another member should support him or her to take notes of the key points in the discussion.

4 Assume you have secured an appointment with a local entrepreneur for an interview on how the business has been coping with the changes in the marketing environment. Brainstorm as a group to decide on the questions that your repre-

sentative will ask her during the interview. Write the questions out and pre-test them on a volunteer from another group.

5 As a group, check any two academic journal articles on marketing-related subjects, one that was written based on qualitative data and the other based on quantitative data. Compare the sampling process and write out the differences and similarities that you can notice in them.

Glossary/Key terms

Descriptive marketing research design: Identifies characteristics of marketing issues such as answering questions about how many customers buy a particular brand of the company's products, what quantity they buy and their perception of the product characteristics

Ethnography: Involves having prolonged engagement with the target group of people in a particular cultural setting for the purpose of studying them

Experimentation: Manipulating independent variables to know the effect a change will have on the dependent variables

Exploratory marketing research design: Usually adopted as the initial step in the conduct of a marketing research enquiry. It often identifies the real nature of the research problem being investigated and provides insight before the conduct of an extensive study

Marketing information system: A set of procedures and methods for the regular, planned collection, analysis and presentation of information for use in making marketing decisions

Snowballing: Contacting a member of the population to be studied and asking him or her to suggest additional respondents

Vocab check list for ESL students

Causal	Hypotheses	Probabilistic	Turbulent
Concomitant	Patronage	Syndicated	Verbatim
Dichotomous	Phenomenon	Systematic	

Definitions for these terms can be found in the 'Vocab Zone' of the companion website, which provides free access to the Macmillan English Dictionary online at www.palgrave.com/business/Gbadamosi

Further reading

K. Fletcher, A. Buttery and K. Deans (1988) 'The Structure and Content of the Marketing Information System: A Guide For Management', *Marketing Intelligence and Planning*, Vol. 6, No. 4, pp. 27–35

The key focus of this article is to show how a marketing system should be considered as a subject or module of a total management information system; it also provides guidance for the development of such a system.

A. Gbadamosi, R. Hinson, T. K. Eddy and I. Ingunjiri (2012) 'Children's Attitudinal Reactions to TV Advertisements: The African Experience', *International Journal of Market Research*, Vol. 54, No. 4, pp. 543–66

The paper shows a clear example of qualitative marketing research, explains the process of collecting and analysing results qualitatively and gives insight into basic ethical issues in marketing research in the context of how children react to TV advertisements.

H. McDonald and S. Adam (2003) 'A Comparison of Online and Postal Data Collection Methods in Marketing Research', *Marketing Intelligence and Planning*, Vol. 21, No. 2, pp. 85–95

This article provides insights on marketing research data collection methods. It specifically reports on a study which directly compares online and postal data collection methods, using the same survey instrument on two samples drawn from the same population of football club subscribers.

N. G. Piercy (2002) 'Research in Marketing: Teasing with Trivial or Rising Relevance?', *European Journal of Marketing*, Vol. 36, No. 3, pp. 350–65

This article explains marketing research in terms of its impacts with diverse audiences, especially in relation to teaching in marketing and practice.

R. S. Sisodia (1992) 'Marketing Information and Decision Support Systems for Service', *Journal of Services Marketing*, Vol. 6, No. 1, pp. 51–64

This paper discusses the relevance of formal marketing information systems for services marketing and examines information technology and its potential for services marketing, presenting a design for an integrated services marketing information system.

References

'AMA Board Approves New Marketing Definition,' *Marketing News* 1, 1985, pp. 1–14

Arber, S. (2003) 'Designing samples' in C. Seale (ed.) *Researching Society and Culture* (2nd edn). London: Sage Publications, pp. 58–82

Armstrong, G. and Kotler, P. (2013) *Marketing: An Introduction* (11th edn). Harlow: Pearson Education

Barnes, E., McClellan, B., Meyer, R., Wieshehöfer, H. and Worsam, M. (1998) *Marketing: an Active Learning Approach*. Oxford: Blackwell Publishers

Bernard, H. R. (2000) *Social Research Methods: Qualitative and Quantitative Approaches*. London: Sage Publications

Bloch, A. (2004) 'Doing social surveys', in C. Seale (ed.) *Researching Society and Culture* (2nd edn). London: Sage Publications, pp. 164–77

Bradley, F. (1995) *Marketing Management: providing communicating and delivering value*. London: Prentice Hall Europe

Brimelow, Z., Gbadamosi, A. and Bamber, D. (2012) 'Women, Beauty, Perception and Consumption Behaviour: Implications For Organisational Studies', paper presented at *British Academy of Management Conference*, Cardiff University, 11–13 September

Bulmer, M. (2003) 'The Ethics of Social Research', in N. Gilbert (ed.) *Researching Social Life* (2nd edn). London: Sage Publications, pp. 45–57

Burns, A. C. and Bush, R. F. (1995) *Marketing Research*. Englewood Cliffs, New Jersey: Prentice Hall

Byrne, B. (2004) 'Qualitative Interviewing', in C. Seale (ed.) *Researching Society and Culture* (2nd edn). London: Sage Publications, pp. 179–92

Chisnall, P. (2005) *Marketing Research*. London: McGraw-Hill Education

Churchill, G. A. Jr. (1996) 'Basic Marketing Research' (3rd edn). Orlando: The Dryden Press

Churchill, G. A. Jr., and Iacobucci, D. (2005) *Marketing Research: Methodological Foundations* (9th edn). Ohio: South-Western

Cronin, A. (2003) 'Focus groups', in N. Gilbert (ed.) *Researching Social Life* (2nd edn). London: Sage Publications, pp. 164–77

Czinkota, M. R. and Kotabe, M. (2001) *Marketing Management* (2nd edn). Ohio: South-Western College Publishing

Denscombe, M. (2003) *The Good Research Guide for small-scale social research projects* (2nd edn). Berkshire: Open University Press

Dillon, W. R., Madden, T. J. and Firtle, N. H. (1994) *Marketing Research in a Marketing environment* (3rd edn). Burr Ridge: Richard D. Irwin

Fielding, N. and Thomas, H. (2003) 'Qualitative Interviewing', in C. Seale (ed.) *Researching Society and Culture* (2nd edn). London: Sage Publications

Fontana, A. and Frey, J. H. (1998) 'Interviewing: the Art of Science', in N. K. Denzin and Y. S. Lincoln (eds) *Collecting and Interpreting Qualitative Materials*.Thousand Oaks: Sage Publication, pp. 47–78

Gbadamosi, A. (2010) *Low-income Consumer Behaviour: A Contextual Focus on Women and Low-involvement Grocery Products*. Saarbrücken: Lambert Academic Publishing

Gbadamosi, A. (2011) 'Entrepreneurship Marketing Environment', in S. Nwankwo and A. Gbadamosi (eds) *Entrepreneurship Marketing: Principles and Practice of SME Marketing*. Oxford: Routledge, pp. 55–78

Glaser, B. and Strauss, A. (1967) *Discovery of grounded theory*. Chicago: Aldine

Jobber, D. (2004) *Principles and Practice of Marketing* (4th edn). Berkshire: McGraw-Hill International (UK)

Kotler, P. and Armstrong, G. (2014) *Principles of Marketing* (15th edn). Upper Saddle River, New Jersey: Pearson Education

Madriz, E. (2003), 'Focus Group in Feminist Research' in N. K. Denzin and Y. S. Lincoln (eds) *Collecting and Interpreting Qualitative Materials*. London: Sage Publications

Malhotra, N. K. and Birks, D. F. (2003) *Marketing Research: An Applied Approach*. (2nd European edn). Harlow: Pearson Education

Marshall, C. and Rossman, G. B. (1999) *Designing Qualitative Research* (3rd edn). London: Sage Publications

May, T. (2001) *Social Research: Issues, methods, and process*. Buckingham: Open University Press

McDaniel, C. and Gates, R. (1998) *Marketing Research Essentials*. Ohio: South Western College Publishing

Myers, J. H. (1986) *Marketing*. Singapore: McGraw-Hill

Proctor, T. (2003) *Essentials of Marketing Research* (3rd edn). Harlow: Pearson Education

Robson, C. (2002) *Real World Research* (2nd edn). Oxford: Blackwell Publishing

Seale, C. (2004) 'Generating grounded theory', in C. Seale (ed.) *Researching Society and Culture* (2nd edn). London: Sage Publications, pp. 239–47

Strauss, A. and Corbin, J. (1998) *Basics of Qualitative Research: Techniques and Procedures for Developing Grounded Theory* (2nd edn). Thousand Oaks: Sage Publications

Tonkiss, F. (2004) 'Using focus groups', in C. Seale (ed.) *Researching Society and Culture* (2nd ed.). London: Sage Publications, pp. 193–206

Welman, C. Kruger, F. and Mitchell, B. (2005) *Research Methodology* (3rd edn). Cape Town: Oxford University Press

Wilkinson, S. (2004) 'Focus Group Research', in D. Silverman (ed.) *Qualitative Research, Method and Practice*. London: Sage Publications, pp. 177–99

Zikmund, W. G. (1997) *Exploring Marketing Research* (6th edn). Forth Worth: The Dryden Press

5 MARKETING STRATEGY: SEGMENTATION, TARGETING AND POSITIONING

UZOAMAKA ANOZIE

BOURNEMOUTH UNIVERSITY

CHAPTER CONTENTS

LEARNING OUTCOMES

The content of this chapter will help you to:

- Define the three main stages of a value-oriented marketing strategy: **segmentation**, targeting and positioning
- Discuss the concept of segmentation and the main bases for the **segmentation** of customer, business and international markets
- Describe how organizations identify attractive market segments and discuss the various market targeting strategies available to them
- Explain the concept of positioning and discuss the factors that are crucial to successful positioning

Marketing in action
Nivea: A global success achieved using a value-oriented marketing strategy

IN AN ERA OF ONGOING INNOVATION IN SKIN CARE products, breakthroughs in technology and changing standards, Nivea has maintained a relevant and competitive position in the industry since its inception in 1911. Originally, Nivea products were targeted at females but, identifying new market segments, Nivea started making men's products in 1922 as well. Nivea's intensive and targeted market research continually reveals significant market segments and its research aids it in understanding these segments and prompts Nivea's new product development. Nivea specifically aims at catering for individuality of the skin and this means that people all over the world are able to find products that suit their individual skin type as well as their needs.

Gradually, Nivea's product portfolio has grown to include bath care, body care, face care, lip care, men's care, deodorants, sun care and gift packs (see http://www.nivea.co.uk/products). Within these product ranges, different varieties exist (see table). For instance, the body care range comes in lotion, moisturizer, hand cream and gel. These ranges have a variety of products, specifically targeted at groups of individuals. There are ten in the sun care range, which come in either lotion or spray, with seven distinct varieties in the ranges based on skin type and the climate where the product is to be used.

Nivea's rich heritage has been handed down from one generation to another for over 100 years. Even in the midst of intense competition from other big players, Nivea is presently one of the world's largest skin care brands and is available globally, serving different needs and purposes. According to Nivea: 'No matter what your age, race, location or culture is, Nivea has you covered'. Segmentation is the tool that allows Nivea to identify different groups of customers and to provide the best possible products to meet individual needs and create value for their customers. Nivea must maintain such value creation, through targeted, innovative and high quality products, if it aims to keep enjoying universal trust and patronage as at present.

Nivea product range and varieties

Product range	Varieties in range
Bath care	23
Body care	15
Deodorant	41
Face care	35
Lip care	13
Men's care	24
Sun care	17
Gift packs	9 for him, 13 for her

Source: Nivea website http://www.nivea.co.uk/products

istock © OlgaMiltsova

INTRODUCTION

Having learnt in previous chapters what marketing is all about, and the significance of understanding consumers and the marketing environment, you will discover in this chapter the main customer-driven and value-oriented marketing strategies used by companies to create significant customer groups in markets they wish to serve (*segmentation*). It also deals with the processes leading to decisions about which groups of customers to serve (*targeting*) and, finally, how to position products or services in the minds of target consumers (*positioning*). This three-pronged approach, sometimes referred to as the STP framework, revolves around the concept of value. This is because the key to being able to figure out or profile the consumer groups that a company might be interested in serving is a clear understanding of the value(s) they share. This includes the consumption decisions they make, the value stimuli to which they are likely to be responsive, the fit between consumer value and producer value and the degree to which the company is able to adapt its systems (such as production, distribution and management) to deliver a bundle of value to consumers.

In dynamically competitive markets, such as the fast-moving consumer goods market, what separates successful firms from less successful ones is often the effectiveness and efficiency with which they design and implement strategies aimed at extending the consumers' value map. Put succinctly, market segmentation may be considered as the process of grouping or classifying consumers according to how they process, express and respond to value maps. It is in this regard that the STP framework is crucially important in developing value-oriented marketing strategy.

Example 5.1:
P&G takes sustainability message to customers

P&G, with its global brands stretching from beauty and health to household goods, and serving about 4.2 billion consumers around the world, is a proactive organization seeking to connect with the sustainability values of growing ecologically sensitive consumer segments. P&G is the company behind such global brands as Gillette, Ariel, Pampers, Head and Shoulders, Vicks and many more. To establish a clear strategic position on the subject of sustainability, the company boldly affirms on its website that 'over 99% of materials entering P&G leave as finished products, or are recycled, reused, or converted into energy'.

To put the strategy into action, and spurred on by lessons learned from its sponsorship of the 2012 Olympic Games, it is partnering Asda in a new campaign to promote safe and clean drinking water. This comes at a time of rising consumer concerns about the effects on the quality of the environment of the products they buy and cynicism around corporate sustainability marketing and social responsibility activities. Thus, by aggressively promoting and communicating its values and principles, the company hopes to keep pace with important consumer segments. According to Irwin Lee, P&G UK Managing Director, the firm has learned that: 'if we build on an idea, and our activities surround things that matter the most, they will have the most impact' (MarketingWeek, 18 April 2013, p. 4). Whatever the intention, P&G's initiative makes sense, especially when put alongside the fact that environmental consciousness is quickly becoming a key differentiator of consumer segments.

VALUE-ORIENTED MARKETING STRATEGY

A value-oriented marketing strategy should naturally flow from the earlier stages of an organization's strategic marketing planning process. While an organization starts to define the objectives and goals of its marketing input, it would probably be faced with the difficult task of translating all the insight and information it has (concerning, for instance, the organization's missions and goals, its present strengths and weaknesses, its target customers and trends in the marketplace) into a basic strategy that would direct its marketing effort over a certain period of time. Such value-oriented marketing strategy is important as it sets out just how the organization will deal with existing and potential market challenges.

For instance, Dell and Sony both manufacture laptops but the way in which they approach customers, position and price their products, advertise themselves and work with distributors is quite different. These different features of style and substance differentiate organizations from one another. The BBC's approach to the news is quite different from ITV's. Primark tackles the retail market differently from Marks & Spencer and both are different from Topshop. Radio 1 is not Capital FM and Oxford University is not Bournemouth University. Many different competing organizations exist in every marketplace, but what makes some organizations stand out more successfully is that they have a unique view of themselves and their role in the marketplace. This distinctive role in the marketplace is captured in a value-oriented marketing strategy with features including:

- **Being customer focused:** The essence of the strategy is not simply to sell a product the organization thinks it needs to sell. Rather, the main focus is to meet the needs and wants of the organization's target audience. Essentially, this means the ability to deliver unique customer value

- **Being different:** The value-oriented strategy will differentiate an organization from its main competitors, thus making the organization stand out from the competition. It will also give its target markets unique and worthwhile reasons to prefer its products to the products of its key rivals

- **Being sustainable:** The strategy will be sustainable in the long term and stand the test of time and competition. Strategies are not applied in an empty space. They are applied amidst existing and potential competition and if they prove successful, competitors will react to them. Thus, the strategy should be such that the organization will most likely anticipate the possibility of competition and be prepared for it

- **Being easily communicated:** The essential features of the strategy should be clear and simple so that both the organization's own staff and intended audiences have a definite understanding of what the strategy really is and why it should be supported

- **Being flexible:** The strategy should be sufficiently broad that it allows for diversity in its implementation by individual staff. Likewise, it should not be so rigid and uncompromising that it cannot be adapted to unforeseen contingencies, which may include change in the market or activities of competitors

- **Being visionary:** A value-oriented strategy should articulate a future for the organization. It should offer a clear sense of direction, including the aims and targets as well as a means of knowing when it meets with expected success

A value-oriented marketing strategy consists of three processes: segmentation, targeting and positioning (see Figure 5.1).

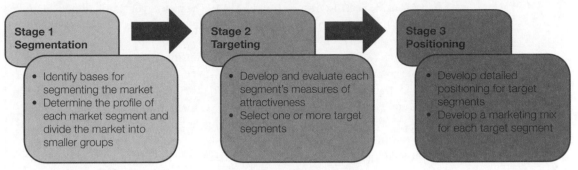

Figure 5.1: The three stages of a value-oriented marketing strategy

MARKETS AND SEGMENTATION

THE CONCEPT OF A MARKET

The word 'market' often has different meanings to different people. The term has been used in many ways in business and economics generally. However, whatever the context in which it is used, the term usually signifies the existence of a demand for a product. Generally, there are three principal features to consider in assessing market demand for any product. These are: the existence of people with needs, purchasing power and buying behaviour. It is in this sense that some authors have defined a market as 'people with needs to satisfy, the money to spend and their willingness to spend it' (Lancaster et al., 2002). Worthy of note is that for marketing executives the market includes not only present customers but also all the people and organizations that may be persuaded to buy the product being offered. In other words, for a marketer, the term 'market' includes both existing and potential customers.

Existing and potential customers of an organization's offerings may be numerous and have varying needs, locations, resources, expectations, buying behaviour and attitudes. This makes it practically impossible for businesses to reach and serve every likely buyer. It becomes necessary, therefore, to split up the whole market into smaller groups, which can then be managed and served more effectively, efficiently and profitably with products or services that suit their distinct needs. The process of breaking down the market into groups of customers with similar needs, so that a business can concentrate its effort on effectively serving the needs of a selected group or groups, is known as market **segmentation**.

General definitions of segmentation

American Marketing Association (AMA): 'The process of subdividing a market into distinct subsets of customers that behave in the same way or have similar needs'

Lilien et al. (2013, p. 61): 'Segmentation is a business process of finding groups of customers who are similar on some specific criterion of relevance to the firm's strategic context'

Pride and Ferrell (2012, p. 161): 'Market segmentation is the process of dividing a total market into groups, or segments, that consist of people or organisations with relatively similar product needs'

McDonald and Dunbar (2012, p. 94): 'Segmentation is the process of splitting customers, or potential customers, within a market into different groups or segments, within which customers share a similar level of interest in the same, or a comparable, set of needs satisfied by a distinct marketing proposition'

Segmentation enables firms to reach their customers more efficiently and effectively with products and services that match their unique needs – in other words, to create value for customers.

MARKET SEGMENTATION AND VALUE CREATION

The marketing concept emphasizes understanding customers and satisfying their needs better than competitors. However, there exists a variety of customers with a variety of needs which cannot be satisfied by treating these customers in the same way. In other words, it might prove tricky if an organization aims to use one product offering to satisfy the various customer needs within the market. Therefore, customers are divided into market segments in order to clearly identify their needs and then provide the goods and services to satisfy these different needs.

A market segment can be seen as a group of customers whose needs are distinct from the needs of other groups for a particular product. Essentially, each customer group in an identified market is most likely to exhibit certain basic characteristics which are special and significant for marketing strategy. Thus, segmentation is a great strategic marketing tool used to divide an organization's customers into distinctive groups in order to enable efficient and effective placement of the organization's offerings.

In order to appreciate how important segmentation is, imagine that the shelves at your local or school library were not segmented, and all the books were displayed by their title and in alphabetical order. You would probably spend hours trying to locate this book you are reading now. Thankfully, segmentation makes it possible for librarians to arrange books into subject categories so that different groups of library users can easily locate the particular books related to their fields of interest. Similarly, imagine the segmentation process that your university or college conducted to provide its various degrees and to aim these degrees at specific groups of students. Students must have been grouped according to degree level (undergraduate or postgraduate), mode of study (taught or research) and perhaps type of student (home or international). In health care, hospitals may segment their patients according to

istock © gbh007

type of treatment needed (surgical, medical or maternity) and by gender (female and male), while preventative medical programmes might find more suitable bases for segmentation to be lifestyle (e.g. drug users and smokers) and age. High service quality standards can only be achieved by organizations when they recognize the differences between various segments in the market. Thus organizations have a better chance of delivering value to customers by serving segments instead of serving the market as a whole.

THE PROCESS OF MARKET SEGMENTATION

Market segmentation is an initial and vital step in the overall process of a value-oriented marketing strategy. It is aimed at enabling an organization to strategically target its customers and to present, measure and market its product offerings to the target group of consumers. Successful segmentation is not a one-off activity but a constant learning process which should be reviewed continuously because of the ever changing needs of customers and the ever more competitive environment. Noting how relevant segmentation is, organizations should not then ask the question 'Should we conduct segmentation exercises or not?' Rather, they should be asking 'When and how do we conduct segmentation exercises?'

EFFECTIVE SEGMENTATION: DETERMINING VIABLE MARKET SEGMENTS

For segmentation to be practical and viable, the segments should be evaluated against certain criteria. Thus, the segments should be:

- **Identifiable or differentiable:** Each segment must exhibit certain common attributes or differentiating characteristics among its members that distinguish it from the general market and warrant the use of a different marketing approach
- **Accessible:** A segment, when identified, should be easy to target and must be reachable with a specific marketing plan and in a cost-effective way. In other words, it is of no use if a potential segment cannot be served because of issues such as communication or distribution, or government or industry regulations

- **Substantial:** A segment must be viable, profitable and big enough to warrant the organization taking any action and to justify any resources needed to target such a segment
- **Measurable:** The size, profits and potential of a segment need to be measurable and known. For example, the size of the smartphone market globally is known to be huge and to be growing very fast. Being able to measure a segment enables an organization to manage that segment and also to assess its performance
- **Actionable:** The organization should be capable of developing programmes that will attract and serve the segment. For instance, a fashion retailer might divide its customers into various segments, but the reality is that it may lack the resources to reach out to all the segments. Segmentation becomes ineffective if it is not actionable

TYPES OF MARKET SEGMENTATION

The type of market is an important consideration in determining the approach to market segmentation. For example, markets may be classified as *consumer markets* (that is, business-to-consumer markets, B 2 C, or consumer-to-consumer markets, C 2 C), *business-to-business* markets (B 2 B) and *international markets*. It is important to note that there is no 'golden rule' for segmenting markets, no right or wrong approach. Marketers are free to develop their own methods depending on the outlook of their organization. They may use various **variables** or a combination of variables to identify the various segments in the overall market. Some of the bases used to segment the different types of markets are discussed below.

SEGMENTING CONSUMER MARKETS

The most common profilers or bases for segmenting consumer markets are **demographic**, geographical, psychological and behavioural profilers (see Figure 5.2).

Demographic segmentation

Demographic segmentation is people-based and utilizes a number of demographic variables. These are mainly descriptive variables and are often used for initial profiling of segments before other types of variable are deployed. For example, age, gender and family size could influence what consumers buy, and how, where and when they buy. Therefore, demographic variables include:

- **Age:** Segmenting consumers on the basis of age bands such as under 6, 12–19, 35–49, 65 and above
- **Gender:** Classifying consumer groups by sex
- **Family size:** Classifying on the basis of the number of people constituting a family unit, e.g. families of 1–2, 3–4, 5 and above
- **Family lifecycle:** Examples may include young and single, young and married with no children, young and married with children, older and married with children, older and married with no children at home
- **Other demographic variables:** These include income, occupation/job type, nationality and religion

Demographic factors should be a vital consideration when segmenting consumer markets and outlining marketing strategies because consumer wants and needs, and even their uptake, depend to a large extent on demographics.

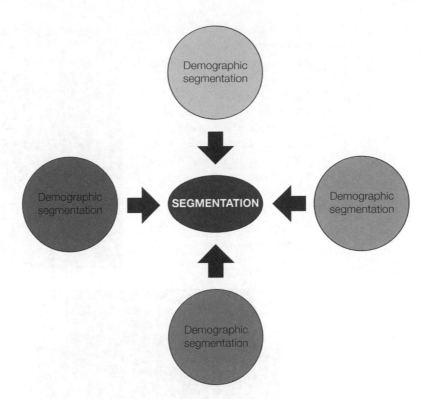

Figure 5.2: Bases for consumer market segmentation

Geographical segmentation

Physical location or location characteristics often influence the sort of product or services demanded by consumers. This means that geographical variables can be important value differentiators and include:

- **Region:** nation, continent, country, state, city or town, etc.
- **Size:** area size, population size, rate of growth, etc.
- **Population density:** rural, suburban, urban, etc.
- **Climate:** for example, weather patterns common to certain geographic regions

It is most likely that geographical frontiers can bring about significant differences in customers' demands, culture, tastes and lifestyle. An organization may therefore decide to operate in one or some of the identified geographical areas. Alternatively, the organization may decide to operate in all the geographical areas but must be mindful of differences in the needs and wants of customers in different areas. Geographical segmentation can influence the strategies of an organization or the marketing mix developed for each chosen segment. For instance, it might influence them in terms of pricing, product development, distribution or communication techniques. Can you think of examples where this might be the case?

Psychological segmentation

Consumers may be segmented according to intangible variables such as personality characteristics, social class and lifestyle (see Figure 5.3).

These characteristics affect the buying behaviour and decision-making processes of consumers and include their values, attitudes, beliefs, opinions, interests, intentions and self-image. For instance, a consumer may be seen as a 'socialite', 'traditionalist', 'rebellious grandmother', 'high-maintenance housewife', 'successful businessman' and so on. You also hear people say things like 'I enjoy active sport', 'I like classical music', or 'I go out most evenings'. These portray the personality, social class and lifestyle of consumers and form segments into which they can be divided.

istock © gregepperson

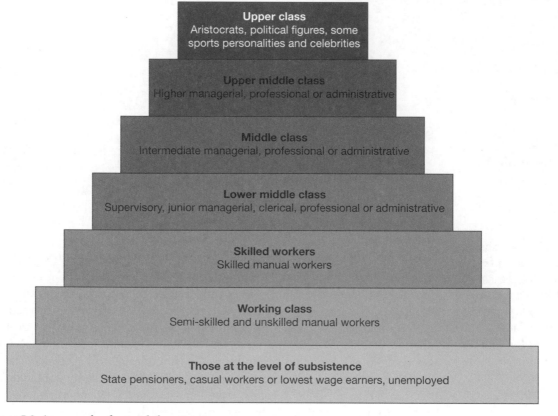

Upper class
Aristocrats, political figures, some sports personalities and celebrities

Upper middle class
Higher managerial, professional or administrative

Middle class
Intermediate managerial, professional or administrative

Lower middle class
Supervisory, junior managerial, clerical, professional or administrative

Skilled workers
Skilled manual workers

Working class
Semi-skilled and unskilled manual workers

Those at the level of subsistence
State pensioners, casual workers or lowest wage earners, unemployed

Figure 5.3: An example of a social class structure

Behavioural segmentation

People express market-mediated values differently and marketplace behaviours are an expression of some deep-rooted values that consumers may hold. Therefore, behavioural segmentation is based on the behaviour of consumers towards products. This includes their attitude and knowledge, uses and response to or of a particular product.

It is quite a helpful tool as it makes use of variables that are linked to the product. Examples include:

- **Benefits sought:** Such as reliability, social benefits, economic benefits, environmental friendliness and time saving
- **Usage rate:** Heavy versus light users, frequent versus occasional users
- **User status:** Such as regular, potential, first-time, non-users, ex-users
- **Purchase occasion:** Certain events encourage purchases, such as Christmas, Eid, Father's Day, weddings and so on
- **Brand loyalty:** Complete loyalty, somewhat loyal, no loyalty
- **Price consciousness:** High versus low as regards the extent to which consumers search for and pay low prices in the marketplace

SEGMENTING BUSINESS MARKETS

How business markets are segmented may be different from what obtains in consumer markets. Business markets consist of buyers who may be individuals (buying for the purpose of further production) or organizations. However, in comparison with consumer markets, business markets are usually fewer in number and involve larger purchases. They also evaluate product offerings in depth (rationality in buying behaviour) and the various decision makers make decisions jointly. Thus, though segmentation can be applied to business markets, the variables used are likely to differ from those used in consumer markets. The variables frequently used to segment business markets are outlined below and shown in Figure 5.4.

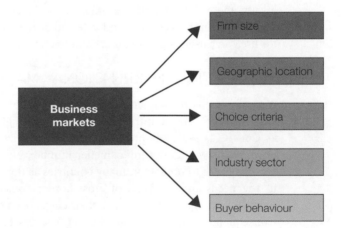

Figure 5.4: Factors to consider when segmenting business markets

Firm size

Criteria used here include the number of employees, market share and turnover or capital employed. The size of firm is significant because it can identify buying/ usage rates, demand and buying processes employed. For instance, smaller firms are more likely to have less formal purchasing processes than larger firms while larger businesses are more likely to purchase products in larger quantities. However, this method has to be treated with caution because a large company will not necessarily purchase large quantities of the product.

Geographic location

Geographic criteria as a basis for segmenting markets may be factors such as rural or urban location, developed or developing country, regions, communities and so on. This segmentation enables sales territories to be identified around certain locations that salespeople can serve easily, and new or small businesses attempting to establish themselves usually use geographic criteria as a basis for market segmentation. However, with the increase in the channels for distribution and communication of products resulting from the Internet, this method is decreasingly relevant.

Choice criteria

An organization may segment its business market on the basis of the type of products the customer seeks. For instance, an estate agent may segment its clients according to businesses that buy properties for use as offices and those that rent office space.

Industry sector

The market may be grouped into retail, services and manufacturing sectors and businesses may also be classified according to the activities they undertake, such as fashion, electronics, food or entertainment. Industry segmentation is useful as the different sectors may have distinct needs for a product. For instance, health care providers, retailers, educational institutions and local governments will have different needs within the computer hardware and software market.

Buyer behaviour

An organization can segment its business customers according to their usage rate, loyalty and order size, among other factors. Examples here would include having segments for non-users and moderate and heavy users. There could also be segments for first-time users, potential users and frequent users.

SEGMENTING INTERNATIONAL MARKETS

A small number of companies can afford the resources and have the will to do business in all or most countries in the world. Though some large organizations such as Coca-Cola sell their products in more than 200 countries, most international businesses pay attention to a smaller number. New challenges exist for businesses that may wish to operate in many countries as there will be wide-ranging variances in the needs and lifestyles of cross-border consumers. Countries, even if close together, can significantly vary in their cultural, economic or political **composition**. Consequently, just as in consumer and business-to-business markets, international businesses need to divide their world market into segments possessing distinctive needs and behaviours. Thus, market segmentation is also crucial in international markets.

Businesses carry out international market segmentation to enable them to conduct country screening and generalize their market research findings, entry decisions and marketing mix policy across a few segments instead of every market. This enables the organization to allocate its scarce resources and determine its positioning strategy. International market segmentation involves grouping countries with similar traits and characteristics together. Some common bases for segmenting the international market are explored below.

Geographic location

Geographic segmentation involves grouping countries into regions such as Africa, Eastern Europe and the Middle East. It is often assumed that countries close to each other will possess similar behaviours, traits, cultural patterns and climatic conditions, so that an organization can develop different strategies and products for each group. However, there are always exceptions, a good example being the US and Mexico, which share a border and yet differ economically and culturally. International market segmentation also offers a convenient organizational structure with regard to administration and cost (Wind and Douglas, 2001) to the advantage of the organization.

Socio-economic factors

Socio-economic factors include level of industrialization, income levels, education levels, rate of economic growth and standard of living. A country's socio-economic composition influences the needs of its people and consequently the potential marketing opportunities. For instance, a region with low standards of living may not have a mass market for luxury goods such as sophisticated electronic products. Also, countries with high literacy and education levels will constitute a better market for medical and health products than countries with lower levels.

Example 5.2:
What class are you?

For a long time, marketers have struggled to come to terms with how to classify consumers in order to work out the potential size of market segments. In the past, consumers used to be classified according to their values and lifestyles, occupation, wealth or education, or through the use of a raft of other economic and socio-demographic variables. Two of the prevalent classification models include 'ABC1' and 'C2', and upper class, middle class and working class. (You are probably familiar with other techniques and the associated proportions of the total population.)

In April 2013, a BBC Lab UK study measured economic capital (income, savings, house value), social capital (the number and status of people someone knows) and cultural capital (the extent and nature of cultural interests and activities). This resulted in seven new classifications, which are:

- **Elite:** The most privileged group in the UK, distinct from the other six classes because of its wealth. This group has the highest levels of all three capitals

- **Established middle class:** The second wealthiest, scoring highly on all three capitals. The largest and most gregarious group, scoring second highest for cultural capital

- **Technical middle class:** A small, distinctive new class group which is prosperous but scores low for social and cultural capital. Distinguished by its social isolation and cultural apathy

- **New affluent workers:** A young class group which is socially and culturally active, with middling levels of economic capital

- **Traditional working class:** Scores low on all forms of capital, but is not completely deprived. Its members have reasonably high house values, explained by this group having the highest average age at 66

- **Emergent service workers:** A new, young, urban group which is relatively poor but has high social and cultural capital

- **Precariat, or precarious proletariat:** The poorest, most deprived class, scoring low for social and cultural capital (about 15 per cent of the population)

Source: Classification taken from http://www.bbc.co.uk/news/uk-22007058

Political and legal factors

Political and legal factors include the type and stability of government, amount of **bureaucracy**, openness to foreign businesses, and monetary regulations, among others. These factors can dictate and influence market demand and opportunities: for instance, placing tariffs and taxes on certain luxury goods will generally weaken the demand for such goods and limit the market to people with higher incomes.

Cultural factors

Cultural factors include common religion, customs and values, beliefs and languages.

This list of bases for segmentation assumes that segments should be made up of clusters of countries. However, a different method, known as intermarket **segmentation**, is used by many international businesses. In this approach, segments are based on consumers who have similar buying needs and behaviour irrespective of their location. For instance, Rolls-Royce targets very rich people in the world while Dark and Lovely hair products target black women around the world.

BENEFITS OF MARKET SEGMENTATION

Whether for consumer, business-to-business or international markets, segmentation affords the marketing organization and its customers benefits without which the segmentation exercise would become pointless. The likely benefits from market segmentation are outlined below.

Effective product strategy

Segmentation forms the basis upon which an organization creates and reviews products and market offerings to make them more suited to the needs of the market. In other words, successful segmentation can inform an organization's product range, product development or merchandizing, thus giving the organization a competitive advantage.

Adequate marketing plan

Segmentation makes available adequate information on the unique needs of customers and helps the organization to develop an effective marketing plan.

Think and discuss

Choose an organization and discuss how it has applied segmentation with reference to its products. How has the organization benefited from market segmentation?

New marketing opportunities

Segmentation enables an organization to distinguish one customer group from another and this could lead to identifying new market segments. For organizations seeking such opportunities, this would lead to greater product differentiation and product variety and consequently greater market share.

Customer-oriented marketing and increased customer satisfaction

The formation of the marketing mix is based on the specified needs of a market segment, enabling an organization to satisfy the needs of its potential customers better. This can lead to greater sales and profitability, thus shaping the future performance of the organization.

Optimal use of resources

Segmentation enables an organization to focus its resources, including its marketing message, on the market segments that have the greatest potential for success. In other words, only the relevant segment(s) are targeted and this helps to reduce the cost of doing business for the organization.

MARKET TARGETING

After segmenting a market to identify segment opportunities, the firm now needs to evaluate each segment and determine how many and which segments to serve. Put simply, a company will have to reflect upon which needs it should serve, which consumer values to address and how well it can profitably or successfully help consumers to maximize the value sought in a market transaction.

EVALUATING MARKET SEGMENTS

To evaluate different market segments, an organization must consider two main factors, namely the overall attractiveness of the segment, and the firm's objectives and resources.

Overall attractiveness of the segment

An organization must first of all determine how attractive the segment is in terms of its size and potential growth and profitability. However, this criterion is subjective because its having the right size and growth potential does not necessarily mean it is an attractive and suitable segment for every organization. It may well be that the segment is too competitive or that the organization has limited resources and skills to cater for it. In this case, it might be more reasonable to target seemingly less attractive or smaller segments which potentially are more profitable to the organization. Also, the organization has to evaluate the attractiveness of the segment in terms of its structure and to consider the factors that are likely to influence long-term attractiveness. Examples of such factors would include the existence of strong and aggressive competitors, the buying power of customers, the presence of many actual or potential substitute products and the presence of powerful suppliers.

The organization's objectives and resources

It is possible that an attractive segment is incompatible with the objectives of an organization or it may be that the organization does not have the necessary resources or capabilities to serve the segment. It is advisable that an organization enters segments where it can fulfil its objectives and offer superior value in order to gain competitive advantage.

MARKET–TARGETING APPROACHES

Once it has evaluated the various segments, an organization can decide which segment(s) it wants to serve and determine its level of involvement with the market. It may very well decide that no substantial segments exist and thus it will cover the entire market with one basic product. This is referred to as an 'undifferentiated marketing strategy' or UMS. Alternatively, the organization may discover some substantial segments and decide to serve all those identified, just a few or only one of the identified segments using different products or a single product. Once segments have been identified, the organization needs to select the approach it is going to use to target them. Common approaches are outlined below.

Undifferentiated marketing strategy

Undifferentiated marketing is also known as *mass marketing*. In this case, an organization ignores the differences between market segments and offers one product to the entire market without any form of differentiation. In order words, the organization does not exploit consumer differences but rather concentrates on what is common to all the consumers. Consequently, the company uses a single marketing mix to cater for the needs of the whole market. By implication, the entire market is treated as a **homogeneous** mass whose needs are met using mass production, mass advertising and mass distribution to serve as many customers as possible. The Post Office's services and staple foods (such as salt and sugar) are obvious examples of the use of UMS to target the market as a whole as there is limited variability within the market.

An advantage associated with this strategy is that it entails relatively low costs because only a single marketing mix is needed to serve a large market whereas the other strategies require more research and periodic updating. Also, because the company uses one product to serve a potentially large market, economies of scale can be maximized. However, a UMS can only be

istock © erminawaters

sustained where demand significantly exceeds supply or in situations of monopoly. When demand decreases or competition is introduced, especially from more focused competitors, such a strategy becomes untenable. Where there is competition, what tends to happen in reality is that some customers will like the product while others will not because it is probably impossible to please everyone. This situation divides the market and automatically creates an 'unintended' segment. However, because the organization has not specifically targeted this unintended segment, its product might not exactly suit the needs of the segment and any competitor who has specifically targeted the segment will attract those customers.

As already noted, pleasing everyone is likely to be impossible so this strategy might be most suitable when products have little psychological appeal – such as in the cases of drinking water, petrol or salt, which we use regularly but to which we attach little psychological importance. For instance, we buy petrol without even seeing it. Our main concern is that it makes our car move regardless of the make or brand of car we drive. Similarly, we purchase table salt with little care except to assume it will fulfil its basic function of adding taste to our food. These sorts of products mostly have a functional importance rather than a psychological bias and the only differences between brands are price, branding, packaging and advertising. Nonetheless, it is important to note that an undifferentiated marketing approach is becoming rarer with the ever changing marketplace and increasing competition. Products that used to exemplify an undifferentiated method no longer do so and variations now exist, possibly in response to market demands. See Table 5.1.

Table 5.1: Differentiation in previously undifferentiated markets

Differentiation in the bottled drinking water market	Differentiation in the petrol market	Differentiation in the salt market
Still water • Spring water • Purified water • Mineral water Sparkling water (also called carbonated or fizzy) • Spring water • Purified water • Mineral water Flavoured water (wide variety exists)	Differentiating the petrol itself • Unleaded • Leaded Differentiating extended products • Providing mini supermarkets • Providing car services such as car wash, change of oil, tyre air pumps • Providing cash machines	Table salt Cooking salt Low-sodium salt Iodized salt Garlic salt Celery salt Sea salt

Differentiated marketing strategy

Differentiated marketing is also known as *segmented marketing*. Here, the organization chooses to operate in a number of market segments. This requires that different products are designed to suit the particular needs of each segment. A differentiated marketing strategy is used in sectors such as the cosmetics, personal hygiene, food, airlines, fashion, mobile phones and car markets. In the automobile industry, for instance, companies target a variety of segments using a range of options such as engine size, automatic or manual transmission, petrol or diesel engine, upholstery and status add-ons (customized, exclusive models). In the personal hygiene market, Colgate's website (http://www.colgate.co.uk/app/Colgate/UK/OralCare/Product Recommender/Toothpaste.cvsp) shows that it has about 26 toothpaste ranges for adults. With regard to the breakfast cereal market, Kellogg's has about 29 brands of cereal and there is also variety within most of the brands in content, taste and size.

An advantage of serving various market segments is that companies anticipate higher sales and a stronger market position within each segment. Having a stronger position in several segments generates more total sales than undifferentiated marketing across all segments (Kotler et al., 2008). In essence, the combined market offerings or brands of a company give it greater market share than any one brand could attain across the entire market. Also, this strategy helps to maintain customer satisfaction as it enables an organization to match its products to the needs of individual segments. In addition, it spreads a company's risk across the market so that if there is a negative change in one segment, the company can still generate revenue from the other segments.

However, differentiated marketing has its downside in terms of increasing the cost of doing business. Research and development for this strategy is more cost intensive than for the other targeting strategies. Also, developing separate marketing plans for different segments and trying to reach these various segments with a different marketing mix increase operational cost with likely **diseconomies** of scale. Companies must therefore weigh their increase in sales against their increase in costs to ensure that using this strategy remains worthwhile and profitable.

Concentrated marketing strategy

Also known as **niche** marketing, a concentrated marketing strategy means that the organization chooses to cater for and concentrate on one or in some cases a few of the market segments. The aim of this strategy is to specialize in serving the chosen segment more effectively and efficiently than the competitors. Organizations that employ this strategy are those that have limited resources to fund their

istock © PaulVinten

chosen strategy (for example, small businesses) or those that simply want to adopt a very exclusive marketing strategy (for example, Rolls-Royce cars or yacht manufacturers, which tend to serve the high-income market segment exclusively).

An advantage of concentrated marketing is that the company can acquire a reputation as a specialist in the market. Consequently, the company attains a strong market position because of its greater knowledge of customers' needs within the niche it serves. Also, costs can be kept down as this strategy requires a single marketing mix to be managed for the niche segment chosen. Many operating economies are enjoyed due to the company's specialization in production, promotion and distribution. If the segment is chosen well, concentrated marketing can be highly profitable with a high rate of return on investment.

However, concentrated marketing does involve higher than normal risks because any change in the market can leave the company vulnerable if there is no fallback arrangement. Such changes could be the entry of capable or stronger competitors into the segment, or a significant change in the purchasing power or buying behaviour of members of the segment. Many companies therefore choose to diversify into several market segments to avoid 'putting all their eggs in one basket'.

Customized marketing strategy

Customized marketing, the newest strategy, is also known as *micro marketing*. Here, a marketing strategy is created for customers individually instead of for each market segment. In other words, each customer is dealt with individually as a 'segment' and to some degree customers are allowed to create their own products. This strategy is more often used in business-to-business marketing (such as in advertising services or market research) or in highly customized products (such as custom-made cars

The automobile industry is probably one of the most adversely affected by the recent economic recession. However, the industry is fighting back and many of the key players are 'pulling all the stunts' to get back on the winning side. Honda is a clear example of how some of the car makers are revamping their marketing strategies, using segmentation approaches in order to gain competitive advantage. Honda, with a 5 per cent share of the UK market, previously dedicated its market-ing budget to product-led, tactical advertising, which seems to have neglected the 'values' driving purchase decisions. This meant that it was only able to target 5 per cent of people actively looking to buy a car at any one time. In the heat of the reces-sion, Honda saw marketing as a huge cost but the mindset is now changing as the company begins to invest significantly in brand marketing – thus demonstrating a clear awareness of 'why' people are actually attracted to the brand. For example, Honda is switching focus and targeting the proportion of the 95 per cent of non-buyers who have key roles as influencers in buying decisions.

or tailored clothing). Other good examples are some computer manufacturers, such as Dell and Cisco, whose modular design and customized manufactur-ing permit the production of individually made-to-order products according to customer specification. These businesses are successfully using this strategy to create more value for their customers and gain competitive advantage for themselves. However, this strategy requires an elaborate system for ascertaining information on the needs and wants of individual customers. In addition, there is a need for a highly flexible system of production and a strong direct-to-customer logistic system (Zipkin, 2001). These can prove expensive and time consuming for an organization and, even then, not all customers are willing to pay for such customization.

CONSIDERATIONS FOR CHOOSING A TARGETING STRATEGY

Having considered some of the advantages and disadvantages of the various target-ing approaches, we should bear in mind that there are a number of other factors that may influence a company's targeting strategy. These include:

- **An organization's resources:** No matter how 'perfect' a strat-egy is, if an organization does not have adequate resources to support and maintain it, then it simply needs to find an alter-native. For example, instead of adopting a differentiated strategy, a small organization may be better advised to adopt a concentrated strategy until it has grown sufficiently to take on a greater coverage of the market

istock © peatalin

Think and discuss

Pick a particular market targeting strategy. Under what circumstances would an organization use such a strategy? Illustrate your answer with examples.

- **Nature of the product:** Certain products suit certain approaches better. For example, products that have high variability and can be varied in several ways, such as cosmetics and mobile phones, tend to be more suited to a differentiated or concentrated strategy

- **Product lifecycle:** The product's stage in its lifecycle affects the choice of strategy for targeting a segment. For example, where a product is still at its introductory stage and neither the customer nor the organization has previous experience of it, it would be more reasonable to use an undifferentiated or concentrated approach. This would allow the company to gain practical knowledge of the behaviour and reaction of the market towards the product. Later, at a mature stage of the product's lifecycle when the organization has learnt from experience, it would become reasonable to use differentiated marketing, especially as competitors might start entering the market

- **Nature of the market:** Where there are no real differences in a market and the market variability is low, an undifferentiated strategy would be more appropriate. Instances would include where most customers have the same tastes, purchase the same quantity and respond similarly to marketing efforts. However, where the market variability is quite high, it becomes more reasonable to use strategies such as the differentiated or concentrated targeting approaches

- **Competitors' marketing approach:** It could be suicidal for an organization to make strategic decisions in isolation from the activities of its competitors. For example, implementing an undifferentiated approach when your competitors are using a differentiated approach might be disastrous. Also, given the existence of competition, an organization can identify the segments where the competition is strong and then consider whether to compete in the same segment or to find another segment that would be more favourable to it (Brassington and Pettitt, 2006).

POSITIONING THE PRODUCT OFFERING

Having divided the market into smaller groups and determined the size and potential of each (*segmentation*), and having also chosen particular target markets (*targeting*), the third and last stage of the STP process should then position a product offering in the target market(s). This is known as positioning. Lancaster et al. (2002) define positioning as 'the act of designing a company's product and marketing mix to fit a given place in the mind of the consumer'. Positioning deals with all the activities undertaken by an organization to create and maintain in the minds of customers the concept of value about its product compared with competitors' products. It enables businesses to distinguish their products in the minds of their customers. According to Ries and Trout (2001), positioning is not about what you do to a product, but about what you do to the mind of a prospect. It concerns the perception that a product produces in the mind of customers when compared with competitors' products and even with other products from the same organization. Perception varies from person to person. For instance, what you perceive as quite expensive might be easily affordable to someone from a richer background or who earns much more than you do. Also, what you perceive as fashionable will be different from your mother's perception or that of a friend of yours. However, it is important to note that there might be similarities in perception among different people.

For positioning to take place, the organization has to determine the basis on which it wishes to compete in its target segment(s). It has to decide how best to combine its assets and competencies in order to create a unique product in the market. There is often an overload of product information that consumers have to cope with and they can only filter this information to distinguish a product based on their perceptions of such products. Positioning should therefore enable consumers to assign a particular position to the product relative to other products in the market. For instance, in the car industry, the Mercedes could be seen as a luxurious car while the Ford may be seen as a more affordable brand. Coca-Cola may occupy a different position from Pepsi in the mind of a consumer. A product can thus acquire its position for a variety of reasons, including product attributes, product origin, usage occasions, product benefits and competitors (Drummond and Ensor, 2000).

The characteristics of a product, the nature of communication about the product and the way these elements merge in the customer's mind play a role in successful positioning. Factors that are therefore crucial for successful positioning include (Drummond and Ensor, 2000):

- **Competitiveness:** The organization should have a unique selling proposition (USP) for the product. In other words, the product should offer benefits that competitors cannot offer to consumers. Why would one decide to fly with British Airways instead of Virgin Atlantic or KLM? Why eat a burger from McDonald's instead of from Burger King or KFC? Why drive a Ford Escape instead of a Toyota RAV4 or a Honda CR-V? Whatever the reason, it might just be the USP the company is offering consumers that competitors cannot offer
- **Credibility:** The target audience has to perceive the attributes used to position the product as believable. For instance, positioning Harrods as a luxury brand is quite believable while it would prove quite a difficult task to position Primark as such
- **Clarity:** The organization's positioning statement has to create a distinct position in the minds of its target market for the product. It should also be a clear value proposition. Statements such as 'Obey your thirst' (Sprite) and 'Every little helps' (Tesco) offer clear value statements to consumers

Think and discuss

Think of breakfast cereals – Kellogg's, Nestlé, Jordans, Quaker Oats, Weetabix or shop brand cereals. Which of these brands do you prefer and why do you buy them? What position do they hold in your mind?

Example 5.4:
'Guardian bids to change press ad model'

This was the headline adopted by the weekly marketing magazine *Marketing Week* (13 November 2012, p. 8) to bring into the open the revolutionary changes in segmentation planning strategy being implemented by *The Guardian* newspaper. *The Guardian* is one of the UK's leading print media companies, with an audience reach of 3.4 million of a possible 12.7 million 'progressive adult' readers. In contrast to other newspapers, *The Guardian*'s audience profile is upwardly mobile and young readers who are sensitive to ethical issues and are willing to spend on new products. *The Guardian*, according to *Marketing Week*, is hoping to leverage its position as the UK's leading quality newspaper in terms of total audience size and 'to boost press spend by making buying advertising with newspaper brands more similar to the way TV trading works'. Put simply, this means changing the way the newspaper sells advertising – which will now focus on audiences rather than platforms (newspaper, desktop, mobile and tablet). This shift of focus signals a more customer-centric approach to marketing and the development of targeting and differentiation strategies around the audience (final consumer) values.

- **Consistency:** The organization's message should be consistent over time as this helps to establish a position against competitors. Regularly changing one's positioning confuses consumers as it makes it unclear what exactly the key attributes and functions of the product are.

POSITIONING MAPS

Positioning maps are also called **perceptual** maps. They are graphs that help to show the relationship between competitors' offerings and the criteria that consumers use when making purchase decisions. In addition, a positioning map enables an organization to know where consumers place them in relation to its competitors. Thus, this tool enables different product offerings to be 'mapped' together so that they can be compared and contrasted. Because they naturally think of particular features when thinking of any product, consumers already have some sort of perceptual map in their minds about one product or the other.

A simple and basic positioning map is plotted on two axes, which represent key variables. Each axis is labelled depending on the products being compared. For example, the variables could be quality (variable 1) and price (variable 2), or efficiency (variable 1) and durability (variable 2). Individual products are then plotted according to these variables. See Figure 5.6, which is a template for a basic positioning map. A more complex positioning map would have more axes and variables used as a basis for comparison.

A major strength of this tool is that it can be used to establish the current situation in the market and identify gaps that an organization could regard as possible areas for new products. For instance, in Figure 5.6, the upper left quadrant is not occupied by any product. Assuming the variables plotted on the axes were high (quality) and low (price), then the gap would not be surprising as these two levels of variables do not usually go hand in hand. An organization may, however, due to its massive economies of scale or as a low-cost strategy, be able to provide high-quality but low-cost products to consumers.

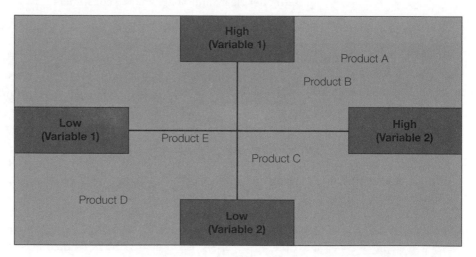

Figure 5.5: A basic positioning map

CONCLUSION

In this chapter, the main value-oriented marketing and customer-driven strategies adopted by companies were explored. These include segmentation, targeting and positioning, which respectively deal with creating significant customer groups in the markets the company wishes to serve, deciding which groups of customers the company should serve and then positioning the company's products or services in the minds of the target customers.

Various types of market segmentation exist including consumer market, business market and international market segmentation and the bases for segmenting in each of these markets were discussed. It was also noted in this chapter that after due evaluation and identification of target markets, companies can use a number of targeting approaches such as undifferentiated marketing strategy, differentiated marketing strategy, concentrated marketing strategy and customised marketing strategy to target their chosen group. Having done that, the company then has to position its offerings in such a way that its products and services create and maintain in customers' minds the concept of value when compared with competitors' products. However, certain crucial factors like the competitiveness of the organization, credibility of product and clarity and consistency of the organization's message have to be present for positioning to be successful.

Undertaking the STP process is one of the most crucial processes companies should undertake both at the onset of a new offer creation and as part of a periodic revision of their offerings and strategies, in order to maintain a value creation and delivery sequence.

Some of the benefits of adopting the STP process include enabling companies to meet customers' needs in addition to identifying new growth opportunities and anticipating changes in the marketplace. It also provides companies with direction and focus for marketing strategies, which strengthens their competitive positions and wards off competition. In addition, companies are able to save costs by more efficiently and effectively matching their resources to targeted market segments.

The STP process is the essence of a value-oriented marketing strategy and, used well, this process not only creates value for the customers but can also significantly contribute to overall company success.

5

Case study
Coca-Cola

FOUNDED IN 1886, THE COCA-COLA COMPANY IS the world's top producer, marketer and distributor of non-alcoholic beverages. It operates in over 200 countries with a vast portfolio of nearly 400 brands and over 3,500 products. It is, however, most famous for its original and landmark soft drink, Coke, other major brands including Fanta, Sprite, Diet Coke and Coke Zero.

Initially, Coca-Cola used a single product – Coca-Cola – and a single size to provide for the mass market. However, this made it more susceptible to competition. In fact, some time in the 1950s, Coca-Cola lost its position as the leading seller of cola drinks in supermarkets to Pepsi-Cola when Pepsi began offering several container sizes. Over time, Coca-Cola has realized that everyone has different choices and it has tailored different products to target and satisfy a variety of groups of consumers in order to stay ahead of the competition. Coca-Cola thus embarks on continuous research to identify these unique groups and to facilitate a successful value-oriented marketing strategy and product development. With increased competition and the ever changing needs and lifestyle of consumers, Coca-Cola's success depends on its ability to provide consumers with a wide variety of options to meet their differing desires, needs and lifestyles choices.

The existing trend for healthier living means consumers are becoming more health conscious and desiring more healthy drinks. In 1982, Coca-Cola launched Diet Coke, which is a sugar-free, low-calorie drink. Although not purposefully aimed at women, females contributed to 80 per cent of Diet Coke sales. A study of male customers showed that men also wanted a low-calorie drink but thought Diet Coke was designed for women since it was traditionally bought by women who wanted to lose weight. Thus they were put off by the feminine image of the drink. In 2005, Coca-Cola's response to this finding came in the form of Coke Zero, which was targeted at young male adults and perceived as a more masculine drink. In 2007, in a bid to attract consumers to nutritional benefits, Diet Coke Plus was introduced. This is a sweeter version of Diet Coke but fortified with vitamins and minerals. Although Coca-Cola generally portrays itself as a drink for the fun-loving youth or young adult, it also uses these sugar-free, low-calorie products to target the elderly, the diabetic, the obese and anyone who is generally health conscious.

Coca-Cola also ascertains the consumption pattern of consumers in terms of where and how particular products are consumed in order to design suitable pack types and sizes. For instance, a two-litre bottle can be consumed at a get-together or by a family at home and a 500 ml bottle consumed on the move. More recently, in 2012, there was a launch of a 375 ml bottle of the MyCoke trilogy. After conducting research into how consumers consume Coca-Cola when they are out and about, Coca-Cola

istock © AlexStar

found out that consumers wanted more choice in addition to having a clear desire to have another size option between the 500 ml bottle and the 330 ml can. Hence the birth of the 375 ml bottle in Britain, which, according to the Market Activation Director Zoe Howorth, 'offers consumers a handy, pocket size Coca-Cola, Diet Coke or Coke Zero to satisfy their thirst at great value'.

Coca-Cola comes in a variety of cans and glass and plastic bottles, with sizes ranging from 150 ml to 3 l and suitable for various occasions. Different types of packaging can be used to target consumers who have different usage rates of Coca-Cola products. For instance, while the large, economy bottles can be marketed to heavy and regular users of the product, the smaller pack sizes can be targeted at light users, or first-time or one-off consumers of Coca-Cola. Packaging can also be used to target consumers with various income levels. For instance, in Kenya, the 200 ml bottle was introduced to address issues of affordability and deepen Coca-Cola's presence in the low-end market during the period of high inflation which eroded purchasing power among low income earners. Likewise, the large, economy bottles can also be targeted at low-income earners as offering greater value for money.

It is important to note at this point that the Coca-Cola Company operates a geographical structure comprising a corporate head office and six pan-global, operating strategic business units (SBUs). This structure recognizes that markets are geographically divided and are at different phases of development. It also recognizes that income, lifestyle, taste, climate, political environment, culture and consumption vary from place to place. Consequently, even though the company thinks globally, it acts locally, bearing in mind regional or country market preferences. This enables it to adapt its marketing mix to suit specific markets. Thus, while the general image of Coca-Cola may be the same across the world, the formulations and ingredients of products are modified according to local tastes.

Also, within certain limitations, the packaging, advertising and promotion may differ from one country to another and in some cases a product may be developed solely for one country. This is the case for the Coca-Cola product Lilt, which is available only in Great Britain and Ireland, and Kuat, which is only available in Brazil. In other instances, even labelled with the same product name, the Coca-Cola Coke in the USA would have a different formulation from that sold in Spain or Nigeria, and the type of advertisements shown in India or China would differ from those shown in the UK.

Within these significant differences in consumer needs and preferences, Coca-Cola endeavours to apply flexibility in order to add value to its services and product offerings and to satisfy the needs of the market.

Questions

1 Why does Coca-Cola, a globally known company, have so many products?
2 Using the case study as a guide, which bases of segmentation are relevant to Coca-Cola's value-oriented marketing strategy?
3 What targeting strategy has Coca-Cola adopted?

Review questions

1 What is market segmentation?
2 Discuss the main bases for the segmentation of customer, business and international markets.
3 Describe how organizations might evaluate the attractiveness of a market segment.
4 Discuss the various market-targeting strategies available to businesses. Use suitable examples to illustrate your points.
5 Explain the concept of positioning.
6 If you were the marketing manager of a five-star hotel, what factors would you consider as crucial to position your organization successfully?
7 When you decide to shop for clothes, what shops do you initially consider? Why do you include these shops as alternatives? Do any of the shops get eliminated along the way and, if so, why? What could those in charge of marketing at the eliminated shops do to keep themselves under consideration?

Group task

Construct a basic perceptual map based on your knowledge of ten different universities. Choose two distinguishing attributes or variables for the map's axes. Bear in mind that there is no right or wrong answer because a perceptual map is designed to visualize consumer perceptions of products. Afterwards, compare your map with those of others and discuss the following:

1 Why do you think the attributes chosen are important? Would you have chosen a different set of variables?
2 Do you think the map shows a significant difference between your perceptions of these universities?
3 How does your map differ from the maps of other students? Why do you think this difference exists?

Glossary/Key terms

Market segment: A group of customers whose needs are distinct from the needs of other groups in relation to a particular product

Perceptual map: Graphs that help to show the relationship between competitors and the criteria that their consumers use when making purchase decisions

Positioning: Creating and maintaining a place of value in the minds of customers

Segmentation: The process of breaking down the market into groups of customers with similar needs so that a business can concentrate its effort on effectively serving the needs of a selected group or groups within the market

Targeting: The process where a firm evaluates various market segments and then chooses which group(s) of customers to serve

Value oriented: The tendency for a firm to create and deliver value (benefits) to its customers.

Vocab check list for ESL students

Bureaucracy	Diseconomies	Perceptual	Segmentation
Composition	Homogeneous	Precarious	Variables
Demographic	Niche	Proletariat	

Definitions for these terms can be found in the 'Vocab Zone' of the companion website, which provides free access to the Macmillan English Dictionary online at www.palgrave.com/business/Gbadamosi

Further reading

S. S. Hassan and S. Craft (2012) 'Examining World Market Segmentation and Brand Positioning Strategies', *Journal of Consumer Marketing*, Vol. 29, No. 5, pp. 344–56
This paper identifies a link between global brand positioning and segmentation factors.

T. K. Bose (2012) 'Market Segmentation and Customer Focus Strategies and their Contribution towards Effective Value Chain Management', *International Journal of Marketing Studies*, Vol. 4, No. 3, pp. 113–21
The paper suggests that market segmentation immensely assists in delivering diversified and customized products and services to customers.

References

Brassington, F. and Pettitt, S. (2006) *Principles of Marketing* (4th edn). Harlow: Pearson Education

Drummond, G. and Ensor, J. (2000) *Strategic Marketing: Planning and Control* (Student Edition). Oxford: Butterworth-Heinemann

Kotler, P., Armstrong, G., Wong, V. and Saunders, J. (2008) *Principles of Marketing* (5th edn) (European edition). Harlow: Pearson Education

Lancaster, G., Massingham, L. and Ashford, R. (2002) *Essentials of Marketing*. Berkshire: McGraw-Hill

Lilien, G., Rangaswamy, A. and De Bruyn, A. (2013) *Principles of Marketing Engineering* (2nd edn). State College, PA: DecisionPro, Inc.

McDonald, M. and Dunbar, I. (2012) *Market Segmentation: How to Do it and How to Profit from it* (4th edn). New York, NY: John Wiley

Pride, W. and Ferrell, O. (2012) *Marketing* (16th edn). Independence, KY: Cengage Learning

Ries, A. and Trout, J. (2001) *Positioning: Battle for the Mind*. New York: McGraw-Hill

Wind, Y. and Douglas, S. (1972) 'International Market Segmentation', *European Journal of Marketing*, 16 (1), pp. 17–25

Zipkin, P. (2001) 'The Limits of Mass Customisation', *MIT Sloan Management Review* 42 (3), pp. 81–7

6 THE PRODUCT AS A POINT OF VALUE

MAKTOBA OMAR & COLLINS OSEI
EDINBURGH NAPIER UNIVERSITY
ROBERT L. WILLIAMS, JR.
SAINT MARY'S COLLEGE, NOTRE DAME
HELENA A. WILLIAMS
MAR–KADAM ASSOCIATES, BALTIMORE

CHAPTER CONTENTS

LEARNING OUTCOMES

The content of this chapter will help you to:

- Define what constitutes a product
- Understand how customers dictate the value of products
- Understand why products are classified in many different ways
- Understand why businesses carry and manage one or more product lines
- Know the difference between consumer products and business-to-business goods or products
- Understand the value of branding and positioning
- Recognize effective packaging and labelling
- Understand the importance of brands and brand equity

Marketing in action
What do David Cameron and Jaguar cars (both British products) have in common?

JUST AS THE CONSERVATIVE party had to project David Cameron as the flag bearer and the best candidate to take the country forward during the 2010 elections, manufacturers and retailers of the Jaguar XJ also market it. It is not just a luxury product, but also offers 'seductive design, intuitive technology and exhilarating performance'.

In fact these two products have more in common than is evident. For example, they both have to be 'sold'. Jaguar sells itself through its design and performance, and David Cameron sells himself by communicating with

Reproduced under terms of the Open Government Licence v1.0

the populace through various kinds of media and by physically interacting with people. The objective of the Conservative Party in 2010 was to present its product, David Cameron, as what the people needed to realize the desired change. Therefore, just as a consumer invests money or other resources to buy a physical product, the consumer also offers support in the form of a vote. They may even campaign for the candidate in order to have a particular person as their prime minister, member of parliament, student representative and so on.

INTRODUCTION

This chapter focuses on what a product is and why people and businesses buy products. Understanding what products are, what determines a product's value and how the value and ultimately the use of products dictate product classifications, all influence how products are marketed. Products are purchased because there is a need or a desire that a particular item, service, person, place or idea fulfils for a particular subset of customers. Products exist because of the value they have to these buyers. The better a product and its customer value are understood, the easier it is to package, label and market it appropriately.

WHAT ARE PRODUCTS?

A product is defined as anything that can be offered to an individual, group of people or organization for use, attention, **acquisition** or consumption to satisfy a need or want (Kotler and Armstrong, 2012). It also refers to what is received in exchange. For some products, this may not be limited to what has already been received but also what will be received in the future. For example, a purchasing decision about a high-involvement product such as a car will hinge on the confidence that there will always be parts and repair services available if necessary and that there will be a trade-in value.

Now let's look at another definition for product. A product is also defined as 'a physical good, service, idea, person, or place that is capable of offering tangible and intangible attributes that individuals or organisations regarded as so necessary, worthy or satisfying that they are prepared to exchange money, patronage or some other unit of value in order to acquire it' (Brassington and Pettitt, 2006, p. 262). This definition has been adopted in the industry because it encompasses a wide range of entities, some of which do not always come to mind when one talks about a product.

Products can be *physical goods*. This type of product is tangible and examples are books, mobile phones, computers, clothes, toys, television sets and cars. Figure 6.3 shows an example of a physical good, a Jaguar XJ car.

Service is also a product but it is intangible. If you go to a tattoo parlour, beauty salon or barber for a haircut, you are buying a (service) product.

Ideas are defined as concepts, images, thoughts, philosophies or issues. If a marriage counsellor offers a couple ideas to improve their marriage, the new ideas become products. The couple offers the counsellor something in exchange for the ideas (product), usually a fee and/or an expression of gratitude. In other words, ideas (new thoughts) were needed, offered, valued and accepted by the couple with the hope that the new way of thinking (this new product they purchased) would help them prevent further marital problems. Ideas can be sold.

A *place* can also be a product. We all know what to expect from holiday locations such as Tenerife, Gran Canaria, Ibiza and even countries as a destination. The media is saturated with travel advertisements that highlight places that promise glorious experiences.

People can also be considered products. For example, a prime minister or celebrity sports star.

Think and discuss

On a piece of paper, list at least 20 examples of what you would call a product.

6

PRODUCT AS A POINT OF VALUE

Products present *value*, both to the company offering them and to the consumer. In order to maximize the value to the consumer, it has to be the right product, and it must be available at the right time and at the right price, and in the right condition.

A birthday card will not be as valuable to the consumer if it arrives days or months after the birthday. In the same way, a consumer will not be very satisfied with a book ordered from eBay if the package arrives and is the wrong title, or some of the pages are missing, or the cover is dirty or damaged.

The satisfaction or dissatisfaction with the product depends on the marketer's promise. To use a common slogan, it depends on the extent to which the product does what it says on the tin. If the marketer's promise was not delivered, consumers may ask for a refund or seek legal advice, and this may have long-term effects on the company's brand perception. With the current rate of technological advancement and the ease of access to information, delivering what consumers perceive as good value is more challenging than ever. If what is promised is not delivered, consumers will not buy.

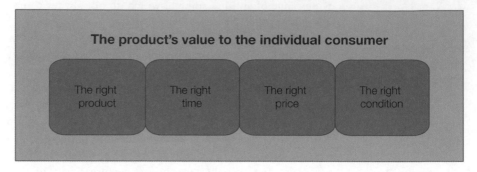

Figure 6.1: Product value to the consumer

For most products, including food, clothes and shoes, consumers are now able to check how they were produced, including whether ethical guidelines were adhered to during their manufacture. What is considered as presenting value to the consumer depends on the product in question and the individual consumer (see Figure 6.2).

For example, two different people may buy the same brand of shoes. One may be satisfied that they fit him or her and feel comfortable. The other, however, may return the product on discovering that child labour was used in their manufacture and that buying the product means they are endorsing or supporting child labour. This type of consumer, called an ethical consumer, influences products offered in The Body Shop, for example.

Figure 6.2: Product value

LEVELS OF A PRODUCT

It is a common mistake to consider only the physical elements of products such as televisions, clothes, shoes or cars as what the customer has paid for. A more useful way to explain the value or the benefits of a product is to look at its layers in order to understand its elements.

As we can see in Figure 6.3, a particular product could be explained as three different but **interrelated** layers. These are known as the core product, the actual product and the **augmented** product. The innermost part of the figure is the 'core product', which is the embodiment of the benefits that customers enjoy. It has been noticed that some small businesses do not really consider how their innovations satisfy the needs of their target market, which shows a lack of understanding of their core product (Gbadamosi, 2011). The 'actual product' contains all the elements that marketers bring together in order to be able to deliver the core product. Examples include brand name, packaging and quality. In the third layer is the 'augmented product', which offers features such as warranty, free delivery and after-sales service that distinguish the offering of a particular marketer. Knowing about these interacting layers is important in managing products competitively in the marketplace.

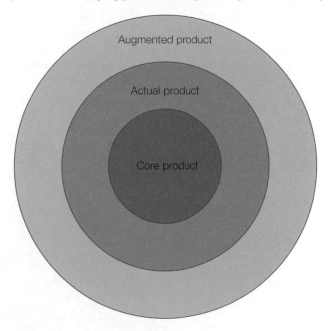

Figure 6.3: The layers of a product

6

Example 6.1:
Offering quality products at Morrisons

The role of quality in the total package of product offerings is significant to customers. It constitutes an important part of what customers perceive in the company's value proposition. This is why customer-focused firms always ensure quality is incorporated into their offerings.

An example of an organization that focuses on making quality products to satisfy its customers is Morrisons, which deals with various product lines. It bakes fresh bread every day, using traditional methods, and it is not surprising that the 'homebaked' smell from the counter attracts visitors to the products. Similarly, customers have also realized that Morrisons prepares its sandwiches in the store, which indicates that they are fresh and communicates to the customer that the retailer cares about the quality of its offer. The same customer-oriented approach applies to how the supermarket handles the 500+ varieties of fruit and vegetables that it sells. This is a clear case of how product quality is linked to customer value, which is the core focus of marketing transactions.

WAYS TO CLASSIFY PRODUCTS

Think and discuss

Make a list of some of the functional products that are used in your home every week. How often are they purchased? List any products that you have considered purchasing that would be classified as innovative. Why would they be innovative as opposed to functional?

Products are classified in various ways and one common distinction is whether a product is considered functional or innovative (see Figure 6.4). *Functional products* are acquired to satisfy basic needs. As these needs do not change significantly and there is the advantage of a long product lifecycle, it is generally easy for marketers to predict demand. That also means that the main challenge for marketers is that new competitors are easily able to enter the market. Functional products include milk, eggs, bread, toilet paper, underwear, fuel and medical services.

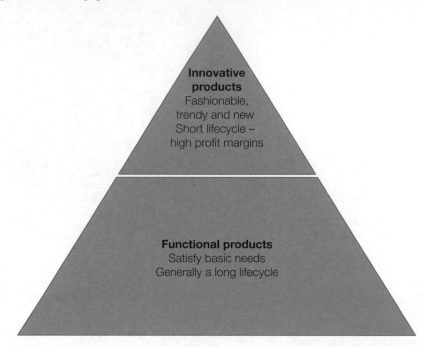

Innovative products
Fashionable, trendy and new
Short lifecycle –
high profit margins

Functional products
Satisfy basic needs
Generally a long lifecycle

Figure 6.4: Classifying products as innovative or functional

Innovative products tend to be fashionable and trendy and to have relatively short lifecycles. New products often fall into this category. The risks for innovative products are very high and demand is also high and variable. However, innovative products can generate very high profit margins, which compensate for the shorter lifecycle. An example can be found in the various innovations and modifications that have taken place in the mobile phone space.

Consumer products are acquired to satisfy the needs of individuals, friends, families and acquaintances. *Business-to-business products* are acquired as part of the operations of an organization or to be used as parts for other products that are for sale. Some products can be used both by individuals and businesses. See Figure 6.5.

From a management perspective, this classification is more useful because it helps in formulating the marketing strategy, since targeting an individual is different from targeting a business (or industrial) organization. Some products may be purchased both as consumer products and at the same time as business-to-business products. For example, a consumer may walk into WHSmith for a box of paper for domestic use. At the same time, an organization such as the National Union of Students may

Example 6.2:
The ethical consumer

The Body Shop business model is built on knowing that the customer's purchasing decision does not only hinge on the physical beauty that is derived from the product, but also on its inner beauty, which is described as coming from the heart. The Body Shop's ethical policies mean that it:

- Does not test its products on animals – it believes this is an example of animal cruelty, which the company detests
- Sources its raw materials from Fairtrade suppliers, from all parts of the world, that demonstrate commitment to caring for farmers and the environment
- Encourages self-esteem through evidence of LOVE ('Learning is Of Value to Everyone') towards its staff. Through this initiative, it

sponsors various learning schemes for staff to develop their skills and achieve self-confidence. The Body Shop also encourages staff to do good within their communities through various volunteering activities

- Actively supports human rights, especially concerning women and children. For example, it assists in dealing with child abuse, HIV and AIDS, and human trafficking, as well as promoting safe sex and facilitating general well-being
- Protects the environment through conservation of wildlife and reduction in the use of electricity, water and general waste

These policies differentiate The Body Shop's products. Although they provide the same physical beauty as competing products might possibly provide, essentially consumers will also obtain inner beauty by becoming ethical consumers.

buy the same product to write to its stakeholders. Effective marketing strategies take this into account. Figure 6.6 develops this further.

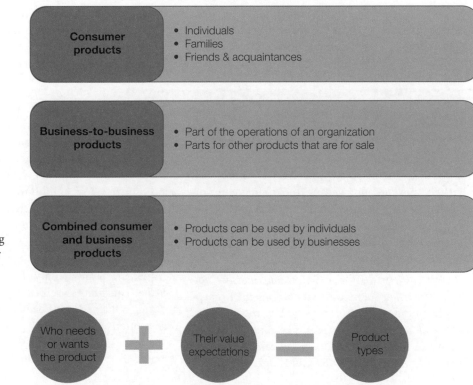

Figure 6.5: Classifying products as consumer or business

Figure 6.6: Creating product types

CONSUMER PRODUCTS

Consumer products can further be classified into durable and non-durable. *Durable goods* (see Figure 6.7) last considerably longer and therefore can be used repeatedly. They are relatively more expensive and the purchase decision process is more involved. Examples of durable products are personal computers, laptops, washing machines, refrigerators, mobile phones, televisions and cars. Just as the **durability** of a product has an influence on the behaviour of firms over time, so it also influences the behaviour of consumers. For example, consumers generally do not need to buy durable goods frequently. How many times will you buy a new television within a year? This type of product also allows flexibility in selling, since there are no concerns about perishability, and this provides value for the producer. For example, the producer may sell a new durable goods product at a high price and gradually reduce the price to respond to market conditions, generally after high profit margins have initially been achieved (Koh, 2005). This is because the utility or value associated with durable goods varies from individual to individual, and from family to family. For example, it is believed that high income levels generally encourage consumers to buy higher cost durable goods (Wang, 2005).

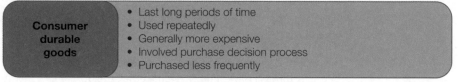

Figure 6.7: Consumer durable goods

Consumer durable goods
- Last long periods of time
- Used repeatedly
- Generally more expensive
- Involved purchase decision process
- Purchased less frequently

On the other hand, *non-durable goods* (products) normally require only a low degree of involvement and are purchased frequently without much thought compared with durable goods (see Figure 6.8). Examples of these are food and groceries, including milk, soft drinks, bread, chocolate bars and chewing gum, and petrol and magazines.

Example 6.3:
The story of Amazon

This case study illustrates what may happen to a product (in this case, a service) if consumers believe they are not getting the right value, or believe they are supporting unethical behaviour by buying or using the product.

In 2013, Ethical Consumer put out the following message to boycott Amazon:

'We all pay our taxes but some companies are not paying their fair share. UK's number one tax avoider is Amazon. In 2011, Amazon's sales in the UK were £2.9 billion but they only paid £1.8 million corporation tax. Consumer power can make Amazon pay a fair rate of tax. Join our Boycott Amazon today'.

With the message, consumers were also given alternatives to Amazon such as Bookbutler.com, Hive.co.uk, betterworldsbooks.co.uk, Oxfam Books, Next, Marks & Spencer, Lush, John Lewis and Debenhams. Consumers were also offered the opportunity to join online forums to discuss the boycott and the unethical activities of Amazon.

Through this campaign, competitors of Amazon are being projected as a better alternative, which gives them free marketing and chips away at Amazon's brand equity. It also highlights the fact that consumers are becoming more powerful and can influence the behaviour and services of organizations.

(**Source:** http://www.ethicalconsumer.org/boycotts/boycottamazon.aspx)

The cost involved in acquiring these products is relatively low and so the risk level is low as well. As a result, consumers do not spend so much time shopping around for the best product and a good deal. This does not necessarily mean, for example, that consumers will not check the nutritional content of food products or check

prices before they buy non-durable goods products. What it means is that because the price is relatively low, and because the purchase is very frequent, consumers generally know where to go and roughly how much the product is going to cost. Even if the consumer is not absolutely certain of the price, he/she knows the price will not be prohibitive. And if a less-than-optimal choice is made for one purchase, before long the consumer has the chance to buy again, and thus easily correct the mistake.

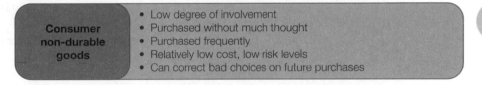

Figure 6.8: Consumer non-durable goods

Consumer non-durable goods
- Low degree of involvement
- Purchased without much thought
- Purchased frequently
- Relatively low cost, low risk levels
- Can correct bad choices on future purchases

INDUSTRIAL OR BUSINESS-TO-BUSINESS PRODUCTS

These products are purchased with very few psychological rewards, if any. They are rationally acquired purely to meet the aims, objectives and goals of an organization. Business products can be further classified into seven main groups, depending upon what they are needed for (Dibb et al., 2012). These categories are raw materials, major equipment, accessory equipment, component parts, process materials, consumable supplies and business/industrial services, as shown in Figure 6.9 and described below.

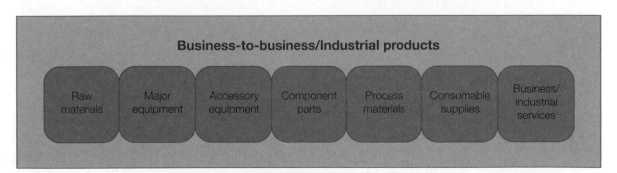

Business-to-business/Industrial products

| Raw materials | Major equipment | Accessory equipment | Component parts | Process materials | Consumable supplies | Business/industrial services |

Figure 6.9: Types of business-to-business/industrial products

Raw materials

These are basic materials that are needed as part of the manufacturing process or in the making of other products. Examples are minerals, agricultural products and chemicals. As organizations manufacture products in high quantities, industrial raw materials are also acquired in high quantities. It must be noted that some products acquired in small quantities may be described as a consumer product whereas the same product acquired in large quantities may be considered an industrial product. For example, whereas pineapples, apples and oranges may be purchased for individual domestic consumption in Ghana, the same products are acquired in high quantities by Blue Skies Holdings Limited, a UK company in Ghana, for the production of fruit juice that will later be sold to other consumers.

Major equipment

Major equipment refers to large machines and tools acquired for the purposes of production that may be used to build or assemble products. Examples are turbines and cranes. These products are very expensive and drain a lot of resources from the buyer. Therefore business-to-business negotiations and bargaining take place for a considerable period of time before a purchasing decision for major equipment is made. The negotiations often involve different stakeholders because the wrong choice of this equipment could be catastrophic for the organization. The advantage of these products, though, is that they are durable and can be used for years. They also usually come with after-sales services, such as training the buyer's personnel to use the product correctly, and there may be installation, repair and maintenance services. Because of the high price involved, the buyer may also negotiate paying in instalments over a period of years.

Accessory equipment

Accessory equipment is needed to help in coordinating the organization's operations but is not part of the production or manufacturing process itself. Examples include telephone systems, computers, office furniture, photocopiers and printers. Compared with major equipment, accessory equipment is relatively inexpensive and is purchased more frequently since it becomes outdated or breaks down relatively quickly. Unlike major equipment, it is fairly easy to install or replace a piece of accessory equipment without causing major disruption to the company's operations for a long period of time.

Component parts

This refers to units that are assembled together to make a product. Though they become part of a product, they are also products themselves and therefore distinctly identifiable. Take a look at a car, for example. This is an end product, but different parts such as the engine, tyres, plugs, screws, lights and wires all come together to make the car perform its function. As with some other industrial products, component parts can function as both consumer products and industrial products, depending upon why they were bought. If a consumer goes to Kwik Fit to get a tyre changed, tyres in this context are consumer products. When Toyota South Africa buys tyres, it will do so in high quantities as part of its vehicle assembly process in Durban and the tyre then becomes an industrial product.

Think and discuss

On a sheet of paper, list a couple of specific products that you feel fit each of the seven categories in Figure 6.9. If you have trouble with any of the categories, the next sections should help.

Process materials

Process materials are used directly in the manufacture of other products, but are not easily identifiable from the finished product in the same way as component parts. For example, consumers can purchase treated wood for various purposes. What is not clear is the chemical that was used – such as Bartoline Creocote Wood Treatment – to protect the wood product from the adverse effects of changing weather. As far as consumers are concerned, they have purchased a quality wood product that has been treated so that it will last for a long time. They may not be aware of what kind of chemical was used in preserving the wood. Therefore the wood treatment process material has now become part of the wood finished product.

Consumable supplies

istock © JanPietruszka

Consumable supplies **facilitate** production and operations but do not become part of the finished product (Dibb et al., 2012). They tend to be used up relatively quickly, even when compared with accessory equipment. To ensure that organizations maintain an adequate level of consumable supplies, they tend to deal with multiple suppliers that can easily be located through numerous outlets. Examples of consumable supplies are paints, paper, print cartridges, pens, pencils and erasers.

Business or industrial services

This refers to intangible resources such as legal, financial, printing, IT management and research services that are needed as part of the operation of the organiza-

6

Example 6.4:
B&Q's consumer and industrial products

B&Q is the largest home improvement and gardening centre retailer in the UK, with 350 stores. The diversity of the types of products it provides is a clear example of how one can appreciate the difference between industrial and consumer products. The company attracts about 3 million customers into its stores every week. Some buy the products for ultimate consumption (such as paints, tools and other DIY items). This group are consumers. Others buy products (such as decking, lighting, insulation, doors and windows) in order to resell them, use them in making other products or use them in home improvement projects for clients. This group are business or industrial customers.

B&Q offers more than 40,000 great value products. Whether it is selling consumer or industrial products, the focus has always been on customer satisfaction. The record of £3.7 billion sales and £187 million profits for the year ending February 2013 is evidence of the fact that the company's focus is to create and deliver value to its customers. This also shows in the various awards it has won, including The Queen's Award for Excellence: Sustainable Development.

tion. Depending upon the cost of acquiring these services, the organization may decide to outsource some of them. This has become easier and sometimes is a less expensive option as many countries continue to remove or lower their cross-border trade barriers. For example, it is possible for a UK company to outsource its IT security and programming functions to a company in India. Obviously this presents value to the organization that is outsourcing the service because it allows it to concentrate on its core competence. It is of no surprise, therefore, that IT outsourcing has become one of the fastest growing businesses in the world (Chadee and Raman, 2009).

PRODUCT MIX OR PRODUCT LINE

Product mix

Product mix refers to the total of all the different varieties of products offered by an organization. A visit to any supermarket, such as Tesco, Asda or Waitrose, will reveal that it offers a one-stop shopping experience where you can get a wide range of both related and unrelated products: food, clothes, electronic and electrical products as well as car insurance, for example (see Figure 6.10).

There are also more specialized shops that only offer products that are related to one another. For example, a visit to Arnold Clark is likely to be for car-related products while McDonald's and Burger King offer related specialized products called fast food. A buyer who wants a burger or a hot dog often also wants fries and generally wants a drink as well. So, for the convenience of the consumer and to boost the profits of the business, related food and beverage product lines are carried in the same fast food establishment (see Figure 6.11).

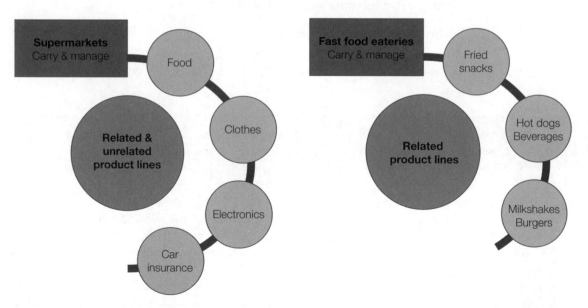

Figure 6.10: The supermarket's related and unrelated products

Figure 6.11: The fast food outlet's related products

Places that only carry related product lines are not likely to be your destination if you are interested in a wider product mix as offered by supermarkets.

Product line

A product line refers to a group of products that are closely related to each other. For example, Heinz's table sauce product line includes tomato ketchup, mayonnaise and salad cream products. Effective product line management is critical for organizations that offer unrelated products to help them establish some kind of order and organization. How does the manager of a supermarket, for example, decide that some products are related and others are not? Products may be put together because a buyer for one normally buys the other. This may or may not be because the products are complementary. For example, if consumers buy a box of tea bags, they may buy sugar as well. If they buy a packet of cigarettes, they might need a lighter to go with it. A shopper may also desire an opportunity to compare different types of wine or different flavours of chocolate. By putting the related products together, the shopping experience becomes easier.

The number of product lines varies from organization to organization. For example, one organization may choose to be a chocolate specialist, and only offer different flavours and sizes of chocolate. This means they have just one product line. Another organization may have hundreds of product lines. For example, Tesco offers different product lines, produced with different technologies and sold to different markets for the satisfaction of different needs.

Over time, some products that were originally considered as belonging to different product lines may come together as one product or product line. For example, according to Brassington and Pettitt (2006), Minolta originally organized its still camera, video camera and photocopier products as three different product lines. Today, however, one can have a single product that can function as both a still camera and a video camera.

6

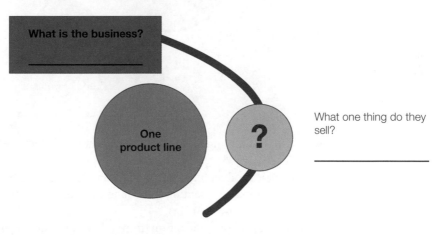

Think and discuss

Using the blank models provided, identify three different businesses that you frequent that carry and manage:

- Just one product line
- Related product lines
- Related plus unrelated product lines

List the product lines for each.

- What are the advantages of carrying and managing just one product line?
- What are the disadvantages?

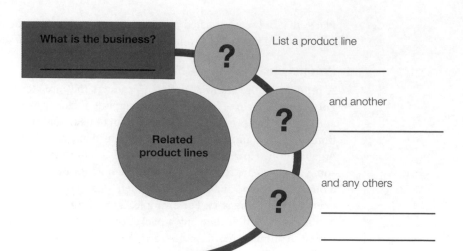

- How are these product lines all related?
- Why does this business carry and manage just related product lines?

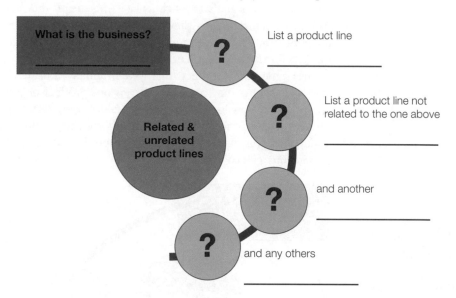

- Why does carrying and managing unrelated product lines benefit this particular business?
- What new product line would you recommend for this business?
- Pretend you are presenting the idea to the business owner: why should the owner consider the new line?
- What value do the products in the new line have? Consider risks as well as benefits.

PRODUCTS CLASSIFIED BY GEOGRAPHICAL COVERAGE

Another way of classifying products and the value they create for both the consumer and the provider is the geographical area at which they are targeted. This can be the local market, international market or global market (see Figure 6.12). Many factors come into play in deciding which geographical market to cover, including the goals of the organization, its resources and the socio-economic, cultural and political factors governing the targeted market. Below is a closer look at these three product classifications.

Figure 6.12: Product geographical coverage

Local market products

Local market products are offered to a single country (Keegan and Green, 2011; Omar, 2009). This may be partly because the company believes there is sufficient untapped market potential within that single country. It may also be because of a realization that the product in question has a unique cultural heritage that is only valuable to the people in that country. The brewery industry offers a strong example of a local market product because there can be a strong local heritage attached to it. An example is the traditional South African sorghum beer known as *umqombothi* (Van Wyk, 2011), which has an estimated market share of over 23 per cent of all commercial beer consumed in the country. This clearly represents a great business potential in a strong emerging market such as South Africa.

It must be emphasized that the company offering the local market product may not necessarily be a local company itself. Global companies such as Coca-Cola and McDonald's have offered local market products in several countries. According to Keegan and Green (2011), Coca-Cola developed both a blended tea called Soken-bicha and a fermented milk drink known as Lactia for the local Japanese market. Similarly, Diageo sells the Gordon's Edge beverage only in the UK.

In terms of value creation, in some cases local market products offer local companies a competitive advantage. This is because these products are offered in response to local tastes, purchasing power, cultural heritage and preferences. Also, where consumers exhibit a strong sense of nationalism, they may prefer local market products to international or global market products (Wang, 2005). It is believed that the preference for local products rather than foreign products contributed to the growth of companies such as Haier (manufacturer of white goods) and Changhong Electric Appliances (manufacturer of televisions) in China. Once companies have established strong brands locally, they may also invest internationally. They sometimes become global brands, as is now the case for Haier, whose markets include Europe, New Zealand, America and the Middle East (Omar et al., 2009).

International market products

This refers to products that are offered in many countries within the same region – for example, 'Euro products'. Sometimes the same product is branded differently in different international markets, as for Unilever, which (until 2000) used to sell Jif household cleaner in the UK, while the same product was named Viss in Germany and Cif in France. Similarly, whereas North Americans have the cleaner brand Mr Clean, the same product is called Maestro Limpio in Latin America, Don Limpio in Spain, Flash in the UK and Mr Proper in a number of other European countries (Pitta and Franzak, 2008). Just as was seen in the case of Haier, above, local market products may evolve to become international and even global market products. The Honda Fit, which is a five-door car, became a successful national market product after it was launched in 2001. However, following its success in Japan, the company decided to widen its market by expanding into other areas including Australia, South Africa, South America and China, thereby making it an international market product.

Global market products

Global market products are developed to satisfy the needs and wants of the global market. For a product to be truly global it must be available in all the regions of the world and it is therefore the case that few products can be considered truly global. Aided by the globalization trend, many companies are increasingly developing global market products as they seek to maximize shareholder value and diversify risks. Global brand awareness helps tremendously in establishing global market products. When a company with a global brand that has strong brand equity introduces a new product, there is a tendency for that new product to be accepted globally as well.

Global companies see the world as one market and so adopt similar policies and methods in their production of goods (Powers and Loyka, 2007). One advantage in terms of value creation is that global market products provide economies of scale for organizations that standardize their products across markets. An example of a global market product is the Fusion razor system, manufactured by Gillette.

MANAGING PRODUCTS

Managing products is very important for both consumers and companies. This is because not all products retain the interest of customers and make profit for producers and retailers for the anticipated period of time. It is believed that between 60 and 90 per cent of all new products end up in failure. In other words, the majority of products do not create the anticipated value. Brassington and Pettitt (2006) identified ways by which a product may be considered a failure:

- When revenue from sale of the products is not enough to cover the cost incurred in making and distributing the products. This may mean that there is not enough demand for the products to generate profit from a high volume of sales
- When consumers reject the product outright

Reasons why some products may fail:

- Products are introduced at the wrong time
- Producers miscalculate the cost of producing and distributing products
- Producers miscalculate the anticipated demand
- There are stronger competitors
- There is a strong substitute for the product

In order to avoid these failures and also maximize value creation for stakeholders, organizations have various ways of managing products. One such way is to appoint a product manager for a product or related products. For example, a supermarket in your town or city may have a product manager responsible for all electronic products. This person will be responsible for making the right volume of products available to the right customer at the right time, in the right location, and at the right price. In doing so, the product manager coordinates various activities with other departments within and outside the organization and with vendors. These activities include market research to know customers' tastes and preferences, ensuring that the offering is of the right quality, developing the appropriate product selection, and orchestrating the most effective marketing communication mix.

It is not always practical to have distinct product managers, especially in small and medium size organizations. In such cases, product management functions and all related functions are performed by the executive management.

NEW PRODUCT DEVELOPMENT

For a moment, consider the fact that many years ago there were no computers. How difficult do you think life would be without access to the internet, mobile phones, television and your favourite movie? Think about the satisfaction and appreciation you have for these products. For a few minutes, think about the value these products have created for the producers in terms of a sense of accomplishment and revenue generation.

It is essential that new products are developed since consumer needs and tastes are constantly changing. Consumers demand the most stylish, efficient, effective and convenient of products, and producers are competing to provide these attributes. If they do not, their competitors will and the company will be disadvantaged.

In order to develop successful new products that satisfy needs, and to be competitive, many organizations have established strong research and development (R&D) departments, and have tasked the marketing department with collecting essential data to generate ideas. This is explored in more detail in Chapter 4. This information may be collected from internal sources such as sales staff, scientists, manufacturing staff, engineers and top executives within the organization, or from external sources such as customers and channel partners. Through market research and analysis of consumer input (complaints and requests), the marketing team establishes what it believes consumers need. Some companies have online tools to enable customers to submit ideas and sometimes products are even made to meet customer specifications. For example, if you order a computer from Dell, you are asked for specific details including your preferred size of screen. Some producers also get ideas from their competitors through analysis of competitors' advertisements and other marketing communication tools. Valuable information may also be collected from distributors.

The steps to developing a new product are:

- Analyse data and ideas from as many available sources of information as possible
- Develop a product concept (attributes of the product)
- Test the concept with consumers and other stakeholders
- Calculate the cost involved and the anticipated value
- Determine the potential for profit
- Develop the product
- Determine the pricing
- Adopt appropriate marketing and promotion strategies

It must be noted that not all companies necessarily develop products for profits. Also, the steps they take in developing and marketing products may not necessarily follow the order above. However, it is important that the product provides the value expected by the producer and the consumer or else it will fail.

PRODUCT LIFECYCLE

Just as living things go through a cycle from birth to decline and eventual death, so do products in what is known as the *product lifecycle* (PLC) theory (see Figure 6.13). The cycle starts with the introduction of the product to the marketplace after all the steps involving new product development have been taken, as outlined earlier. The product grows if it continues to produce value for the consumer and the producer. It matures because the producer and more customers continue to nourish it with the right investment and volume of purchases. However, if stronger alternatives are introduced to the market or if customers' tastes and preferences change, the product may go through the decline stage. Here, consumers do not buy the product as they used to, and producers discover that it is no longer profitable to support the product with their resources. According to the PLC theory, the product may go through these stages:

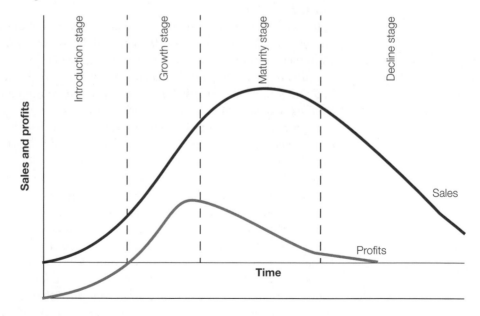

Figure 6.13: The product lifecycle

- Introduction
- Growth
- Maturity
- Decline

Introduction stage

At the introduction stage, the product first appears on the market with no sales and no profit. In fact, the product will be generating a loss at this stage because of the investment that was put in through the development stage. Also, the company needs to spend significant resources in marketing and promotion (various forms of advertising and distribution). The pricing strategy at the introduction stage may vary depending upon the type of product and the anticipated market response. For example, the initial price may be high in order to break even as quickly as possible. Also, if the product is unique, customers who are innovators may acquire the product even if the price is high. However, the company may reduce prices for a period as part of the promotion strategy in order to generate interest, and then increase the prices afterwards. The majority of products do not make it past this stage. For example, it is believed that 80 per cent of products from the food and drink industry fail at this stage (Dibb et al., 2012).

Growth stage

At the growth stage, sales from the product quickly rise, and the profit also accelerates rapidly. It is important that those entrusted with the responsibility of managing the product work really hard at this stage. Their success or failure will determine whether the product has a long or short life span. At this stage, desirably, consumers are now aware of the attributes of the product and are rapidly purchasing it. However, undesirably, competitors are also aware of the product and therefore offer the market alternatives in order to take away as many customers as possible. The company may respond by adding more features to the product in order to appeal to customers even more. They must also make efforts to improve brand loyalty. In spite of this, profit tends to fall during the latter period of the growth stage as a result of the activities of competitors to win more customers, which in some cases compels the company to reduce prices.

Maturity stage

At the maturity stage, the sales of the product peak and begin to decline, and profit margins also continue to decline. The competition for market share at this stage becomes intense. Product managers at this stage emphasize the attributes of the products and how they differ from what competitors can offer. They do this through communication with consumers as well as distributors, to convince them that their products offer the best value, relative to those of competitors. Consumers at this stage are experienced and are able to make informed purchasing decisions. Due to the intense competition, some competitors may be unable to survive and will have to withdraw their market offering or sell it to other competitors.

Decline stage

During the decline stage of the product lifecycle, sales fall very quickly. This may be because competitors have become stronger and offer better value for customers. It

6

may also be because customers' tastes have changed. For example, due to technological advancement and change of consumer needs, we rarely see people using floppy disks. In fact, very few computers nowadays have a compartment for a floppy disk and most users prefer USB sticks for data storage.

istock © bedo

When a product reaches the decline stage, the organization has a difficult decision to make. One option is to prune the product of some of its features that are preventing it from being profitable, thereby reducing the cost of production. Another option is to sell the product to another company that may be able to revive it or maintain the product if it helps in promoting interests for the organization's other products. The company may consider selling the product in international markets where it may still be in the early stages of its lifecycle. This situation is what is referred to as the international product lifecycle. When colour television was introduced in developed countries to replace black and white television sets (which then were in the mature/decline stage), some companies continued to sell black and white televisions to less developed countries. At the same time, companies must be working towards gradual development of new products to replace those at the decline stage.

STANDARDIZATION AND ADAPTATION OF PRODUCTS

Companies investing in international markets have to make an important but difficult decision regarding the extent to which the products they are offering in an international market are similar to those offered in the host country. This is a question of standardization and adaptation.

STANDARDIZATION

When the product offered in different countries is similar to that offered in the company's home country, this is described as standardization (Powers and Loyka, 2007). The use of a standardization strategy offers the company a number of advantages (see Figure 6.14). First, it offers the market a consistent product, which then helps in strengthening the brand. It also helps to reduce costs as it offers economies of scale. Also, it ensures better coordination between headquarters and subsidiaries, and therefore facilitates the monitoring process of the subsidiaries. For example, to save costs Revlon exported its products to foreign markets without any substantial changes to the formulation of the product, how it was advertised and even how it was packaged. A company may also use standardized products because of industry and practical specifications. There is no point changing the size specifications of a CD if it is not going to fit in a standard CD player or a computer.

Figure 6.14: Reasons for standardization of products

ADAPTATION

On the other hand, adaptation refers to the extent to which products offered in different markets are modified to respond to environmental conditions which are different from those within the host country. These conditions may include economic, political, social, legal, industry or company factors. For example, Unilever sells fast-moving consumer goods (FMCG) in smaller packaging sizes in Africa than elsewhere in order to make them affordable for consumers who do not have high incomes (Smith, 2008). Companies may also make changes in response to consumers' tastes and preferences. Because the product was manufactured as a direct response to environmental conditions, it is more likely to satisfy the needs of the targeted market. Adaptation does have its disadvantages, however. First, it reduces the possibility of achieving economies of scale and therefore increases operational cost to the company. Second, it is relatively more difficult for the headquarters and other subsidiaries to keep track of what is happening in the group if the product is not standardized. Finally, not all products can be easily modified.

PRODUCT DESIGN

Product design is a multidisciplinary process involving many stakeholders, where expertise helps companies to become more competitive and can contribute to higher product sales. If a product is designed well, the company and consumers will benefit. With the increasing power of consumers and the availability of improved technology, companies are now able to involve consumers in the co-creation process as new products are being designed or existing products (services, experiences, ideas) are being modified or redesigned.

Before the design department or team works on the aesthetics of the product, it may collect information about what customers want to see, how they want to use the product and what can be done to improve the efficiency of the product. Companies that communicate with consumers during the design process will

Think and discuss

Pick a product that you feel would need to be adapted if it were to be marketed outside your country. List the reasons why it would be better to adapt the product. What possible disadvantages would need to be considered?

be in a better position to meet consumer preferences and specifications and will ultimately be more competitive. For example, manufacturers may ask consumers how to shape a toothbrush in order to offer the user a better grip. In addition to thinking about products to satisfy current customer needs, it is important that designers are also creative to anticipate what design criteria consumers might want in the future.

BRANDING, POSITIONING AND PACKAGING

Think and discuss

What tangible product (a physical item) that you own would you like to have been able to co-create? What consumer input would you have provided to the product design team?

In Greek and Roman times, there were signs or route descriptions to shops, carved out in stone, and there were even brand markings applied to pieces of silver (Riezebos, 2003, p. 1). The signboards of the shops often showed pictures of the products sold because this was the best way to communicate effectively with consumers in an age when literacy was mostly for the few (Murphy, 1990). According to Keller (2003) and Riezebos (2003), branding has been around for a long time as a means of distinguishing one product from another. The English word 'brand' is derived from the Old Norse word 'brandr', which means 'to burn'. Brands were and still are the means by which owners of livestock mark their animals to identify them. Its modern form dates from the Middle Ages.

It is important to contrast a brand and a product. According to Kotler and Armstrong (2003), a product is anything that can be offered to a market for attention, acquisition, use or consumption that might satisfy a need or want. Thus, a product may be actual goods, a service, a retail store, a person, an organization, a place or an idea. Branding is the way for a business to communicate a product's value. It conveys information and certain perceptions about the product or product line to both consumers and businesses.

Product brands can have long lives. Major brands such as Coca-Cola and Gillette have been around for over a hundred years, and one of the oldest brands in the UK – Bass Ale – was established in 1777. The sustainability of a particular brand depends on tangible and intangible attributes that establish and maintain loyalty from stakeholders such as employees and customers. The strength of a brand is usually built up by advertising and promotion campaigns that are based on the brand's foundations, such as quality, innovation, superior services, customer satisfaction and value (Keller, 2003).

To brand a product, it is necessary to teach consumers:

- *Who* the product is, by giving it a name (labelling it and using other brand elements to help identify it)
- *What* the product does
- *Why* consumers should care

Riezebos (2003, p. 32) defines brand as 'every sign that is capable of distinguishing the goods or services of a company'. A sign may be a word, picture or mark. The brand name is that part of the brand that can be pronounced. In its most basic form, a brand name can serve as a characteristic in the recognition of the branded article. A branded article should minimally entail a product (goods or services) and brand (name, picture or form mark). An article not provided with a mark is called a generic product. Among others, the extrinsic attributes are price, packaging, information about the country of origin and information about the year of market introduction of the brand.

According to the American Marketing Association (AMA), the key to creating a brand is to be able to choose a name, logo, symbol, package design or other attribute that identifies a product and distinguishes it from others. These different components of a brand that identify and differentiate it are called brand elements and will be discussed further (Keller, 2003). Kotler and Armstrong (2003, pp. 418–19) state that brands represent lasting assets which can take on a range of different meanings.

A brand is a complex symbol that can convey up to six levels of meaning:

- **Attributes:** A brand brings to mind certain attributes. Mercedes suggests expensive, well-built, well-engineered, durable, high-prestige automobiles
- **Benefits:** Attributes must be translated into functional and emotional benefits. The attribute 'durable' could translate into the functional benefit 'I won't have to buy another car for several years'. The attribute 'expensive' translates into the emotional benefit 'The car makes me feel important and admired'
- **Values:** The brand also says something about the producer's values. Mercedes stands for high performance, safety and prestige
- **Culture:** The brand may represent a certain culture. The Mercedes represents German culture, which is characterized as being organized, efficient, high quality
- **Personality:** The brand can project a certain personality. Mercedes may suggest a no-nonsense boss (person), a reigning lion (animal) or an austere palace (object).
- **User:** The brand suggests the kind of consumer who buys or uses the product. We would expect to see a 55-year-old top executive behind the wheel of a Mercedes, not a 20-year-old secretary

What functions do brands perform that make them so valuable? One can take a couple of perspectives to uncover the value of brands to both consumers and firms themselves.

BRAND NAME STRATEGIES

The brand name has been defined as a word (or phrase) or illustration that differentiates a company's market offering. In developing a brand name strategy, a marketing manager has to develop a product image to project across the market. For example, Birds Eye projects the image of healthy food and caring about the consumer. Its slogan is 'Who cares if you eat well? Birds Eye cares'. According to Burca et al. (2004, p. 280), for companies to operate in a global market the following brand name options are available to develop image:

- Use the same brand name worldwide: This option is suitable when the company markets one product and has wide international distribution for it. At this stage the company should make sure there is no conflict between the brand name and the culture of the host country
- Modify the brand name in each market: This option is appropriate when the marketing strategy is to identify with the local market. While the same brand name is used, add-on words create local identification: for example, Sunsilk shampoo
- Different names in different markets: This option is required when it is difficult to translate into the local language or when the company has decided to create a local identity

Think and discuss

Pick an intangible product (a service, idea, experience or place). If you were a consumer on the design team for that product, what would be important to you? What might be critical to the business investing the funds to create and market the product?

6

Example 6.5:
Next brand in action

The Next brand was created in 1982. From the outset, it was considered aspirational but still affordable and positioned to communicate distinctive style, good quality and value. It is a good example of a brand name that is easily spelled, easily pronounced and distinctive and there is no doubt that the name contributes strongly to the increasing popularity of the fashion retailer. Next was confirmed as the official clothing and home-ware supplier for the London 2012 Olympic and Paralympic Games and produced outfits for Team GB for both the opening and closing ceremonies. Whether in-store, online or on the phone, the Next brand is a reassuring name that gives customers the confidence that they have made the right choice of product which will give them value compared with competing offerings. Next celebrated its 30th year jubilee in 2012 in the same year that its online trade spread to more than 50 countries worldwide.

- Company name as a brand name: Many companies allow the use of different brand names in different countries and use a standard trademark for their entire product. The trademark, which acts as a form of corporate identification, is made of letters, symbols and logos which distinguish both the product and the company, and often communicates a stronger corporate message to the consumer than the brand by itself

Changing brand names

In some cases, it becomes essential for a company to change a brand name, either globally or just for the host market. The decision to rename is not taken easily because of high advertising costs in communicating the new name to consumers and the possibility of creating confusion and **alienation** in the minds of existing and potential customers, especially when it comes to very loyal and dedicated customers (Kotler and Armstrong, 2012). A company renaming strictly as a strategic decision, without any merger influence, is said to be carrying out 'an action which changes identity as a means to alter image in order to create utility through the sharing of names that have been learned and graded' (Williams, 2012, p. 242).

There are several reasons why companies might change brand names, generally for growth or prestige, or just to maintain stability:

- The associations with the brand name damage the value of the brand. For example, Kentucky Fried Chicken uses 'KFC' to avoid the negative connotations of the word 'fried'
- The material or immaterial brand associations learned by consumers damage the value of the brand
- Added-value differences between brands may belong to the same company
- The current name has limited possibilities when it comes to using it for products in other product classes
- The brand name is different in different languages or areas. Three situations are possible here. First, it may not be possible to pronounce or translate the brand name correctly abroad. 'Snickers', the US brand of chocolate bar, sounds like 'knickers', a woman's undergarment, in the UK. 'Sears', when spoken in Castilian Spanish, sounds very much like 'Seat', the Spanish automobile company. Second, a company may have similar branded articles in different countries, but use differ-

ent brand names in those countries. Third, as a result of positioning differences between countries, parallel import will take place in the country where the price is highest

- Mergers, acquisitions and joint ventures may mean each of the partners wants to see its old brand in the new brand name so that existing customers of the original companies will feel more familiar with the new brand name
- There is a legal problem with the brand name. For example, when Yves Saint Laurent introduced the performance brand, Champagne, it needed to change the name because it was a protected brand name for the sparkling wine from the Champagne district of France.

Relationship between brand and offering; brand extension

The relationship between the brand and the offering (product, service or 'experience') can be measured by the **correlation** between them. For a specific referral to a certain offering, it can be seen that the distance between the offering and the brand is small. Where the correlation between the offering and the brand is vague, the distance is larger.

It is important to know what the relationship between the brand and the offering is or will be. Two aspects are very important: the type of positioning and possible plans for extension. When a brand is distinguished from other brands on functional grounds, it is best to choose a brand name that refers to the product or to advantages of the product. A brand also can relate to different products, but for many brand names the association is with a certain product. Duracell equals batteries; Heineken is lager. Sometimes the brand name itself already gives information: Vidal Sassoon Wash & Go indicates a shampoo. The same brand can also be used for different products: Peugeot is used for cars, scooters and bicycles.

Besides the positioning of the brand, possible plans for brand extensions should also be taken into account. Brand extension refers to the use of an existing success-ful brand to enter into a new product category, sector or market (Srivastava and Sharma, 2012; Martinez et al., 2008). It gives the firm a much better chance to establish a wider presence in international markets. A well-recognized brand name can also allow a product to come into the market with low advertising expenses. Brand extension can include launching the same product in a different form, adding the brand name to related products often used together, building on the company image and expertise, and communicating unique and designer attributes. However, extending the brand image to an undesirable product can damage the image of the original brand (Terpstra and Sarathy, 2000). Companies therefore have to assess the likelihood of success before selecting this strategy. The key considera-tions are whether they have positive brand equity, and whether the brand equity is transferable from the customer's perspective. This will then determine the will-ingness of customers to purchase the product or service offered through brand extension.

The use of brand extension is still an interesting and attractive option for compa-nies. This is particularly so because the success rate of introducing new products and brands is not encouraging. For example, it is reported that in the US market as many as 85 per cent of new products fail to succeed. This presents huge costs to the affected companies (Srivastava and Sharma, 2012). Brand extension therefore offers companies the opportunity to introduce products at a relatively low cost and with less risk.

The difference between global and local brands

Brand names are critical elements in making an impact on customers and one question is whether a company should have one international brand or different brands for each market. Naturally, there is concern about whether the brand names are able to travel well and create positive images in the minds of international customers (Burca et al., 2004, p. 277). When companies expand their activities to encompass international markets, they will have to decide whether they want to create a standardized global brand or manage a portfolio of different, locally adapted brands. Hollensen (2008) refers to the former as international or universal brands. A subset of this is what has been referred to as a 'Eurobrand', where the brand is only targeted at European markets with profound similarities. Similarly, it is believed that companies such as Varig Airlines of Brazil and Shangri-La Hotels and Resorts of Hong Kong have pursued regional rather than global branding (Gillespie and Hennessey, 2011).

On the other hand, some factors may dictate the preference of local brands rather than regional or global brands. Gillespie and Hennessey continue that Unilever had a different brand for the same product in different markets simply to ensure easy pronunciation. For example, while it originally had Jif household cleaner in the UK, the same product was named Viss in Germany, Cif in France and Vim in Canada. Similarly, whereas North Americans have Mr Clean, the same product is called Maestro Limpio in Latin America, Don Limpio in Spain, Mr Proper in a number of other European countries and Flash in the UK (Pitta and Franzak, 2008).

Ellwood (2002) argues that, in the case of a standardized product for different markets, a global brand is likely to yield the higher benefit whereas for adapted products, separate brand identities are generally more suitable. There are salient general arguments for each approach, as can be seen in Table 6.1.

Table 6.1: Global versus local branding
Source: Aaker et al., 1995, p. 267

Global brands	Local brands
Economies in the development of advertising, packaging, promotion, etc. Exploitation of: • Media overlap • Exposure of customers who travel Associations of: • A global presence • The 'home' country	Names, symbols and associations can be: • Developed locally • Tailored to local market(s) • Selected without the constraints of a global brand Reduced risk from 'buy local' sentiments

On a general level, Gregory and Wiechmann (2002) indicate a strong propensity towards global brands, which results from five major market trends:

- A growing need for economies of scale as a result of high differentiation costs
- The desire to capitalize on experience and knowledge transfer
- The wish to benefit from rapidly spreading local brand images
- A continuous struggle for growth opportunities
- The ongoing internationalization and consolidation of the retail trade

Global branding has the advantage of providing economies of scale in advertising and the uniform image can appeal to globe-trotting consumers. Global brands are also important in securing access to distribution channels because they give the company a strong position from which to convince the retailer to carry their product rather than that of their competitors. Having an international brand means additional sales overseas, which in turn justifies additional expenditure to create a new global brand and define the established one. A strong, distinguished brand name will enable easier market entry for the offering (Terpstra and Sarathy, 2000).

The top 25 global brands in 2011 are ranked in Table 6.2. (Note: to be ranked, the company must have publicly available marketing and financial data.) According to Business Week/Interbrand, a global brand should receive about one third of its revenue from outside its own country, and be recognizable outside its base of customers.

Table 6.2: Top 25 global brands
Source: Business Week/ Interbrand Top 100 Global Brands 2011

Rank	Brand	Rank	Brand	Rank	Brand
1	Coca-Cola	10	Hewlett-Packard	19	Honda
2	IBM	11	Toyota	20	Oracle
3	Microsoft	12	Mercedes-Benz	21	H & M
4	Google	13	Cisco	22	Pepsi
5	GE	14	Nokia	23	American Express
6	McDonald's	15	BMW	24	SAP
7	Intel	16	Gillette	25	Nike
8	Apple	17	Samsung		
9	Disney	18	Louis Vuitton		

Planning and implementing a brand marketing programme

Building brand equity requires a brand that consumers are sufficiently aware of and with which they have strong, favourable and unique brand associations. In general, this knowledge-building process will depend on three factors:

- The initial choices for the brand elements or identities making up the brand
- The marketing activities and supporting marketing programme, and the manner in which the brand is integrated into them
- Other associations indirectly transferred to the brand by linking it to some of the brand entity

Choosing brand elements

A brand element is visual or verbal information that serves to identify and differentiate a product. The most common brand elements are brand names, logos, symbols, characters, packaging and slogans. A number of options exist and a number of criteria are relevant for choosing brand elements, which can be chosen to enhance brand awareness or facilitate the formation of strong, favourable and unique brand associations. The best test of the brand-building contribution of brand elements is to consider what consumers would think about a product or service if they knew only its brand name, associated logo, and so forth. Because different elements have different advantages, a subset or even all of the possible brand elements are often employed.

Although the judicious choice of brand elements can make some contribution to building brand equity, the primary input comes from the marketing activities related to the brand. Strong, favourable and unique brand associations can be created in a variety of ways by a marketing programme.

Brand associations may themselves be linked to other entities that have their own associations, created by linking the brand into another node of information in memory that conveys meaning to consumers. For example, the brand may be linked to certain source factors, such as the company (through branding strategies), countries or other geographic regions (through identification of product origin) and channels of distribution (through channel strategy), as well as to other brands (through ingredients or co-branding), characters (through licensing), spokespeople (through endorsements), sporting or cultural events (through sponsorship) or other third-party sources (through awards or reviews).

Brand equity and brand flux

Through the skilful design and implementation of marketing programmes that capitalize on well conceived brand positioning, strong brand leadership can be obtained. Maintaining and expanding on that brand equity, however, can be quite challenging. *Brand equity management* concerns those activities that take a broader and more diverse perspective of the brand's equity, regarding how product line branding strategies might have to be adjusted to reflect corporate concerns, geographic boundaries or unique market segments. Managing brand equity involves managing a product brand within the context of the corporate brand, as well as managing product brands over multiple categories, over time and across multiple market segments, based upon the outcomes from a brand audit.

As shown in Figure 6.15, in the brand flux model (Williams, 2012) the x axis 'Change in branding' refers to changes in marketing aesthetics (such as logo, slogan and packaging), intended to create a new identity and designed to alter the image of the brand with the consumer. The y axis represents an organization's 'Change in positioning', such as when it targets a different market segment.

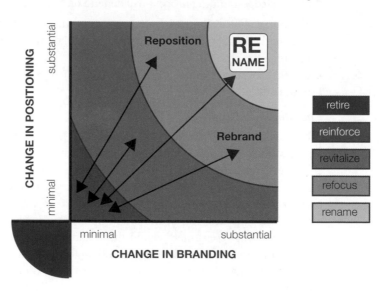

Figure 6.15: Brand flux model
Source: Williams, 2012

Think and discuss

Think of a product or service that has recently changed its name. What changes in positioning do you feel the company was trying to convey with the name change? What were its marketing efforts to reinforce this branding change? Who do you think was the target customer for the branding effort? Do you think the marketing efforts worked?

As companies make more substantial changes than just regular *reinforcing activities*, they can *revitalize* the brand. Organizations that implement more substantial changes in branding combined with minimal changes in position are shown in the model as *rebrand*, while organizations that implement more substantial changes in position along with minimal changes in branding aesthetics are portrayed as *reposition*, with gradients in between. These rebranding and repositioning actions are referred to as *refocusing*, as they are more substantial than a revitalization of the brand. The most substantial change in branding involves *renaming*. After any brand change (revitalize, refocus, rename), it is important to reinforce the change with increased marketing efforts. Thus the brand flux model can clarify all the various brand management terms and activities in relation to changes in branding (x axis) or changes in positioning (y axis). Note that there is no path depicting *retirement*, since the product no longer exists.

Protecting the brand name

From the manufacturer's standpoint, a lack of brand name protection can result in sales lost to imitators (for example, Coalgate versus Colgate), which is considered to be unfair competition as well as misuse of the name. Reduced sales mean reduced investment and innovation, so consumers will also suffer. The following is a summary of the different kinds of signs that can be protected as trademarks in Europe:

- Word marks: The most common type of trademark is the word trademark. Words are pre-eminent signs that can be used to make products or services recognizable – for example Mars, Intel, Nike, PricewaterhouseCoopers, McKinsey and Microsoft
- A combination of characters: It is not only words that have distinguishing capacities. A combination of letters can also function as a trademark – for example, BMW, IBM and KLM
- A combination of numbers: This can also function as a trademark – for example, 4711 (cosmetics) and 911 (Porsche)
- Words written in a certain style: Some trademarks are protected for the specific way they are written – for example, Coca-Cola, Harrods and Marlboro
- Logos: These are used to make products recognizable – for example, Apple's apple, KLM's crown
- Slogans: Phrases can make the product distinguishable even when the trademark name is not included – for example 'Just do it' (Nike) or 'Let's make things better' (Philips)
- Colours: Singly or in combination, colours can be distinguishing as a trademark – for example, Shell's red and yellow colours and IBM's blue and white stripes
- Layout on packaging: This enables consumers to recognize products from the layout of words or illustrations – for example, Marlboro and After Eight
- Packaging designs: Some products can be recognized by the design of the packaging itself – for example, Coca-Cola and Odol bottles
- Product design: Design can be viewed as a trademark if the consumer recognizes a product from its design – for example, Apple iPod
- A gesture: This can be a trademark if it is a distinguishing sign and can be registered as such – for example, the Twix scissoring gesture with two fingers
- Sound and scent: A music jingle is protected by the Office of Harmonization in the Internal Market (European Union). However, it is not certain yet whether it

is protected by various EU members. A certain scent might well be a distinctive mark of a specific product such as a stationery brand

It may also be necessary to explain or clarify the brand meaning of a product to potential consumers. This includes creating mental structures or perceptions about the product and helping consumers to organize their knowledge about a product, service, experience, person or idea in a way that assists their purchasing decision making and, in the process, provides value to the business as well.

Whenever and wherever consumers are deciding between alternatives, brands play an important decision-making role. Accordingly, marketers can benefit from branding whenever consumers are in a situation of choice. Given the myriad choices that consumers make each and every day, it is no surprise that branding has become pervasive. Although businesses provide the impetus for brand creation through their marketing programme and activities, ultimately a brand is something that resides in the minds of consumers. A brand is a perceptual entity that is rooted in reality, but it is also more than that, reflecting the perceptions and perhaps even the **idiosyncrasies** of consumers.

Think and discuss

Which commodities are now highly marketed through effective branding? How have consumer perceptions of a particular commodity been differentiated?

Brands that were once commodities

A commodity is a product so basic that it cannot be differentiated in the minds of consumers. Over the years, a number of products that at one time were seen essentially as commodities have become highly differentiated as strong brands have emerged. Some notable examples (with brand pioneers in parentheses) are: coffee (Maxwell House), bath soap (Ivory), flour (Gold Medal), salt (Morton), oatmeal (Quaker), pickles (Vlasic), bananas (Chiquita), chickens (Perdue), pineapples (Dole) and even water (Perrier).

These former commodity products have become branded in various ways. The key success factor in each case was that consumers became convinced that all the product offerings in the category were not the same and that meaningful differences existed.

In some instances, product makers convinced consumers that a product was not a commodity and actually would vary appreciably in quality. In these cases, the brand was seen as assuring uniformly high quality in the product category on which consumers could depend. A recent example of this approach is Intel, which has spent vast sums of money on its 'Intel inside' promotion to brand its microprocessors as delivering the highest levels of performance (for example, power) and dependability (through offering upgrades, for example) possible.

In other cases, because product differences were virtually non-existent, image or other non-product related considerations led to brand creation.

Product positioning

Positioning a product or product line means making decisions about where and how the product should be distributed (sold). This becomes a strategic business decision that requires the marketer to understand the potential customer's motivations.

Marketers need to avoid three major product positioning errors:

- **Under-positioning:** Failing to position the product or product line at all. Some companies discover that buyers do not know about their product or product line
- **Over-positioning:** Giving buyers too narrow a picture of the product line. Consumers might have thought that the Steuben Glass company made only fine glassware costing $1,000 or more, when in fact it had a product line that made affordable fine glassware starting at around $50
- **Confused positioning:** Leaves buyers with a confused image of a product or product line. This might suggest that a company has so many messages that it confuses customers so they forget the main purpose of the product

The real task is to decide which differences to promote. Businesses must differentiate their products clearly from those of their competitors and the product distinctions they plan to emphasize should satisfy all or most of the following criteria. The distinction:

- Is a highly valued benefit to the target market
- Is not on offer from competitors: your product is more distinctive than the competitor's similar product
- Is superior in other ways
- Is communicable and visible to buyers
- Is pre-emptive: competitors cannot easily copy the difference
- Is affordable: buyers can afford to pay for the difference
- Is profitable: the company can introduce the difference profitably

PACKAGING AND LABELLING

Packaging and labelling are very important in marketing management in creating value for consumers, producers and retailers. On one level this involves the use of logos and graphics in order to present the product in an attractive and acceptable way for the consumer (Brassington and Pettitt, 2006). *Packaging* has been described as the development of a container, a label and graphic design for a product (Dibb et al., 2012). *Labelling* can be very simple or complex, depending upon the intent of the message. For example, if a company wants to portray itself as 'green' and to show that it conforms to environment-friendly guidelines, it will use an eco-labelling strategy (Clemenz, 2010).

This visual perceived value can dictate whether or not a consumer buys the product at the point of purchase. Think about the many items you have purchased from a supermarket that you did not initially set out to buy. How and why did you become convinced that the product would represent value and that you needed to have it, even though it was not on your shopping list?

This impulsive decision is a function of how the product has been packaged and labelled to gain consumer attention and perceived value. In other words, the package serves as a marketing communication tool at the point of purchase. It is believed that 70 per cent of packaged goods purchasing decisions are made at the point of purchase (Holmes and Paswan, 2012).

One of the functions of a label is to identify the product. It may also provide information such as the manufacturer, location of production, components or ingredients, functions and when it expires. Retailers are aware of the effects of labelling and some of them significantly use their own labelling in order to transfer the value consumers

Think and discuss
Think and discuss

What was the last impulsive buy you made? What influenced you to make the purchase? Was it the packaging and labelling, the marketing display or something else?

6

associate with the retailer to the product. For example, in the UK, Sainsbury's own labels account for about 60 per cent of its total sales (Omar, 2009).

In packaging products, the following are some of the factors that must be taken into consideration: new production technology, material development, environmental factors, logistics requirements, and consumer tastes and preferences (Rundh, 2009). It is important that the marketer or the designer of the product package tries to create value in reference to all these factors. Failure to do so may result in reactions from various stakeholders. For example, ethical consumers may boycott products or stage a protest if the packaging does not comply with environmental or ethical standards, which may have a long-lasting detrimental effect on the brand. Also, some consumers may choose products with paper packaging, as opposed to plastic packaging, especially if there is huge negative media coverage of the effects of the use of plastic packaging.

CONCLUSION

This chapter has emphasized the 'product', both tangible and intangible, as a point of value, and the use of the brand to distinguish one product from another. It has discussed the activities designed to create, protect, adapt and enhance a brand's equity over the product lifecycle and laid out the definition of the product as a point of value to the individual as well as to the organization. The chapter has also established that products can be classified in many different ways, and the perceived value of the product is influenced by the type of product it is and how it is branded. The value of the product depends on the extent to which a consumer perceives the

Example 6.6:
No value, no product

Consumers' perceptions of products as offering value is key to product survival. Consider the case of Coca-Cola's launch of Dasani water in the UK in 2004. Over £6 million was spent on the promotion of the product alone. It is therefore not surprising that the financial resources spent on making the product available to the UK consumer were huge. Prior to launch, Dasani pure water had been hugely successful in the USA. An excellent return on investment was therefore anticipated, though there were strong competitors in the UK such as Volvic, Highland Spring, Evian, Vittel and Aquafina. Judging by the huge success in the US and the fact that Coca-Cola is a huge brand, UK consumers could have been forgiven for assuming that Dasani would be of high quality. The product was described as 'pure' but during the early stage of the product lifecycle it was discovered that Dasani

was no more than purified tap water, though consumers had to pay high prices for it because of its high perceived value. It also contained excess levels of bromate, which could increase the risk of cancer.

UK consumers and the media were furious that they were being sold this product with very high mark-up even though it was not as pure as it claimed it to be. The media therefore published numerous articles exposing the defects of the so called 'pure' water. In the end, the product had to be withdrawn from the market because consumers did not want it, and retailers wanted it out of their shops – not only to create space for other products, but also to minimize any negative associations from offering this product. A lot was promised and anticipated in terms of value for both the consumer and Coca-Cola, but in the end not much was delivered and the product had to be added to the statistics of products that failed to succeed in the current competitive market.

product in terms of personal taste, preferences, availability and affordability, which all come together to determine whether the product offers value for money (or whatever is exchanged for it).

Case study
Samsung: Managing product lines in a competitive environment

THE WORLD OF TECHNOLOGY HAS CHANGED DRAStically in recent years as the players in the industry compete with one another. The stiffer the competition gets, the more choices are available to consumers. One of the key players in this industry, Samsung, has been in the business for over 70 years, seeking to make a better world through its many product lines, which include domestic appliances, home electronics, mobile devices and accessories.

Reproduced with permission of Samsung

Although the actual products often look appealing to consumers, evidence has shown that what consumers are really buying in Samsung's products is the core product – that is, the benefits that these gadgets give users. Samsung periodically gives its customers certain offers to distinguish its products from those of competitors, such as a two-year guarantee and free delivery.

Samsung as a brand has really become a household name. The name is easy to pronounce, and easy to identify among competing brands, and has been associated with good quality over the past seven decades. Since the company mostly uses brand extensions, whenever consumers see the name Samsung, it communicates quality, value and excellence. This reflects in the company's sales records. Evidence shows that Samsung is taking the world in imaginative directions. Its flagship smartphone, Galaxy S III, unveiled in May 2012, has been widely acknowledged as a significant addition to the world of communication by consumers. The company announced that, as at January 2013, this phone and its predecessors Galaxy S and Galaxy S II will have achieved more 100 million sales. This is clearly a remarkable achievement and it results from the fact that the offerings

serve as points of value for consumers. Samsung smartphones are easy to use and display photos and videos with ease on dazzling screens, and the associated designs are elegant.

Samsung's key position in the industry shows that the company does not just rush to turn ideas into products; these ideas generated from various internal and external sources are screened thoroughly to be sure that the eventual products to be released will be commercially successful and resonate with consumers. Some of the clear examples of this are its recently released cameras, WB250F and WB200F, which have an impressive 18x optical zoom and built-in wi-fi connectivity. Also, its NX300 is the first single-lens system that can capture 2D shots as well as having the capacity to capture still images and full-motion video in 3D.

For those wondering how Samsung has achieved its remarkable success during the global economic recession, the answer lies in the company's total package of offerings, including the branding, packaging, labelling and quality, which are brought together to deliver value for customers all over the world. In the 2013 annual international Consumer Electronics Show (CES) at Las Vegas, attendees were thrilled with the features of the Samsung S9 UHD TV, especially the picture quality. This is good news for Samsung because, in marketing parlance, customers are the ultimate judge and boss.

In developing new products, it is clear that Samsung positions its products to meet specific consumer needs in the marketplace. Laundry, refrigeration, vacuum cleaners, ovens, air conditioning and other products in the home appliances product line are well favoured by consumers. Other items in the

6

company's product mix are similarly well received. This shows the company is consistent about its five core value areas as an organization. It states that its values revolve around excellence, people, change, integrity and co-prosperity. So, when introducing new products, Samsung uses all of these collectively to ensure that the products survive the threats associated with the introduction stage and move into the growth stage to maintain a strong presence in the marketplace. This effort includes the use of various marketing communication tools, including its noteworthy use of sponsorship. Since 1997, Samsung has been supporting sports and it is no wonder that it was given global marketing rights for the 2012 Olympic Games. This is an example of how Samsung creates awareness for its new and existing products among its various consumer segments.

By Dr Ayantunji Gbadamosi,
University of East London, UK

Questions

1 Identify three Samsung product offerings and explain their core benefits. How are these different from the actual products?
2 What are the main factors that account for the success of Samsung's products despite the keen competition in the electronics industry?
3 Explain the term 'product lifecycle'. Explain why Samsung will want to engage in significant marketing communication efforts when the product is at the introduction stage.
4 What advice would you give to the new product development team at Samsung in respect of a planned new product development project scheduled for the next business year?
5 In a recent discussion, a friend has argued that for Samsung to increase its profit, it could reduce the quality of the packaging, especially as this is not the main product the consumer is buying. To what extent do you agree with this standpoint?

Review questions

1 Define product and product value.
2 Distinguish between international marketing and marketing in the domestic market in relation to product value.
3 Discuss competitive advantage in relation to product and product value, and summarise the reasons why it is important.
4 How can a local company compete against a global firm? How might it apply competitive advantage to the foreign competitor?
5 How can a company identify its competitors, and how can it assess them?
6 What are the factors to bear in mind in packaging and labelling a product?
7 What are the biggest advantages of carrying and managing related and unrelated product lines?
8 When should a company decide to retire a brand? Using the Brand Flux model as a guide, what steps should a company consider before it makes this decision?
9 Explain what it means to manage a product line's brand. How is this related to brand equity?
10 Describe how and why a company may develop a new product.

Group tasks

1 Brainstorm in a group to develop a new automobile product. Remember to highlight what you consider to be the unique selling proposition (USP) of this new product and why you think it will be commercially successful.
2 Select any three brands from different business sectors. Identify what you consider to be similar among them and discuss why each survives the turbulent marketing environment.
3 Take a look at the list of products you were asked to make on page 20 again. Did you include any services, ideas, places or people? If you did, good for you!

Now circle anything on your list that was not a physical good. If you don't have at least two examples for each of the categories listed above, add more products to your list.

Glossary/Key terms

Business-to-business products: Products acquired as part of the operations of an organization or to be used as parts for other products that are for sale.

Consumer products: Products acquired for the satisfaction of the needs of individuals, friends, families and acquaintances.

Durable goods: Products that can last for long periods of time and therefore can be used repeatedly.

Functional products: Products acquired for the satisfaction of basic needs.

Product line: A group of products that are closely related to each other.

Product mix: The total of all the different varieties of products offered by an organization.

Vocab check list for ESL students

Acquisition	Commodities	Facilitate
Alienation	Correlation	Idiosyncrasies
Augmented	Durability	Interrelated

Definitions for these terms can be found in the 'Vocab Zone' of the companion website, which provides free access to the Macmillan English Dictionary online at www.palgrave.com/business/Gbadamosi

6

Further reading

Päivi Eriksson and Keijo Räsänen (1998) 'The Bitter and the Sweet: Evolving Constellations of Product Mix Management in a Confectionery Company', *European Journal of Marketing*, Vol. 32, No. 3/4, pp. 279–304
    The paper discusses the product mix in relation to how it was shaped by groups of marketing and production managers, general managers and owner-managers.

Dennis A. Pitta (2008) 'Product Innovation and Management in a Small Enterprise', *Journal of Product and Brand Management*, Vol. 17, No. 6, pp. 416–19
    This paper describes a product innovation and management approach that is in use by one small enterprise.

John A. Quelch, Paul W. Farris and James Olver (1992) 'The Product Management Audit', *Journal of Product and Brand Management*, Vol. 1, No. 2, pp. 5–18
    Through an actual audit survey, this article shows how an organization used an audit to identify and solve problems within its product management system.

References

Aaker, D. A., Kumar, V. and Day, G. S. (1995) *Marketing Research* (5th edn). Chichester: John Wiley and Sons

Brassington, F. and Pettitt, S. (2006) *Principles of Marketing* (3rd edn). Harlow: Pearson Education

Burca, De B., Fletcher, R. and Brown, L. (2004) *International Marketing, An SME Perspective*. London: Pearson Education

Chadee, D. and Raman, R. (2009) 'International Outsourcing of Information Technology Services: Review and Future Directions', *International Marketing Review*, 26 (4), pp. 411–38

Clemenz, G. (2010) 'Eco-labelling and Horizontal Product Differentiation', *Environmental Resource Economics*, 45, pp. 481–97

Dibb, S., Simkin, L., Pride, W. M. and Ferrell, O. C. (2012) *Marketing: Concepts and Strategies* (6th edn). Andover: Cengage Learning

Gbadamosi, A. (2011) 'Managing Products in Small and Medium-sized Enterprises: A Customer-oriented Perspective' in S. Nwankwo and A. Gbadamosi (eds) *Entrepreneurship Marketing: Principles and Practice of SME Marketing*, pp. 108–26. Abingdon: Routledge

Gregory, J. R. and Wiechmann, J. G. (2002) *Branding Across Borders: a Guide to Global Brand Marketing*. New York: McGraw-Hill

Hollensen, S. (2008) *Essentials of Global Marketing*. Harlow: Pearson Education

Holmes, G. R. and Paswan, A. (2012) 'Consumer Reaction to New Package Design', *Journal of Product and Brand Management*, 21 (2), pp. 109–16

Keegan, W. J. and Green, M. C. (2011) *Global Marketing* (6th edn). Upper Saddle River, NJ: Pearson Education

Keller, K. L. (2003) *Strategic Brand Management*. New York, NY: Prentice Hall

Koh, W. T. H. (2005) 'Household Demand, Network Externality Effect and Intertemporal Price Discrimination', *Journal of Economics*, 84 (1), pp. 49–69

Kotler, P. and Armstrong, G. (2012) *Principles of Marketing*. Harlow: Pearson Education

Martinez, E., Polo, Y. and de Chernatony, L. (2008) 'Effect of Brand Extension Strategies on Brand Image: a Comparative Study of the UK and Spanish Markets', *International Marketing Review*, 25 (1), pp. 107–137

Murphy, J. (1990) *Brand Strategy*. New York: Prentice Hall

Omar, M., Willliams, R. and Lingelbach, D. (2009) 'Global Brand Market Entry to Manage Corporate Reputation', *Journal of Product and Brand Management*, 18 (3), pp. 177–87

Omar, O. (2009) *International Marketing*. Baskingstoke: Palgrave Macmillan

Pitta, D. A. and Franzak, F. J. (2008) 'Foundations for Building Share of Heart in Global Brands', *Journal of Product and Brand Management*, 17 (2), pp. 64–72

Powers, T. L. and Loyka, J. J. (2007) 'Market, Industry and Company Influences on Global Product Standardisation', *International Marketing Review*, 24 (6), pp. 678–94

Riezebos, R. (2003) *Brand Management*. New York, NY: Prentice Hall

Rundh, B. (2009) 'Packaging Design: Creating Competitive Design with Product Packaging', *British Food Journal*, 111 (9), pp. 988–1002

Smith, D. K. (2008) 'Interview with Mr Felix Ohiwerei, former Chairman of Nigerian Breweries, Unilever Nigeria and Virgin Nigeria', *Journal of African Business*, 9 (2), pp. 327–36

Srivastava, K. and Sharma, N. K. (2012) 'Consumer Attitude Towards Brand Extension Incongruity: the Moderating Role of Need for Cognition and Need for Change', *Journal of Marketing Management*, 28 (5–6), pp. 652–75

Terpstra, V. and Sarathy, R. (2000) *International Marketing*. Fort Worth, TX: Dryden

Van Wyk, B.-E. (2011) 'The Potential of South African Plants in the Development of New Food and Beverage Products', *South African Journal of Botany*, 77, pp. 857–68

Wang, J. (2005) 'Consumer Nationalism and Corporate Reputation Management in the Global Era', *Corporate Communications: An International Journal*, 10 (3), pp. 223–39

Williams, R. (2012) 'Branding through Renaming for Strategic Alignment in Service Organizations', PhD thesis, Edinburgh Napier University

7 PRICING STRATEGIES

EMMANUEL OHOHE

LONDON METROPOLITAN UNIVERSITY

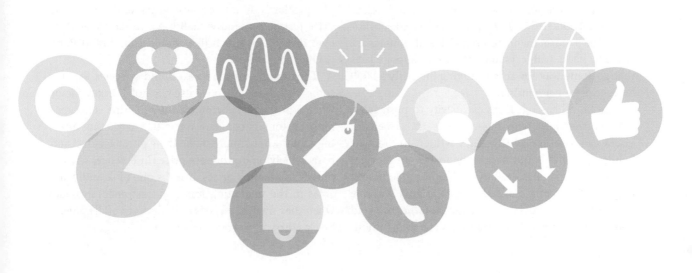

CHAPTER CONTENTS

LEARNING OUTCOMES

The content of this chapter will help you to:

- Define price, understand its characteristics and appreciate its relationship with value, cost and quality
- Explain the factors that influence pricing decisions in different kinds of organizations and how consumers and customers perceive price
- Understand the application of pricing strategies and pricing methods
- Explore approaches to developing value-based pricing
- Understand how to coordinate pricing decisions with other elements of the marketing mix
- Discuss the stages for setting prices

VERTU MADE ITS NAME MORE THAN A DECADE ago by producing mobile handsets encrusted with precious stones and providing a personal concierge service for its users, accessed at the touch of a button. Launched in 1998, it is a UK-based subsidiary of the handset manufacturer, Nokia. Its phones are made by hand, with crystal displays and sapphire keys that go some way towards justifying the hefty £4,000 average price per handset.

The brand has relied on exclusivity to push sales, with partnerships with big names such as Ferrari. Users can also access ringtones written by popular bands. Widely coveted and endorsed by several celebrities, Vertu has established itself as a dominant player in the luxury smartphone arena. It is available in 120 branded stores in 70 countries and has sold 300,000 units since 2002. Handsets are sold without contracts in Vertu-branded retailers and jewellers, and delivered in lavish boxes, with additional services including concierge and craftsman servicing. The product's desirability was visual and tactile, the price justified by individuality. Vertu has created its own mythology, much like audio-visual brand Bang & Olufsen in the past.

The example of the Vertu brand suggests that for some customers price by itself is not the key factor when a purchase is being considered. This is because most customers compare the entire marketing offering and do not simply make their purchase decision based solely on a product's price. In essence, when a purchase situation arises, price is one of several variables in the marketing mix that customers evaluate when they mentally assess a product's overall value.

Source: Marketing Magazine, 16 May 2012, p. 21

INTRODUCTION

The word 'price' tends to have different meanings for different people. To the average person, the price of anything is the amount of money which has to be paid to acquire that thing. Price may be called different names in different contexts. Universities and colleges charge tuition fees, hotels quote a room rate, charities seek donations, employees want a wage and banks want interest for a loan to customers. In business terms, price is the value placed on physical goods, services or ideas that can be offered to target customers. To a marketer, price is a component of the marketing mix.

This chapter explores price as an important component of the marketing mix and as a revenue generator. In doing so, it provides a framework for understanding value-oriented pricing decisions.

DEFINING PRICE FROM A VALUE PERSPECTIVE

Price is the amount of money charged for a product or service; it is the sum of the values that customers exchange for the benefits of having or using the product or service.

This definition suggests that price plays two distinct roles for consumers:

- It is a measure of sacrifice, such as monetary value or non-monetary components, such as time and risk

- It is an information cue: The information effect for some customers means price perceptions guide consumer behaviour in the sense that some consumers may equate higher prices with higher quality or higher expected value

The theory of price is not new. Price and pricing have their origins in classical economics, with links to the concept of demand and supply curves, elasticity and marginal costs and revenue. In the discipline of accounting, the approach to pricing tends to emphasize fixed and variable costs and financial considerations such as shareholders' dividends. It is important to differentiate prices from costs. In business, costs are important and must be covered through prices. However, costs are a matter of fact, whereas prices are a matter of policy and are often a marketing consideration. For marketers and marketing-oriented organizations, price is one of the most important marketing mix decisions, being the only variable that generates revenues and has an immediate and direct effect on buyer behaviour (Rao, 1984; Nagle and Holden, 1995). Therefore 'price is what a customer must give up to get the benefits offered by the rest of a firm's marketing mix, so it plays a direct role in shaping customer value' (Perreault et al., 2010). As a result, the key issues related to price are practical ones such as the pricing methods used in businesses and how they are determined in order to satisfy the needs of the target customers and provide value.

Value refers to the perception of benefits received for what a customer must give up. Since price often reflects an important part of what someone gives up, a customer's perceived value of a product will be affected by a marketer's pricing decision. Price also relates to anything that is not money but has a perceived value. For example, if you exchange any of your personal items or provide services in exchange in a transaction without money changing hands, such trade is called *bartering*.

An easy way to see this is to view value as a calculation:

$$\text{Value} = \frac{\text{perceived benefits received}}{\text{perceived price paid}}$$

For the buyer, the value of a product will change as the perceived price paid and/or the perceived benefits received change. For example, the Vertu brand, with a £4,000 average price per unit, includes concierge and craftsman servicing, products delivered in lavish boxes, association with premium brand names and celebrities, and so on.

In other words, a marketing-oriented business treats price and pricing as a key creative decision area and not as an accounting or cost responsibility.

Other marketing mix variables such as product, place and promotion are discussed in other chapters. The price component is discussed and explored not as a mechanical process determined in isolation but as a process that should be compatible with and lend support to the other key marketing elements of product and services marketing.

THE IMPORTANCE OF PRICE TO MARKETERS

Academics and practitioners are in agreement that the selling price of products and services represents one of the most important decisions businesses have to make.

For commercial organizations to earn a profit, marketers must arrive at a price that is neither too low nor too high. In other words, they must set a price that equals the perceived value to the target or potential customers. If a price is set too low, the consumer may perceive the product or service as being of great value, but the business may lose revenue that could have been earned. On the other hand, if the price is high in the consumer's mind, the perceived value may be less than the cost and potential sales may also be lost.

REVENUE GENERATION

The selling price of goods and services relates directly to the generation of total *revenue* (= price multiplied by units sold). This is primarily because the price component is the most adjustable of all marketing mix decisions. Unlike product, promotion and distribution decisions, which may take months or years to change, price can be changed very quickly. The flexibility of pricing decisions is particularly important in times when the marketer seeks to stimulate demand quickly or to respond to competitor price actions. For instance, a marketer can agree to their salesperson's request to lower a price for a potential prospect during a phone conversation. Likewise a marketer in charge of online operations can raise prices on fast selling products with the click of a few website buttons.

As noted earlier, whilst the other marketing mix elements relate to costs (such as spend on new product development, advertising, setting up distribution networks, paying salespeople and the field salesforce), price is the only marketing mix element that generates revenues and has an immediate and direct effect on buyer behaviour. So price can be a major determinant in the quantity of goods sold and can influence total costs through that impact on quantity sold.

For example, marketers often have to adjust the price of their products and services either as part of sales promotions to rid themselves of perishable stock or for old stock to make way for new. This often results in a decision to lower prices, which may represent value and attract some customers. In other cases, attempts may be made to raise an initially low-priced product to a higher price. Such changes are sometimes met by resistance as customers may feel the marketer is attempting to take advantage of them.

Prices set too high can also impact revenue as they prevent interested customers from purchasing the product. In relation to buyer behaviour, price has been reported as having a psychological impact on customers. By raising prices, the quality of the product can be emphasized, particularly when such effort is backed by attempts to emphasize design, reliability, durability or prestige. Also, by lowering prices, marketers can emphasize a bargain, thus affecting cost, quantity sold and revenue generation. However, marketers must guard against the temptation to increase or reduce prices too frequently because this could result in confusion about the real price and value of the product to the target and potential consumers. Continually increasing and decreasing price can lead customers to anticipate price reductions and, consequently, withhold purchase until the price reduction occurs again. As will be discussed later in the chapter, decisions on setting the right prices are influenced by a number of factors, including market knowledge, with regard to setting prices for new products.

Other reasons for the importance of price to marketers

There has been an increase in customer knowledge over the years about products and marketing. Increased competition in most markets has led to the launch of new products and services. Consumers are often aided by the internet, which has made comparison-shopping easier. This has led to potential buyers being able to evaluate prices carefully and evaluate the value of products and services.

In industrial or organizational markets, where customers include both businesses and governments, buyers are becoming price sensitive and better informed, particularly with the growth and availability of bargain-priced private and generic brands of products. Improved communications and the increasing use of direct marketing, ecommerce and computer-aided selling have opened markets and sectors to new competitors. All these have put downward pressure on overall prices. In this market, prices are often affected by the relationship between price and cost, and by value management. Research suggests that in industrial markets quality is the factor most often sought by buyers and price is a major motivator required to prompt a currently satisfied buyer into making a change. The second factor most often sought is reliable delivery. In business-to-business markets, price discounting, geographical pricing, transfer pricing, price discrimination and economic value to the customer are additional pricing concerns.

Many businesses are trying to adapt to changing marketing conditions to maintain or regain their market share by cutting prices. The UK, Europe and elsewhere in the developed world have all been in recession since 2008 and have still not achieved recovery in 2013. Most economic forecasts suggest that the current recovery will be slow and will not be achieved until 2015. This trend will continue to put pressure on consumer spending and prices.

PRICE AND COMPETITION

Organizations can adopt one of two approaches to price in relation to the competition.

Price competition

Firms adopting this policy emphasize price in the marketing of their products and services and attempt to match or beat their competitors' prices. In this case, the company seeks to attract customers solely on the basis of product price. In price competition, marketers seek to influence customer demand primarily through changing the prices of their products.

Non-price competition

Businesses using a non-price competition policy choose to differentiate their products by non-price means – for example, by quality, style, delivery methods, locations or special services. Non-price competition is often practised by firms that desire to differentiate virtually identical products. Companies producing cigarettes, over-the-counter medications or food products spend large sums on non-price competition. Luxury brands also spend a lot on differentiating and promoting their brands and are often very selective in their promotion and distribution.

Non-price competition may adopt the following tactics:

- Reinforce the quality image of the product
- Reinforce the desirability of the product benefits
- Use extended warranty to help customers think they are getting more for their money
- Emphasize the longer-term cost saving derived from using this product rather than the immediate price advantage
- Provide customer loyalty cards
- Provide incentives for purchasing off peak or out of season
- Offer internet shopping
- Offer home delivery systems

PRICE AND SERVICES

In service markets, the influences on prices are related to some of the distinct characteristics of service (intangibility, heterogeneity, perishability and inseparability) and these are discussed in detail in Chapter 10. However, in relation to prices, research by Hoffman et al. (2002, p. 1016) noted seven distinct categories and considered how these affect prices for services:

- **Demand:** For example, the demand for services tends to be more inelastic than the demand for goods
- **Cost:** For example, cost-oriented pricing is more difficult in services
- **The consumer:** For example, service consumers are more likely to use price as an indication of quality
- **Competition:** For example, comparing competitive prices is more difficult in the case of service
- **Profit:** For example, price bundling makes the determination of individual prices in a bundle of services complicated
- **Product:** For example, product line pricing tends to be more complicated in the case of services
- **Legal issues:** For example, the opportunity for illegal pricing practices to go undetected is greater in services

The same authors have argued, based on this list, that the organization's pricing strategies and objectives for services will be different from those of physical products.

PRICE AND NON−PROFIT ORGANIZATIONS

The non-profit or not-for-profit sector is made up of different and diverse types of organizations such as charities, political parties, hospitals, cities, social clubs and churches that are not allowed to distribute their net earnings, if any, among the individuals who operate the organization. Many organizations operate non-profit projects because of the value or perceived value of such projects to society or the organization's members rather than their potential to generate monetary profits. In other words, they are not set up to generate and distribute profits.

Some non-profits such as hospitals and universities charge for the goods and services they provide to their service recipients; others provide free services that are financed by a complex variety of donations, grants and other income sources. But they all need revenues and funding to run their operations. Over the last 20 years, non-profit organizations in the UK, particularly universities and voluntary, religious and charitable institutions, have been adopting the marketing concept and integrating fully the principles and practices that could benefit their operation. In relation to price, when a non-profit does charge a fee, the fee may deliberately not cover the costs of the service. This contrasts with commercial firms that only sell things for less than cost if forced to do so by market apathy. Obviously, it is more difficult for non-profits to raise prices, partly because of public expectations and partly because of the economic need of the organization's constituents. Therefore, in non-profit markets, there are different objectives relating to the price of a product or service.

FACTORS INFLUENCING PRICING DECISIONS

Pricing decisions are often complex and are affected by many interrelated and varied factors that marketers must take into account. Some of these factors are within the control of the organization and the marketing manager; others are outside the control of the organization and the marketer but can equally impact on any pricing decision. As a result, some researchers have suggested that managers require a pragmatic approach to setting prices, which incorporates not only demand and supply-driven issues but also strategic factors (Jobber and Shipley, 1998). These factors can be grouped into two distinct categories: internal and external factors (see Figure 7.1). This section explores how each element in these two categories enters into price decision making.

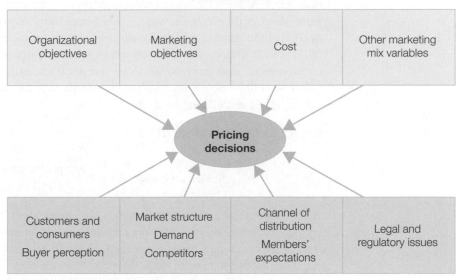

Figure 7.1: Internal and external factors affecting pricing decisions
Source: Based on Dibb et al., 2009, p. 358

INTERNAL FACTORS

Internal business factors such as organization objectives, costs and marketing objectives influence pricing decisions.

Organization objectives

Marketing decisions, including those about pricing of products and services, are not made in isolation but are guided by the overall objectives of the organization. Every organization has objectives. These objectives include performance measures that are used to evaluate the results of different aspects of the business to determine whether the organization is achieving its stated mission. In this regard, pricing can play a role in achieving long- and short-term corporate objectives. Marketers are also tasked with setting marketing objectives that are consistent with the organization objectives, goals and mission.

Marketing and pricing objectives

Marketing objectives are a statement of what is to be accomplished through marketing activities. According to Jobber (2010), marketing objectives are often expressed through two types of activity – strategic thrust and strategic objectives:

- Strategic thrust dictates which products should be sold in which markets
- Strategic objectives determine product-level objectives, such as which products to build, hold, harvest or divest from

In a highly competitive market, one of the key elements in strategy and marketing mix decisions is the desire and ability to differentiate you from competitors. In other words, marketers can become successful if they can create and differentiate their products and brands from the rest of the market. To achieve this, they must address the issue of pricing at any given time and over the life of their products and services. Therefore, marketers need pricing objectives that are specific, attainable and measurable. And they need realistic pricing goals that require periodic monitoring to determine the effectiveness of the company's strategy (Lamb et al., 2012). This is because a price based on differential advantage over competitors may need to change over time as competitors gradually begin to reduce a company's differential advantage (Palmer, 2012, p. 325). There are four key objectives in which price plays a central role: *return on investment*, *cash flow*, *market share* and *profit maximization*. In most situations only one of these objectives may be followed, though the marketer may have different objectives for different products.

Return on investment (ROI)

$$\text{Return on investment} = \frac{\text{Net profits after taxes}}{\text{Total assets}}$$

A firm may set as a marketing objective the requirement that all products attain a certain percentage return on the organization's spend on marketing the product. This level of return, along with an estimate of sales, will help determine appropriate pricing levels needed to meet the ROI objective.

Lamb et al. (2012) note that a company with a target ROI can predetermine its desired level of profitability. They added that the marketing manager can use a standard, such as 10 per cent ROI, to determine whether a particular price and marketing mix are feasible. However, research suggests that most pricing objectives based on ROI are achieved by trial and error. Also, companies often do not account for all the costs that ought to be allocated to their products when prices are set.

Cash flow

Cash flow means the incomings and outgoings of cash that represent the operating activities of an organization. In this context, cash flow is concerned with pricing decisions that will lead to the selling of more goods and services.

Some organizations may seek to set prices at a level to ensure that sales revenue will at least cover product production and marketing costs. This is most likely to occur with new products where the organization objectives allow the product simply to meet its expenses while efforts are made to establish it in the market. This objective allows the marketer to worry less about product profitability and instead directs energies to building a market for the product. As Dibb et al. (2012) note, some companies set prices to recover cash as fast as possible, especially when a short product lifecycle (PLC) is anticipated or the capital spent to develop products needs to be recovered quickly. However, the use of cash flow and recovery as an objective oversimplifies the value of price in contributing to profits. A disadvantage of this pricing objective could be high prices, which might allow competitors with lower prices to gain a large share of the market.

Market share

Market share is defined as a company's product sales as a percentage of total sales for that industry (Lamb et al., 2012, p. 695). The pricing decision may be important when the firm has an objective of gaining a hold in a new market or retaining a certain percentage of an existing market. For new products under this objective, the price is set artificially low in order to capture a sizeable portion of the market and will be increased as the product becomes more accepted by the target market. For existing products, firms may use price decisions to ensure they retain market share in instances where there is a high level of market competition and there are competitors who are willing to compete on price.

Sales-oriented pricing objectives are based on attempts to increase either market share or sales volume. Many companies believe that maintaining or increasing market share is an indicator of the effectiveness of their marketing mix. Some researchers (Lamb et al., 2012) report that larger market share often means higher profits, thanks to greater economies of scale, market power and ability to compensate top management.

Think and discuss

To what extent can marketers rely on price as the key differentiator of their offerings? Think about examples of different products to illustrate your arguments.

istock © torque

Some companies set pricing objectives to maintain or increase a product's market share in relation to total industry sales. For example, car companies such as Volkswagen have been known to cut prices on existing models when introducing new ones, to boost share of the car market (Dibb et al., 2012). Pricing for market share, for example, is an objective that was frequently associated with Japanese companies in the 1990s (Bradley, 1995, p. 575). Dibb et al. (2012, p. 600) noted that maintaining or increasing market share need not depend on growth in industry sales and a company can increase its market share even though sales for the total industry are decreasing. On the other hand, if the overall market is growing, a business's sales volume may actually increase as its market share decreases.

Profit maximization

Profit maximization is the desire and ability of a company to achieve a maximum profit with low operating expenses. Profit-oriented pricing objectives are where the objectives centre on profit maximization, satisfactory profits and returns on sales and investment. Older products that appeal to a market that is no longer growing may have a company objective requiring the price to be set at a level that optimizes profits. This is often the case when the marketer has little incentive to introduce improvements to the product (for example, if demand for the product is declining) and will continue to sell the same product at a price premium for as long as the market is willing to buy.

If the objective is maximization of profits, Lamb et al. (2012) suggest that managers can try to expand revenue by increasing customer satisfaction, or they can attempt to reduce costs by operating more efficiently. A third possibility is to attempt to do both. For example, a company can maintain or slightly cut costs while increasing customer loyalty through customer services initiatives and loyalty programmes. Other authors note that although businesses often claim they aim to maximize profit, in practice this objective is difficult to measure. The reality is that profit objectives tend to be set at satisfactory levels, with specific profit objectives often stated in terms of actual monetary amounts or in terms of percentage change relative to previous profits (Dibb et al., 2012). In some cases, rather than

Example 7.1:
Profit maximization

If profit maximization is the objective, an organization may adopt one of the following approaches:

- Charge a high price with a high mark-up (where the 'mark-up' is the difference between the cost of the product and the selling price). This may mean low sales but each product will be making a profit. This is often used as a strategy where the product or brand is of a

istock © rustemgurler

high value, rarely purchased or has some unique attributes (such as Rolls Royce, Rolex, Vertu)

- Charge a low price with a low mark-up. Here the profit on each product may be low but volume sales might lead to a higher overall profit. This is a strategy often adopted by marketers who sell products that have a quick sales turnaround (such as Lidl, Aldi and Netto grocery products where the idea is to 'pile them high and sell them cheap') or no-frills short-haul air travel (such as Rynair and EasyJet) maximizing profits, the company may strive for profits that are satisfactory to the shareholders and management. In this case, the focus will be on a level of profit that is consistent with the level of risks the organization faces. In a risky industry, a satisfactory profit may be 35 per cent return. In a low-risk industry, it might be as low as 7 per cent (Dibb et al., 2012, p. 313).

Maintenance objectives

Maintenance objectives are concerned with issues such as price stabilization in the market and with meeting competitive pricing behaviour.

Some more pricing objectives:

- **Survival:** A fundamental pricing objective is survival. Most businesses will tolerate difficulties such as short-run losses and internal upheaval if they are necessary for survival. Because price is a flexible and convenient variable to adjust, it is sometimes used to increase sales volumes to levels that match the company's expenses
- **Product quality:** A company might have the objective of product quality leadership in the industry. For example, the construction equipment manufacturer JCB aims to be ranked as one of the leading companies in its industry in terms of product quality and customer satisfaction. This normally dictates a relatively high price to cover the high product quality and/or the high cost of research and development
- **Status quo:** In some cases, a business may be in a favourable position and may simply wish to maintain the status quo. Such objectives can focus on maintaining a certain market share, meeting (but not beating) competitors' prices, achieving price stability or maintaining a favourable public image. Such an approach can reduce a company's risks by helping to stabilize demand for its products. The use of status quo pricing objectives sometimes leads to a climate of non-price competition in an industry

Source: Dibb et al., 2012, p. 600

Cost

Cost represents a multifaceted concept to producers of goods and services, and to marketers. In some cases, the selling price of a product or service may have little to do with the total cost of producing it. This is because, as indicated earlier, a business may choose to price products below cost to *survive*, *generate cash flow*, *increase market share* or *match the competition*. However, before marketers can determine or set prices for their products or services, they must understand the relationship between cost, demand and revenue. This cost should not be confused with *marketing cost* – which is the total cost associated with delivering goods or services to customers. The marketing cost may include expenses associated with transferring title of goods to a customer, storing goods in warehouses pending delivery, promoting the goods or services being sold, and the distribution of the product to points of sale. (This is covered in detail elsewhere.) Cost consideration is very important because reducing cost is one of two ways a company can increase its profitability. The other is to increase price, which is not always possible. In this section we look at the different types of costs that marketers must consider in their pricing decision.

Fixed costs

These are the costs associated with the production of products and services. These costs do not change in the short run as a result of changes in sales volume. For example, the annual depreciation on the manufacturing plant and salaries of full-time employees are considered as fixed costs. Other examples are rents, rates and loan interest payments.

Variable costs

This type of cost varies directly with the number of products and so changes in proportion to the sales volume. For example, the costs of running the plant, materials and power are variable costs.

Marginal costs

These are variable costs consisting of labour and material costs, plus an estimated portion of fixed costs (such as administration overheads and selling expenses). In companies where average costs are fairly constant, marginal cost is usually equal to average cost. However, in industries that require heavy capital investment (such as automobile plants, airlines and mines) and have high average costs, it is comparatively very low. The concept of marginal cost is critically important in resource allocation because, for optimum results, management must concentrate its resources where the excess of marginal revenue over the marginal cost is maximal.

Total costs

These represent all the costs incurred by an organization in manufacturing, marketing, administration and delivering the product to the customer. Total cost is the sum of fixed and variable costs.

Research shows that companies consistently undercharge for products despite spending millions to develop or acquire such products. This is because many

Example 7.2:
Competitive pricing

Amazon sells its devices, including its Kindle e-reader, for less than it costs to make them, aiming instead to make profits through sales of books, music and movies in its online Kindle store.

The iPad formula of selling high-quality technology at mid-range prices has helped its success. Its most basic tablet models may seem expensive at £399, but executives at major technology companies complain privately that they have found it impossible to build a strong competitor at the same cost.

istock © PIKSEL

companies want to make a quick grab for market share or ROI. With high prices, both objectives can be harder to achieve (Marn et al., 2003).

Marketing mix variables

As stated earlier, higher prices are usually associated with higher quality. This price–quality relationship does influence customers' image of a brand of product or service. As a result, consumers may be prepared to pay high prices for Armani jeans because they believe this is a high-status product with high or perceived high value.

The pricing decision adopted by a marketer may influence and increase the number of competing brands in the product category. When a new product enters the market with a relatively high price and commands high unit sales, it will attract the attention of competitors in the product category. The opposite may also be true if the prices are fixed low and profit margins are also low.

The same principle applies to the channels of distribution adopted for a product. The channels used to distribute premium-priced products are either exclusive or selective while lower-priced products are intensively distributed.

Also, the promotional strategy adopted for a product would affect the price. Price is naturally emphasized in promoting products that compete on price, particularly bargain prices. This is not often the case in premium products. Also, high-quality and highly priced products are more likely to require personal selling.

In relation to marketing orientation, this suggests that price is just one factor in the consumer's buying decision and is not necessarily the most important. This is especially so if the other elements in the marketing mix are adding value and a competitive edge. See Table 7.1.

Table 7.1: Influences of relative perceptions and elements of the marketing mix

Product	Those perceived by consumers as high quality have a superior design and superior components or ingredients compared with competitors' products. This is the case in fashion brands for clothes, and their accessories such as perfumes and fragrance
Price	More expensive products are commonly perceived by consumers to be higher in quality than less expensive products. Therefore they are likely to command premium prices. If the product strategy is differentiation through a high-quality, 'upmarket' brand image, the pricing strategy would be to price high so as to reinforce the desired image. Armani, Brioni and Lanvin, are examples of brands that set premium prices for their clothes to enhance an image of product luxury
Promotion	Promotion and advertising tell consumers what is special or unique about a particular brand, which influences consumers' perceptions. Conversely, price can be used in sales promotion to offer incentives such as short-term discounts, money off, easy and interest free credit terms
Place	The place and manner of distribution of a product also affect the perception of the product – for example, a high-quality product is mainly sold in upmarket retail outlets. A few years ago, Levi's jeans successfully stopped Asda from stocking and discounting its products because it was argued that the downward interference with price, as well as the cut-price image of Asda, would cause damage to its luxury product image

PRODUCT LIFECYCLE AND PRICE

Stages in the product lifecycle also influence pricing decisions.

Introduction stage

Management may set high prices during the introduction stage, partly to recover its development cost quickly and partly to cater for the core market, which may not be price sensitive. If the target market is highly price sensitive, the price will be set at the market level or lower.

Growth stage

At this stage the product may begin to appeal to a broader market and competitors may have entered the market, thus increasing supply. Economies of scale mean lower costs and the savings are passed on to consumers in the form of lower prices.

Maturity stage

At the maturity stage there are further price decreases as a result of competition. High-cost competitors are also eliminated. Those who are left in during the later stages of maturity offer similar prices. Any price increases are cost initiated rather than demand led. Also, price reduction at this stage does not necessarily stimulate demand.

Decline

There may be a scrabble by remaining competitors to tap the last pockets of demand. Prices might rise for certain products or brands if they move into a speciality product category, such as for vinyl records.

Marketing strategy of the organization

As already stated, not all organizations view price as a key selling feature for the different products in their product mix and portfolio. For some products that are market leaders in their category, the emphasis will instead be on a strategy that highlights non-price benefits such as quality, durability and service. Such non-price competition can help the company avoid price wars, which often break out between competitive firms that follow a market share objective and use price as a key selling feature.

EXTERNAL FACTORS

External factors such as customers and consumers, demand and price elasticity, legal and regulatory, channels of distribution, and competitors affect pricing decisions.

General economic conditions often have a strong impact on any organization's pricing strategy. This is because boom, recession, inflation and interest rates can affect consumer spending and the company's cost of producing and selling products. In times of economic well-being, there is a high 'feel-good factor'; consumer demand and spending tend to be high and move towards value added. Conversely, during a downturn in the economy, consumer demand tends to fall, moving towards price and away from value added. These changes are beyond the control of any business but they affect the price of goods and services and must therefore be given consideration in marketers' pricing decisions.

Customer and consumer perceptions

Marketing decisions cannot be made without thinking about price from the perspective of the customer or consumer. This is primarily because the selling price of a product may be interpreted in a different way by consumers. For example, a low price may attract some consumers while others may interpret low price as meaning low quality and be deterred. Equally, high selling prices may signal superior quality to some customers while others may interpret them as too expensive. This means marketers must have a good understanding of the feelings and sensitivities of the end buyer. As noted in Brassington and Pettitt (2013, p. 258) different market segments react to price levels and changes differently, depending on the nature of the product, its desirability and the level of product loyalty established.

Also, Dibb et al. (2012, p. 602) suggest that when making pricing decisions marketers should be concerned with two vital sets of questions:

● How will customers interpret prices? Interpretation in this context refers to what the price means or what it communicates to customers. Does the price mean 'high quality' or 'low quality', or 'great deal', 'fair price' or 'rip-off'?
● How will customers respond to the price? Customer response refers to whether the price will move customers closer to the purchase of the product, and the degree to which the price enhances their satisfaction with the purchase experience and with the product after purchase

The authors suggest that, in the context of price, buyers can be categorized according to the three degrees of consciousness: value consciousness, price consciousness and prestige sensitivity.

● **Value-conscious consumers:** Are concerned about both the price and the quality of the product. Recent economic difficulties have altered the purchasing habits of many consumers and business customers, with many more placing value for money high on their list of key customer values when making a purchase decision
● **Price-conscious consumers:** Strive to pay low prices
● **Prestige-sensitive consumers:** Focus on purchasing products that signify prominence and status

Perceived value for money

Perceived value for money is an important consideration when setting prices. As indicated earlier in the chapter, consumers do not tend to regard price purely as the monetary value being demanded in exchange for goods or services (see Table 7.2). Other important considerations include: the quality of the item, its brand image, purpose, usage and overall appeal, along with the consumer's previous experiences of the product. They may also consider certain tangibles such as interest-free credit and warranties. All or some of these factors may dictate the consumer's view of the value for money.

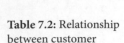

Table 7.2: Relationship between customer costs and values

Customer costs	Customer values
Affordability	Acceptability
Alternatives	Aesthetics – look, feel, sound, taste, smell
Cost of use	Conformance to standards
Installation	Credit and terms
Life span of product	Dependability
Monetary price	Durability
Service costs	Economy of purchase
Time needed to search for purchase	Image perception
Transportation	Performance and features
	Safety and security
	Serviceability
	Variety

What Table 7.2 suggests is that buyers' perception of price is not static in the sense that price has different associations in the minds of different buyers. However, in determining price, marketing managers must understand the cost involved, the alternatives available and the response of the different customer groups and the value they place on the product or service.

Market structure, demand and competition

After marketers establish pricing objectives, they must set specific prices to achieve those objectives. The price adopted is influenced by factors such as production costs, the nature and strength of demand, and competitors' prices. Very often the price arrived at has a combination of all three elements.

Market structure

The structure of the markets will affect the ability of the organization to set and control the price (see Table 7.3).

Demand

Demand is the amount of a particular good or service that a consumer or group of consumers will want to purchase at a given price. The demand curve is usually downward sloping, since consumers will want to buy more as price decreases. Demand for a good or service is determined by many different factors other than price, such as the price of substitute goods and complementary goods. In extreme cases, demand may be completely unrelated to price, or nearly infinite at a given price. Along with supply, demand is one of the two key determinants of the market price.

Table 7.3: Economic markets and prices

Type of markets	Characteristics	Role of price
Perfect	Many producers and buyers Unrestricted entry to the market Cartels/oligopolies may form Producers are homogeneous Buyer/seller indifferent about whom to trade with	Price uniformity – only one price in the market at any given time, subject to minor variations One firm or customer cannot affect price
Imperfect	Many producers/buyers Restricted entry to the market Products are differentiated Back-up promotion and product innovation utilized	Price not uniform Firms may change prices, thereby affecting other firms Price war my occur, often destructive
Oligopoly	Small number of large producers controlling the total market	Firms control the price, but compete against each other
Duopoly	Only two suppliers in a market, e.g. Unilever and P&G have over 80 per cent market share of the detergent business	Two companies regulate price, depending on market share
Monopoly	Only one manufacturer of a product, which can control supply	Company can stipulate price (but subject to regulatory bodies investigating if this is against public interest)

Source: Adapted from Hutchings, 1995, p. 255

A demand and supply curve, as in Figure 7.2, is a graphical or mathematical diagram that shows the relationship between the price and quantity of a product that consumers are willing to buy. In business, demand curves are useful when testing and measuring the *supply and demand* of certain products within a competitive market. Graphed over time, demand curves assist businesses in determining whether a certain product is actually profitable at the pricing point on the curve where it is in demand.

Understanding the impact of price changes on the market requires the marketer to have a firm understanding of the concept economists call 'elasticity of demand', which relates to how purchase quantity changes as prices change.

Elasticity deals with two types of demand scenarios:

- **Elastic demand:** Products are considered to exist in a market that exhibits elastic demand when a certain percentage change in price results in a larger and opposite percentage change in demand. For example, if the price of a product increases (decreases) by 10 per cent, the demand for the product is likely to decline (rise) by more than 10 per cent
- **Inelastic demand:** Products are considered to exist in an inelastic market when a certain percentage change in price results in a smaller and opposite percentage change in demand. For example, if the price of a product increases (decreases) by 10 per cent, the demand for the product is likely to decline (rise) by less than 10 per cent

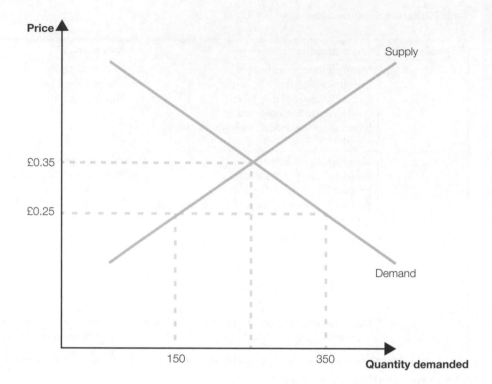

Figure 7.2:
Relationship of price
and demand

For marketers, the important issue with elasticity of demand is to understand how it impacts company revenue. In general, the scenarios shown in Figures 7.3 and 7.4 apply to making price changes for a given type of market demand.

In *elastic markets*, increasing price reduces total revenue while decreasing price increases total revenue.

In *inelastic markets*, increasing price raises total revenue while decreasing price reduces total revenue.

The concept of price elasticity is a good measure of how consumers respond to price changes. It is an important concept in pricing decisions if it can help the manager decide on the most appropriate price to charge for the organization's products and services. Also, if managers know what determines price elasticity of demand, they will be in a better position to estimate how consumers will respond to price changes, and to decide on the price to charge for their products and services.

Competition

Competitors: Pricing
under different market
structures

In terms of competition, marketers agree that it is vital to know competitors' prices and to price or adjust their prices accordingly or to offer differentiation. Rochford and Wotruba (2000) suggest that value may be added on the basis of attributes, benefits or brand image. For example, many car companies are able to add value by offering superior performance, trim or a strong brand image. This does not mean that a company should necessarily match competitors' prices; it may set its price above or below theirs. It is also important for marketers to assess how competitors

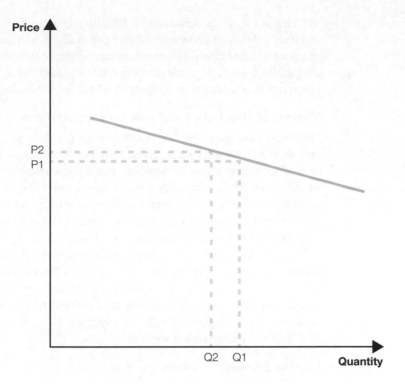

Figure 7.3: Elastic demand curve

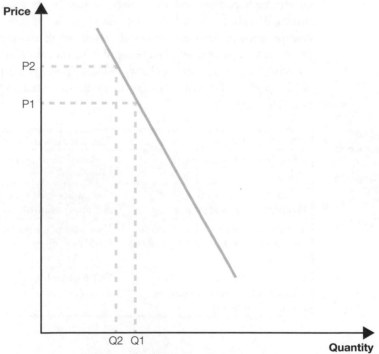

Figure 7.4: Inelastic demand curve

will respond to price adjustments. Will they change their prices (some may not) and if so, will they raise or reduce them? For example, when a bank or building society stresses its interest rates on loans, competitors often do the same. This suggests that, in a competitive market, very little advantage can be gained through price cuts. If an organization cuts its price to gain a competitive advantage, others are likely to follow suit.

Channel of distribution and members' expectations

Marketing managers who use middlemen to get their products to end-users must include these elements when making pricing decisions. A producer must consider what distribution channel members (such as wholesalers, retailers and dealers) would expect. These intermediaries or channel members certainly expect to receive a profit for the functions they perform. The amount of profit depends on the amount of time resources expended and on an assessment of what would be gained by handling a competing product instead (Dibb et al., 2012).

In most cases, channel members expect producers to provide discounts for large orders and quick payment. In other cases, resellers expect producers to provide support activities, such as sales training, repair advisory services, cooperative advertising, sales promotion and a programme for returning unsold merchandise to the producer. These support activities clearly incur costs, so a producer must consider these costs when determining prices.

Legal and regulatory issues

Government actions and the powers vested in its agencies influence marketers' pricing decisions. To curb inflation, for example, the government may invoke price controls such as 'freezing' prices at certain levels to determine the rates at which prices can be increased. Following the privatization of public utilities, the UK government also set up regulatory bodies that regulate pricing and billing. Some of the bodies also have powers to establish maximum and minimum charges (see Table 7.4).

Table 7.4: Legal and regulatory influence on pricing
Source: Adapted from Dibb et al., 2012, p. 604

Ofwat for water	Ofgem for gas and electricity
Ofcom for the telecommunications industry	Marketers must also refrain from fixing prices
Companies must develop independent pricing policies	Companies must set prices in a way that does not involve collusion
The UK Competition Commission prevents the creation of monopolistic situations	The consumer is protected by the Trade Descriptions Act
Countries in the EU follow EU legislation to protect consumers within the community	VAT payments as required by law

METHODS OF SETTING PRICES

In the previous section we discussed the different influences on pricing decisions. Here the focus will be on basic methods of setting prices. It has long been reported that marketers have different methods of setting prices. Shapiro and Jackson (1978) identified three distinct methods that are widely used by managers to set prices. These are cost-based pricing, competition-based pricing and market-oriented pricing.

COST-BASED PRICING

In cost-based pricing, the marketer sets a floor price that is the minimum price acceptable to the firm so it can reach a specified profit goal.

According to Jobber (2010, p. 423), businesses mostly use two cost-based pricing methods. These are:

- Full-cost pricing
- Direct-cost (or marginal) pricing

Full-cost pricing

Full-cost pricing seeks to set a price that takes into account all relevant costs of production. The marketing manager looks at the full average cost of production of a brand (fixed and variable overheads) and adds a profit margin to arrive at the selling price. This approach is favoured by service providers such as solicitors and accountants where it is difficult in some cases to compute the costs in advance. One drawback is that this method does give an indication of the minimum price required to make a profit. This could be calculated as follows:

$$\frac{\text{Total budgeted factory cost} + \text{Selling}}{\text{Distribution costs} + \text{Other overheads} + \text{Mark-up on cost}}$$

Direct-cost (or marginal) pricing

Unlike full-cost pricing, direct-cost (or marginal) pricing includes only costs that can be directly traced to producing specific goods or services. The focus is on the direct costs such as labour and raw materials plus a mark-up to arrive at the selling price. In the context of retailing, the retailer adds merchandise and retail operating costs and adds a profit margin to these figures. It is generally agreed that this method of pricing is not customer oriented. Other forms of cost-based pricing are:

- Break-even analysis
- Target rate of return
- Return on investment
- Payback period

The point at which the cost of producing a product equals the revenue gained from selling it is called the *break-even point*. Figure 7.5 shows the relationship between costs, revenue, profits and losses. Calculating the point at which the product breaks even means that a unit price has to be previously determined.

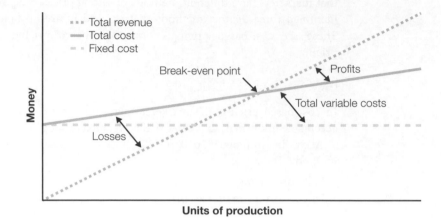

Figure 7.5: The relationship between costs, revenue, profits and losses

COMPETITION–BASED PRICING

Competition-based pricing shows the average around which most firms' prices are set. In other words, it involves setting prices based on knowledge of the competition, their behaviour and cost (see Table 7.5). In this context, a marketer sets prices based on what competitors charge for similar products, sometimes with less attention paid to the company's own cost or demand. In applying this method, the marketer may charge the same as or more or less than its main competitors. The major forms of competition-based pricing are:

Table 7.5: Reacting to competitor price changes

	Increases	**Cuts**
When to follow	• Rising costs • Excess demand • Price-insensitive customers • Price rise compatible with brand image • Harvest or hold objective	• Falling costs • Excess supply • Price-sensitive customers • Price fall compatible with brand image • Build or hold objective
When to ignore	• Stable or falling costs • Excess supply • Price-sensitive customers • Price rise incompatible with brand image • Build objective	• Rising costs • Excess demand • Price-insensitive customers • Price fall incompatible with brand image • Harvest objective

- **Competitive benchmarking:** The supplier benchmarks against major competitors and chooses whether to sell at the same price or above or below. Here, other variables such as product quality and consumer perception will play a part in pricing decisions
- **Going-rate pricing:** With no product differentiation, producers are forced to accept the going rate, as in the case of bread or newspapers. Yet, in reality, there is always scope to offer something different about a product
- **Competitive bidding:** The supplier will price according to a specification drawn up by the purchaser. Usually, but not always, the supplier chooses the lowest (most competitive) price tendered

MARKET– OR DEMAND–ORIENTED PRICING

Rather than using cost or competition as the basis for setting price, marketers may base it on the intensity of demand as expressed by consumers or users of a given product. In this scenario, the objective is to charge higher prices for the same products to consumers who are willing to pay more. In other words, strong demand may lead to high price, and weak demand to low price. This is called *price discrimination* or *differential pricing*.

Some examples of differential prices:

- **Pricing by market segments:** Some marketers market their services at different prices in different geographical areas. Some services such as cinemas or hairdressers are available at lower prices to senior citizens or children

Table 7.6: Conditions for effective price discrimination
Source: Adapted from CIM Study Text, 2004, p. 160

1.	The market must be *segmentable* in terms of price, and different sectors must show different intensities of demand. Each of the sectors must be identifiable, distinct and separate from the others and be accessible to the firm's marketing communications
2.	There must be little or no chance of a *black market* developing so that those in the lower segment can resell to those in the higher segment
3.	There must be little chance that *competitors* can and will undercut the firm's prices in the higher-priced (and/or most profitable) market segments
4.	The *cost* of segmenting and administering the arrangements should not exceed the extra revenue derived from the price discrimination strategy

- **Pricing by product segment:** Software is written top-down and the full version is sold at a premium price. However, for less advanced users, software companies can take features out at little extra cost and charge a lower price

Example 7.3:
Maximizing revenue not price

'Airlines have perfected the science of yield management, concocting complicated pricing schemes that not only defy consumer comparison but also permit revenue maximization on a flight, despite the fact that the average fare might be lower. Many airlines now use their Website to sell tickets on slow-to-fill or ready-to-leave fights, either on specials or on ticket auctions. They also make use of external services such as priceline.com to both discern market conditions and sell last minute capacity. Apart from their own Websites, airlines, hotels, restaurants and theatres can also use sites such as lastminute.com to market seats, rooms, tables and tickets a day or two before due date.'
Source: Pitt et al., 2001, p. 49

istock © ssuaphoto

- **Pricing by time:** Travel companies use price discrimination by charging more for peak-time/rush-hour commuters and travellers whose demand is inelastic at certain times and periods of the day or year. Other examples are off-peak travel bargains and telephone charges

PRICING STRATEGIES

There are two generic pricing strategies: price skimming and penetration pricing.

PRICE SKIMMING

Think and discuss

Airlines offer price discrimination in some circumstances; how do you think they justify this strategy? Is this approach sustainable, during unfavourable economic situations?

Price skimming involves charging a relatively high price for a short time where a new, innovative or much-improved product is launched onto a market. A major disadvantage is that it encourages new entrants.

A variation of price skimming is *rapid skimming pricing strategy*. This involves launching a new product with a high price and supporting the product with high levels of promotional expenditure, such as in case of a new product called Sunny Delight, launched by P&G in the in UK in 1998. This product eventually failed because of false health claims and was withdrawn from the market.

Conditions for charging high prices include:

- Product provides high value
- Customers have high ability to pay
- Lack of competition
- High pressure to buy

PENETRATION PRICING

Penetration pricing involves setting lower rather than higher prices in order to achieve a large or dominant market share. It is often used by businesses wishing to enter a new market or build on a relatively small market share.

A successful penetration pricing strategy may lead to large sales volumes and market share and therefore lower costs per unit. A variation of penetration pricing is *rapid penetration pricing strategy*, which involves launching a new product with a low price and supporting the product with high levels of promotional expenditure in order to gain an initial share of the market. This is organized on a large scale in the washing and liquid soap markets.

Conditions for charging lower prices include:

- Lack of differential advantage
- Market presence or dominance
- Economies of scale
- Objective of making money later
- Strategic use of a loss leader to attract customers
- Attempting to create a barrier to entry

Trial pricing involves pricing a new product low for a limited period of time in order to reduce the risk to customers. The idea is to win customers' acceptance first and make profits later. Trial pricing also works for services. Health clubs and other service providers may offer trial membership or special introductory prices. The hope is that the customer tries the service at a low price and is converted to using the service at the regular price.

CONCLUSION

This chapter began by discussing the meaning of price to marketers and consumers. It then focused on discussing the influences on pricing decisions by providing an understanding of how controllable and uncontrollable forces influence pricing decisions. It went on to show how pricing decisions work with other components of the marketing mix to create something of value to the customer. Overall, the chapter has provided a foundation for understanding the objectives of price and the policies guiding decisions and price-setting processes.

Case study
'Value for Money': A key focus in Primark's pricing strategy

PRIMARK IS ONE OF THE WIDELY KNOWN fashion retailers that have had significant impacts on British society in recent times. Its product lines include menswear, womenswear, childrenswear, and items for the home such as bed linen, duvet covers, candles and bath mats. As at February 2013, it had 161 stores in the UK alone. The main factor that people associate with this organization is its focus on providing its customers value for money. This is why it states categorically on its website that the word 'value' means two things to the organization – value for its customers and value for its employees.

As the effects of the current unfavourable economic conditions in society show in what people consume and how they spend their hard-earned money on goods and

istock © visionchina

services, many more fashion-conscious customers are now turning to Primark because its offerings are found to be relatively cheap and give them an opportunity to still embrace fashion despite the economic downturn. Some people will be wondering how it is possible that Primark is able to offer its products at such low prices in the marketing environment where other firms have to charge far higher prices to be able to break even or survive the threats in the marketing environment. Primark offers a clear message on how it does this in its Frequently Asked Questions (FAQ). It uses a variety of cost-saving strategies. For example, while many of its competitors would use a number of marketing communication tools to promote its products to its various customer groups, Primark relies heavily on 'word of mouth' communication. So, it allows the customers to do the talking about its products. Besides, as a firm that has over 210 stores in various countries including Germany, Holland, Belgium and the United Kingdom, it has the buying power to buy in bulk. The fashion retailer also ensures that it keeps its overheads low wherever it can. All of these give Primark the opportunity to save costs and pass the saving back to the customers.

As its operations indicate, Primark knows that while all of the marketing mix elements are important to the overall success of an organization, the role of price in this arrangement is considerable. Price gives the customer an indication of value in their transactions, and it is the only element in the marketing mix that revolves around revenue while others relate to costs. When it comes to deciding the price of its products, Primark looks both inward and outward as it acknowledges that various factors will be involved when determining how to offer customers value for money and remain in business. Even in its recent trial to sell its products online with the fashion retailer Asos, as reported in the media in June 2013, Primark remains resolute in focusing on customer value as it knows that when customers' needs are met, the possibility of their making a repeat purchase and becoming loyal to the organization is very high.

It has become clear to customers that Primark positions itself against competitors using price as a leading factor among many others that distinguish the organization in the marketplace. The budget fashion retailer targets the value-conscious customers who demand for fashion products at cheaper prices. The bond between Primark and its customers seems to be getting stronger by the day. This shows in the huge interest customers have shown in the company's recent competition in conjunction with Disney in respect of the film called Monsters

University. So, Primark shows that the impact of price on relationships between firms and their customers can be far-reaching. It is therefore not surprising that Primark has bagged several awards including the Best Affordable Fashion Award for 2012 at the ITV Lorraine High Street Fashion Awards and the Overall Best Retailer of the Mall Blackburn Award at the The Mall Blackburn Awards in the same year.

**By Dr Ayantunji Gbadamosi,
University of East London, UK**

Questions

1 Given that interest in Primark's offering has increased in recent times as a result of its low prices, do you think its competitors that charge higher prices can still get good patronage in their business? Give justification for your views.

2 The case study shows that Primark considers both internal and external factors while determining its prices. Mention what you think these factors are and categorize them accordingly.

3 Explain the term 'price elasticity' with appropriate illustration from the information provided in this case study.

4 The case study shows that one of the factors which explain why Primark is able to charge low prices is because it operates on low costs. Give examples of what could be the fixed costs and variable costs of this fashion retailer.

5 Assume that a friend of yours is contemplating going into the fashion business but with the plan to target customers with a taste for luxury. She has been advised to use market skimming as the pricing strategy but has no understanding of how this works. Briefly explain this to her in relation to the fashion industry.

Review questions

1 What is the importance of price to marketers?
2 Why is the price of a product or service not always the most important consideration to consumers?
3 What are the internal and external factors that influence pricing decisions?
4 Outline the key considerations in deciding on a pricing method.
5 Compare and contrast price skimming and penetration pricing strategies.

Group tasks

1 In groups, visit any price comparison website to compare the APRs of various credit card offers. Record specific differences between the competing products as highlighted on the website. Discuss the implications of these in relation to customer value.

2 Assume you are a group of entrepreneurs contemplating the introduction of your new brand of soft drinks in the British marketing environment. Compile a list of factors that will influence your decision about the appropriate price of this new product, separate the factors into internal and external and discuss what you can do to overcome the challenges associated with the ones categorized as external.

Glossary/Key terms

Business-to-business (B2B) online marketing: Businesses using online marketing to reach new business customers, serve current customers more effectively and obtain buying efficiencies and better prices.

By-product pricing: Setting a price for by-products to make the main product's price more competitive.

Captive product pricing: Setting a price for products that must be used along with a main product, such as blades for a razor and games for a videogame console.

Competition-based pricing: Setting prices based on competitors' strategies, prices, costs, and market offerings.

Discount: A straight reduction in price on purchases during a stated period of time or of larger quantities.

Economy pricing: No frills, low prices, for example supermarket 'economy' brands.

Fixed costs (overheads): Costs that do not vary with production or sales level.

Geographical pricing: Different prices for customers in different parts of the world.

Market-skimming pricing (price skimming): Setting a high price for a new product to skim maximum revenues layer by layer from the segments willing to pay the high price; the company makes fewer but more profitable sales.

Off-price retailer: A retailer that buys at less-than-regular wholesale prices and sells at less-than-retail. Examples are factory outlets, independents and warehouse clubs.

Online marketing: Efforts to market products and services and build customer relationships over the internet.

Optional product pricing: A favourite with BMW, which adds optional extras.

Penetration pricing: Offers a low price to gain good market share and then increases the retail price to meet demand.

Premium pricing: Uses a very high price, but in return it is hoped that the consumer receives an excellent product or service, for example Vertu phones.

Price skimming: During the introduction phase of a new product, prices will be high. They are then reduced as the product is adopted by consumers, and competitors launch their own similar products.

Pricing by behaviour: Many companies will price by customer behaviour, offering the heavy or regular user a loyalty bonus or price discount off product purchased, for example the Tesco loyalty card, now used by 6 million customers. Past users of products might also be targeted and offered price reduction for re-using the product, for example re-ordering *The Economist* magazine at a 50 per cent discount if contracting for three years.

Pricing by delivery method: Some organizations will price by the method of delivery, for example if you collect and install you pay one price, if we deliver and install you pay another. This could lead to the growth of a 'cash and carry' type of retailer where the customer could choose to collect at a lower price all sorts of products from computers and fridges to garden sheds and houses. The seller would offer delivery and installation but at a stipulated price.

Pricing by distance: The price charged will often vary according to the distance between the supplier and the customer, for example radius bands of 5, 10 and 50 miles from the outlet; the greater the distance, the higher the price. When selling abroad different prices may well be charged depending on where responsibility for the product is taken on. This might be at the factory gate, at the docks before shipment, at the docks after shipment, when delivered to the customer and with or without insurance. The customer is able to choose, or often negotiate, the best method for them.

Pricing by method of payment: Price can be used as an incentive to encourage payment by a method favoured by the producer. This might be discount for cash or for early or immediate payment. Similarly, extra might be charged for the use of credit card, cheque book or credit terms. Price, as a form of extended credit, is also used to encourage purchase. This might be interest-free credit or 'buy now pay in six months.'

Pricing by sociodemograpy: Many organizations will offer lower prices for larger quantities purchased. This is used to encourage the purchase of more products or a range of products. Some organizations are making this facility increasingly available to the consumer, for example Sainsbury's buy three and get one free or Bottoms Up offering an extra 5 per cent off ten bottles of wine. However, quantity discounts tend to be used predominantly in business-to-business and trade negotiations.

Pricing by time: Different prices can be charged for the product or service at different, underutilized, times of the day, night, week and month of the year. Thus railway companies charge lower prices out of the rush hour, in the evening, on weekends and at bank holidays.

Pricing variations: For example, off-peak pricing on summer holidays or discounts for booking early. At Christmas everything goes up but in the January sales it is all sold at half price!

Product-bundle pricing: Sellers combine several products at the same price. This is often used to move old stock such as books and CDs.

Product line pricing: For example, a consumer buys an individual packet of crisps for 50p, a pack of four for 99p and a family pack of 20 for £2.

Product line strategy: Marketing-oriented companies need to take account of where the price of a new product fits into its existing product line. Where multiple segments appear attractive, modified versions of the product should be designed and priced differently, not according to differences in costs, but in line with the respective values that each target market places on a product.

Profit: The surplus amount of money generated by sales once fixed and variable costs have been removed.

Promotional pricing: For example, buy one get one free (BOGOF) or buy two get the third free.

Psychological pricing: Consumers buy for emotional reasons rather than rational ones – for example, in the case of a product priced at 99p instead of £1 we can say 'I got this for under a pound'.

Revenue: The amount of money generated by sales.

Value pricing: Used to promote pricing during difficult economic conditions, for example, McDonald's and M&S offer value meals from their food stores.

Variable costs: Costs incurred in relation to selling or producing the product (e.g. raw materials, transportation, commissions, part-time staff).

Vocab check list for ESL students

Concierge	Monopoly	Optimum	Tactile
Duopoly	Multifaceted	Periodic	
Heterogeneity	Oligopoly	Perishable	

Definitions for these terms can be found in the 'Vocab Zone' of the companion website, which provides free access to the Macmillan English Dictionary online at www.palgrave.com/business/Gbadamosi

Further reading

Anna Codini, Nicola Saccani and Alessandro Sicco (2012) 'The Relationship between Customer Value and Pricing Strategies: An Empirical Test', *Journal of Product and Brand Management*, Vol. 21, No. 7, pp. 538–46
This paper explores the relationship between the customer value, which is a key element in marketing, and the pricing strategy.

Paul T. M. Ingenbleek and Ivo A. van der Lans (2013) 'Relating Price Strategies and Price-setting Practices', *European Journal of Marketing*, Vol. 47, No. 1/2, pp. 27–48
This article explores the relationship between price strategies and price-setting practices. It also shows that price strategies are visible in the market, while price-setting practices are concealed behind the boundaries of a firm.

References

Bradley, F (1995) *Marketing Management: Providing, Communicating and Delivering Value*. Upper Saddle River, NJ: Prentice Hall

Brassington, F. and Pettitt, S. (2013) *Essentials of Marketing* (3rd edn). Harlow: Pearson Education

CIM Study Text (2004) Certificate stage 1, Paper 1 'Marketing Fundamentals'. London: BPP Professional Education

Dibb, S., Simkin, I., Pride, W. and Ferrell, O. C. (2012) *Marketing Concepts and Strategies* (6th edn). Andover: Cengage Learning

Dubois, P.-L., Jolibert, A. and Muhlbacher, H. (2007) *Marketing Management, A Value-creation Process*. Basingstoke: Palgrave Macmillan

Hoffman, K. D., Turley, L. W. and Kelly, S. W. (2002) 'Pricing Retail Services', *Journal of Business Research*, 55 (12), pp. 1015–23

Hutchings, A. (1995) *Marketing: A Resource Book*. Salisbury: Pitman Publishing

Jobber, D. (2010) *Principles and Practice of Marketing*. New York, NY: McGraw Hill

Jobber, D. and Shipley, D. D. (1998) 'Marketing-orientated Pricing Strategy', *Journal of General Management*, Summer 98, 23 (4), pp. 19–34

Lamb, C. W., Hair J. F. Jr, and McDaniel, C. (2012) MKTG 6 (Instructor edn). Independence, KY: Cengage Learning

Marn, M. V., Roegner, E. V. and Zawada, C. C. (2003) 'Pricing New Products', *McKinsey Quarterly*, Issue 3, pp. 40–49

Nagle, Thomas T. and Holden, Reed K. (1995) *The Strategy and Tactics of Pricing*. Englewood Cliffs, NJ: Prentice Hall

Palmer, Adrian (2012) *Introduction to Marketing, Theory and Practice* (3rd edn). Oxford: Oxford University Press

Perreault, W. D. Jr, Cannon, J. P. and McCarthy E. J. (2010) *Essentials of Marketing: A Marketing Strategy Planning Approach* (International edn) (12th edn). New York, NY: McGraw-Hill

Pitt, L., Berthon, F. P., Watson, R. T. and Ewing, M. (2001) 'Pricing Strategy and the Net', *Business Horizon*, 44 (2), pp. 45–54

Rao, Vithala R. (1984) 'Pricing Research in Marketing, The State of the Art', *Journal of Business*, 57 (1), S39–S60

Rochford, L. and Wotruba, T. R. (2000) 'New Product Pricing Strategy and the Sales Environment: An Exploratory Study', *Marketing Management Journal*, 10 (2), pp. 101–111

Shapiro, B. P. and Jackson, B. B. (1978) 'Industrial Pricing to Meet Customer Needs', *Harvard Business Review*, Nov/Dec, pp. 119–27

8 VALUE-ADDED DISTRIBUTION STRATEGIES

DULEKHA KASTURIRATNE & HUGH D. CONWAY

UNIVERSITY OF PLYMOUTH

CHAPTER CONTENTS

LEARNING OUTCOMES

The content of this chapter will help you to:

- Define a distribution channel and understand how it can operate in both a business-to-consumer (B2C) and a business-to-business (B2B) market
- Put the role of distribution into context in the marketing mix and comprehend its contribution to product and service value
- Discuss the complexity of the relationships between partner companies in the distribution chain and how they can add value for the end-customer
- Differentiate between traditional supply chains and vertical distribution systems
- Appreciate the demands of both buyers and sellers throughout a chain
- Identify the factors that contribute to an efficient and effective distribution channel

Marketing in action
J. Sainsbury

As a prime exponent of supermarketing, Sainsbury's is at the forefront of developments in supply chain management. It currently has 21 depots around the UK and approximately 1,000 stores, including the supermarkets and convenience stores, and those stores stock approximately 30,000 products. The largest of the depots makes around 2,000 deliveries a week to 83 stores. World-class systems, updated with sales data every 15 minutes, ensure they know exactly what to deliver and where (www.j-sainsbury.co.uk).

Products are sourced from all over the world: fresh food and meat from suppliers in the UK, flowers from Holland, packaged goods from China. Some of these have long shelf lives and some, especially the fresh produce, need to be in and out of the distribution depots within the same day. Although Sainsbury's does not buy direct from farmers, it works hard to maintain a strong relationship with farmers and growers through the Partnership in Livestock and Partnership in Produce schemes.

Supporting the logistics **infrastructure** are highly sophisticated computer systems that track products into and out of the depots. This ensures that the right products are shipped to the right store at the right time. Products must be shipped out in a strict order and in most cases operate under a 'first in, first out'

(FIFO) principle. The data management process is closely linked to Sainsbury's Brand Match, which price checks 14,000 branded products each day against leading competitors, and the Nectar loyalty card, which has over 11 million active users. From all this data, the company can track trends in product sales and help identify potential new outlets that will enhance the distribution network.

In common with other major supermarkets and retailers, Sainsbury's offers online products supported by a 'click and collect' service. This adds another layer of complexity to the distribution process. The general merchandise website offers more than 6,000 branded products. Standard deliveries are guaranteed within 3–5 days but products can be delivered next day or on a named day if required. Not only does the logistics operation have to pick and pack the orders but also the transport operation has to ensure the products are delivered to the right household.

From a single shop founded in 1869 by John James Sainsbury, the company has become a highly sophisticated retail operation with global connections and a vast network of suppliers, stores and online customers, all of whom need to be supported by the distribution system.

Source: Sainsbury, 2012

INTRODUCTION

In this chapter we will consider the nature of the distribution process and the complex networks of value-adding partner companies involved in delivering finished goods and services to customers.

Distribution is the 'P' (Place) in the marketing mix concerned with ensuring the product that a customer wishes to buy is in the right place at a time convenient to him or her. In the past, distribution has been viewed as purely functional. Today, it is seen by marketers as a means of adding value not only for the final consumer but also for the members of the distribution network.

For example, many fast moving consumer goods (FMCG) have timelines within which they must be on display or consumed (a sell-by date). For the local supermarket, the supply chain must facilitate delivery to that supermarket in order to ensure adequate shelf time. The supply chain must also ensure there is sufficient stock in store to meet the demands of the supermarket manager for each day's trading. Bear in mind that in this case the demand will vary not only by day but by the time of year, so we must take account of seasonal trends. Or in the case of durable goods, the demand predictions will more likely be on a weekly or perhaps monthly basis. On the other hand if buying from the web, it is of little or no concern to the customer where the stock is held as long as the promised delivery time is not exceeded.

The process of ensuring that distribution is efficiently and profitably managed involves a number of stakeholders: manufacturers, professional buyers, professional sellers, independent distribution and logistics companies, warehousing organizations, transport companies and **intermediaries** such as agents and wholesalers, retailers and resellers (see Fig. 8.1).

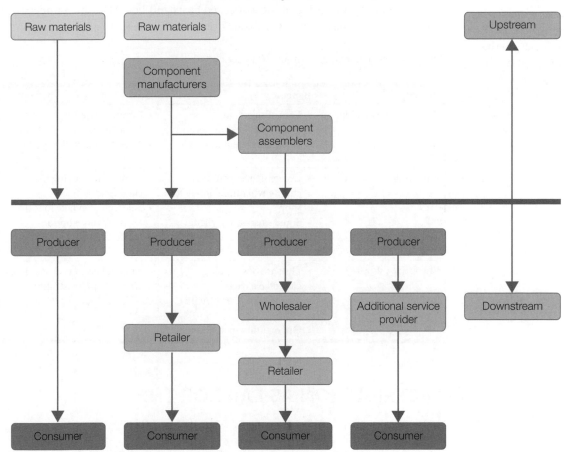

Figure 8.1: The supply chain structure

Each link in the supply chain is an opportunity for the organizations to create relationships, and the stronger those are, the greater the opportunity to create value for the end-consumer. There is a flow up and down the channels of information, data, finance and risk, and throughout the network there are personal relationships. Distribution is a blend of business-to-business (B2B) and business-to-consumer (B2C) marketing. The successful organization will be the one that recognizes the value in these activities and can maximize the potential for added value throughout the distribution channels. The value in a delivery chain comes from the suppliers, distributors and ultimately customers who contribute to the partnership 'relationship'.

The notion of value is central to distribution just as it is to the other elements of the marketing mix. Essentially, it is the difference between the benefits the customers realize from using the product and the costs they incur in finding and using it (Hollensen, 2003). It is generally perceived from the customer's point of view in relation to the transactions. For example, if a busy female executive needs to buy a new jacket, her options are to: look in a Boden catalogue recently sent to her through the post; go online and search through familiar sites including Boden and its competitors; or visit a shop close enough. Her choice in this scenario will be significantly influenced by the weighting of the associated costs and benefits, which underscores the fact that consumers' actions are value driven (see Table 8.1).

Think and discuss

As we experience significant improvements in the technological environment, do you think the services of marketing intermediaries will still be necessary in the near future?

Table 8.1: The benefits and costs of a transaction

Activity	Benefit	Cost
Buy from the catalogue	• Ease of selection • Quick: can be done as and when the time is available	• Cannot try it on • Delay in delivery • Need to return if it is not right
Buy online	• Convenience: you can choose what time of day to shop • Some sites have a virtual model to enable clothes to be 'tried on'	• Same as for buying from a catalogue • Selection can take longer as many more options considered
Buy from a shop	• Pleasure of shopping • Can take a friend • Trying on will ensure it is right • Opportunity to accessorize	• Time taken to visit the shop • Car parking frustrations

THE ROLE OF DISTRIBUTION AS PART OF THE MARKETING MIX

Peter Drucker, writing in 1962, pointed out that the distribution function can account for 30–50 per cent of the total cost of the manufactured product (Drucker, 1962). In contrast, advertising typically accounts for 5–7 per cent. It is still largely the case that the demand chain is seen as a functional operation and not an integral part of the marketing mix; it remains a largely neglected topic in marketing. However, with more and more channels open to customers, and retailers increasingly using multichannel strategies, such strategies are becoming a source of competitive advantage.

The balance of importance of any one of the Ps in the marketing mix is often difficult to determine and will change from one market environment to another. In some cases, such as the market sector in which retailers Poundland and 99p Stores operate, price might be considered the most critical from the consumer's perspective. On the other hand, in an upmarket restaurant, service and physical evidence may well be of the highest priority to the clientele.

Place will always remain a critical element of the marketing mix. Reputations can be very easily damaged through a failure in the delivery of a product or service. This applies much the same in both B2B and B2C environments.

As well as handling physical goods, demand networks handle all sorts of services and in doing so can provide added value for the customer. Distributing things is a service, but so is the distribution of services: restaurants, insurance companies, hairdressers, consultants, water and electricity companies, telecoms. British Gas provides a boiler maintenance service, delivered in the home, and the important criteria are the quality of the service and the accuracy of the time of delivery. This type of service will add little value if the consumer, who has taken time off work to be at home for 1pm as arranged, is made to wait until 3pm for the engineer to turn up.

A failure in the delivery of a product or service will tend to reflect more on the supplier than on the delivery agent. So, if you order from a catalogue and the item takes five days to arrive instead of the promised three days, the tendency is to blame the catalogue company not the Post Office or delivery organization. Companies such as DHL, Amtrak and many retailers offer customers online tracking of the delivery of products. So, you can tell where your recent purchase is in the delivery system. The intention is to manage the customer's expectations, but it also has the advantage to the delivery organization that the customer can act as a controller and immediately highlight when a problem (that is, a delivery failure) occurs. However, this adds another layer of complexity to the process and a reliance on technology which needs managing to ensure customer expectations are met.

Think and discuss

What factors do you think consumers will be looking for in selecting a particular retail outlet for their shopping? Do you think these factors will be different from those that will be used by a business to select the manufacturer whose products will be chosen among competing offerings?

8

istock © lisafx

Consumers are an integral part of the distribution process. For example, in the case of resort holidays, the family may travel by car or fly to the destination before they experience the product. The traditional high street retailers also rely on the customer contributing to the process. Retail stores that advertise their products rely on the consumer making a decision to visit the store, which may include a car or public transport journey. This decision will be influenced by many things, in particular the value the purchaser will place on the shopping experience itself.

The cost of distribution is such a significant part of many products and services that where significant savings are achieved compared with competitors there is the potential to create a strong sustainable competitive advantage (SCA). If you assume the cost of distribution is 40 per cent of the total product cost, a 10 per cent saving or increase in efficiency will represent a reduction in the product cost of 6 per cent. However, if you assume the cost of promotion to be 10 per cent of the total product cost, then a 10 per cent saving is a reduction in the product cost of only 1.5 per cent. Furthermore, a 10 per cent cut in promotional expenditure is likely to have a significant effect on sales enquiries and turnover. A 10 per cent saving on the logistics, if done selectively, will not directly affect sales, but can serve to make the product more competitive. Anderson and Narus (1996) suggest that stock levels can be reduced by 15–20 per cent as a result of better use of channel partnerships.

The cost of the transaction will also impact directly on the value added to the sale. As shown in Figure 8.2, the low-cost transactions of the internet sales add little value to the product whereas the value that a sales person can bring to a transaction is considerable, hence the high cost of direct sales through a salesforce.

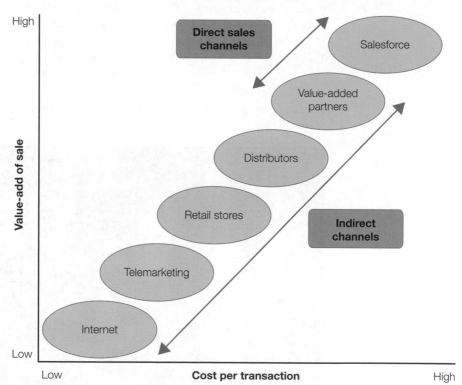

Figure 8.2: Adding value to the sale

Efficient channels will improve the place, possession and time utility. Place utility means ensuring the products are available where the consumer wants them, which increasingly means delivered directly, following an online purchase. Possession utility means that customers should be able to access a product, or indeed store it for future use. For instance, should you want to hire a car you are much more likely to rent from a company who will deliver the car to your door than from one that requires you to use public transport, or a friend, to get to the rental company. Time utility means the demand chain has to be organized in such a way that products are available to the customer when they want them. Remember that in the channel each member is a customer of the member above in the chain. The channel that can deliver a product or a service most efficiently will be in a position to offer the greatest value.

DEMAND CHAIN FLOWS

In a complex demand chain there are a number of important flows, as shown in Figure 8.3 and outlined below.

Product flow: The flow of products from the manufacturer to the end-user. This is downstream of the manufacturer (see Figure 8.1)

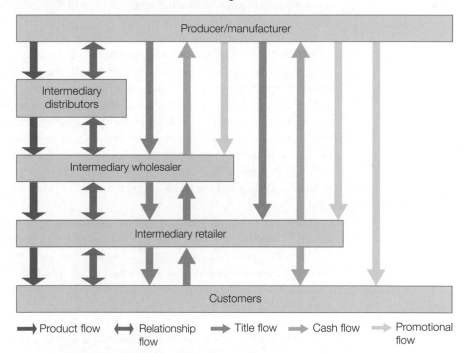

Figure 8.3: Demand chain flows

Ownership flow: Although a product may pass through a number of hands on its journey to the consumer, the ownership of the product may not follow. Different organizations have different rights under their contracts. A distributor may hold and organize the transportation of a product, whereas a wholesaler will buy the products in bulk before reselling to retailers.

Payment and cash flow: Cash flow is the lifeblood of a commercial organization, whether it is marketing a product or a service. In a cash transaction, the cash flow will mirror exactly the product flow. In a B2B transaction there will most often be a credit period involved in which the seller allows the buyer a period of time (30 days, 60 days or perhaps 120 days) in which to fulfil the payment terms.

Information flow: Information flow is less predictable than other flows and often relies on the relationship between the parties. It can be formal in the sense that information or data is reported that relates to the market and the behaviour of organizations and consumers within the demand network. This can be a contractual obligation. If it is informal it will result from the working relationship established by the people involved. So, a warehouse manager might make comments to a sales executive on the flow of products through the operation that is significant to the future flow of products. Information like this, of course, needs to be captured in order that a company can act on it.

Promotional flow: The extent of the flow through the demand network will be determined by the push or pull promotional strategies adopted by manufacturers and producers (dealt with in more detail elsewhere). These strategies are largely adopted by the owners of the products as they establish communication links with the target consumer audience. There are also promotional flows within the demand network. Companies involved in logistics, such as UPS and DHL, will promote their services to other partners in the chain.

In general, it is the case that the goods flow is accompanied by an information flow. *Logistics* concerns the flow of goods, all the way from extraction of raw material, manufacturing of components and assembly, to finished goods made available to the buying organization or household (Gummesson, 2008). It includes the transfer of material, its transportation, security, money flow, detail recording, warehousing, inventory, material handling and delivery to the ultimate point of sale or delivery. Logistics cuts across functional and hierarchical borders and seeks to provide a seamless transition, which may now include reverse supply to meet recycling requirements. According to Gummessen, logistics is a marketing strategy.

Wholesalers are organizations that act as a channel for a range of products, often linked by a common factor, for example household durable goods. As an intermediary, they will take ownership of a product and hold volume stocks of a range of products from a wide source of suppliers. The prime advantage of a wholesaler is the reduction in the number of communication links between producer and customers, as shown in Figure 8.4.

The wholesaler acts as a communication link as well as a channel for the products. In this example, the number of links between each producer and its markets is reduced by 30 per cent, making for a potentially much more efficient system.

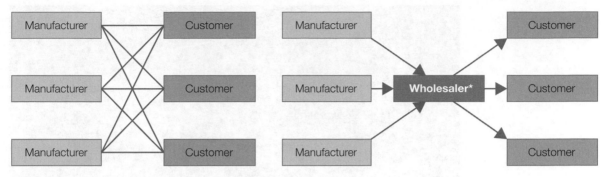

* Note: A wholesaler can reduce the lines of communication from nine to six.

Figure 8.4: The role of the wholesaler
Source: Based on Kotler and Armstrong, 2012, p. 366

SUPPLY CHAIN MANAGEMENT

The use of the phrase *supply chain* implies that the chain starts with the supplier of raw materials, together with a manufacturing capacity. We prefer to think of it as a *demand chain* because this implies that we are **cognizant** of the consumer needs (Kotler and Armstrong, 2012). Throughout this chapter we will generally consider the distribution of products and services from the consumer's point of view. Ultimately, it is the needs and preferences of the end-consumer that all stakeholders in the demand chain must consider. In this chapter we will also differentiate between the *customer*, who makes the purchase, and the *consumer*, who benefits from the purchased product or service. They may be one and the same but can be different. This applies in the B2B sector as well as the B2C market.

At each stage of the process there is a seller and a customer. So, ultimately, the farmer growing food crops will be meeting the needs of the family shopping in their local supermarket. The farmer also needs to meet the requirements of the supermarket buyers for preparation, packaging and delivery. The supermarket must understand the preferences of the family for the type of foods it stocks, but at the same time the professional buyer needs to take into account the circumstances of the farmer. There is value in having a good relationship with the supplier because this value can be passed on to the consumer.

A car manufacturer will contract with a network of component manufacturers and assemblers that will run into thousands of types of relationship. Each component manufacturer in turn sources other components or raw materials. And often the component manufacturer will seek to supply a number of car manufacturers, so increasing the complexity of the demand chain. The conclusion we reach is that demand chains are not linear but are a complex and wide-reaching network. With the advent of new technologies, there are many different ways a customer can access a product – via the retailer, direct from the supplier, via a website, from an independent mobile retailer (such as fish vans), by home delivery or a web-based buy and collect.

'*A large Sainsbury's store stocks approximately 30,000 products and an increasing number of stores also offer complementary non-food products and services.*'

(J Sainsbury FAQ)

8

istock © RainerPlendl

There are two types of demand channel structure: traditional multi-owner channels and owned or contracted channels, referred to as vertical marketing systems (VMS).

In a traditional *multi-owner channel network* there is little or no control on the profits of each supplier and the focus is on the individual channel partners' profits and sustainability. The ability to retain customers provides benefits back up the chain and of course this means the producer is reliant on the partners in the chain to maintain their customer bases. That is why producers will employ 'pull' strategies in their promotions to try to ensure customers' loyalty. A good example of this is Intel with its 'Intel inside' advertising.

In the case of *owned channels*, full control is maintained over the profit centres and the producer can focus the whole channel on delivering customer satisfaction.

CONVENTIONAL DISTRIBUTION CHANNELS

Bucklin (1965) argues that consumer demand will determine what services are required and what value is placed upon them, and this will result in the evolution of the most efficient and cost-effective channel structure.

The efficiency of the traditional multi-owner channel will largely depend on the relationship between the partners. Figure 8.5 shows the relationships that can exist between producer and retailer. The strength of these relationships will determine the sustainability of the channel network. Essentially, if each partner recognizes the value in the network and contributes to the operation of the network in a manner that offers a fair return on investment, whilst at the same time strengthening the relationship, then all partners will benefit.

The distribution of products and services needs to match the expectation of customers, which in turn is driven by the changes in both shopping and lifestyles. Shopping is no longer simply the **utilitarian** function it used to be and marketers have for some time now been aware of the hedonistic factors (Tauber, 1972) that affect retailing. For many consumers it is a social activity and the term 'retail therapy' has become familiar. Consider, for example, the rise of some supermarkets as late-night centres for 'singles' to meet.

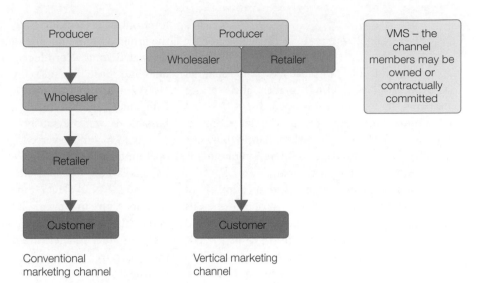

Figure 8.5: Demand channel structures
Source: Based on Hollensen, 2003, p. 533

In some market sectors the retailer must support the selling of products with a service that provides consumers with advice and technical knowledge. The computing industry is a typical case where a retailer such as Dixons will not only sell you a laptop, PC or digital camera, but will also help programme the equipment and even install it in your home if required. In addition it will provide online and telephone after-sales support. This activity can extend the supply chain from producer to wholesaler to retailer and finally right to the consumer's home.

For both small and large retailers selling white and brown goods (fridges, freezers, cookers and televisions), there is a need not just to install the new but also to manage the removal and disposal of the old. The growing demand for sustainable marketing means the retailer must assume a responsibility for disposing of or recycling the unwanted product. This is known as *reverse distribution* (see Figure 8.6).

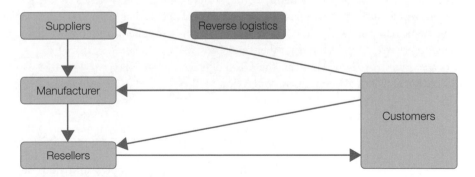

Figure 8.6: Reverse distribution

A company's network of relationships with channel partners can provide incremental sales and access to new markets, and allow the firm to leverage its competencies in additional areas (Doyle, 2000). The problem that companies face in establishing a demand chain is that there are many options available and often the resultant strategy is a combination of a number of those options.

Example 8.1:
Dixons Retail: Reverse logistics

Dixons Retail is a leading specialist multi-channel electrical and computing retailer and service company. Its first store was opened in 1930 and the company first registered by Charles Kalms in 1937. His son, Stanley joined the family business in 1948 and capitalized on his interest in photography to set up a mail order company.

Through organic growth and a number of acquisitions, notably the Currys group in the 80s and a growing group of London stores branded PC World, Dixons Retail has grown to be the UK market leader. In recent years the company has focused heavily on its supply chain and services, launching a new end-to-end service brand KNOWHOW.

Dixons Retail has also extended its reach into Europe, having market-leading positions throughout the Nordics, the Czech Republic, Slovakia and Greece, as well as a pan-European pure play brand (PIXmania) and operations in Italy and Turkey.

Throughout the years of growth and achievement Dixons has operated a returns policy that has enabled customers to easily and quickly return damaged or faulty products. Since 2011 customer support has been provided by its services company KNOWHOW. From a simple returns counter, KNOWHOW has become a highly complex operation which not only handles Currys/PC World products but also white and brown goods from customers who bought them at other retailers.

Described by Tim Allinson, the UK Logistics Director at Dixons Retail, as an operation at the forefront of reverse logistics, KNOWHOW offers the group a highly flexible range of exit routes for unwanted, unused products, damaged recoverable ones and those beyond economic repair. KNOW-HOW maintains a wide network of partner companies which refurbish, recycle and where possible recover previously sold products.

Key to making reverse logistics a cost-effective operation for a multifarious organization like Dixons is how fast and efficient the process can be made. KNOWHOW manages the operation from its centre in Newark, Nottinghamshire. From here white and brown goods bought by customers from other retailers are despatched direct to a third-party recycling operation. Faulty goods are returned to suppliers. Unwanted electronic gifts together with refurbished items that have been cleaned of all data are sold to consumers through clearance stores in Manchester and London and via an eBay site. The last exit route option is through jobbers, who are companies specializing in recovery and recycling.

In a retail environment that is rapidly moving to multichannel shopping and away from the conventional high street store, the ability to maximize the potential from reverse logistics is increasingly important for retailers, not just in the electrical and electronics sector, but also in clothing and non-grocery retailing. Reverse logistics is critical to the relationships an organization has with its many stakeholders: customers, suppliers and others throughout its network of associates.

Source: http://www.dixonsretail.com (accessed 26 March 2013)

VERTICAL MARKETING SYSTEMS

Channel structures can be highly complex and may be of a formal, contractual nature, as in the vertical marketing system (VMS), or an informal arrangement that is kept loose to suit the customer organization. For example, a company that frequently uses couriers to despatch products may negotiate a long-term contract that gives it favourable terms based on volume and delivery patterns. A company that only occasionally requires a despatch company will buy the service on an ad-hoc basis and may well not be loyal to any one supplier.

The structure of a VMS is dependent on the element of control that the partners wish to exert. Full control over the demand chain will be achieved through ownership. The success of Spanish clothing company Zara is in part due to the fact that it owns its entire manufacturing and distribution operation. Clothes are designed by the in-house team, at least 50 per cent of the clothing is manufactured in-house and the products are delivered to the retail stores by Zara's modern distribution system. The high-technology system can handle up to 80,000 items per hour. Zara's competitive edge is maintained through getting new designs into its stores very quickly. Controlling the whole system makes Zara highly efficient. The organization often creates a new design and delivers it to stores worldwide in less than a month (Kotler and Keller, 2013).

However, such a VMS comes at a cost. To develop a fully integrated distribution system takes considerable capital expenditure and a management commitment to making a long-term investment. It also takes management expertise, so it may well be that a company that decides to establish a wholly owned VMS will also need to employ specialist managers and significantly enlarge its workforce and salary costs. The return on the investment needs to be considered carefully.

There are a number of options for the structure of a VMS, outlined below.

Corporate or wholly owned

A corporate or wholly owned demand structure enables a producer company to control, through ownership, the entire system from manufacture to the retail environment. In this case, the system will be linear with each part of the channel accountable for its operation to the company's central management. The advantages of control and cost management need to be set against the high levels of financial commitment to the infrastructure and personnel. Corporate ownership of the channel also enables a company to manage the risk (that is, the uncertainty) element of distribution better. The greatest risk in demand chain management is low inventory levels – in other words, failure to have enough products in the right place at the right time. Technology developments in stock control systems are contributing to a reduction in the risk factor, but they cannot be removed altogether. Central management can further reduce the risks.

Contractual or franchise organizations

According to the British Franchise Association (BFA), franchising has been used to describe many different forms of business relationships, including licensing, distributor agreements and agency arrangements. In its most familiar sense, the term has arisen from the development of what is called 'business format franchising'. This is the granting of a licence by one person (the franchisor) to another (the franchisee) that entitles the franchisee to trade as an independent business under the brand of the franchisor, following a proven business model. The franchisee also receives a package that comprises all the elements necessary to establish a previously untrained person in the business and to run it with ongoing assistance on a predetermined basis (including a predetermined agreement length, with renewal options).

In the US there are 1,500 franchise businesses and 883,000 franchise outlets (Kotler and Armstrong, 2012, p. 370). In the UK, according to the NatWest/BFA 2011 survey, there were 897 franchisors and approximately 36,900 franchisees.

The automotive industry typifies the *manufacturer-retailer franchise* – for example, Ford operates worldwide through a network of exclusive dealers. In exchange for an exclusive commitment to Ford, the company offers its franchisees minimum stocking levels, access to main dealers and national stocks, reduced administration, full signage showing status as a member of the Ford Dealer network and full training and support (Ibrahim, 2007).

In a *manufacturer-wholesaler franchise*, the franchisee is permitted to manufacture and distribute the product of the franchisor. An example of this would be the distribution of bottled drinks such as Coca-Cola.

In a *wholesaler-retailer franchise*, the retailer, who is the franchisee, goes to a wholesaler, who is the franchisor, and buys products for sale in retail. Sometimes a cooperative of a large number of franchisee retailers forms a wholesaling company from which retailers have to buy their products. Examples of this include stores that sell automotive products and hardware products.

In a *retailer-retailer franchise*, the franchisor markets a product or service, using a standardized system and common name, through a huge network of its franchisees. This format is the most common and is often seen in the service sector – for example, Burger King, Toni & Guy, Fit4less and CarpetKare UK.

The opportunities for franchising are diverse and include national and international options. The benefits of entering a franchise agreement include the use of an established brand name, a proven business model and administrative support. For the franchisor, it is a way of building a distribution network quickly, using other people's funds and without making a significant investment in the distribution infrastructure. There is, though, a price to be paid in that the profit margins will be lower than if the demand network were wholly owned. There are also management issues with enforcing contractual obligations.

In an *administered VMS*, one partner in the network will exert leadership through its relative size and superiority. The structure is informal in that there are no written contracts or ownership. The power can come through the volume of goods being moved, as in a major retail chain such as Walmart, or through the strength of the brand – for example, companies such as Unilever and P&G.

Example 8.2:
Avon and Tupperware

Many franchised operations have very long established histories. Avon Cosmetics was established over 120 years ago by American door-to-door salesman David McConnell. In 1886 Mrs P. F. E. Albee of Winchester, New Hampshire joined him to help found what has become a global cosmetics business that still uses Avon representatives door to door. Of course, it has now added e-commerce to its demand chain and continues to grow. Avon Products Inc. reported full-year sales for 2010 of $10.9 billion, 6 per cent higher than in 2009.

Similarly Tupperware, the giant producer of plastic food containers, started in 1946 when Earl Tupper invented a container with an airtight seal. It did not sell well through retail outlets because consumers did not understand how it worked. As a result, the Tupperware Home Party was born in 1948. Today, Tupperware is a global company with a salesforce of 2.7 million in almost 100 countries and sales revenues of $2.6 billion in 2011, a 12 per cent increase compared with 2010.

Sources: Avon, 2012, and Tupperware, 2012

CHANNEL STRATEGY

Customers demand value from the retailers from whom they buy. As discussed earlier, the value is the difference between the price paid and the cost of acquiring the product or service. In meeting the demands of customers, whether in high street shops, on the internet or over the telephone, manufacturers and retailers have to take into account changes in buyer behaviour and the growing range of alternative delivery systems.

Retailers want products that will sell well and provide a good return on the investment in stock. Manufacturers want outlets that will sell all that can be made. So, over-demand and under-demand are both issues. The channel strategy will be determined by analysing customers' needs and considering the resources available and whether it is possible to utilize existing channel structures or whether it will be necessary to invest in new ones. There are three channel strategies we can consider. The final choice will depend on the marketing strategy adopted for each product in a company's portfolio and the related channel objectives.

Intensive distribution: Intensive distribution involves maximizing the coverage to ensure the products are distributed as widely as possible. Typically, FMCG will be distributed this way. Volumes will be high and the business objective will be to achieve the best possible turnover. The distributor will need to manage short-term demand for stock and, in the case of the major supermarkets, provide a distribution service 24/7.

Selective distribution: Selective distribution means that a limited number of outlets are chosen. This reflects either the perceived value of the goods (for example, distributing Seiko watches only through high-quality jewellers) or where selection may be on a geographic basis (if, for instance, the marketing strategy is to target only the UK).

Exclusive distribution: Exclusive distribution involves the distributor only handling one manufacturer's products. The major motor manufacturers all operate exclusive dealerships, for example, and Apple has 28 stores in the UK that sell exclusively Apple products.

Setting a channel strategy is a commitment to the long term. Whilst it is relatively easy, for instance, to increase or decrease expenditure on promotions or switch between various media, making changes to the demand chain can take a long time, especially if there are complex contractual negotiations to undertake. Companies may well review their strategy and conclude that they can achieve better results with a shorter, more direct channel and fewer partners. This process is known as **disintermediation** or, in common **parlance**, 'cutting out the middle-man'. Whilst this can be a deliberate strategy, it can also be driven by the consumer. With the growth of web-based retailing, there has developed a new feature of consumer behaviour which the retail industry refers to as 'showrooming', in which customers use physical stores to examine a product before buying it somewhere else, either online or via their mobile device, for the sake of cheapness or convenience (*Retail Week Technology*, September 2012, pp. 9–10).

8

SELECTING CHANNEL MEMBERS

Unless the producer is in direct contact with the customer, as would be the case in a business-to-business context when the manufacturer's salesforce is visiting customers' premises, the channel network is also the communication link between manufacturer and customer. Implicit in the channel network is a level of trust between the channel partners that each is conducting his business in a manner that benefits both the individual partner and the total demand chain. Hence, the management of the demand chain is crucial to the long-term success of the manufacturer and ultimately is to the benefit of the consumer.

Consumer purchase decisions can be influenced by the channel strategy. For example, a person will buy a computer from a retail outlet if they think they need technical advice. On the other hand, if they are technically competent and confident they may choose the direct route. The growth of shoes and clothing retailing over the web has only been facilitated by solid returns policies which give the consumer confidence that if an item does not fit or is the wrong colour it can be returned without **quibble**.

If we consider the choice of channel partners from the manufacturer's perspective, the critical points are:

- Can the channel partner manage the volume of business? Does it have an established track record?
- Does the partner have adequate resources to provide the expected level of service? This might include inventory systems, warehousing facilities and own or contracted transportation
- Does the partner's network extend to the geographic coverage necessary now and to meet the future ambitions of the manufacturer? For example, a good network coverage of the UK may meet current needs, but if the producer is due to embark on an export strategy this needs to be considered
- Is the partner now, or likely to be, contracted to a competitor manufacturer? This is not necessarily a negative. For example, if the partner in question is a retail chain, it may have generic product expertise that can be used to promote the manufacturer's products. The question, then, is how to ensure the manufacturer's products are the customer's first choice
- Do the respective business cultures match? When the marketing strategies and implementations skills of the two trading partners fit well together, there is a strong relationship **synergy**

If we then consider the issues from the perspective of the channel partner:

- Are the resources sufficient to manage the expected volume or will there need to be additional investment?
- Is the manufacturer a competitor to an existing customer, in which case can both be managed, or will the new partner manufacturer replace the current one?
- Is there any legal restraint in place with any other partner company?
- Does the product fit with the portfolio of products currently handled, which would enable the existing resources to be used more efficiently?
- What level of service support is expected by the manufacturer and can it be met or, preferably, exceeded?

When establishing a demand channel, the producer and the channel partners need to agree the terms and conditions under which they will operate. These will cover pricing policies, territorial rights and how sales enquiries will be handled. There should also be a detailed course of action in the event of a service failure. No system is perfect and failures will occur; the strength of the relationships between channel partners will determine how well they overcome failures when they do happen.

MOTIVATING CHANNEL MEMBERS

'Firms with superior ways of thinking about and making decisions about distribution relationships possess a competitive advantage as long as they can sustain their channel-relationship thinking advantage over their rivals' (Dickson and Nielsen, 1997).

In an ideal world channel members will appreciate the added value of working closely with other members and accept their share of the value of the relationship between producer and customer. However, if competitive business practice gets in the way, we have channel conflict.

So, where does the responsibility for motivating the demand channel lie? Much depends on the relative strengths and weaknesses of the partners. A distributor working with a major brand will have very little influence on the business relationship unless the distributor has something valuable to offer. Management is made easier if there are contractual obligations such as in a VMS. If the partnership is a conventional distribution network in which the partners are independent, then the motivation will be very much a two-way exercise. The primary value in a channel partnership is the reward, which might be profit or might be the leverage the relationship offers in respect of other organizations. A wholesaler that has built a reputation for managing a range of high-value brands will find it easier to add a new brand to the portfolio than if the wholesaler has a short track record and little visibility in the trade.

A manufacturer that recognizes the effort a partner puts into the relationship to provide a high-quality service will be more likely to provide that partner with additional support or an increase in business, which will benefit both parties. A wholesaler that stocks a range of competitor products will come under a lot of pressure to favour one manufacturer over another, depending on the down-channel service the wholesaler provides. A manufacturer that adopts a push strategy to their promotional activity will be reliant on the performance of the channel partner for the success of the business. Conversely, a manufacturer that can demonstrate a substantial investment in a pull strategy is more likely to be supported by its channel partners, who will see the added value of building the relationship.

The strength in a relationship between channel partners lies in the communication between the parties. This will happen at many levels, as shown in Figure 8.7. Each partner is a stakeholder in the channel network and should be included in every partner's internal marketing activity. Supplementing the formal flow of information relating to flow of goods and services is a flow of informal communications. Keeping channel partners aware of developments within a company can be very important in building the relationship and social media can be a conduit for maintaining this

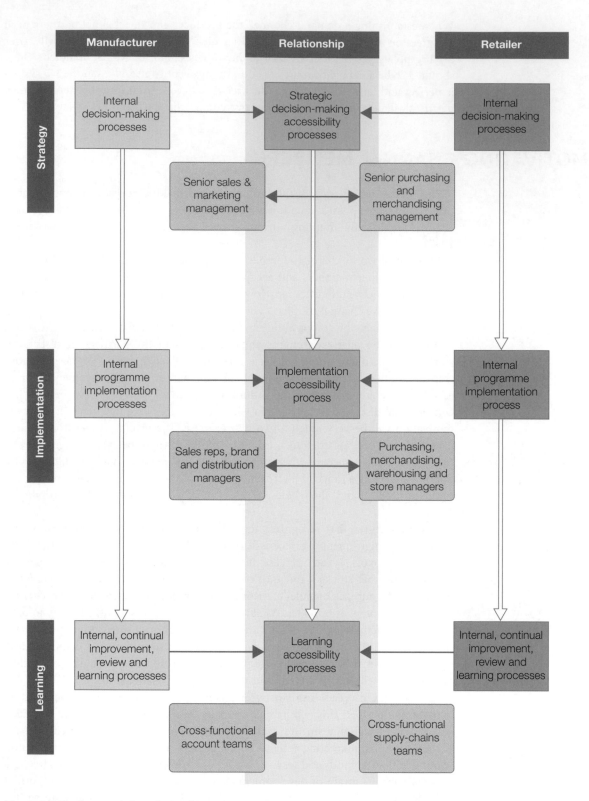

Figure 8.7: Producer–retailer relationships

Example 8.3:
Exporter–importer relationships in the tea industry

Kasturiratne (2007), in her study of the tea industry, found that one of the factors that contributed to the strength of the relationship between channel partners is timely, relevant communication. She noted that exporter–importer relationships were stronger, more effective and less subject to conflict and control when there was a good flow of information communication between the two parties, making daily dealings between them more

transparent, thereby also increasing mutual trust and satisfaction. Such mutually beneficial relationships meant that they were interdependent, avoiding power struggles and increasing commitment.

This is doubly important when the product in question is considered a commodity rather than a value-added one. Mutually beneficial relationships which are viewed as sharing equal power enable a reasonable negotiation of price of the product without the more powerful party dictating terms to the less powerful party.

Source: Adapted from Kasturiratne, 2007

'conversation'. If partners are encouraged to take an interest in a company, the staff will develop an empathy towards each other and collectively this will add value to consumers' experiences.

It is also vital that demand channel partnerships are reviewed on a regular basis. Objectives can change as market conditions and economies change. New products are launched and new demand channels open up; some existing channels may become redundant. The problem facing Royal Mail

is that the handwritten letter is rapidly being replaced by keyboard-generated email. So Royal Mail is facing competition from other distributors for the lucrative sections of the mail business as well as changes in the demand for letter delivery. Producers seeking the most efficient way of reaching customers will be constantly reviewing the options available to them.

MARKETING LOGISTICS

As we have said, logistics is concerned with the flow of raw materials to production and on to delivery of the finished product wherever it is required and by whatever means it is demanded by the consumer.

We have suggested that whereas the term 'supply chain' implies consideration of the process from the manufacturer's perspective, we prefer the phrase 'demand chain' because it implies consideration from the point of view of the customer.

In the past the management of the supply chain has been seen as a purely functional operation – how can we move products from A to B at the lowest cost? Now, the focus is on delivering added value not only for the customer but also for the individual partners in the demand chain.

The objective of marketing logistics should be to meet the service demands of the customer in the most efficient and cost-effective manner. This implies first researching exactly what are the demands of the customer in terms of delivery expectations and perceived value commensurate with product or service price expectations. To ensure a demand chain is sustainable, each partner (or link) in the chain needs to ensure it makes a profit. Logistics management will seek to design a system that meshes seamlessly *warehousing, inventory management, transportation* and *logistics information* and *data transfer*. Companies will look critically at all these areas to ensure that at all times the right level of stocks are maintained to meet the demand of the next link in the chain. A *just-in-time* logistics system will keep inventory levels as low as possible, thus minimizing investment in stockholding. To achieve this, accurate forecasting is required, which means close ties with the marketing team predicting consumer demand.

Retailers use *electronic data interchange* (EDI) to provide data to product suppliers that can track consumption patterns and tailor their manufacturing and warehousing stock levels to meet real-time needs. In some cases, suppliers are required to manage the ordering and delivery system for their customers. Large retailers such as Walmart and Home Depot work very closely with major suppliers using a *vendor-managed inventory* (VDI) system. Using VDI, the supplier takes on full responsibility for ensuring timely deliveries of products to the point of sale.

As technology improves and systems are developed that closely control the transition of products through the demand network, partners are able to share information and improve the whole-channel distribution. Successful companies will use these resources to build strong and enduring partnerships that collectively create competitive advantage whilst at the same time contributing to a sustainable and profitable business.

CONCLUSION

As marketing is about creating and delivering value to the customers, the role of distribution becomes essential in this system. This is because while producing goods in the right form, as desired by customers, gives them form utility (which explains the satisfaction associated with the product in its form), this cannot be actualized if the products produced cannot get to the ultimate consumers. Hence, the distribution role in the marketing system offers the customers, place, time, and possession utility.

Marketers have a number of options in terms of how to distribute their offerings to the target market. The channel strategy will be determined by analysing the needs of the customers and considering the resources available to see if it is possible. Basically, there are three channel strategies, which are intensive distribution, selective distribution and exclusive distribution. The choice will depend on the marketing strategy adopted for each product in a company's portfolio and the related channel objectives. Nonetheless, the ultimate factor in the selection of distribution strategies is that the choice should be customer-focused and enhances the value of the target market.

Case study
Relationships in the tea value chain

SRI LANKA ENJOYED DECADES AT THE HELM OF the tea industry as the largest exporter, renowned for its top-quality, flavourful teas. However, changes in consumption trends, over-supply in the global market and increasing competition from countries such as Kenya, India and Indonesia have resulted in reduced market share and low prices in the international market, thereby threatening Sri Lanka's position. The declining competitiveness of the Sri Lankan tea industry is an example of shifting competitive advantage in agribusiness. Firms in such markets are becoming increasingly aware of the limitations of arm's-length exchanges and of the benefits of more cooperative relationships. A case study based on the tea industry, conducted by Kasturiratne in 2007, analysed how buyer–seller relationships can be utilized as a valuable organizational resource whereby firms can create value to gain a competitive advantage.

istock © hadynyah

The tea industry in Sri Lanka is one of the oldest industries introduced during the British regime in the 19th century, following the demise of the earlier coffee plantations due to disease problems. It consists of a sophisticated network of supply chain links, as shown in the diagram.

The diagram demonstrates how the tea leaves are bought from the estate by a supplier or are sold directly to a factory where they are processed. This tea is then purchased by a broker and sold via an auction or through other means of sale to an exporter or to an overseas buyer. The supply chain can take many routes before reaching the final consumer, depending on the type of tea, methods of trade, market structure and type of buyer.

Following the trading systems that were in place in the 19th century, the British produced commodities in occupied countries while all other value-adding activities such as packaging, distribution and promotion took place in the UK. Most Sri Lankan traders were engaged in supplying tea, either in bulk form or for private label brands. This meant that large and dominant overseas labels such as Tetley, Twinings and PG Tips exercised their power over less powerful suppliers. This is further emphasized when there are a small number of powerful buyers and a large number of less powerful suppliers because the buyers have the choice of purchasing from a large selection of suppliers.

Traditionally, interorganizational exchanges between firms have been conducted at arm's length, with individual firms looking to achieve cost reductions or profit improvements – sometimes to the detriment of both buyers and sellers. However, many researchers such as Christopher (1998), Spekman et al. (1998) and Morgan and Hunt (1994) have identified that successful firms recognize the limitations of such **adversarial** approaches of exchange and instead promote long-term, cooperative relationships that are beneficial for both parties. The occurrence of patterns of cooperative, interfirm exchanges has become much more common in many industries such as food, automobiles and wood products since the last decades of the 20th century.

The power relations between Sri Lankan tea exporters and UK tea importers mostly characterized the dyad as transactional, rife with conflict, opportunism and independent behaviour, as opposed to relational dyads portraying trust, timely communication, commitment and interdependence. Where there

8

were high levels of interaction and social bonds these were found to strengthen the quality of the relationships, providing mutual benefits to both the exporter and importer. The buyers benefited from saving time and an improved consistency and quality of product, and by gaining specialist knowledge from expert Sri Lankan suppliers. The suppliers benefited by being able to gain and enter new markets, negotiate price and gain access to demand and trend information of consumer markets. Benefits of such relationships were identified as difficult for competitors to duplicate, thus creating strategic value and leading to long-term competitive advantage for both the buyer and seller.

Source: Kasturiratne, 2007

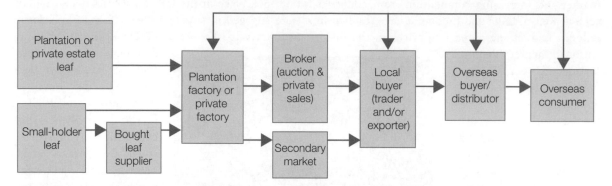

References:

Christopher, M. (1998) *Logistics and Supply Chain Management: Strategies for Reducing Cost and Improving Service* (2nd ed.). London: Financial Times, Pitman Publishing

Spekman, R., Kamauff, J. and Myhr, N. (1998) 'An Empirical Investigation into Supply Chain Management: A Perspective on Partnerships', *International Journal of Physical Distribution and Logistics Management*, Vol. 28, No. 8, pp. 630–50

Morgan, R. M. and Hunt, S. D. (1994) 'The Commitment-Trust Theory of Relationship Marketing', *Journal of Marketing*, Vol. 58, No. 3, pp. 20–38

Questions

1 Identify the importance of intermediaries in a value chain. How does this apply to the tea value chain discussed in this case study?

2 If intermediaries or 'middle-men' were eliminated, what advantages and disadvantages would there be for a value chain? Would this apply to the tea value chain?

3 Identify two characteristics each of arm's-length, adversarial relationships and cooperative, long-term relationships in value chains.

4 Identify two advantages each to the tea exporters and importers of cooperative, long-term relationships.

5 Identify the impact on a value chain when there are a large number of less powerful suppliers and a small number of dominant buyers.

6 Discuss how value chain relationships can be a source of competitive advantage.

7 Discuss the types of value that intermediaries can add to a product.

8 Discuss how cooperative, long-term value chain relationships can assist tea exporters in negotiating the selling price.

Review questions

1 We referred in the chapter to a preference for the term 'demand chain' rather than 'supply chain'. What is the key driver for this change in focus and how can this new paradigm offer benefits for all partners?

2 The efficiency of a demand chain can be greatly increased through the application of relationship marketing techniques. Discuss the major benefits and disadvantages of this approach.

3 Supply logistics is a network function rather than a linear one. Consider the ways in which any member of the network can add value to the product or service that is ultimately delivered to the consumer.

Group tasks

1 Give three specific examples of vertical marketing systems (VMS) that you are aware of. Cite specific reasons why you think they should be categorized as such. Discuss these reasons in your group.
2 Make a list of products that you consider appropriate to be distributed using intensive, selective and exclusive distribution strategies.

Glossary/Key terms

Exclusive distribution: Involves the distributor handling only the one manufacturer's products.

Intensive distribution: Involves maximizing the coverage to ensure products are distributed as widely as possible.

Product flow: The flow of products from manufacturer to end-user.

Selective distribution: Involves choosing a limited number of outlets, reflecting either the perceived value of the goods or a restricted geographic area.

Value-added reseller (VAR): A company or other organization that adds features or services to an existing product, then resells it (usually to end-users).

Vocab check list for ESL students

Adversarial	Infrastructure	Quibble
Cognizant	Intermediaries	Synergy
Disintermediation	Parlance	Utilitarian

Definitions for these terms can be found in the 'Vocab Zone' of the companion website, which provides free access to the Macmillan English Dictionary online at www.palgrave.com/business/Gbadamosi

8

Further reading

John Fernie (1992) 'Distribution Strategies of European Retailers', *European Journal of Marketing*, Vol. 26, No. 8/9, pp. 35–47
This journal article shows that UK-evolved strategies are clearly different from their continental European counterparts, and argues that the difference is the result of a significant sector of retailers with pan-European aspirations.

Gabriel Gazzoli, Woo Gon Kim, Radesh Palakurthi (2008) 'Online Distribution Strategies and Competition: Are the Global Hotel Companies Getting it Right?', *International Journal of Contemporary Hospitality Management*, Vol. 20, No. 4, pp. 375–87
The focus of this article is to compare online room prices of global hotel chains across online distribution channels and their own brand websites. It discusses pricing in relation to intangible offering.

Kangkang Yu, Jack Cadeaux, Hua Song (2012) 'Alternative Forms of Fit in Distribution Flexibility Strategies', *International Journal of Operations and Production Management*, Vol. 32, No. 10, pp. 1199–227

The article discusses distribution flexibility and the downstream supply chain in relation to how marketers make strategic choices among different distribution flexibility strategies.

References

Anderson, J. C. and Narus, J. A. (1996) 'Rethinking Distribution: Adaptive Channels', *Harvard Business Review*, 74 (4), pp. 112–20

Avon Products Inc. (2012) *2012 Annual Report*. Available at: http://investor. avoncompany.com (accessed 20 April 2013).

Bucklin, L. P. (1965) 'Postponement speculation and the structure of distribution channels', *Journal of Marketing Research*, 2 (1), pp. 26–31

Doyle, P. (2000) 'Value-based marketing', *Journal of Strategic Marketing*, 8 (4), pp. 299–311

Drucker, P. (1962) 'The Economy's Dark Continent', *Fortune*, 72 (103), pp. 265–70

Gummesson, E. (2008) *Total Relationship Marketing*. Oxford: Elsevier

Hollensen, S. (2003) *Marketing Management: A Relationship Approach*. Harlow: FT Prentice Hall

Ibrahim, D. (2007) Ford Motor Group: 'Do you have the drive to succeed?' *The Franchise Magazine*. Available at: http://www.thefranchisemagazine.net (accessed 3 May 2012)

Kasturiratne, D. (2007) 'Value, Relationships and Competitive Advantage in the Sri Lankan Tea Industry', unpublished PhD thesis, Imperial College, University of London

Kotler, P. and Armstrong, G. (2012) *Principles of Marketing* (Global edn) (14th edn). Harlow: Pearson Education

Kotler, P. and Keller, K. L. (2013) *Marketing Management* (14th edn). Upper Saddle River, NJ: Pearson

Morrel, L. (2012) 'Stores Go Multichannel', *Retail Week Technology* (September) pp. 9, 10. Available at: http://issuu.com/emap_/docs/rw_tech_sept2012 (accessed 20 June 2013

Sainsbury (2012) J Sainsbury plc FAQs. Available at: www.j-sainsbury.co.uk/extras/ faqs/media/ (accessed 19 April 2013)

Tauber, E. M. (1972) 'Why do people shop?', *Journal of Marketing*, 36 (4), pp. 46–55

Tupperware Brands Corp (2012) News release 1 February 2012. Available at: http://ir. tupperwarebrands.com/results.cfm (accessed 20 April 2013)

9 MARKETING COMMUNICATIONS STRATEGIES

LINDA PHILLIPS & SUE CLEWS

STAFFORDSHIRE UNIVERSITY

CHAPTER CONTENTS

LEARNING OUTCOMES

The content of this chapter will help you to:

- Appreciate the role of integrated marketing communications in connecting consumers' and producers' values
- Understand the communication process
- Be aware of the steps in developing communications strategy
- Recognize the factors impacting on marketing communications decisions
- Understand the role and characteristics the communications mix tools

Marketing in action
Innocent

IN A MARKETING ERA WHEN ADVERTISING campaigns and general marketing information appear to overwhelm consumers (who are becoming increasingly selective in what they pay attention to), Innocent seems to have broken out of the mould and achieved a unique market position.

Founded in 1999 by three Cambridge graduates (Richard Reed, Adam Balon and Jon Wright – all in their twenties), the company enjoys a very strong market position in the soft drinks industry, largely based on its ability to communicate unique brand values. Partly through the simplicity of its product messages (for example, 'no rubbish', 'no funny things', 'no nasty things'), the company has been successful in gaining consumers' attention. In fact, there is something approaching 'cult consumer patronage' because of how Innocent has sought to embed issues around sustainable consumption in its marketing communications.

Reproduced with permission of Innocent Drinks

According to Richard Reed, the company is driven by a business philosophy that aims to make Innocent 'a global brand and take its ethical values to the world's consumers'. The ethical positioning, which includes donating 10 per cent of profits to charity, has touched a chord with general consumer sensitivities regarding sustainable consumption (especially at a time when there is a growing concern about food additives and unhealthy eating). A consumer who posted on the company's website has this to say about the company: 'their fresh approach to marketing has been an inspiration and as a consumer of their products I must admit that I enjoy the packaging as much as I do drinking the contents. Not sure how many other food and drink products I could say that about.'

Reproduced with permission of Innocent Drinks

As a mark of its success, between 2008 and 2012 the company doubled its turnover to £209 million. In a situation that may look as if Innocent is a victim of its success, Coca-Cola took over control of the company in February 2013 by increasing its stake to above 90 per cent. However, the founders have rebutted any claim of a 'sell-out' by insisting that the relationship with Coca-Cola has been 'beautiful', and saying that the company will benefit from taking advantage of its marketing and buying power. According to Mr Reed, 'because of Coke, we were the official smoothie of the Olympics'. For Coca-Cola, it makes sound business sense to fully commit to Innocent's founding ethical ideals, part of which read as follows:

We sure aren't perfect but we're trying to do the right thing.

It might make us sound like a Miss World contestant, but here at Innocent, we want to leave things a little bit better than we find them. We strive to do business in a more enlightened way, where we take responsibility for the impact of our business on society and the environment, aiming to move these impacts from negative to neutral or (better still) positive. It's part of our quest to become a truly sustainable business where we have a net positive effect on the wonderful world around us.

(**Source:** www. innocentdrinks.co.uk)

Reproduced with permission of Innocent Drinks

INTRODUCTION

Businesses have a growing interest in value creation perspectives and, importantly, how these should be communicated to consumers. It is not enough for a company to claim the high ground in its value standings; this must be seen to be shared with consumers, who must 'buy into' such value positioning for it to be effective. This is the basis of market differentiation. Therefore, effective marketing communications are vital to the successful organization. A strong brand presence in the market, recognized by users and non-users alike, says a lot about the role of marketing communications in an organization.

Successful companies tend to use a variety of promotional tools (such as advertising, public relations, personal selling, digital marketing, sales promotion, direct marketing, sponsorship, events and experiences) to position their organizations and products in the minds of consumers. This means that such companies are able to effectively connect consumers' values with the value embedded in the companies' offerings. As the popular saying goes, 'a good product sells itself' but it still depends on effective marketing support that convinces consumers that the product will appropriately deliver satisfaction to them. Brands such as Starbucks, Coca-Cola and McDonald's, which have become household names, exhibit common features in the pervasive role of their marketing communications strategies. For example, Innocent was voted the top 'social' brand in May 2012 by social agency Headstream for communicating and engaging with consumers through a variety of channels whilst maintaining a lighthearted but consistent tone of voice. Benetton achieved a high market visibility by connecting with 'diversity values'.

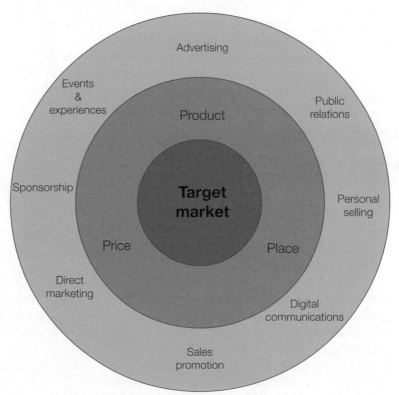

Figure 9.1: The relationship between the marketing mix and the marketing communications elements

Marketing communications are also known as promotion, one of the original four Ps of the marketing mix. Promotion is the mix element that is instrumental in establishing product positioning in the eyes of the consumer to gain competitive advantage. Its role is to inform, persuade and remind consumers and potential consumers of product benefits with the aim of obtaining a response, changing behaviour or influencing opinion. Figure 9.1 demonstrates how the marketing communications elements may be used to envelop and portray the three other key marketing elements (product, price and place) to the target audience.

THE COMMUNICATIONS PROCESS

Think and discuss

Think of organizations such as Coca-Cola, Innocent, McDonald's and Nike. List at least three common features that differentiate them from the competition. In particular, highlight the 'core value' which they seek to communicate to their target markets.

The process by which individuals receive and act on communications is not straightforward. Individuals exist within complex and dynamic environments and are exposed to a multitude of communications from a wide range of sources, all competing with each other to be seen, heard and acted on. An individual will selectively perceive and retain messages that are meaningful and important to them at a particular point in time. The rest will be ignored and thus rendered ineffective. It is important for marketers to understand the communications process. One of the simplest models of communications was developed by Schramm (1954), cited in Brassington and Pettitt (2006); see Figure 9.2.

The model attempts to explain the complexity of the route a message will take between the originator and the receiver. The message is developed (encoded) by the sender (organization or individual) and a channel is selected to carry the message to the intended receiver(s). Noise represents interruption to the communications process. This can happen when the message is being developed (for example, selection of the wrong media channel) or when it is being received and decoded (for example, competing messages and distractions). Feedback is the term given to the message response and can take the form of a purchase, a visit to a dealership or a change in attitude, perception or behaviour. Feedback can be measured – for

Example 9.1:
Findus brand damaged by horsemeat scandal

The scandal about horsemeat contamination has poisoned many ready-meal brands. Findus is one of the most prominent brands in the firing line as consumer confidence in meat products plummets. The intensity of the scandal leaves many market watchers wondering whether names like Findus have become toxic.

For over 50 years, Findus has been established as a successful company in the frozen ready-meal market, with global sales in excess of £1 billion in 2011. In the aftermath of the horsemeat scandal, sales plunged – its beef lasagne was taken off the shelves after being found to contain a large proportion of horsemeat. Brand experts say that the future of Findus will depend on how the company responds to the fallout from the scandal. Whether the situation is recoverable or proves to be terminal for the company remains an open question. What is not in doubt, however, is that the company's marketing communications will be severely tested. In fact, it may well be that the future of the company rests on the effectiveness of its marketing communications strategy in shoring up consumer confidence in the brand.

example, through sales volume or formalized market research such as brand preference surveys or awareness of advertising, or from the number of 'likes' on Facebook.

The way in which organizations apply the model above (the communications process) is by using various communication tools. McDaniel et al. (2013) refer to this as a promotions mix and it includes advertising, public relations, sales promotion, personal selling, social media, events and experiences, and sponsorship. If each of these communication approaches is managed individually, it may result in a range of mixed messages to the target market, causing confusion and misinterpretation. Individually, the communications may be very effective. However, if they are not fully understood by the target audience, all of the money, time and effort expended in developing them may be wasted. Historically, in large organizations each communication tool has been managed separately. For example, personal selling has been carried out by the sales team, advertising by an agency, publicity activities by a public relations team. This can lead to variations in the message transmitted to consumers. The purpose of integrated marketing communications is to ensure coordination between each element of the communications mix to deliver a **coherent** message to the target market.

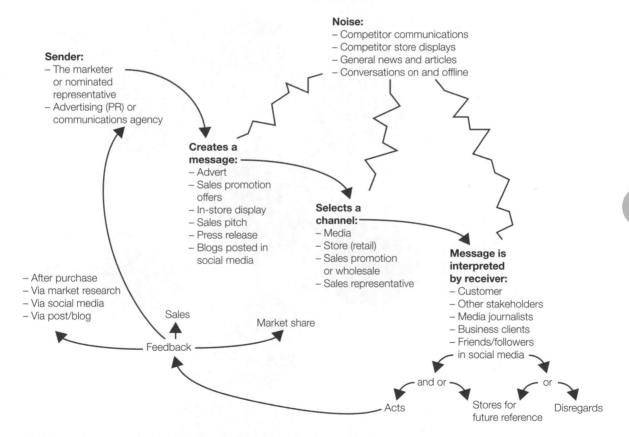

Figure 9.2: The communications process
Source: Based on McDaniel et al., 2013

THE NEED FOR INTEGRATED MARKETING COMMUNICATIONS

Integrated marketing communications have been defined by Dibb et al. (2012, p. 795) as 'the coordination and integration of all marketing communication tools, avenues and sources within a company into a seamless programme that maximizes the impact on consumers and other end users, at minimal cost'.

Organizations communicate with their target audience(s) primarily to inform, persuade and remind. Before any message can be created or media selected to carry the message, it is important to have information about the consumers belonging to each target audience group, from a number of perspectives.

The following section focuses on the factors affecting strategic communication decisions relating to consumer behaviour, the product and the market.

STRATEGIC COMMUNICATION DECISIONS

Figure 9.3 illustrates the factors influencing strategic communication decisions, which are discussed in this section.

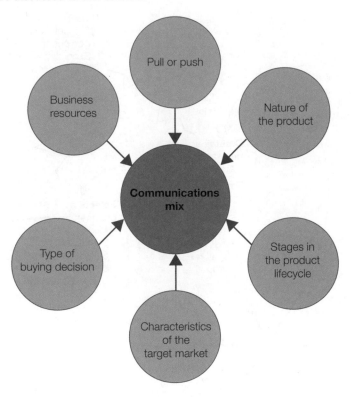

Figure 9.3: Factors influencing strategic communication decisions

TARGET MARKET: MARKET SIZE AND CONCENTRATION

The characteristics of the target market strongly influence communications strategy, such as:

- Where it is located geographically

- How large the market is
- Market composition such as socio-economic characteristics (Dibb et al., 2012)

Each of these has an impact on how the message is created and also which media are selected to convey the message to the target audience (see Table 9.1).

Table 9.1: Effect of target market characteristics on marketing communications

Characteristics	Implication	Example
Geographic location	Limits the range of tools available	Widely dispersed consumer markets may require mass media communication Widely dispersed business markets may require personal selling and publicity
Size of the market	Influences media selection	In large markets, mass media tools such as advertising are economically viable because the cost per person is low
Market composition and knowledge of buyer behaviour	Affects how the message is formulated and transmitted	Toothpaste adverts focus on different benefits according to buyer's age, life stage, etc.

PUSH/PULL STRATEGIES

These are two distinct approaches to developing a communications strategy. A 'push' strategy focuses on promoting products between levels in the distribution chain. For example, a toothpaste brand is promoted by the manufacturer to the wholesaler (using the sales team to engage with wholesalers to negotiate sales and using point-of-sale material). The wholesaler then promotes to the retailer (using the point-of-sale material and trade sales promotion activities). The retailer presents the product in store (point-of-sale material, product samples and promotional offers) and online to the consumer. A 'pull' strategy involves communicating directly with the end-user of the product, who is incentivized to visit a retailer to make a purchase (advertising, public relations activities or direct marketing).

In reality these two strategies tend to overlap and are often used **simultaneously** to engage with the end-user and achieve organizational objectives. This is known as a profile strategy.

Think and discuss

Use product examples to distinguish between 'push' and 'pull' strategies. Under what conditions would each of the strategies be more effective?

9

NATURE OF THE PRODUCT (CHARACTERISTICS)

The nature of the product has a direct influence on the approach taken to communication.

Business products often use personal selling as a key communication tool, particularly for customized or bespoke products. The relationship between buyer and seller requires regular two-way communications in the form of virtual and face-to-face meetings. As the relationship develops, a wider group of staff form part of the sales process – for example, mechanical and electronic engineers acting as design consultants and technical support. This is often supported by advertising in trade journals, editorial including articles on product applications, and participation in trade exhibitions. Exhibitions are an excellent way of meeting competitors and customers or potential customers in a neutral environment. Conferences often run alongside trade exhibitions, providing the opportunity to give presentations on company developments and product applications to a clearly defined and receptive audience.

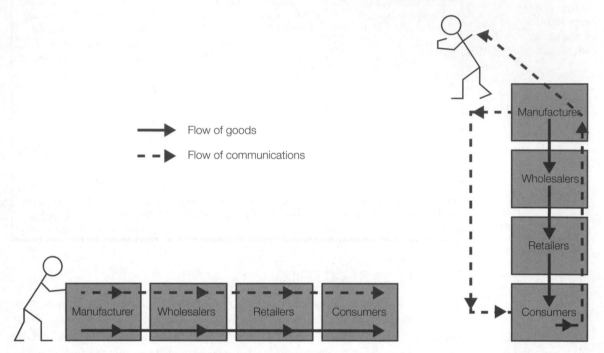

Figure 9.4: Push versus pull marketing communications strategies

Consumer products use a range of communication tools including advertising, public relations, personal selling, digital marketing, sales promotion, direct marketing, sponsorship, events and experiences. Brand owners of fast-moving consumer goods (FMCG) – everyday products such as shampoo, soap, bread and chocolate – utilize advertising to raise awareness of new products and to remind. Whilst traditional mass media (TV, magazines, posters and so on) continue to be significant, new technologies have provided many other opportunities not only to advertise but also to interact and engage with the brand, fostering greater consumer brand involvement. Advertising can carry direct marketing and sales promotion messages to encourage the consumer to move to trial or action.

Organizations producing consumer durables face different buying conditions. For example, for most individuals, buying a computer, laptop or iPad is a significant investment that requires greater thought and commitment in comparison with purchasing everyday household items. This has ramifications for the communications required to support the consumer through the buying process. In these situations, retail sales staff – whether in person, in call centres or online – can provide product solutions for customers.

Risk increases for consumers buying higher-value items such as cars and homes, and communications have a role to play in supporting the consumer's decision making. This may involve a broader range of communications such as advertising, publicity and sales promotions used strategically to persuade the consumer – such as car manufacturers waiving VAT for consumers for a short time period.

istock © monkeybusinessimages

Of increasing importance today is the support offered by web-based communications. An organization's website may provide online help in the form of an online shop assistant (as in the case of IKEA), FAQs (for example, Microsoft), telephone helplines (such as for BT internet services), value-added information (such as Sainsbury's recipes) and social media coverage (for example, through Facebook and Twitter).

STAGES IN THE PRODUCT LIFECYCLE

The product lifecycle can guide the marketer in developing an appropriate marketing mix for each stage of the lifecycle, which influences the selection of communications tools.

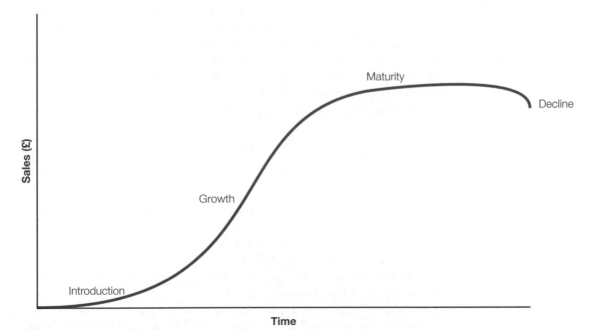

Figure 9.5: Product lifecycle

During the *introduction* stage the focus is on public relations and advertising to create awareness of the product or service. Sales promotions and free samples may be used to encourage trial. If a push strategy is being adopted, personal selling will be used to establish distribution outlets and provide communications support such as sales promotion and point-of-sale materials.

During the *growth* phase, advertising and public relations are still important to encourage repeat purchase. New purchases will still be made, based on word-of-mouth recommendation from those who tried the product during the introduction phase.

Maturity represents the point at which sales level off. Here, competitive activity is generally at its peak, so advertising, reinforced by sales promotion, is used to remind consumers of the product's competitive superiority.

During the *decline* phase, the company will make strategic decisions on whether to rejuvenate or discontinue the product. For example, car manufacturers often add value by providing additional features such as bluetooth, satellite navigation or reversing sensors to encourage the sale of cars that are about to be replaced by a newer design. Sales promotion and advertising may be used to clear stock.

TYPE OF BUYING DECISION

The type of buying decision is affected by product choice and the level of involvement and risk associated with the purchase. Consumers engage in day-to-day routine buying situations that involve little thought and risk, such as buying crisps, soft drinks, shampoo and bread. They will be affected by sales promotions as a stimulus to buy but will also be predisposed towards certain brands, dependent on how their perceptions have been formed from other communications messages delivered by the brand owner. For example, there has been a growth in the use of events to encourage engagement with the brand in a fun, relaxed way.

On occasion, consumers will be involved in more complex buying situations that involve a high degree of involvement, personal risk and time – for example, with high-cost purchases such as property, cars or expensive holidays. This often requires sequenced communications to guide consumers through the buying process and to reassure them post purchase to prevent cognitive dissonance.

Impulse purchasing may occur as a result of a sales promotion or an immediate, urgent need such as a damaged tyre or environmental conditions such as poor weather.

BUSINESS RESOURCES

There are a number of constraints that have an impact on media and message choices. These include:

- **Time:** The time available for the development of the campaign may be affected by competitors' activities
- **Budget:** This can be approached in a number of ways but will essentially limit the communication opportunities available
- **Human resources:** Factors such as in-house capability and expertise may affect the decision to buy in campaign specialists
- **Externalities:** Legal constraints, for example, such as those in Europe that restrict promotions aimed at children and those in the USA where some states forbid the use of competitions as a sales promotion activity

Example 9.2:
Tesco prepares for price war to communicate its customer value strategy

Tesco started out as an East End market stall and made its name on a unique selling strategy of 'piling them high and selling them cheap' to a generation of cash-strapped housewives. It has since grown to crush its rivals, achieving the 'No. 1 spot' as Britain's biggest supermarket and outperforming Asda (No. 2) and Sainsbury's (No. 3).

Riding on a wave of growth against the tide of a sluggish economy, with profits topping £2 billion a year, the company in 2012 invested £1 billion to face off fierce competition from rival chains. Apart from its expansion strategy of 'being everywhere', it has continued to deepen its distinct ranges of own-brands, from *Value* to *Finest*, which are priced to attract all types of shoppers. As an industry analyst commented: 'Whether you are a prince or a pauper you can go into Tesco and find something you want.'

Additionally, the company is using its Clubcard to reward loyal customers and is refunding any price differentials offered by rivals. By monitoring price movements of goods carried by competing firms on a daily basis, with strong commitment to match or beat competitor prices, the company lives out its business credo – '*giving you more for less*'. In March 2013, Tesco launched its 'Clubcard TV', which will use real-time customer data to serve viewers' ad needs. According to the Managing Director, 'we look at what customers buy from us and then show them ads that are relevant to them' (*Marketing Week*, 7 March 2013).

istock © monkeybusinessimages

Once all of the above have been taken into consideration, the marketing manager selects the most suitable communications elements from the marketing communications mix in order to achieve the communication objectives (for example, to persuade, remind, reinforce).

9

THE MARKETING COMMUNICATIONS MIX

Marketers rarely use only one method of communication to reach their target audiences. Ideally the elements selected from the diagram in Figure 9.6 should, once put into motion, seamlessly merge to present one cohesive brand message – much as the diagram would blur into one visual mass if it were spun at speed.

ADVERTISING

Advertising comprises structured impersonal messages which usually inform, persuade or remind consumers about products, services or ideas. They are paid for by the organization initiating the advertisement.

There are many ways in which advertising can be presented to consumers. Traditionally, advertising is delivered through media such as TV, newspapers, magazines, posters, bill boards, radio, cinema, vehicles and transit boards. For example, the

Monkey Forest in Stoke-on-Trent paid for the rear of a single-deck bus to feature a monkey encouraging other road users to follow the bus to the venue. This provides the opportunity for one-way communication to consumers. The growth of online and mobile media provides a wider range of options for companies to engage and interact with their customers, such as static advertisements on websites, banner or skyscraper advertisements, pop-ups, videos that can become 'viral' and fan pages on Facebook. Further developments include SoLoMo (social, local/location, mobile), which combines GPS data and online behavioural information to target consumers with specific adverts. For example, at a football match (where the stadium has wi-fi access) spectators may be able to see **augmented** reality scanned adverts on seat backs or coffee cups via their mobile, vote for the man of the match on their mobile or have their own Facebook image displayed on the stadium screen (Derrick, 2012). This is in addition to advertising digital interchangeable messages around the pitch perimeter, sponsors' logos on football kit and background boards used during match news interviews with players and managers. Advertising is often integrated with other forms of communication such as direct marketing and sales promotion, which will be discussed later in this section.

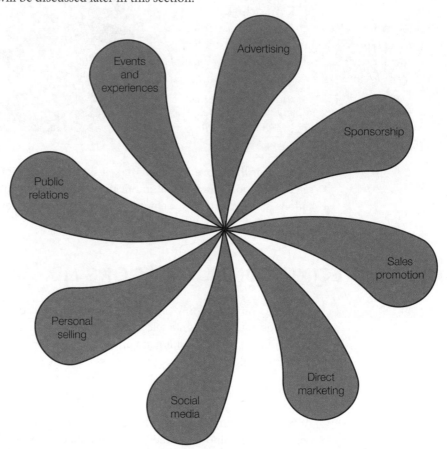

Figure 9.6: Blending the marketing communications elements

Ambient advertising includes unusual or unexpected hosts for the advert such as inflatable items, T-shirts, reverse of car park tickets and shopping receipts, people, supermarket floors, shopping trolleys and so on.

As consumers have become more adept at using online sources, and devices have been developed to facilitate use on the go (smart phones and tablets), evidence suggests that consumers are competently multitasking – in other words, they are poly-chronic. Consumers are watching TV, searching online and texting/tweeting simulta-neously. This means that a consumer can respond to an advertising message instantly, which in turn may impact on online retail sales or on the company's reputation.

SALES PROMOTION

Sales promotion is an enticement to consumers or trade buyers to purchase products or services. Whilst sales promotion often results in increased sales of products in the short term, it does not always result in an increase in total sales over time. Promo-tions will appeal to existing consumers, who may bring their purchasing decision forward to take advantage of a good offer and stock up on the product. For example, you may only need to buy toothpaste every two months but if the manufacturer offers a special price or multiple product deal, you may take up the offer and then delay further purchases for some time. However, organizations combine sales promotion with other tools such as advertising in order to build brand loyalty and encourage non-users to switch to the brand. Other objectives of sales promotion include new product trial and increasing frequency of purchase – for example, by offering coupon or token collection over a specific time period.

There are two key approaches to implementing sales promotions, either direct to the consumer or through trade or intermediary channels. See Table 9.2 for an outline of consumer promotion techniques.

Table 9.2: Consumer sales promotion techniques

Consumer promotions	Examples
Multi-buy promotions	'3 for the price of 2' offers provide a short-term boost to sales, e.g. Muller Crunch Corners, two multipacks for £5
Money-off coupons	50p off when you buy a specified item. This could be obtained from a pack of the product, a newspaper or magazine advert, mobile message or download from the internet, e.g. Groupon Supermarket vouchers for money off your total shop, acquired when paying for shopping and for use within a limited time frame to encourage repeat store visits, or from regular use of a store loyalty card e.g. Tesco Clubcard and Marks & Spencer Master Card/points card
Point of sale (POS) items	Signs, displays used in-store to attract attention or provide samples of products In-store TVs showing product advertisements Interactive displays, both physical and online e.g. Argos click and collect
Premiums	Bonus items either free or at a low cost, offered in conjunc-tion with a purchase of a standard item Free samples delivered to home/store location
Price offers	Short-term reduction in price to boost sales
Prize promotion	Competitions, draws or games (Jobber and Fahy, 2012)
Giveaways at events	T-shirts, pens, pads, bags, mouse mats, etc.

9

Sales promotions are viewed as a short-term inducement and are measurable, enabling organizations to track and review the impact of each promotion – for example, the number of coupons redeemed and consequent sales or market share increase.

PUBLIC RELATIONS

Public relations is 'A planned and sustained effort to establish and maintain goodwill and mutual understanding between an organization and its stakeholders' (Dibb et al., 2012).

Stakeholders are all groups with an interest in the organization, as illustrated in Figure 9.7. Each may require different forms of communication to deliver the appropriate message.

Public relations involves a strategic approach to managing various methods for communicating with an organization's stakeholders, such as publicity, press releases, stunts, events and press conferences. It is an indirect form of communication, as the organization is not perceived to be the message sender unless the message takes the form of corporate advertising. Messages are delivered by a third party – for example, press releases are submitted by the organization to a journalist or editor, who then decides what to include in their newspaper or magazine; articles are commissioned on product applications such as electronics and engineering products in the business-to-business market. An alternative approach is to commission a short film to portray a special event at the organization, to demonstrate product features or the variety of production techniques, or even to showcase the organization in its entirety. An example of a corporate presentation produced on behalf of Swanline Print (Swanline Print's Corporate Presentation teaser) can be found at www.youtube.com/watch?v=y9cKWPg_gG0.

Press conferences are often linked to exhibitions, especially where new products are launched such as at motor shows or clothes shows. At these types of exhibitions, prolific and renowned consumer bloggers are invited to provide a commentary on the show/exhibition to generate interest amongst the wider public and encourage visitors to attend. Twitter feeds provide a similar stimulus. The danger for the organization is that these messages are not controlled and could provide negative information.

Social media provides an exciting opportunity for viewers to relive the show – for example, Top Shop's February 2013 London Fashion Week show was filmed and shared on YouTube and Google+. Bloggers were invited to the show to cover proceedings and provide a buzz of excitement around the show and clothes.

Public relations are utilized to manage dangerous or crisis situations. These can spark from a small incident, such as a brief argument between footballer and team manager, or from a major disaster, such as the Hudson River plane crash in 2009.

As can be seen from the above, public relations are used by an organization to develop and maintain a reputation with its many stakeholders, whether external (such as consumers and investors) or internal (such as employees).

SPONSORSHIP

Sponsorship involves paying for the right to be associated with an organization or an event (BDS Sponsorship, 2013). Sponsorship has grown significantly in the recent past. It is valued as a method of communication in that it provides an alternative way of engaging with stakeholders. Fenton (2012) identifies that the European Sponsorship Association (ESA) finds a ratio of 67:33 in sport to non-sport sponsorships (Brand Meets Brand, 2012). Fenton argues that there is so much expenditure on

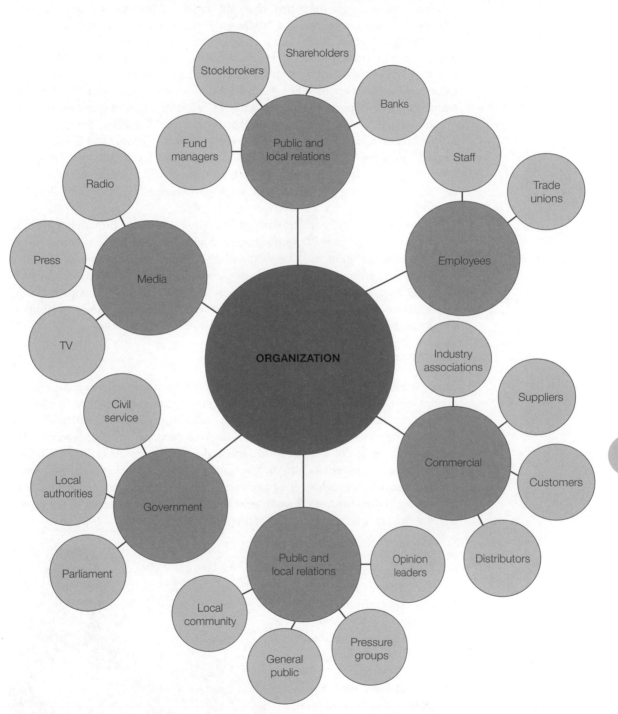

Figure 9.7: Organization stakeholders

sponsorship (€26.5 billion in Europe in 2011) that it is becoming a key element of the communications mix.

Sponsorship enables organizations to demonstrate their interest in activities and businesses or their support of charitable causes. Whilst the sponsor's brand is evident, there is no **overt** message driving an observer to buy or modify their behaviour. Sports such as football, tennis, rugby, athletics, Formula 1 and darts attract intense sponsor interest due to their popularity and audience appeal. This also means that they will receive extensive media coverage and hence further brand exposure. Other organizations sponsor non-mainstream or extreme sports – such as Red Bull, whose gamble to support the space jump of Felix Baumgartner in October 2012 paid off handsomely with media coverage (that is, publicity) following the jump worth £10 million in the UK and up to £100 million worldwide (Rowley and Clancy, 2012). Reduced government funding for the arts in recent years has highlighted the importance of sponsorship as a means of survival for the arts. For example, recent sponsors of the Natural History Museum include Anglo-American, GlaxoSmithKline and Starbucks.

Corporate sponsorship, particularly of sports-related events, provides opportunities for staff to engage with customers in a different setting and environment and can help to foster good working relationships. For example, companies may take trade buyers to an open golf championship. Partners would be entertained in a city whilst the buyers were taken to the championship tournament. This approach links well with sales promotion. The event itself provides sponsors with an opportunity to distribute giveaways as a longer-lasting reminder of the organization.

PERSONAL SELLING

Personal selling involves face-to-face communication between sellers and buyers and is most often used in business-to-business selling situations. This type of communication facilitates discussion and support for complex buying situations – for example, where custom-made products, systems or services are being produced. For example, the design of a battery for a medical ventilator or defibrillator will have distinct design requirements and specific quality standards. During such discussions, numerous specialists such as design engineers, financial managers, buyers and even the managing director from the buying organization may be involved in the project development and in choosing the appropriate battery supplier. The buying team are likely to be involved in similar discussions for the other components of their products, systems or services. In other organizations, equipment users might also be involved for their feedback on product proposals relating to potential purchases. A key objective of these meetings is to demonstrate the technical excellence of the selling team in meeting the requirements

istock © AndreyPopov

of the buyer and to secure an order for the development and eventual manufacture of the seller's product.

Whilst this approach is predominantly used in business to business, there are instances in consumer markets where sales personnel are involved in consumers' complex buying situations – for example, financial products, cars and houses. There may also be instances where the consumer's buying decision relates to high-risk or high-involvement situations, such as for expensive clothing, jewellery or perfume, where the retailer assists in the buying process. As an extension of this, some stores (for example, John Lewis) employ personal shoppers to provide advice and guidance and make suggestions on product choices to help the consumer reach a decision and perhaps try something new or out of the ordinary for them.

Identification and **clarification** of customer needs are a fundamental part of the selling process. In a selling situation it is important for the sales person to present themselves well, but they must also be a good listener and empathetic to be able to pick up and respond to verbal and non-verbal cues from the buyer and others influencing the buying decision. This will allow the seller to respond to clients' objections, whether implicit or explicit, and possibly overcome them and lead to a greater likelihood of achieving the sale. Once the sale is complete, it is important for the sales person to return to the buyer to measure their satisfaction with the product and to facilitate the development of a good working relationship. This is beneficial to future sales and for the prevention of cognitive dissonance in buyers. In the consumer market, this may take the form of a letter, email or other direct communication rather than a personal visit.

Sales management involves a number of key areas including the allocation of work to the sales team, remuneration, motivation, evaluation, training and continuing professional development. There is a decision to make on how to allocate work and this will depend to some extent on the buying situation, type of product and geographic spread of customers. Salesforces can be organized, for example, according to territories, industry or product group, key accounts and size of order. It should be noted that sales teams are expensive to run – their costs include salary, expenses, transport and subsistence costs. Choice of method of communicating with the customer needs to be related to the objective of each communication and to the buying situation.

DIRECT MAIL

Organizations use personal approaches to customers in a less direct manner than personal selling by sending letters direct to the customer's home or business. An alternative is to use the phone. These methods are frequently used to support the salesperson in business-to-business markets. In consumer markets, direct mail and phone contact are used either to initiate a relationship or to make a sale (for example, double glazing) or to build and extend a relationship with an existing customer (for example, after a car purchase). The diffusion and adoption of the internet has led to increased use of email rather than direct mail to keep in contact with customers. This is discussed in more detail below. The organization's knowledge of customers and their ongoing relationship is stored in a database of personal information that may evolve into a customer relationship management (CRM) system.

Think and discuss

In a group of 3–4, choose a company affected by a scandal such as meat contamination (Tesco, McDonald's, Findus). Suggest how the company could use marketing communications to turn around consumers' wavering values about ready-meal meat products.

9

Example 9.3:
Dunlop drives sales with digital campaign

Dunlop has had a long and chequered history in the solid tyre business, stretching over 120 years. According to company records, it was started way back in 1888 by John Dunlop, a Scottish vet who lived in Belfast. The history of the company is inextricably linked with innovation, which has enabled the building of a brand with a strong reputation among car and motorcycle users globally. (See, for example, www.dunlop.eu/dunlop_uk/what_sets_dunlop_apart/corporate_info/120years.jsp).

Not resting on its laurels, the company in early 2013 launched a digital campaign to strengthen relationships with consumers. This focused on extending travel experience and consumer value by the deployment of cutting-edge technological innovation. The campaign is simple but effective. Using social media and online resources, consumers are signposted to a virtual site that enables them to plan their 'ultimate road trip' and experience the journey online. With a strong online following, the company proactively supports the growth of Dunlop's brand community. The long-term goal is to create a more cost-effective marketing campaign to stimulate sales in a market dented by tough economic conditions.

istock © svedoliver

EVENTS AND EXPERIENCES

Events and experiences are becoming an increasingly popular element of the communications mix. This was demonstrated in the London Olympics 2012 when this major event offered not just sponsorship rights but also 'brand immersion'. Brand houses were set up throughout London and key customers and clients were invited to these locations. For example, in Hyde Park, Cadbury used three purple inflatable structures to serve as hospitality locations (Bull, 2012). At the O2 arena in London, Nissan held an event where visitors could interact with various displays pertaining to the vehicles and their technology. Entrance to the event was free and visitors were invited to register with their name and address on entry. Various **experiential** activities were situated within the arena space, such as games and challenges. There were staff on hand to help the less technologically able with some of the games and there was also a mock-up of the vehicles and a special promotional batman vehicle. The final activity was designed to collect email addresses, inviting visitors to enter their email address to win an iPad. This is a win-win event for both Nissan and visitors – the former have a database of potential customers while the latter had free entertainment.

DIGITAL COMMUNICATIONS

All of the communications methods discussed so far – advertising, sales promotion, public relations, sponsorship, personal selling, events and experiences, and direct mail/phone – are enhanced and supported by digital communication via the internet.

The internet is used to communicate not just to customers but also to all of the organization's stakeholders. Its impact over the last few years has been phenomenal, changing the way in which communication and commerce are conducted. This area is subject to constant change and innovation. One area of rapid growth is the development and adoption of mobile devices (smartphones and tablets), which allow for constant access to the internet wherever individuals may be (subject to internet availability). Use of such mobile devices allows organizations to target consumers specifically, particularly where GPS is enabled on an individual's phone. This provides an opportunity for companies to distribute a myriad of messages such as adverts, vouchers, advertainment, games and emails and allows for interaction with customers and potential customers rather than the one-way communication of traditional media (see Figure 9.2). whilst they are in a specific location.

THE INTERNET

The World Wide Web (www) and email are the primary media of the internet.

The World Wide Web

The vast majority of organizations have a website as the basis for their digital communications. This is further developed by some to include ecommerce, enabling order processing and fulfilment, as in the case of Amazon, Next, Argos, Marks & Spencer and John Lewis. Support can be provided to customers through virtual assistants (in the case of IKEA), order and logistics tracking (for example, from FedEx), FAQs (for example, HM Revenue and Customs) and customer reviews (such as on tripadvisor.com and bookings.com). Financial services providers, such as those offering debit and credit cards, have needed to develop their services to satisfy consumers' fears about giving confidential financial details online. Earlier in the development of the internet this was a major barrier to purchase for some customers and target groups.

In addition to its customer-facing function, the internet/web can be used extensively within an organization, in particular to facilitate communications with employees through an intranet. This is a secure area of the website for internal staff use. Information can be restricted to onsite viewing only and may include personnel documents and quality procedures. The intranet is used as a public relations tool (internal marketing) to foster a community of employees and to engage them in the ethos and vision of the company, which they in turn embody in their communications with customers and other external stakeholders.

The easiest way to find something on the web is to search for a keyword or term through a search engine such as Google or Bing. Organizations must therefore understand their customers and use these keywords and phrases on their websites to enable them to be found by the search engines. This area of activity is known as *search engine optimization* (SEO). This is where a company identifies the key terms or phrases a customer will use when searching for a specific product or service. SEO is important to organizations in that it will influence where the company appears in the list returned by search engines. A first-page position is preferable as it is thought that those searching will often not look beyond the first page of results.

There are a number of different ways for organizations to communicate with customers, potential customers or stakeholders via the web, as shown in Table 9.3.

Email communication

Email communication is simply an electronic version of direct mail (referred to in the previous section) sent via the internet. To be effective it needs to be carefully targeted to relevant market segments and each receiver needs to have given permission to the sender before emails can be transmitted. In the UK this is a legal requirement. Not only are special offers sent to customers, but emails can also be sent at any stage of the customer relationship cycle from initial contact through to fostering long-term relationships. The point that the customer has reached in the relationship cycle affects the message emailed to that person. Dependent on the market segment, it may still be necessary to use more traditional forms of communication to keep in touch with customers, such as in the case of older members of the population, who have not necessarily adopted the internet and email.

Table 9.3:
Communication via the web
Source: Adapted from Semenik et al., 2012

Paid search (SEO)
Display and banner ads
Sponsorship
Pop-up, pop-under ad
Rich media/video and audio
Corporate/brand home pages
Widgets
Second life/virtual worlds
Video games
Coupons
Competitions
Social media
Email
Voice over internet protocol (VOIP), e.g. Skype

From a marketing perspective, email is often used in connection with promotions or offers for a company's products or services and can be very successful when linked to an attractive offer. For example, Ocado discounts by 10 or 15 per cent when a customer orders within two days of receipt of the offer. Tesco offers free delivery to encourage repeat business and Premier Inn has £29 per night bookings available during offer periods. Email is also used in other ways. The Chartered Institute of Marketing (CIM) uses electronic magazines to update its members. Others, including Brand Republic and the Academy of Marketing, run webinars to update registered users on research.

DIRECT MARKETING

Direct marketing allows for interaction between the organization and its customers, so it is a two-way form of communication. Because of this, the general response to any campaign is measurable and can be justified in terms of its return on investment. Therefore direct marketing encompasses the means of communication previously discussed, which are direct mail and email communication.

DEVELOPING A MARKETING COMMUNICATIONS STRATEGY

Marketers face a choice between all the communications methods available in order to select the most appropriate for the products they are managing. There are several approaches to developing a communications campaign and Figure 9.8 illustrates a basic planning process. This comprises a number of steps, which form an outline plan for the key elements of communications. The steps can be taken in sequence or, when necessary, companies will work on one or more steps at the same time – for example, selecting the media channels and engineering the impact that the communications messages have on each other.

Figure 9.8:
Steps in effective communications planning
Source: Adapted from Kotler and Keller, 2006

The first step is to identify the target market. This involves producing a customer profile from the information already collected for the marketing plan. This profile influences the objectives, creation of the communications message and the channels and media mix being selected.

Human behaviour is always complex and this needs to be taken into account when making communications decisions. In particular, each customer is likely to be at a different stage of readiness in relation to the buying decision. In order to generate an effective communications campaign, the marketer needs to understand where the customer is in this process and have an objective either for what they require the consumer to do or how they wish them to respond. The AIDA model can be helpful in understanding the potential stages of a purchase decision.

THE AIDA MODEL

AIDA stands for attention (awareness), interest, desire, action (see Figure 9.9). These are steps a consumer must progress through before a purchase or change in behaviour can be made. In conjunction with customer profile details which show where the consumer is in the buying decision process, the AIDA model provides a framework for sequencing objectives.

Attention (Awareness): The consumer may not be aware that a product exists or know about its features or benefits. Therefore communication at this stage requires a focus on creating awareness and knowledge of the product and its availability.

Interest: Awareness of a product is not usually enough to persuade a customer to buy, and companies create interest in their products in different ways. For example, Boots launched its 'protect and perfect' range of skincare, which was featured in a BBC Horizon programme that verified its proven anti-ageing properties. This created a high level of interest to the point where the stores were unable to stock enough of the product to meet demand. This demonstrates taking the customer from the interest to the desire stage, where they try the product.

Desire: This is the stage where customers include the brand within their preferred brand set.

Action: At this stage, the consumer makes a purchase or changes their purchasing behaviour.

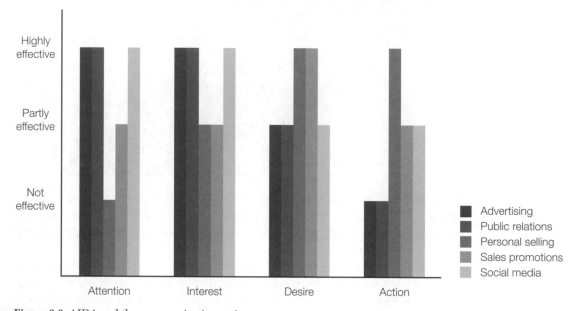

Figure 9.9: AIDA and the communications mix

Communications objectives drive the plan forwards and are written in a clear, concise manner to be SMART (specific, measurable, actionable, realistic and timed). Marketers can use the AIDA model in creating their communications objectives.

There are conflicting views about when the *budget* should be determined – whether before any decisions are made or after the media have been selected. There are a number of methods for establishing the budget. In general, the favoured method is 'objective and task' which requires the marketer to outline clearly the communications actions required, to price them accordingly and make adjustments if too excessive. It should be noted, however, that when times are tough during a **recessionary** period, communications budgets are among the first to be reduced.

Encouraging *creative approaches* to message design is critical to campaign success in competitive markets, where many organizations are competing for consumers' attention, such as in fast-moving consumer goods. It is important to cut through

Think and discuss

In a group of 3–4, choose a company affected by a scandal such as meat contamination (Tesco, McDonald's, Findus). Suggest how the company could use marketing communications to turn around consumers' wavering values about ready-meal meat products.

the noise created by other campaigns and be seen to be innovative in motivating consumers to progress from awareness through to action (on the AIDA model). Key decisions in this area require organizations to agree the message, design the visuals and accompanying words (whether they are spoken or written) and match these to the media selected. Crucial decisions are about:

- The 'big idea': For example, L'Oréal's big idea, sometimes known as a strapline or platform, is 'Because you're worth it'
- The advertising appeal: This can be rational or emotional, appealing to the head (cognitive) or the heart (affective/feeling)
- The execution style: How the appeal is conveyed to the target audience – for example, using humour, slice of life, straight sell, animation, comparison, demonstration, testimonial, imagery, dramatization or any combination of these styles

The selection of channels (media) will be influenced by the campaign objectives, target audience and budget. This stage will involve selecting one or more media from those given in the section on the marketing communications mix, above. The internet has grown in importance as a medium over the last few years. The World Advertising Research Centre (WARC) forecasts that, in the UK, advertising on the internet will take a 35 per cent share of total advertising expenditure by the end of 2013 (WARC, 2012). However, traditional media such as TV are still used extensively for mass market products in the UK.

Within each media channel the marketer may be faced with a choice of media vehicles. For example, within TV as a channel there are multiple stations that could carry the company's message. This is also the case with radio and even more so with magazines. The choice is based on target audience characteristics and budget.

Completing the integrated marketing communications campaign is not the end point. Once the plan has been agreed, *tasks and responsibilities* must be allocated. The success of the campaign requires *monitoring and evaluation*, with adjustments made as necessary to ensure that the plan objectives are met and that changes in the general business environment are responded to. The monitoring and evaluation stages may necessitate a return to the start of the process and a revision of the plan. This should be a constant cycle of activity.

Throughout the planning process, it is important to remember that the other elements of the marketing mix also communicate – such as pricing level, product attributes and packaging, distribution strategy and service providers. The plan must therefore integrate all elements if it is to be successful and provide a competitive edge.

9

CONCLUSION

The primary role of marketing communications is to establish the organization's brand position to facilitate differentiation in target markets. A secondary role is to provide the voice of the company in terms of establishing its credentials to consumers and other stakeholders. An understanding of the communications process helps marketers to deal with the challenges in developing successful communications strategy. It is important that communications are carefully planned, coordinated and integrated to present a consistent message to all stakeholders. This means all factors influencing communications decisions should be considered in the planning process such as characteristics of the target market, nature of the product, business resources and others. This forms part of a marketing communications strategy situation analysis, which is generally followed by the development of objectives, in other words what the company wants its communications to achieve within a specific target market. Strategy comprises creative and media approaches utilizing specific media tools to best effect from a range of tools such as sales promotion, advertising, public relations and digital marketing. The final steps in any communications strategy are to monitor, evaluate and revise as required on the basis of response to the campaign.

Case study
The Katharine House Hospice

KATHARINE HOUSE HOSPICE (KHH) IS LOCATED in the grounds of Stafford Hospital. It caters for 10 inpatients and 15 daycare patients, and costs around £2.6 million a year to maintain. The hospice serves the mid-Staffordshire region, which has a population of approximately 150,000. (See www.khhospice.org.uk.)

KHH is financed by funding from the government, trusts, corporations, shops, a lottery and individual donations. Because of the economic situation, generating funds from these sources has been extremely challenging.

Fundraising activity is a fundamental element of hospice management. KHH income streams come from:

- **Ticketed events**
  Annual Ball, Vegas Evening, Ladies' Luncheon, Festive Fun, Grown Up Skool Disco, Mixed Golf Day, Ladies' Golf Day, Dining Events
- **Sponsored events**
  10 k Run, Endurance Challenge, Skydive, Cycling Challenge, Winter Walk, London Marathon, Midnight Walk

- **Annual appeals**
  Light up a Life, Big Cuppa, Sponsor a Nurse, Circle of Friends
- **Community fundraising**
  Collecting boxes, store collections, home boxes, community asks, schools fundraising, support groups, Open Gardens
- **Corporate fundraising**
  Sponsorship, payroll giving, Charity of the Year, cartridge recycling, Dress Down Day
- **Plus**
  Gifts in wills, In Memoriam giving, Gift Aid, Trust Fundraising, regular giving, Make a Will month

Over the last 11 years, gross fundraised income has increased from £200,000 to £1 million per year, attributed to the hard work put into developing this much wider range of fundraising activities. Fundraising for 2012/13 is anticipated to be £675,000 net.

Fundraising is perceived by the hospice as a long-term relationship development activity rather than as the genration of one-off contributions. Every donor is thanked for their contribution as quickly as possible, with different types of personalized 'thank you' letters.

One of the most significant funding increases was seen in the 'Light up a Life' Christmas campaign where supporters pay to have a light on the Christmas tree lit in memory of a loved one. Donations have risen from £1,000 to £30,000 and 70 per cent of these donations are repeat gifts. The average donation tends to vary between £16 and £18, and in 2012 there were nearly 1,700 donors to this scheme. It is felt that this fundraiser is in the maturity stage of the product lifecycle and requires product innovation and/or a widening of the target market. Current communications activity includes direct mailings to existing supporters (no paid-for adverts), banners (of the vinyl type) outside shops and the hospice, and flyers in local shops.

New fundraising activities are in process, two of these being a Film Premiere evening at the Stafford Apollo cinema, and a Summer Tea Party. The Film Premiere will be for a new (blockbuster) film scheduled for release next year. It will be a 'black tie' event, with champagne and canapés, and a red carpet entrance for all guests. Tickets will be £35 each. The hospice hopes to secure the use of the theatre (and staff) free of charge.

There are around 25,000 names on the donor database, including lottery participants. Mailings to different segments of this list for different initiatives can see response rates ranging from 5 per cent to 85 per cent. A cold mailing exercise was ineffective as a funding driver, yielding an extremely poor response rate (less than the 1–2 per cent industry norm).

The majority of hospice (and charity) supporters tend to be women over the age of 50 years. With the introduction of a variety of initiatives, the hospice has seen its audience diversify. The hospice has more than 2,850 followers on Facebook, its page being maintained with little input from the hospice fundraisers. There is no proactive advertising or public relations activity via the internet and this is an area where much development is required.

Question

Your task is to create an advertising or public relations plan for the hospice for either the Light up a Life annual Christmas campaign or the Film Premiere evening.

General objectives:

- To grow the database
- To increase the number of supporters in younger age groups (without alienating the existing core supporters/donors)
- To raise awareness of the hospice amongst the mid-Staffordshire population
- To grow the number of Facebook followers by 15%

Specific objectives:

- Film Premiere evening: To sell 200 tickets, 50 of which will be to new donors
- Light up a Life: To grow income by recruiting 200 new donors to the scheme

Sources

The sites below may be of some use to you when you are researching for background information on the target market and scenario:

www.institute-of-fundraising.org.uk – A one-stop shop for fundraising info

www.institute-of-fundraising.org.uk/Codes_and_regulation/Codes/codes-directory – The codes that fundraisers try to operate within, mainly fundraising- rather than marketing-specific

www.helpthehospices.org.uk/welcome – General information about hospices

www.fundraising.co.uk – Fundraising news and info

www.sofii.org – Examples and case studies of fund-raising in action

9

Review questions

1 How might an organization use its marketing communications strategies to strengthen its value positioning in the market?

2 The principal role of marketing communications is to help organizations build relationships with their customers. Do you agree with this statement? Use examples to illustrate your answer.

3 How can marketing communications be used to support and develop branding strategy?

4 Direct marketing allows for interaction between the organization and its customers. Explain the role of digital marketing in direct marketing. Does digital marketing reduce the overall marketing budget by reducing reliance on traditional distribution channels? Give examples to support your answer.

5 Assume the role of a marketing manager in a small business-to-business company. Which communications elements (tools) would you propose to assist the company in its market growth objective? Find examples of businesses that have used these communications elements.

6 Go to www.thinkbox.tv and select an advert from the 'Thinkboxes Winners' icon link. Using this advert, explain what makes a good ad. Can you suggest any other 'good' ads? What makes them 'good'?

7 Offering a positive brand experience is becoming an expected part of the brand package. Which brands offer you a good/positive experience? How was this created? Compare your answers with a friend's. Do your answers differ? Why?

Group tasks

1 Design an advertisement for a product of your choice. Specify your 'big idea' and whether your advertisement has an emotional or rational appeal. What objectives would your advert meet? (Hint: use the AIDA model to frame your response.)

2 Chocolate Heaven is a new high-end chocolate supplier that produces high-quality, high-value chocolate products designed for affluent consumers or as special occasion gifts. Advise the company on its options when developing a marketing communications campaign. Then develop a campaign based on one of your options, making sure that you consider all stages in the marketing communications planning process. Be prepared to present this, justifying the choices you have made.

3 Using the Katharine House Hospice case study, plan an event for the Summer Tea Party. Assume it will be held in the grounds of the hospice. (Note for tutor: this can be further developed into an integrated communications plan by asking students to coordinate plans for other marketing communications activities alongside the event.)

Glossary/Key terms

Advertising: A paid-for form of communication, usually by the advert sponsor, delivering impersonal messages.

Advertising appeal: How a message is crafted to appeal to either the heart (emotional) or the mind (rational).

AIDA: A communications model, used to help design communications objectives. It stands for attention (awareness), interest, desire, action.

Ambient advertising: Unusual or unexpected hosts for adverts, such as petrol pump nozzles.

B2B: Business-to-business, or organizational marketing.

Communications process: The way in which the consumer receives and acts on messages from the brand sponsor or owner, delivered via one or more media. It is illustrated by use of a model/diagram.

Digital communications: The use of the internet to facilitate communication with target audiences, using email, the web and social media (e.g. Facebook, Twitter, Google+).

Direct mail: A form of direct marketing that makes personal approaches to customers. It involves sending letters or emails direct to the customer's home or business.

Direct marketing: A two-way form of communication between an organization and its customers. When managed effectively, it can add value and lead to a valuable relationship with the customer.

Events and experiences: Staging an event or creating a customer experience is becoming an increasingly valuable means by which organizations can enable customers to engage with the brand.

Execution style: How the appeal is conveyed to the target audience.

Integrated marketing communications: Facilitated by creating a plan to merge the various ways of communicating with the target audience to form a cohesive and synergistic series of messages.

Marketing communications mix: The range of communications approaches a marketing manager can select from to deliver the brand message in the most appropriate and cost-effective manner to the target audience. Also known as communication tools, or the promotions mix. Includes advertising, public relations, sales promotion, sponsorship, personal selling, digital communications, direct marketing, events and experiences.

Marketing communications strategy: Involves formulation of a plan based on well researched data to ensure that the right message is delivered to the right people at the right time.

Mass media communication: Use of media channels that enable the message to be delivered to a large number of consumers, e.g. TV, newspapers, magazines, posters.

Media: The channels through which marketers relay messages to target audiences.

Message: What the sponsor wishes to communicate to the target audience based on the positioning strategy.

Personal selling: Face-to-face communication between sellers and buyers, most often used in business-to-business selling situations, but also in retail.

Platform: The big idea that an advertising campaign is based on and revolves around. It can become the brand's strapline.

Promotion: The mix element instrumental in establishing product positioning in the eyes of the consumer to establish competitive advantage. Also known as **marketing communication**.

Public relations: A strategic approach to managing various methods for communicating with an organization's stakeholders.

Pull strategy: Communicating directly with the end-user of the product to encourage them to visit a store and ask for the product, i.e. make a purchase.

Push strategy: Promoting products between levels in the distribution chain to encourage channel intermediaries to stock the product.

Sales promotion: An enticement to consumers or trade buyers to purchase products or services.

SoLoMo: A combination of social, local/location and mobile technologies that uses GPS data and online behavioural information to target consumers with specific adverts.

Sponsorship: Paying for the right to be associated with an organization or event.

Stakeholders: The various groups the public relations department should be aware of which have an interest in the organization and therefore may require communicating with in some way.

Target audience: The section/group of consumers within the target market selected to receive a message from the brand owner or sponsor.

9

Vocab check list for ESL students

Augmented	Experiential	Recessionary
Clarification	Formidable	Simultaneously
Coherent	Overt	

Definitions for these terms can be found in the 'Vocab Zone' of the companion website, which provides free access to the Macmillan English Dictionary online at www.palgrave.com/business/Gbadamosi

Further reading

The following texts focus more specifically on aspects of marketing communications and provide a useful extension to the chapter. For interest, specialist events and tourism communications texts are also included.

W. F. Arens, D. H. Schaefer and M. F. Weigold (2011) *Advertising*. McGraw-Hill International

G. A. Belch and M. A. Belch (2011) *Advertising and Promotion*. McGraw-Hill International

G. Masterman and E. Wood (2005) *Innovative Marketing Communications: Strategies for the Events Industry*. Elsevier

S. McCabe and C. Lashley (2007) *Marketing Communications in Tourism and Hospitality*. Elsevier

T. Morris and S. Goldsworthy (2012) *PR Today*. Palgrave Macmillan

T. A. Shimp (2010) *Integrated Marketing Communications*. Cengage Learning

R. Tench and E. Yeomans (2009) *Exploring Public Relations*. FT Prentice Hall

A. Yeshin (2012) *Integrated Marketing Communications*. Butterworth Heinemann

References

BDS Sponsorship (2013) www.sponsorship.co.uk (accessed 7 January 2013)

Brand Meets Brand (2012) www.brandmeetsbrand.com (accessed 24 February 2013)

Brassington, F. and Pettitt, S. (2006) *Principles of Marketing* (4th edn). Harlow: Financial Times Prentice Hall

Bull, R. (2012) 'The Rise of Brand Houses', *Marketing*, 24 October 2012

Derrick S. (2012) 'Right Here, Right Now', *Marketing*, 31 October 2012

Dibb, S., Simkin, L., Pride, W. M. and Ferrell, O. C. (2012) *Marketing Concepts and Strategies* (6th edn). Andover: Cengage Learning

Jobber, D. and Fahy, J. (2012) *Foundations of Marketing* (4th edn). New York, NY: McGraw-Hill

Kotler, P. and Keller, K. (2006) *Marketing Management* (12th edn). Upper Saddle River, NJ: Pearson Prentice Hall

McDaniel, C., Lamb, C. W. and Hair, J. F. (2013) *Introduction to Marketing* (International 12th edn). Independence, KY: Cengage Learning

Rowley, E. and Clancy, R. (2012) 'Red Bull's Space Jump Stunt with Felix Baumgartner "Worth £100m" in Ad Spend', *Daily Telegraph*, 19 October 2012

Semenik, R. J., Allen, C. T., O'Guinn, T. C. and Kaufmann, H. R. (2012) *Advertising and Promotions: An Integrated Brand Approach* (6th edn). Andover: South-western Cengage Learning

10 SERVICES MARKETING

HSIAO–PEI (SOPHIE) YANG & SANJIT KUMAR ROY

COVENTRY UNIVERSITY

CHAPTER CONTENTS

LEARNING OUTCOMES

The content of this chapter will help you to:

- Understand what is meant by the term services
- Distinguish characteristics of services
- Explain what is meant by services marketing
- Define what is meant by service quality
- Explain the SERVQUAL model
- Understand customer-perceived service value
- Explain relationship marketing in services
- Understand the service delivery process

Marketing in action
Zappos.com: Competing through customer service

ZAPPOS.COM GROSSED $1 BILLION IN SALES IN 2009. From the time of its inception in 1999, the stupendous success of this online retailer has had its roots in the excellent customer service which the company provides. One of the ten core values of Zappos is to create a 'wow' experience for customers through service. The company's transparent, open and honest culture is geared towards creating employee happiness, which in turn aids in the creation of customer happiness.

In order to offer best customer service, Zappos controls the entire value chain from value creation (for example, placing an order) to value delivery (for example, order fulfilment). The company is known for its work environment and unique approach to for customers by reducing the time between order placement and order delivery. Zappos customers are encouraged to speak to company executives. According to Tony Hsieh, 'At Zappos, we want people to call us. We believe that forming personal, emotional connections with our customers is the best way to provide great service.' The company also makes heavy use of the social media platform to bond with its customers.

The company always takes an extra step to make its customers happy, such as through surprise upgrades to faster shipping or sending gifts to customers on their birthdays and other important occasions. The company strongly believes that if its customers are happy they will create a positive

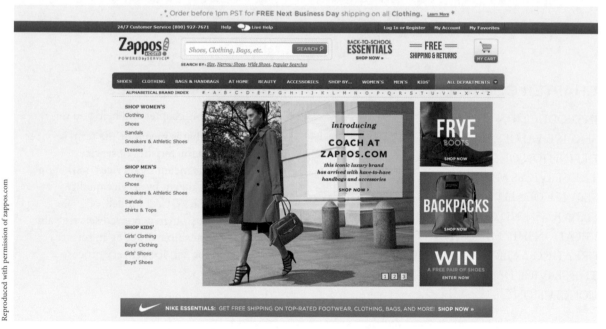

customer service. Zappos aims to develop long-term relationships with its customers by providing a unique, attractive and memorable shopping experience for a wide assortment of shoes, clothing and household products. The company offers free shipping, a free 365-day returns policy, 24/7 availability, and high-quality customer service. The fast shipping offered by Zappos helps to create instant gratification reputation for Zappos by word of mouth amongst their peers and friends. According to Alfred Lin, CFO/COO of Zappos, 'The customer is more powerful than paid advertising.' With over 75 per cent of purchases made by repeat customers, it is evident that Zappos' mission to 'provide the best customer service possible' is working well for the company.

INTRODUCTION

Services have become the heart of value creation for customers all over the world. We live in a service economy (Lovelock and Wirtz, 2011, p. 27). Forty-one European companies were ranked in the world's top 100 companies in 2011 (Fortune, 2011). Out of these, 25 were service companies (such as banking services, financial services and telecommunication services). The contribution of services to EU gross domestic product (GDP) is about 73 per cent and to UK gross domestic product it is about 76 per cent (CIA, 2011). The contribution of services to world GDP is also increasing steadily and even in the emerging economies it constitutes a significant percentage. Thus, with the dominance of services in our economies, there is a need to understand and evaluate how services can be managed to achieve competitive advantage.

SERVICE VALUE

Customer-perceived value is widely recognized as an important determinant in developing marketing strategy and in the study of consumer behaviour. According to Sánchez et al. (2006), despite its importance, no universal conceptualization of customer value exists. Value is considered as an important constituent of relationship marketing and the ability of a company to provide superior value to its customers is regarded as one of the most successful strategies of the 1990s. This ability has become a means of differentiation and a key to the conundrum of how to achieve a position of sustainable competitive advantage.

Service value has become a critical concept in the field of services marketing. There is a great deal of debate on the conceptualization and measurement of service value. Bolton and Drew (1991) define service value as a mere trade-off between consumers' evaluation of the benefits and cost involved in using the service. According to Holbrook (1994), the factors that lead to customers' evaluation of service value are efficiency of service, service quality, social value, playful environment, aesthetics and altruistic value. Efficiency includes consumers' monetary cost, time and effort related to the service experience and is measured by comparing what the consumer receives in an exchange relationship with what he/she gives for the purchase. Quality or excellence involves a reactive appreciation of an object's or experience's potential ability to accomplish some goal or perform some function. Social value captures the dimensions of status (success, impression management) and esteem (reputation, materialism, possessions). Play involves the feeling of having fun and thereby characterizes the intrinsically motivated side of the familiar distinction between work and leisure. Aesthetics or beauty is a concept difficult to define and operationalize, but it brings the feeling of pleasure and personal enrichment to the consumer. And, finally, altruistic value refers to the notion of ethics and spirituality in consumer behaviour.

For example, in the context of a hospital, the service value scale consists of functional values of installation, quality, price and professionalism, and emotional values of novelty, control, hedonics and social value. In the case of the tourism industry, service value consists of six underlying factors, which are: functional value of the travel agency (the tangible facilities); functional value of the travel agency's contact personnel (professionalism); functional value of the tourism package purchased

Think and discuss

Identify and compare the different service value components for banking and restaurant services.

10

(quality); functional value of the price; emotional value; and social value. The job of the service provider is to manage the factors that lead to service value, because service value managed properly has the capability to impact customer satisfaction and customer loyalty positively. In the next section we define services and explain their characteristics.

DEFINITION OF SERVICES

Unlike goods, services are actions, processes and performances that offer benefits to consumers. Pure services are intangible, cannot be inventoried and are consumed at the point of sale. Examples of commonly purchased services include banking, education, insurance and medical treatment.

Services can either be provided to consumers in their own right (such as entertainment or passenger transport) or be a significant part of a tangible good (such as car insurance or a finance package that adds value to car offers). In real life, companies often utilize services to create values and differentiate tangible product offers from the competition. For example, car manufacturers provide various after-sales services to attract consumers.

Figure 10.1 shows that pure services have low physical content and a high element of service (those shown at the bottom of the figure), while pure goods have high physical content and a low element of service (those shown at the top of the figure). For example, medical treatments, education and travel agencies provide a high level of services with low physical content. On the other hand, pure goods such as fast-moving consumer goods (FMCG), electronic goods and cars could still require after-sales services. Yet, the level of service needed for pure goods is much lower. Following the service itself (after an operation or after completing a course), a consumer might simply receive a letter from a doctor or a certificate from a training institution (the physical content). However, the benefits the consumer receives are mainly intangible and are hard to evaluate before purchasing the service. On the other hand, FMCG, electronic goods and cars have a high physical content and low element of services, so consumers can evaluate the tangible goods with all five senses before purchase. Having defined services, we will discuss their distinguishing characteristics next.

Think and discuss

Based on Figure 10.1, come up with more examples of services that have either a high physical content or a high service element.

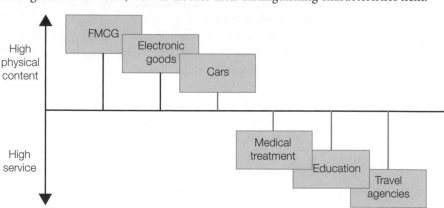

Figure 10.1: The product/service spectrum

Example 10.1:
Ocean Green: Value creation in a small/ medium-size service firm

Offering services as a core business is becoming increasingly popular all over the world. The challenges associated with doing this are enormous because such transactions revolve around intangible offerings. While this is the case for big organizations such as British Telecom (BT) and HSBC, the number of small businesses in the service sector is also on the increase. However, it is noteworthy that irrespective of their size and the length of their existence, what is common to successful service-oriented firms is their focus on value creation.

An example of a small service-oriented firm is Ocean Green, a UK-based firm that engages in diverse service businesses including international freight forwarding and logistics, sale of travel tickets, and international money transfers. The owner-manager, Kola Lambo, emphasizes the focus of this enterprise: 'Our businesses are designed principally to help other businesses achieve efficiency in their administrative tasks, thereby cutting down on wasted hours whilst simultaneously increasing productivity.' Even though the marketing environment is increasingly volatile and competitive, Ocean Green is able to survive the turbulence because the firm offers excellent service delivery, which gives its customers the value they desire in their transactions.

CHARACTERISTICS OF SERVICES

Services differ from goods/products because of the unique characteristics they possess. These characteristics call for managing services differently from goods/products. The characteristics are termed intangibility, inseparability, perishability and heterogeneity and are explained with more examples below.

Intangibility

Intangibility is considered to be the main distinction between goods and services. Services are considered to be intangible because they are performed rather than being objects, and there is a lack of ownership. Services cannot be seen or touched like physical goods and are experiential. For example, restaurant services are composed of steps of action (such as order taking, serving food and bill payment) performed by the service providers and directed towards the customers visiting the restaurant.

Inseparability

Inseparability means that the production and consumption of services happens simultaneously, whereas in the case of products or goods the production and consumption are two separate activities. Usually, products are first produced and then consumed, but services are sold first and then produced and consumed simultaneously. For example, restaurant services cannot be provided unless they are sold and the dining experience that customers receive is produced and consumed at the same time.

Perishability

Perishability refers to the fact that services cannot be inventoried, saved and returned. Services can only be provided if there is a demand and the formidable

10

challenge for service providers is to balance the supply and demand. For example, in the case of hotel bookings, if some hotel rooms remain unoccupied on a particular date, they cannot be stored and sold at a later date. Similarly, unsold airline seats for a given flight and date cannot be inventoried and added on to a plane during the peak holiday season, when seats are in short supply.

istock © mikdam

Heterogeneity

Heterogeneity is another important differentiator between goods and services. It refers to the fact that service performance varies from one service encounter or transaction to the next one. Heterogeneity also occurs because no two customers are the same in evaluating the same service provided at the same time. For example, an income tax consultant may provide a different service experience to different customers on the same day of service delivery. This depends upon individual requirements and personalities.

Having discussed the characteristics of services, we will present what is meant by services marketing.

DEFINING SERVICES MARKETING

Services dominate developed economies. About 70 per cent of GDP is accounted for by service sectors in developed countries such as the USA, UK and Australia (Bureau of Economic Analysis, 2006). The marketing of services focuses on the marketing of activities and processes rather than objects. Therefore, the marketing mix is usually an extension of the traditional '4 Ps' framework in that three additional Ps (*physical evidence*, *people* and *process*) are added to *product*, *price*, *place* and *promotion*.

THE SERVICES MIX

For a hotel service, the four traditional Ps include:

- **Product mix** refers to the decisions a firm makes about the products, services and benefits it should offer to a group of customers. The decisions on service features, quality level and branding of a hotel should be decided first for meeting customers' needs
- **Price mix** is the value of a product or service determined by a firm. For a hotel, the overall costs include expenditure on service design (product), advertising and salespeople (promotion) and distribution channels (place), which should be evaluated as a part of the price mix
- **Place mix** involves decisions on distribution channels and their management, the location of outlets, methods of transportation and inventory levels for any physical goods. For a hotel service, a firm decides the channel type, use of intermediaries, hotel locations and the management of different channels to avoid conflicts
- **Promotion mix** refers to decisions on advertising, personal selling, sales promotions, public relations, direct marketing and online promotion. For a hotel, it is important to decide the promotion blend between the different types of promotional tools mentioned above. Key advertising decisions also include the most appropriate media types and types of ads utilized to target potential audiences

The three additional Ps for services:

- **Physical evidence mix** is the environment in which the service is delivered and where the firm and customer interact. In other words, any tangible components that facilitate performance or communication of the service are included. For a hotel, the facility design, equipment, signage, employee dress and other tangibles, such as reports and business cards, are a part of the physical evidence mix
- **People mix** refers to all human actors who play a part in service delivery and thus influence consumers' perceptions. Therefore, the firm's personnel, the customer and other customers in the service environment are included. For a hotel, decisions on the people mix include recruitment, training, motivation and rewards of employees. When customer self-service is a part of the services, education and training of customers is also crucial for firms
- **Process mix** refers to service delivery and operating systems, which are the actual procedures, mechanisms and flow of activities by which the service is delivered. For a hotel, decisions on process mix include the flow of activities, number of steps/stages and level of customer involvement.

Table 10.1 presents the services marketing mix and the next section examines the concept of service quality.

Think and discuss

Select any two services that you have experienced at least twice in the past. Discuss the associated marketing mix elements as specifically related to these services when you first experienced them.

10

Table 10.1: Expanded marketing mix for services

Product	Place	Promotion	Price
Physical goods features	Channel type	Promotion blend	Flexibility
Quality level	Exposure	Salespeople	Price level
Accessories	Intermediaries	Selection	Terms
Packaging	Outlet locations	Training	Differentiation
Warranties	Transportation	Incentives	Discounts
Product lines	Storage	Advertising	Allowances
Branding	Managing channels	Media types	
		Types of ads	
		Sales promotion	
		Publicity	
		Internet/web strategy	

People	Physical evidence	Process	
Employees	Facility design	Flow of activities	
Recruitment	Equipment	Standardized	
Training	Signage	Customized	
Motivation	Employee dress	Number of steps	
Rewards	Other tangibles	Simple	
Teamwork	Reports	Complex	
Customers	Business cards	Customer involvement	
Education	Statements		
Training	Guarantees		

Source: Adapted from Wilson et al., 2008, p. 20

SERVICE QUALITY

The concept of service quality has received a great deal of attention from both academics and practitioners. Historically, most practitioners have associated the term with manufactured goods and products. However, from the beginning of the 1980s, the term quality was broadened to cover services as well as goods and products. It is more difficult to define quality for services than for products because services are intangible and variable. Consumers most often lack the information they need to evaluate service quality. For example, it is relatively easy to evaluate the quality of cars and other major appliances before making a purchase, whereas for services such as financial services, healthcare and educational services, it is very difficult. This makes service quality a critical element of the customer perception.

DEFINING SERVICE QUALITY

Service quality is defined as the overall assessment of a service by its customers. Parasuraman et al. (1988, p. l6) define perceived service quality as 'global judgment, or attitude, relating to the superiority of the service'. Service quality is conceptualized as perceptions resulting from the comparison of customer expectations and actual service performance. Perceptions of service quality are not solely the outcomes of service, but also involve the evaluation of the service delivery process by the customers. Lehtinen and Lehtinen (1982) conceptualized service quality as

Think and discuss

Select any two services that you have experienced at least twice in the past. Discuss how the provider could improve any elements that have not improved (or that have got worse) since your first experience.

Example 10.2:
DIY Doctor: The marketing mix of a small/medium-size service firm

The systematic interconnection of the marketing mix elements, also known as the 7Ps, is very important in service-oriented transactions. Firms must look into how their service offerings are priced and promoted, and look at the activities of marketing intermediaries that mediate between them and the target market where applicable. Moreover, it is imperative for them to look at the processes involved in their offerings to be sure that customers are delighted by the speed involved in serving them. Since services are essentially intangible, marketers are also expected to consider the physical evidence element, which could be in the form of furniture, colour, uniform or many other factors. The people element is also crucial in the marketing mix. If firms aim to delight employees, the task of making customers happy will be easier.

All of these form the focus of DIY Doctor, a service-oriented firm in the UK which offers free DIY advice on the web. After running a building company for 25 years, Mike Edwards, the MD, became aware of the number of jobs the company was being called to where the home owner had tried some DIY that had gone horribly wrong. Then in the year 2000, he thought 'What if we were to build a small website offering to answer people's DIY "how to" queries free of charge? Then, when they ask us a question about proposed work which is clearly in contravention of the Building Regulations, we could tell them that legally they should not be attempting the job and offer to quote to do it for them.'

Reproduced with permission of DIY Doctor Ltd who retain the rights and trademark of the logo

This approach was taken and by 2003 the firm had a database of thousands of questions and answers. So, it took photographs of every job it did and added them to the website content written by the tradesmen, giving instructional 'how to' answers to all of these questions. These were then published as 'project' pages on the website. As the number of users of these web pages increased, selling advertising space on the pages became very easy. In 2006, DIY Doctor was turned into a limited company and the building company was sold so that the free advice service on the website became the only means of revenue. The firm later introduced the use of social media. These efforts proved successful and by November 2010 the number of unique users on the website was over 400,000. Essentially, the firm's success is linked to its commitment to having a perfect mix of its product, price, place, promotion, people, physical evidence and processes.

10

a three-dimensional construct that is physical, interactive and corporate. Physical quality is the quality dimension that originates from the physical elements of service, such as the physical product and physical support. Interactive quality indicates the interaction between the customer and the service organization and corporate quality is symbolic in nature and indicates customers' perceptions of the image of the organization. Garvin (1988) provided a comprehensive definition of service quality comprising all the attributes of performance, features, conformance, reliability, durability, aesthetics, serviceability and customers' perceived quality. Simply put, service quality is defined by Asubonteng et al. (1996, p. 64) as 'the difference between the customers' expectations of service performance prior to the service encounter and their perceptions of the service received.' Companies' ability to create and sustain competitive advantage depends upon the high level of service quality given by the service provider. Perceived service quality is the extent to which a firm serves the needs of its customers successfully.

SERVQUAL AND GAP ANALYSIS

After an extensive research programme, Parasuraman et al. (1988) came up with an instrument to measure service quality and termed it SERVQUAL. This is the most frequently used, yet also a highly debated, measurement instrument for service quality. According to this study, the five dimensions of service quality from the customer's perspective are reliability, assurance, tangibility, empathy and responsiveness, and the acronym RATER can be used to denote them:

- **Reliability** refers to the ability of the service provider to deliver its services dependably and consistently
- **Assurance** refers to the competence of the firm, the courtesy of the employees and the ability to create trust and confidence in customers' minds
- **Tangibility** considers the service provider's physical facilities, employee appearance and equipment
- **Empathy** refers to the willingness of the service provider to help customers and provide prompt customer service
- **Responsiveness** reflects the willingness of employees to help and provide service in a timely fashion

Research on service quality has shown that reliability is the most critical dimension, followed by responsiveness, with empathy being the least important (Parasuraman et al., 1988). As defined earlier, service quality is the difference between what customers expect and what they receive. Customer perceptions are influenced by a series of 'gaps', defined as follows:

Example 10.3:
Managing service quality at NatWest

Driven by the enduring problems associated with managing service quality, especially when consumer views are not easy to establish, NatWest, one of the popular banks in the British banking sector, encourages its customers to give the organization ideas on how the firm can create and deliver value effectively. A visit to the bank's website will reveal how the huge number and diverse types of ideas that customers have sent in are used. This customer-oriented approach has proved successful and positioned the bank strategically in the marketplace.

Basically, NatWest has its products in various categories specifically tailored to meet the needs of different customer groups. Whether in personal banking, private banking, business banking or commercial banking, NatWest is committed to hearing from customers and addressing their needs efficiently and effectively in order to maximize customer lifetime value. The firm acknowledges the variability in the nature of service offerings. It recognizes that the quality of services provided depends on those providing them, how they are provided, where they are provided, and when. So, it addresses these issues through its recruitment policy and training and development programmes for employees. In the bid to extend customer value, the primary focus has been to create and deliver customer value consistently both in normal weekday and Saturdays (SatWest) transactions.

- **Gap 1 (the service gap):** This is the most important gap between customers' expectations of the service and their perception about the service delivered. The job of the service provider is to reduce this gap as much as possible
- **Gap 2 (the knowledge gap):** This is the difference between customers' expectations of a service and management's perceptions of those expectations
- **Gap 3 (the standards gap):** This is the difference between management's perception of customers' expectations and the quality specifications required for proper service delivery
- **Gap 4 (the delivery gap):** This is the difference between the quality standards set out by management for service delivery and the actual quality of service delivery
- **Gap 5 (the communications gap):** This is the difference between the actual quality of the services delivered and the quality specifications as mentioned in the firm's external communications.

The importance of these gaps lies in allowing the management to make analytical assessments of the reasons behind poor service quality. Service providers that aim to deliver excellent customer service need to focus on reducing all these gaps. Relationship marketing of services is presented next.

RELATIONSHIP MARKETING OF SERVICES

Drucker (1954) states that 'There is only one valid purpose of a business ... that is to create and keep a customer.' This statement highlights the importance of customer acquisition and retention for firms, especially for service firms. The complex nature of buyer–seller interactions in today's business environment is heavily dependent on relationship creation and nurturing. Relationships add to the service benefits of a product. In this context, relationship marketing is defined as 'the identification, specification, initiation, maintenance and (where appropriate) dissolution of long-term relationships with key customers and other parties, through mutual exchange, fulfilment of promises and adherence to relationship norms, in order to satisfy the objectives and enhance the experience of the parties concerned' (O'Malley et al., 1997, p. 542). Relationships between companies and customers are like marriages. The success of the marriage depends on the mutual understanding of the other party's need in the relationship. The goal is to create value for individuals in the relationship in the long run. In this context, Levitt (1983) states that 'the sale merely consummates the courtship. Then the marriage begins. How good the marriage is depends on how well the relationship is managed by the seller.' This sums up the essence of relationship marketing in the case of services.

According to Berry (1995), relationship marketing is most applicable to services if the following three conditions are fulfilled:

- There is an ongoing need for the service from the service customers. For example, mobile telecommunications service, internet service and transportation services
- Service customers have control over the selection of service providers. For example, choosing a dentist or a mobile telecom service provider
- A number of service providers exist in the market, the cost of switching from one to another is low and switching is commonplace. For example, for restaurant services or airline services

Think and discuss

For which dimensions of service quality have you most often experienced a large gap between your expectations and your perceptions of the service performance? What do you think might be the underlying causes?

Think and discuss

Find out the importance of relationship marketing strategies for retail stores in your locality. You may interview the store personnel.

10

The above three conditions exist in most services, hence the importance of attracting new customers and retaining existing ones is heightened. Service firms can use the various relationship marketing strategies to differentiate their service offerings from those of their competitors. One of the most important elements of the relationship marketing of services is the creation of the service product, which is presented next.

CREATING A SERVICE PRODUCT

A service product has two components which are the core product and the supplementary services.

CORE PRODUCT

The core product is defined as the core set of benefits and solutions delivered to customers. For example, the core product in the case of a hotel is 'a good night's sleep' and for restaurant service it is 'good food served'. According to Lovelock and Wirtz (2011, p. 87), the delivery process around the core product consists of the following four elements:

- **The nature of the service process:** This refers to the people processing the service request. The service delivery process will be discussed further in another section
- **The role of the customer:** This refers to what customers are supposed to do for themselves. For example, what customers need to do in a self-service restaurant
- **The scheduling:** This refers, for example, to the length of time the room will be occupied before another customer comes in
- **The level of service:** This refers to the type and range of services provided. For example, a hotel will make the bed, supply bath towels and clean the room

SUPPLEMENTARY SERVICES

These are the additional services-related activities which add value to the core product of the service offered. For example, in the case of a hotel, the supplementary services consist of room service, meals, parking facilities, phone usage, pay TV, portering and check-in and check-out services. Similarly, for a restaurant, the supplementary services consist of the ambience and cleanliness, the courtesy of the employees, the billing process and hospitality.

Supplementary services are being used by service firms to differentiate their core product from that of their competitors. Service firms create a value proposition by combining the elements of core product, the supplementary services and the service delivery

istock © iofoto

process. A service firm needs to add more and more supplementary services to its core product if it aims to enhance the perceptions of service quality in customers' minds. For example, the Dubai-based airline company, Emirates, offers supplementary services such as goodie bags to pacify highly active children in the aircraft. They also offer other in-flight entertainment such as cartoons and video games to occupy kids so that parents have less stress during the flight. Service firms that compete on lower prices offer fewer supplementary services. For example, Southwest Airlines is a 'no-frills' airline.

For the success of the buyer–seller relationships in the context of services, there are two crucial enablers, which are trust and commitment. Research has found that there is a direct correlation between these two factors and the business performance of service firms (Morgan and Hunt, 1994). Trust is an important factor for the long-term relationship between the service provider and its customers. Trust nurtures confidence in the exchange partner's integrity and reliability. For example, there has to be a high level of trust between financial service providers, such as banks, and their customers, so that the customer feels confident in investing money safely.

Commitment is central to any relationship and is an important enabler for long-term buyer–seller relationships in the case of services. It is defined as a desire by the relationship partners to maintain the relationship. Research has shown that trust in a partner leads to commitment in the relationship partner (Morgan and Hunt, 1994). For example, if a bank is committed to providing excellent and safe banking services to its customers, those customers will have a highly committed and long-term relationship with the bank.

In summary, to create competitive advantage and differentiate the service from the competition, in addition to creating a service product, service providers should use the relationship marketing strategies of creating trust and commitment amongst their customers.

THE SERVICE DELIVERY PROCESS

In order to compete, firms need to focus on superior service quality. This section explains the utilization of blueprinting and servicescapes in the service delivery process and how they help firms to provide superior service quality.

Blueprinting is important in providing superior service quality as it acts as a communication tool for service designers and managers to identify potential problems and develop possible contingency plans (Harvey, 1998). The blueprinting approach is effective in managing the *process* mix. Servicescapes also play a great role, not only acting as a cue for the expected service quality, but also influencing customers' evaluation of other factors that determine perceived service quality (Reimer and Kuehn, 2005). They are useful for managing the *physical evidence* mix.

Due to the high variability of services, services firms utilize a 'design brief' to manage the service delivery process and 'service encounter'. Service encounter refers to the moment of interaction between the customer and the firm, and a well-specified service delivery process increases customer-perceived value and quality. Two commonly used approaches, blueprinting and servicescapes, are discussed next.

10

Briefly, blueprinting is effective in managing the *process* mix, whereas servicescapes are useful for managing the *physical evidence* mix.

BLUEPRINTING

Following Shostack's work (1984), service blueprinting was further developed by Kingman-Brundage et al. (1995) and widely used to identify service encounter points where consumers directly interact with, and are exposed to, visible evidence of the service. Blueprinting allows firms to 'fully and accurately portray any service system in its entirety, so that the system can be understood objectively and dealt with on that basis' (Shostack, 1992, p. 77).

A blueprint provides a visual representation of a service delivery process, presenting a two-dimensional service process. The horizontal axis identifies the chronology of actions conducted by the customer and the service provider. The vertical axis divides different areas of actions. The simplified version of blueprinting covers four key zones:

- Service functions and stages in the process
- Timing and sequencing of the process
- Participants involved, both staff and customers
- Visible front-office activities and invisible back-office activities

Blueprinting involves specifying sequences of activities and correlating the service encounter with activities that take place in the back office. It requires firms to think in detail about who and what is involved in delivering the service at the service design stage. Blueprinting acts as a communications tool between service designers and managers to identify potential problems and develop possible contingency plans (Harvey, 1998). For example, at the phase of pre-service, management can employ a service blueprint to define or refine service concepts, allocate resources and co-ordinate service functions (Kingman-Brundage et al., 1995). Blueprinting can also act as a training tool for a firm to inform all service providers about the 'who, what, how and when' of the service delivery, providing a holistic picture of the service delivery process.

SERVICESCAPES

Servicescapes, a term coined by Bitner (1992), is the second approach that is useful for managing the service delivery process. Because of the intangibility and inseparability of services, customers' service evaluations are affected by the tangibles in the physical or 'built' environment. Servicescapes are defined as 'the environment in which the service is assembled and in which seller and customer interact, combined with tangible commodities that facilitate performance or communication of the service' (Booms and Bitner, 1981, p. 56).

In general, there are two facets to servicescapes – the facility exterior and facility interior. Take hotel service as an example. The facility exterior includes the exterior design of the hotel building, exterior signage, parking, landscaping, the surrounding environment where the hotel is located. On the other hand, the facility interior includes the interior design of the hotel, its equipment, interior signage, layout, air quality, temperature, sound, music, scent and lighting. Firms should consider the importance of servicescapes in the service delivery process and their impact on customer-perceived value in order to design and manage service delivery and build a service brand. Figure 10.2 provides an example of the servicescapes of a restaurant.

istock © RenéMansi

Figure 10.2: Part of the servicescapes of a restaurant

Servicescapes have four key roles (Bitner, 1992):

- Package of a service: Servicescapes convey customer expectations and influence customer perceptions of service quality. Therefore, similar to the package of goods, servicescapes are equivalent to the package of a service
- Facilitator of a service: Servicescapes facilitate the flow of the service delivery process by providing information to show customers how to act. For example, the floorplan and signage of a department store or a museum facilitate the customer purchasing process and customer flow to direct customers how to act
- Socializer of a service: Servicescapes encourage or nurture interactions between customers and employees as well as between customers and fellow customers. For example, a lower height of counter encourages interactions between customers and employees in a bank more than a higher counter does. A round dining table allows customers to talk to each other more easily than a long table
- Differentiator of a service: Servicescapes set a firm apart from competition in the mind of the consumer. They help to segment the market, targeting appropriate customers and positioning the firm by communicating how it is distinct from competitors. For example, the servicescapes of a high-end French restaurant would differentiate it from competitors in both the facility exterior and interior

10

CONCLUSION

This chapter included the key concepts in services marketing. In summary, services are actions, processes and performances that offer intangible benefits to consumers. Because of their intangibility, inseparability, perishability and heterogeneity, they add three Ps (physical evidence, people and process) to the traditional 4 Ps framework of product, price, place and promotion. Service quality is the overall assessment of a service by customers, and the SERVQUAL model offers the management of a firm a basis on which to make an analytical assessment and increase service quality by reducing gaps in five key areas (service, knowledge, standards, delivery and communications). Because of the importance of customer acquisition and retention, relationship marketing is crucial for services. Trust and commitment are the two central enablers that contribute to the success of the buyer–seller relationship in the context of services. Finally, blueprinting and servicescapes are two common approaches that manage service encounters and facilitate the service delivery process.

Case study
Marketing of services: The McDonald's way

McDonald's India entry

MULTINATIONAL COMPANY (MNC) OWNERS OF restaurant chains had struggled consistently to adapt to the needs of India's many markets from their earliest investments in India. Some pulled out of the country after ventures that did not work out or failed miserably. At the time, consolidation of the hugely fragmented Indian retail sector had also slowly begun but would Indians prefer foreign foods such as burgers and fries to local food offerings? When McDonald's India launched in 1996, Indians in Mumbai and Delhi ate out three to five times a month. In the next 12 years, that average frequency doubled and analysts predicted that by 2011 the Indian quick-service restaurant market would be worth 30,000 crore (about US$6.3 billion at October 2008 exchange rates) (Fahad, 2010).

However, in the intervening decade, McDonald's continued to open new outlets in the country, and evolved its marketing strategies through impressive endeavours even though there were minor protests from existing political parties (Lahoti, 2010). After the first Indian McDonald's outlet in Mumbai in 1996, outlets had begun trading in metropolitan and Tier II towns across the country. By September 2008, McDonald's had completed 12 years of operations in India and had a presence in Mumbai, Delhi, Bangalore, Chennai, Hyderabad, Ahmedabad, Baroda, Nasik, Pune, Indore, Surat and other Tier I and Tier II cities (Indian Franchise, 2010). Meanwhile, there had been a significant increase in the Indian eating out habit. 'The past decade has witnessed a marked change in Indian consumption patterns, especially

in terms of food. Households in middle, upper, and high-income categories now have higher disposable income per member and a propensity to spend more,' said Jatia, one of the founders of McDonald's India (Kaimal, 2009).

Services marketing strategies

In the year 2000, McDonald's India came out with its first television campaign. It featured a child who suffers stage fright and is not able to recite a poem. On entering McDonald's, he recites it properly in the store's familiar and easy environment without any reluctance. A similar campaign featured a child and his family moving into a new, unknown place. The child misses his previous surroundings until McDonald's provides something familiar and homely and makes his world a better place to live in. The first TV commercial, 'Stage fright', attempted to establish an emotional connection between the (Indian) family and the brand together with the aim of establishing McDonald's as a familiar place. The storylines of the campaigns were all supported by other creative initiatives. The company promoted a one-minute service guarantee which attempted to reinforce its reputation for quick, friendly and accurate service and it also ran in-store events for mothers and little children. It was found that 'to kids, sitting on the Ronald McDonald bench [and] pumping sauce from the sauce machine became brand rituals' (Chaturvedi, 2008).

K. V. Sridhar is National Creative Director of Leo Burnett, McDonald's American advertising agency in India. (Leo Burnett Worldwide opened in Chicago in 1935 and started its two first major advertising projects for Kellogg's and P&G in 1950.) Of the McDonald's campaign, Sridhar says, 'In the launch phase, the communication focused solely on building brand and product relevance. The brand's scores on relevance to families and kids were very high.' Furthermore, the introduction of the toys and other little gimmicks that came along with the meals appealed to the children and they all craved more (Kaimal, 2009).

In 2004, McDonald's realized the strong potential in the youth audience, which considered McDonald's to be expensive and mainly for children. Thus the Happy Price Menu was launched, with a value message for a younger audience, and for the first time McDonald's India saw an upsurge in young people entering the restaurants (Adgully Bureau, 2011). In 2008, the latest impressive campaign from the McDonald's-Leo Burnett stable used father-son duos from Bollywood (the informal term for the Hindi-language film industry based in Mumbai) to rejuvenate the theme of 'yesteryear's prices'. It featured Bollywood stars from past decades along with their sons, with the message that prices of fast food had not risen in line with the onslaught of time (Exchange4media, 2008).

McDonald's has also explored strategic tie-ups with Indian sports events in the country such as the Indian Premier League professional cricket tournament (Business Standard, 2009). Jatia from McDonald's remarked, 'The eating out market in India is very large and has huge potential fuelled by rising disposable incomes. There are many Indian and international fast-food companies who have entered the market since the last decade and unbranded food chains have also grown significantly. The Indian consumer has seen value in what we have to offer at our restaurants, which is a testament to our model.'

Products, pricing and distribution

In the early days, McDonald's India made efforts to change Indian consumers' perceptions completely because they related the brand to being 'foreign' or, often, 'American'. Consumers typically had the feeling of not knowing what to expect, which made India a more challenging market, as did local dietary preferences for non-meat dishes. India was the world's vegetarian paradise with nearly one billion people who eat meat only occasionally or never at all (Petrun, 2007).

McDonald's India thus invested time and effort to develop a customized menu for India, a menu that reflected both the taste and beliefs of the natives. In the words of Bakshi, another founder of McDonald's India, 'it really doesn't make sense to sell beef in a country where 85 per cent of the population doesn't eat it or will even shun a restaurant where beef is served'. The second largest community, the Muslims, did not eat pork. To establish a market in India, McDonald's managed to design a menu that included only chicken, fish and mutton products. McDonald's in India also devised a comprehensive range of vegetarian products with the addition of Indian spices, as a large population in north India preferred a Vedic style of eating which propagates vegetarian food (Sameer, 2011). Jatia told his co-workers, 'What moms tell us is that typically it's very hard to get their kids to eat vegetables, rice on its own. But when it's put together in a patty, and then you get it in a burger format, then kids absolutely love it' (McDonald's India, 2007).

McDonald's used the most creative forms of innovation to make their efforts palatable and catchy so that even the kids would love them. The names of the burgers (such as the Maharaja Mac) had an Indian connotation and so were more acceptable to the customers of the country. Jatia revealed that products such as the McAloo Tikki burger, Veg Pizza McPuff and Chicken McGrill burger were formulated and introduced using spices favoured by Indians. He added that the menu development team was responsible for special sauces which used local spices that did not contain beef or pork. Other products, too, did not contain eggs and were 100 per cent vegetarian. 'The Indianized products have been so well received that we even export [the] McAloo Tikki burger and Veg Pizza McPuff to the Middle East,' exclaimed Jatia, though certain flagship items like McNuggets were served in both the US and India (Kulkarni et al., 2009).

Sridhar remarked that 'When McDonald's launched, we took a conscious call of not introducing any beef or pork in our products. Thus, when controversies around McDonald's products started during the early and growth stages of the Indian business, we reacted quickly. We educated our customers about the build of our products and did extensive kitchen tours for our customers. We showed them how we

10

use separate vegetarian and non-vegetarian platforms for cooking – a first in any market for McDonald's' (Chaturvedi, 2008).

McDonald's kept the prices of its products low, which was made possible by strategies such as bulk buying, manufacturing efficiencies and long-term vendor contracts. The launch of the Happy Price Menu in 2004 meant that products were priced as low as INR20 (Chaturvedi, 2008). For individual products, McDonald's adopted value pricing strategies and went for bundling strategies for the combo meals, which typically consisted of a burger, french fries and coke. In September 2009, when food prices were on the rise, McDonald's further reduced its prices by about 25 per cent for its lunch and dinner menus (Case Study Inc., 2009).

Apart from typical fast-food restaurants set up all across India, McDonald's also launched home delivery services. 'The key idea is convenience. We are a quick service restaurant available at high-traffic locations. But there is a large number of people who find it difficult to travel. By offering home delivery we can reach out to them and increase our penetration,' said Jatia. There were no restrictions on the minimum order for home delivery, but a flat fee of INR10 was charged per delivery order, irrespective of the size of the order (Ganapati, 2004). McDonald's India also started a single nationwide McDelivery number (66-000-666) in an effort to upgrade its home delivery service (India Retailing).

McDonald's wanted to recognize itself as 'Indian' and a promoter of 'family values and culture', and as being 'comfortable and easy'. Thus the brand projected that, operationally, it was seriously committed to maintaining a good quality service and cleanliness, and to offering complete value for money.

Sources

Adgully Bureau (2011) 'McDonald's Happy Price Menu Spreads Happiness', www.adgully.com, 17 February 2011

Business Standard (2009) 'McDonald's Launches Special Offer to Cash IPL Frenzy', 23 April 2009, www.business-standard.com

Case Study Inc. (2009), 'McDonald's Pricing Strategy in India,' http://www.casestudyinc.com/mcdonalds-pricing-strategy-in-india

Chaturvedi, Preeti (2008) 'How McDonald's Evolved its Marketing in India' http://ipm.ge/article/How%20McDonald's%20evolved%20its%20marketing%20in%20India_ENG.pdf

Exchange4media (2008) 'McDonald's Carries Forward the Baap-beta Saga', 29 March 2008 www.exchange4media.com

Fahad, Mohd (2010) 'Feasibility Study of Opening a Maggi Restaurant at Jalandhar-Phagwara Highway', www.scribd.com

Ganapati, Priya (2004) 'Home Delivery from McDonald's Now!' 8 April 2004, www.rediff.com

Indian Franchise (2010) 'Growth of the India Fast Food Industry and the Opportunities it Offers', 17 May 2010 www.indiafranchiseblog.blogspot.com

India Retailing (2007), 'McDonald's tie up with Customer Corporation', http://www.indiaretailing.com/food_mcdonald.asp

Kaimal, Sreejit (2009) 'A Study of the Marketing Strategies of McDonald's with Special Reference to Indore', 5 September 2009, www.managementparadise.com

Kulkarni, Smita; Lassar, Walfried; Sridhar, Chandan and Venkitachalam, Akhila (2009) 'McDonald's Ongoing Marketing Challenge: Social Perception in India', OJICA-Online Journal of International Case Analysis, Vol. 1, No. 2, 31 January 2009

Lahoti, Nitin (2010) 'McDonald', 29 January 2010 www.scribd.com

McDonald's India (2007) 'No meat!' 15 December 2007 www.worldsgreatesthamburgers.com

Petrun, Erin (2007) 'Where's the Beef? Meatless McDonald's Burgers in India, 2 April 2007, www.cbsnews.com

Sameer (2011) 'McDonald's Spices op Products for Indian Vegetarians', 6 February 2011 www.buddingmarkets.com

Questions

1 How did McDonald's India overcome the characteristics of services by modifying its product, pricing, distribution and promotional mix when entering the Indian market?

2 Discuss Indian customers' perceived values and consumer behaviour in selecting fast-food services and the McDonald's approach to offering superior values to its customers.

Review questions

1 Using an appropriate example, discuss the concept of service quality and how it is embedded in the marketing activities of a company of your choice.
2 Apply the SERVQUAL model to your chosen company and examine the five dimensions included in the model. How might the gaps you found be reduced?
3 Apply Table 10.1, the expanded marketing mix for services, to a company of your choice. How are the 7 Ps utilized by the firm to provide superior customer value?

Group tasks

1 Based on Table 10.1, discuss the 7 Ps in relation to banking services.
2 Choose one service and come up with a service blueprint process and the key facets of the servicescapes for your chosen service.
3 Meet the manager of a bank in your locality and interview him/her to find out how they define service quality in the case of banking services.
4 Because of the distinguishing characteristics of services, marketing aims to overcome their intangibility, inseparability, perishability and heterogeneity. Come up with some possible approaches that reduce the impact of intangibility, inseparability, perishability and heterogeneity on services.

Glossary/Key terms

Relationship marketing: The identification, specification, initiation, maintenance and (where appropriate) dissolution of long-term relationships with key customers and other parties, through mutual exchange, fulfilment of promises and adherence to relationship norms, in order to satisfy the objectives and enhance the experience of the parties concerned.

Service quality: The difference between customers' expectations of service performance prior to the service encounter and their perceptions of the service received.

Service value: A trade-off between consumers' evaluation of the benefits and the cost involved in availing themselves of the service.

Vocab check list for ESL students

Aesthetics	Conceptualization	Gimmicks
Ambience	Dissolution	Inception
Components	Facets	Integrity

Definitions for these terms can be found in the 'Vocab Zone' of the companion website, which provides free access to the Macmillan English Dictionary online at www.palgrave.com/business/Gbadamosi

Further reading

Roland T. Rust, Peter J. Danaher and Sajeev Varki (2000) 'Using Service Quality Data for Competitive Marketing Decisions', *International Journal of Service Industry Management*, Vol. 11, No. 5, pp. 438–69

Using an empirical study, the authors of this article propose a simple theoretical framework of how market share changes result from changes in service quality, by the focal firm and/or by a competitor.

Evert Gummesson and Christian Grönroos (2012) 'The Emergence of the New Service Marketing: Nordic School Perspectives', *Journal of Service Management*, Vol. 23, No. 4, pp. 479–97

The article discusses how the new marketing theory, as seen through the lens of the Nordic School of Service, emerged.

Randi Priluck (2003) 'Relationship Marketing can Mitigate Product and Service Failures', *Journal of Services Marketing*, Vol. 17, No. 1, pp. 37–52

This research suggests that relationships make up for increasingly strong negative encounters in service marketing and provide a level of insulation for the marketer.

References

Asubonteng, P., McCleary, K. and Swan, J. E. (1996) 'SERVQUAL Revisited: A Critical Review of Service Quality', *Journal of Services Marketing*, 10 (6), pp. 62–81

Berry, L. L. (1995) 'Relationship Marketing of Services, Growing Interests and Emerging Perspectives', *Journal of the Academy of Marketing Science*, 23 (4), pp. 236–45

Bitner, M. J. (1992) 'Servicescapes: The Impact of Physical Surroundings on Customers and Employees', *Journal of Marketing*, 56 (2), pp. 57–71

Bolton, R. N. and Drew, J. H. (1991) 'A Multistage Model of Customers' Assessments of Service Quality and Value', *Journal of Consumer Research*, 17 (4), pp. 375–84

Booms, B. H. and Bitner, M. J. (1981) 'Marketing Strategies and Organization Structures for Service Firms', in J. H. Donnelly and W. R. George (eds) *Marketing of Services*. Chicago: American Marketing Association, pp. 51–67

Bureau of Economic Analysis (2006) *National Economic Accounts* www.bea.gov/national/index.htm#gdp (accessed 11 June 2012)

Drucker, P. (1954) *The Practice of Management*. New York: Harper Business

Fortune (2011) http://money.cnn.com/magazines/fortune/bestcompanies/2011/full_list/

Garvin, D. A. (1988) *Managing Quality: The Strategic and Competitive Edge*. New York, NY: The Free Press

Harvey, J. (1998) 'Service Quality: A Tutorial', *Journal of Operations Management*, 16 (5), pp. 583–97

Holbrook, M. (1994) 'The Nature of Customer Value: An Anthology of Services in the Consumption Experience', in R. T. Rust and R. L. Oliver (eds) *Service Quality: New Directions in Theory and Practice*, Thousand Oaks, CA: Sage Publications, pp. 21–71

Kingman-Brundage, J., George, W. R. and Bowen, D. E. (1995) 'Service Logic: Achieving Service System Integration', *International Journal of Service Industry Management*, 6 (4), pp. 20–39

Lehtinen, U. and Lehtinen, J. R. (1982) 'Service Quality: A Study of Quality Dimensions,' unpublished working paper. Helsinki: Service Management Institute

Levitt, T. (1983) *The Marketing Imagination*. New York, NY: The Free Press

Lovelock, C. and Wirtz, J. (2011) *Services Marketing: People Technology and Strategy*. Boston: Prentice Hall

Morgan, R. M. and Hunt, S. D. (1994) 'The Commitment-trust Theory of Relationship Marketing', *Journal of Marketing*, 58 (July), pp. 20–38

O'Malley, L., Patterson, M. and Evans, M. J. (1997) 'Intimacy or Intrusion: The Privacy Concerns of Relationship Marketing in Consumer Markets', *Journal of Marketing Management*, 13 (6), pp. 541–60

Palmer, A. (2008) *Principles of Services Marketing* (5th edn). London: McGraw-Hill

Parasuraman, A., Zeithaml, V. A. and Berry, L. L. (1988) 'SERVQUAL: A Multiple Items Scale for Measuring Consumer Perceptions of Service Quality', *Journal of Retailing*, 64 (1), pp. 12–40

Reimer, A. and Kuehn, R. (2005) 'The Impact of Servicescape on Quality Perception', *European Journal of Marketing*, 39 (7/8), pp. 785–808

Sánchez, J., Callarisa, L. R., Rodriguez, R. M. and Moliner, M. A. (2006) 'Perceived Value of the Purchase of a Tourism Product', *Tourism Management*, 27, pp. 394–409

Shostack, G. L. (1984) 'Designing Services that Deliver', *Harvard Business Review*, 62 (1), pp. 133–39

Shostack, G. L. (1992) 'Understanding Services through Blueprinting', *Advances in Services Marketing and Management: Research and Practice*, 1 (1), pp. 75–90

10

11 MARKETING PLANNING FOR VALUE DELIVERY

ZUBIN SETHNA

UNIVERSITY OF BEDFORDSHIRE

CHAPTER CONTENTS

LEARNING OUTCOMES

The content of this chapter will help you to:

- Define marketing planning and understand why adapting to market trends is a key organizational issue
- Outline the seven steps on the marketing planning ladder
- Discuss a variety of marketing metrics and their use in marketing planning
- Understand the importance of developing a strategy for 'value delivery through marketing planning'

Marketing in action
T. rex: Band and beast

MY FAVOURITE DINOSAUR IS THE *T. REX*. IT IS big, strong and powerful, or rather it *was* …

Another way of looking at the phrase 'staying ahead of the game' could be 'survival of the fittest'. This was first used by Charles Darwin in his theory of evolution. But it remains very true for organizations of all sizes in the world we live in today, too. Many a management briefing has quoted this term, but the meaning of the word 'fittest' has often been somewhat **misconstrued**. According to studies of Darwinian English, one would have to assume that the term means 'that which fits best'. What does this actually mean for our organizations? Well, that can be answered in two ways. First of all, what Darwin meant by the word 'fittest' was 'better adapted for the immediate, local environment' by differential preservation of organisms that are better adapted to live in changing environments. So, given the current context and using Darwin's theory, the 'survival of the fittest' does not mean that it is the big, strong and powerful that will survive. Rather, it means that the species that best fits into its environment will survive. In other words,

istock@LeventKonuk

bigger and stronger is not necessarily better – hence *T. rex* became a *was* rather than an *is*!

Of course, *T. rex* is not the only species to have failed to adapt to changing environmental conditions. And in the business world there are innumerable examples of corpses that lie **strewn** across the corporate landscape. Examples of UK 'deaths' in 2012 include Aquascutum, Clinton Cards and the Game Group. It can be argued that these companies died because they did not embrace change – and, in a changing world, change itself is the only constant. So, relying on the strategies and actions that worked last year is a misguided pathway to be on, as there are no guarantees that they will work as well in the coming year. And so the race is on! Every company now enters into a race in which the marketing environment changes daily and is increasingly competitive in all sorts of ways, whether it is for consumer spend in pounds and pence or for the human resource that drives the business. Those companies that forget to run or are slow off the mark either get left behind or, worse still, are disqualified.

INTRODUCTION

This chapter is about the role of marketing planning, and understanding the strategic marketing decisions that input into the marketing planning process and therefore greatly impact the strategies used for value delivery. It investigates issues that marketers in the real world have to deal with: identifying and adapting to market trends; selecting and understanding target markets and the value required by each of them, creating superior value to competitors, prioritizing marketing objectives and strategies, and finally assessing the possible financial consequences of actions taken, using marketing metrics. It is this planning process that focuses the minds of

Example 11.1:
Practice perspective: a practitioner view

Early on in my career as an eager young junior marketer working for a professional services firm, I had the pleasure of attending a conference called the 'Accountants Boot Camp' where I heard a management consultant called Paul Dunn famously say:

Those that aim at nothing usually hit it with surprising accuracy!

Those words have been resonating with me ever since ... and so we need a plan!

However, in my experience, planning is never straightforward. Whilst we may be able to predict the future to some extent, organizations are complex. This means that accurate predictions are difficult to make, even after detailed research. In the words of General Dwight D. Eisenhower, Supreme Commander of the Allied forces at the time of the D-Day invasion in 1944:

Plans are nothing – planning is everything!

Think and discuss

You already know from Chapter 4 how to organize focus groups; you need to find out what *all* your stakeholders think about the service and value you provide. Canvass their opinions and attitudes.

marketing managers and provides a framework that is sufficiently flexible to allow for the unforeseen.

Therefore what every company needs, just like a runner in a race, is a race plan, only we call it a marketing plan. And we are going to start, here and now! There are two things that you should consider before you start to run the race:

istock © morganl

1 What do other people think about your chances of winning?
2 Which direction are you running in and what position do you want to end up in?

Now all you need to do is to write a strategic marketing plan – your one- to five-year race plan that will enable you to realize your vision. But as anyone who has ever watched a fast-paced Formula 1 race will know, even the best-laid race plans (which have details of the specific changes you intend to make during the race) will change depending on how the race is being run. Adaptations might include changing the timing of the pit-stops, navigating a route past accidents, having the *bottle to* **throttle** through the hair-pin bends and holding your nerve when overtaking without knowing what is around the next corner. Hence the *race directors* are constantly changing their outlook; the process of adaptation lies in their hands. They can choose to act or they can choose to retire out of the race. What will you and your company choose?

11

DEFINING MARKETING PLANNING FROM A VALUE PERSPECTIVE

Before we start to focus specifically on the marketing planning issues, I will ask you to revisit Chapter 1 and refresh your memory of the definitions that currently exist to describe the discipline we call the *marketing* function – for example, you might look at the CIM (2009) definition, or the one offered by the American Marketing Association (2007).

The links between these two definitions are the words 'profitably' and 'value'. The Oxford English Dictionary (Oxford Minidictionary, 1991) defines value as 'the amount of money or other commodity etc. considered equivalent to something else; usefulness, importance; thing's ability to serve a purpose or cause an effect'. And so we can safely conclude that the value we are talking about here is the difference between the benefits received and the perceived total price. That said, there's an interesting article that appeared in the *Daily Telegraph* back in 2001 which shows the differing perspectives on value (Pook, 2001).

This *difference* between the benefits received and the perceived total price is further alluded to by a group of eminent marketing scholars. First, Dibb et al. (2006) proposed that 'Marketing consists of individual and organisational activities that facilitate and expedite satisfying exchange relationships in a dynamic environment through the creation, distribution, promotion and pricing of goods, services and ideas.' Second, Kotler and Keller (2006) defined the marketing concept thus: 'The key to achieving organisational goals lies in determining the needs and wants of target markets and delivering the desired satisfactions more efficiently and effectively than the competition.' But that is the definition of the raw marketing *function* in theory.

Think and discuss

Chapter 5 showed you how to develop a long-term vision for your company. Now you need to develop that vision and set out exactly what you aim to achieve.

Example 11.2:
Sex shop is fined because its videos are 'too tame'

A sex shop owner who sold 'hardcore' pornographic films was ordered to pay £5,826 because they were not explicit enough.

Customers of Little Amsterdam, in York, and The Adult Shop, in Grimsby, owned by Nicholas Griffin, paid up to £50 a time for erotic videos. But when they got the films home they discovered they were distinctly tame.

One video, *Secrets of a Sensuous Nurse*, was a 30-year old comedy starring Ursula Andress and Jack Palance. *Confessions of a Sex Maniac* told the innocent story of an architect who wanted to build an office block shaped like a pair of breasts. *Talk Naughty to Me* proved to be equally 'softcore'.

Michael Taylor, prosecuting, said the charges against the company were only samples of numerous breaches. He added: 'These videos can be seen on late night terrestrial television. They were not the more interesting videos these people were seeking, and in simplistic terms it is clearly a breach of the Trades Descriptions Act. The public have been misled.'

Colin Rumford, head of trading standards in York, said: 'We responded to complaints from the public, both men and women. They felt embarrassed and reluctant to come forward, but also felt cheated. They did not know exactly what they had bought until they settled down to watch the films. In many cases they must have got a shock, hence the complaints.'

Griffin said: 'I am amazed people have the audacity to complain about things like that.'

Source: Pook (2001)

What about when one gets to the organizational level? (See Sethna et al., 2013.) What about marketing as an organizational orientation? If we take Narver and Slater's (1990) seminal work on *marketing orientation*, they conclude that it consists of five key aspects:

● Customer focus
● Competitor focus
● Integrated functional coordination
● Organization culture
● Long-term profits

Of course, in reality, the organization needs to manage and coordinate its resources vis-à-vis this list of foci before it achieves any sort of 'satisfying exchange relationship' or indeed 'competitive advantage'. This coordination could move forward by using three dimensions outlined by Kohli and Jaworski (1990):

1 The generation of market information about the needs of customers and external environmental factors
2 The dissemination of such information among organizational functions
3 The development and implementation of strategies in response to the information

This framework puts the customer at the centre of the entire process and therefore, just like an axle, the customer becomes the pivot around which the organization turns (see Figure 11.1). Blythe and Megicks (2010, p. 4) call this 'the business philosophy of customer centrality'.

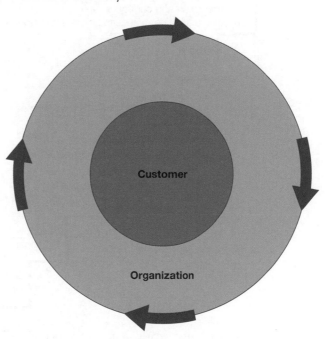

Figure 11.1: Customers at the centre of the organization

And so the last definition we look at is specifically focused on marketing planning (also see McDonald, 2007), which Svend Hollensen (2006) defined thus:

Marketing planning is the structured process of researching and analysing marketing situations, developing and documenting marketing objectives, strategies and programmes, and implementing, evaluating and controlling activities to achieve the objectives.

Thus, what we have in this final definition is the process of marketing planning outlined very well indeed. Let us not forget Paul Dunn's quote from earlier in this chapter!

In time-honoured 'traditional marketing speak', marketers need to ask the three crucial questions:

Figure 11.2: Seven steps of the marketing planning ladder

Q1. Where are we now?	Answer 1. ANALYSIS Research and analyse the current situation
Q2. Where do we want to be?	Answer 2. PLANNING Develop the organization's aims, objectives and strategies
Q3. How are we going to get there?	Answer 3. IMPLEMENTATION AND CONTROL Implement, evaluate and control the marketing activities

THE MARKETING PLAN

There are seven steps on the marketing planning ladder (see Figure 11.2).

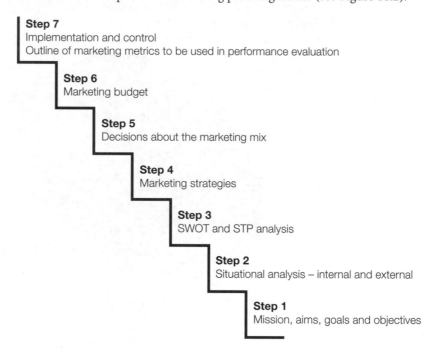

Step 7
Implementation and control
Outline of marketing metrics to be used in performance evaluation

Step 6
Marketing budget

Step 5
Decisions about the marketing mix

Step 4
Marketing strategies

Step 3
SWOT and STP analysis

Step 2
Situational analysis – internal and external

Step 1
Mission, aims, goals and objectives

STEP 1: MISSION, AIMS, GOALS AND OBJECTIVES

This first step is crucial in its role to establish the clear reasoning for the organization's existence. Whether it is a 'financial profit' or a 'not-for-profit' role, the organization needs to articulate its character and identity along with its reason for existence. The widely accepted definition of *mission* is one which Campbell et al. (1990) conjured up:

A mission exists when strategy and culture are mutually supportive – an organization has a mission when its culture fits with its strategy.

'Aims' and 'goals' are terms that are somewhat interchangeable and denote the direction in which the organization is generally heading. An 'objective' usually has a measurable outcome (and, incidentally, *all* objectives should conform to the acronym 'SMART', which stands for specific, measurable, achievable, realistic and time-bound). For example, take a small business that I know called Kumon Wembley Central, which provides Maths and English tuition for children aged between 3 and 18 years. The company might instigate a local, short-term promotional campaign with the aim of recruiting more students onto the programme. This would then become an objective only if the business owner says, for example, that she wants to increase student recruitment by 20 per cent as a direct result of the current three-month campaign.

Table 11.1: General categories of objectives

Customers	Objectives here are concerned with all things customer-related: which section of the market or 'market segment' they come from, how they are 'targeted' and how the company is seen in their minds, i.e. how the company 'positions' itself in the minds of the customer
Competitors	Rather than 'matching' what competitors are doing, objectives here should be concerned with understanding the company's performance 'relative' to that of the competition. This could be done at a strategic level, for example by pursuing a new market development strategy in a particular geographic region, or at a tactical/functional level, for example by using a marketing communications campaign to highlight the 'price point' differences between two leading brands
Target markets	Understanding which specific markets the company will be targeting and why. Is it because there is a proven demand and, at the same time, the distribution of products is manageable in that particular market?
Technology, research and development	What objectives does the company have as regards the use and application of new technology? Which 'functional areas' will the new technology aid? How will the new technology enable the company to develop a 'competitive edge'?
Products, production and services	In a marketing-oriented company (one in which every decision is approached with the customer in mind), setting objectives for outputs is usually done from within the marketing department as *they* understand and forecast customer demand, and hence can plan ahead
Finance	These objectives are very easy to measure and are usually the starting point for most organizations. For example, 'we want to increase turnover by 10 per cent over the next year'. This is then further translated into marketing objectives (e.g. promotional campaigns to increase market share or promotions for point of purchase) which will facilitate that increase in turnover
Environment	This comprises a number of elements such as internal environment, external environment and environmental scanning. Whilst the information on the internal environment may be readily available, it might not be so easy when it comes to the external environment. What this also means is that the data may be difficult to measure. Objectives for 'environmental scanning' may exist in order to keep a constant updated picture of what is happening around the organization. Inputs into this picture will come from a variety of functions and levels within the company

11

McDonald (1984) said that, in setting objectives, a company should move from the general to the particular, from the broad to the narrow, and from the long term to the short term. And so, at this stage, it is also useful to start thinking about the kinds of objectives that the company is seeking to achieve in various categories of marketing process. For example, we can see from the list in Table 11.1 that there are a **plethora** of areas that need careful consideration.

STEP 2: SITUATIONAL ANALYSIS – INTERNAL AND EXTERNAL

Marketers should 'audit' and analyse both the internal and the external environments within which they work. These are sometimes referred to (see Table 11.2) as 'macro-environmental factors' (forces that have an impact upon the whole organization and over which the organization has no direct control) and 'micro-environmental factors'.

Table 11.2: Macro and micro environments

Macro-environmental factors	Micro-environmental factors
Political-legal	Customers
Economic	Competitors
Socio-cultural	Value-chain members
Technological	Products
Environmental/ecological	Place (distribution)
Demographic	Promotions

Table 11.3 is by no means a comprehensive checklist but it will get you to start thinking about the effects on the company from various forces. How will your company address them?

There are a number of different models and frameworks that are used by marketers to classify the forces that surround an organization. One of the most frequently quoted is Porter's 'five forces model' (Porter, 1990). Porter surmised that an organization should have a thorough understanding of competition in existence in its market *before* it develops any assertions about the industry's attractiveness.

We can use this to understand how to analyse the industry that we are in. Whilst, undoubtedly, there are potentially many sophisticated ways of doing this, I would like you to try to answer the following questions for your own organizations.

The *intensity of rivalry* between competitors depends on a number of factors. What is the structure of both competition and costs within the sector? To what degree do the competitors differ – that is, are their products highly differentiated? Do you know what kind of strategic objectives your competitors are pursuing? Are the barriers to exit – to leave the industry sector – high or low? And finally, but perhaps most importantly, are the switching costs high or low?

Taking the *threat of new entrants* as the next point, do you know who they are or could be? What *size* are they compared with your operation? Have they established economies of scale throughout their functions (such as marketing, finance and production)? Do they have existing market share? How does the brand awareness of their brand(s) compare with yours? Does this affect brand loyalty and, if so, how will you fare? Do you have any advantages over them as regards channels of distribution (physical or digital)?

Moving onto the opposite side of the model and taking a look at *the threat of substitutes*, we already know that unless an organization is extremely 'environmentally savvy' (aware of anything that is a potential 'substitute'), it is often very difficult to plan for such eventualities. Competition is relatively easy to define when seen in terms of physical products or services. However, it becomes increasingly difficult for

Table 11.3: Checklist of effects on the company

☑	Political-legal	Current and proposed legislation; local, national and international government actions; climate and stability
☑	Economic	Demand, taxation, inflation and interest rates; workforce and unemployment; credit availability
☑	Socio-cultural	Language; social trends, cultural norms; values and beliefs; societal attitude changes
☑	Technological	Advances in product, process and communications technologies; development of generic substitute products; internal and external attitudes towards technological change
☑	Environmental/ ecological	Cost of conservation; effects of pollution and the availability of natural resources
☑	Demographic	Population make-up vis-à-vis age, gender, ethnicity, religion, education, occupation, household size, income
☑	Customers	Purchasing and consumer behaviours; awareness of and attitude towards competitors
☑	Competitors	Strategies employed and actions taken; size and intensity; new players, trends and tactics
☑	Value-chain members	Suppliers with the availability of resources; efficiency of distributors and dealers in servicing the main trade channels; availability and efficiency of supplementary functions/services such as distribution, communications, transport and finance
☑	Products	What does the current product portfolio look like? Are there elements which will be kept/dropped/improved? What are the legislative effects on product liability, quality, etc?
☑	Place	Are we distributing adequately to the markets that we wish to cover? How well are the value-chain/channel members performing? Which other channels should we be aware of? What are the effects of digital media and online markets?
☑	Promotions	This could include a variety of marketing communications activity such as advertising, sales promotion, direct and digital marketing/sales and public relations. Are the assigned strategies and tactics for each suitable for the accomplishment of the overall marketing plan? Do they 'fit' with the assigned budget? Is the chosen medium relevant? Have we planned appropriately for the requirement of staff at particular times?
☑	Price	Has the company given any thought to its current pricing strategy? What is its origin and does it 'fit' within the current environment? Has it identified the synergies between the '4 Ps' (product, place, promotion and price)? If it changes the price, what effect will it have on the others as well as on the company's strategy and, ultimately, profits?

11

a consumer to compare when organizations offer their products as a part of a 'bundle' where the product and service is wrapped up to include a plethora of '*added value*', which will hold a different meaning for different audiences. (This may be a reason why we have seen a multitude of 'comparison websites' emerge over the past five years, such as www.comparethemarket.com.) How easily definable is your offering? Is the value you offer easily identifiable or is it wrapped in a 'value bundle'?

In order to ascertain the *bargaining power of suppliers*, the organization needs to know who the main suppliers are. What is the make-up of the supplier industry – are there many or just a handful? What is their financial influence on the supply/ value chain (that is, how much of the pricing is taken up by their margins? Can they be trusted to deliver what they say they will deliver (Sethna, 2006)? The answers to these questions will help us to develop an understanding about the strength of the suppliers that currently exist and their bargaining power. Who is calling the shots here – the suppliers or the buying organizations?

This takes us swiftly into looking at the *bargaining power of the buyers*. It stands to reason that the collective bargaining power of buyers is greatest when there are a few very dominant buyers in the market, but many sellers. There are a number of other situations which enable buyers to hold the 'upper hand'. Are the products in your sector standardized? To what degree is your sector 'price sensitive'? Is it able to increase its prices freely without having a **detrimental** effect on demand and there-fore on sales (*elasticity of demand*)? Of course, there are also other considerations such as brand loyalty, quality and quantity that impinge upon the price, but the key point here is that the forces of 'buyer' competition could ultimately erode profitabil-ity for various players in the industry.

STEP 3: SWOT AND STP ANALYSIS

As outlined in Chapter 1, 'SWOT' is one of the most commonly referred to market-ing models in the marketing planning process. To remind you, the SWOT analysis is usually depicted as a matrix (see Figure 11.3).

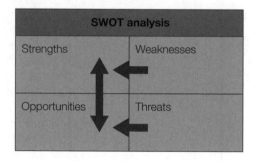

Figure 11.3: The SWOT model

The SWOT (strengths, weaknesses, opportunities, threats) analysis enables an organ-ization to evaluate its external and internal situation from the previously collected information (see Step 2) in a very structured and particular way. First and foremost, it **endeavours** to harmonize its internal marketing strengths with the opportunities that are present. Second, it will highlight areas of the organization where weaknesses could be converted into strengths and threats into opportunities.

Table 11.4 is an example of a completed SWOT analysis for the London-based service company, Kumon Wembley Central.

Table 11.4: Example of a completed SWOT analysis

SWOT analysis	
Strengths: • Quick responses • Recognized (industry award) dedicated customer service • Some staff have a strong reputation in the market • Able to change strategy and direction quickly due to size of company • Low overheads and so can offer value for money to customers and other stakeholders	Weaknesses: • Market share is shrinking • Small number of staff have low skills base in some areas • Susceptible to staff turnover, absence • Cashflow often an issue, with very little support from the bank • Internal technology (e.g. customer relationship management databases) are not maintained and consequently staff are missing either vital data or relationship links
Opportunities: • A continually steady market sector • An ability to decrease fixed costs as the customer base grows • Increasing sales opportunities as a result of ongoing marketing communications and brand awareness campaigns	Threats: • Competition from other local franchisees due to misallocation of geographic territory • A change in local transport infrastructure will disrupt customer base sufficiently to divert customers to competitors

So what are the three things you need to look out for when completing a SWOT analysis?

● When making a list of your organization's strengths and weaknesses, make sure that you not only include those that are unquestionably 'absolute' but also those that are relative as compared with your competition – that is, does the competition also have them?

● The strengths and weaknesses of your resource base and organizational capabilities should most definitely be 'valued' by your customers. Therefore, saying that you have 'great customer service' is subjective unless, of course, as in the example SWOT in Table 11.4, your company has won an industry award for its *dedicated customer service* and is therefore 'valued' by the people that matter!

● Remember that the second section of SWOT, which deals with the opportunities and threats, should investigate the factors that are *external* to the organization and that have, or could have, an impact on organizational performance

Segmentation, targeting and positioning (STP)

Let's now revisit Chapter 5, where you looked at segmentation, targeting and positioning, known to marketers as 'STP'. The first question that comes to mind is 'why is there a need for this?' Well, over the past 20 years, we have seen our world move away from 'mass marketing' and towards 'segment marketing', focusing on a particular segment/sector.

Where is the value-add in this? Segmentation allows you to focus your resources on the most appropriate opportunities (given the time, budget and resource allocations/availabilities). We find as a result that, if you get your STP strategies right, it will improve both marketing efficiency and effectiveness.

11

The first decision that you have to make here is identify whether you are segmenting consumers or business markets. Tables 11.5 and 11.6 will give you an indication of the kinds of variables you need to be mindful of.

Table 11.5: Examples of consumer segmentation variables

Behavioural and attitudinal	Benefits and value sought, purchase occasion/behaviour, product usage and attitude, sensitivity towards price, buyer readiness stage
Demographic	Age, gender, wealth, educational attainment, income distribution, occupation, ethnicity, religion and nationality
Geographic	Location, climate, distance
Psychographic	Lifestyle, personality

Table 11.6: Examples of business segmentation variables

Identifier profile used by firms to establish segments *a priori* or before any direct data is collected (Day, 1990)	Demographics, operations, product required, purchasing situation
Response profile used by firms to understand the way in which other stakeholders will respond *a posteriori* or after the first contact with the customer	Vendor product attributes, customer variables, product application, and the personal characteristics at play in the organization's decision-making unit (DMU)

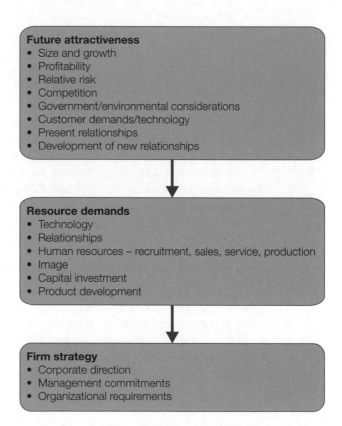

Figure 11.4: Selecting target segments
Source: Adapted from Freytag and Clarke, 2001

Now let us move on to 'targeting'. A target market is a particular segment of the whole market that a company chooses to pursue and sees as being relevant to and accepting of their offering. Each time an organization identifies a potential segment, it must be evaluated on the basis of the relevance and overall 'fit' with the firm's objectives, resources (financial, human and operational) and core competences. See Figure 11.4.

The last element of STP is 'positioning', which is embedded in the theory of branding. It is the process of creating a perception of a brand relative to competing brands. So, in simple terms, what kind of place does your brand/organization occupy in the mind of your consumer? This can be measured using a 'high-low scale' across several dimensions – price, reliability and quality.

For example, we can see from the 'perceptual map' in Figure 11.5 how six competing retail brands are seen by customers, using the dimensions of price and quality. It shows that the retail brands C and F are close rivals and have quite a distinguishable perceptual positioning. They are both in the low-quality and low-price sector compared with the other four brands (A, B, E and D). Using these consumer perceptions, an organization may make strategic decisions to change the positioning of its brand – usually using a variety of marketing communications.

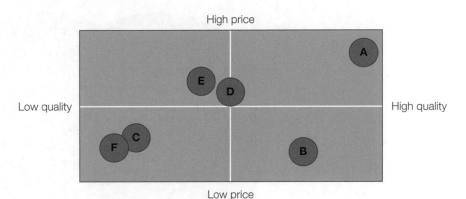

Figure 11.5: Perceptual map

STEP 4: MARKETING STRATEGIES

In simplistic terms, marketing strategies can be viewed in two ways, which are not mutually exclusive. First, as we have seen earlier in this chapter, the organization chooses its target market – the customers it feels that it has a 'fit' with. Hand in hand with this, the organization also needs to consider its 'competitor targets' by analysing the perceptual positioning map as shown in Figure 11.5.

Porter (1985) proffered a model of marketing strategy which was based on three possible strategies:

● **Differentiation:** The main aim of this strategy is to *differentiate* in a way that leads to a price premium paid by the customer that is over and above the actual cost of differentiating. Thus organizations can portray to customers that their offering is significantly different from that of their competitors, prove the added value that customers are set to glean and then charge a premium for this. The added value can be developed in two ways. There are the *real* differences in the product that a company can prove, but there are also the communications and promotions

11

messages which can *allude* to differences

- **Cost focus:** The basis of this strategy is that an organization tries to find a *cost advantage* with a specific target market(s) rather than with the whole market. Thus, the organization may find particular economies of scale (or *savings*) that their competitors, which are targeting the whole market, may have missed
- **Cost leadership:** Organizations that succeed in implementing this strategy have done so because they have achieved the lowest cost position in a given industry sector. They have therefore minimized their production, distribution and sales costs, and offer their customers a lower price (the organization has a price advantage) without diminishing their profit margins. In recent years we have seen examples of this from organizations such as Dell (PCs), Ryanair (air travel), Lidl (retail supermarket) and Tata (the 1 lakh automobile)

Value disciplines

An alternative to the Porter strategy was proposed by Treacy and Wiersema (1993), who identified three strategies or '*value disciplines*' which they believe increase customer value (see Figure 11.6).

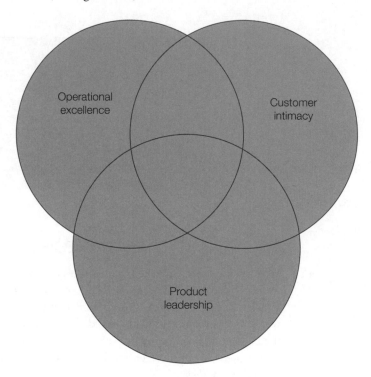

Figure 11.6: Value disciplines
Source: Treacy and Wiersema, 1993

Value discipline 1: Operational excellence

An organization following this strategy tries its best to lead the industry sector in 'price and convenience'. These organizations will not stop until they have found ways 'to minimize overhead costs, to eliminate intermediate production steps, to reduce transaction and other "friction" costs, and to optimize business processes across functional and organizational boundaries'.

Value discipline 2: Customer intimacy

So, whilst organizations that are actively chasing operational excellence concentrate all their efforts on making their operations lean and efficient, those pursuing a strategy of customer intimacy continually tailor and shape their offering, thus precisely meeting the needs of their highly segmented customer requirements. Getting to know one's customers with this level of detail is not cheap, but these organizations know that they have to spend the money in order to develop customer loyalty, which translates internally as the customer's lifetime value (CLV is further described later under *marketing metrics*). In their ledgers, the column housing details of the *one-off transactions* has been erased!

Value discipline 3: Product leadership

Product leadership is all about organizations that endeavour to keep ahead of the technology curve and continually produce leading-edge, state-of-the-art products and services, thus repeatedly rendering both their own and competitors' products obsolete (see also 'cannibalization' under 'Marketing metrics' later in this chapter). The keys to such strategies are:

- Creativity: Being able to recognize new ideas from the wider environment
- Commercialization: Getting ideas quickly to market
- Innovation: Relentless pursuit of new solutions to the problems that the (own) latest product or service has just solved

An example of this is undoubtedly Apple. Its creative foresight in developing market-changing, innovative products that it commercializes with meticulous planning surely fits with this model of 'product leadership'. Burgess (2012, pp. 28–42) argues that the design philosophy, marketing and business models behind the iPhone (and now the iPad) 'have decisively reframed the values of usability that underpin software and interface design in the consumer technology industry, marking a distinctive shift in the history and contested futures of digital culture'.

The BCG Matrix

The Boston Consulting Group (Henderson, 1979) developed a key model and simple technique that was traditionally used by many organizations to classify a product or even a business according to the features of the market and the features of a product. This in turn was used to allocate resources. The model is commonly known as the BCG matrix (see Figure 11.7).

Using this model, products are ranked by analysts according to their relative market share and growth rates. The four quadrants where products could be 'charted' are typically:

- **Cash cows:** Products that enjoy a high market share and where the market growth is relatively low/slow so that these products are high revenue generators and can be 'milked'!
- **Dogs:** Products that are stuck in slow-growing markets that have a low market share. These products barely break even – that is, they generate just about enough revenue to maintain the business's market share without adding any profits to the firm. From an accounting viewpoint, these 'dogs' should perhaps be sold off. From a marketing viewpoint, they continue to give the firm a presence in the market and therefore should be thought about somewhat strategically

11

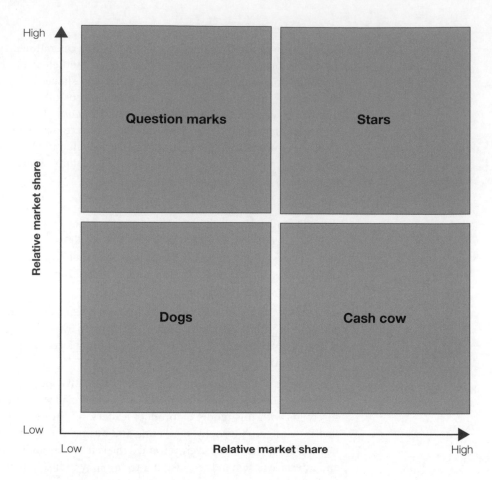

Figure 11.7: Boston Consulting Group matrix

- **Question marks:** These products have low market share but operate in a high-growth market. There is the potential for these products to become stars if sufficient resources are primed. However, the firm should make a decision in the light of the overall strategy and the relationship with other products
- **Stars:** These products are defined by having high market share in a growing market. It is likely that these products are the leaders in the firm and the market but that does not mean that they do not still need a lot of support or promotion

STEP 5: DECISIONS ABOUT THE MARKETING MIX

We have already looked at these in some depth in earlier chapters. The point of revisiting the mix (also referred to previously in this book as the '4 Ps' or the '7 Ps' – product, price, place, promotion, people, process and physical evidence) is that there are some crucial decisions to be made that impact the nature and direction of the marketing plan. You could call these the 'tactical' aspects of the marketing plan. The ways in which the organization will develop and implement the marketing mix activities will very much depend upon the segments that it has already specified as being of interest.

Vital questions that will enable you to make decisions about the marketing mix and include (but are not limited to):

- Which products and services will we develop in the short and medium term, and for which markets?
- What are our pricing objectives, current approaches and policies to set future pricing?
- How will we distribute and deliver our products and services to our customers?
- Which channels will we use? Which ones *can* we use? Which ones *should* we use?
- How will we promote the benefits of our product to our markets?
- How do we use, value, train, promote and nurture our human resource – the people?
- Do we understand and periodically review our business processes? How do they impact our current and future operations, quality standards and therefore eventual market share?
- Where the service element of our offering dominates the physical product, how do customers and key stakeholders judge our capabilities? What physical, tangible evidence do we provide to create and reinforce the ideas of quality, reliability and consistency?

Thus, once the decisions have been made as regards the elements of the mix, the organization will *position* itself in its chosen market with its chosen offering.

STEP 6: MARKETING BUDGET

In *buy-to-let* property markets, there is an old adage that says, 'The three most important elements in a property are location, location and location', as success in this market is all about the location of a property. We can borrow and adapt from that here and say that the marketing budget is all about 'resource, resource, resource'!

This is because the marketing budget not only offers a **mechanism** for allocating amounts of money to translate the previously set marketing objectives/goals into actual marketing actions, but also acts as control mechanism.

However, this is a two-step process. The first step is to decide upon the method of resource allocation (see Table 11.7).

'Budgets turn objectives into actions'

(Anon.)

Table 11.7: Methods of resource allocation

Method	What it means
This-is-how-much-I've-got method	We totally disregard the task in hand, but take the perspective that we will spend whatever is available, or whatever can be secured from reducing other activities
Percentage of sales method	We use a fixed percentage of the company's profits to be allocated as the marketing budget, regardless of what is happening in the wider marketing environment within which we work
Competition matching method	We mirror/copy the amount our competitors spend, in the hope that they are doing it correctly. What it does not account for is that we do not know about why they are doing what they're doing!
Objective and task method	We identify and establish how much it will cost to achieve the objectives and goals which we have set out earlier in our plan. We then allocate the financial resources to meet those demands

11

Example 11.3:
Vintage Image: Using the past to plan for the future

Glamorous images from a long-gone era now adorn the homes of many a UK home. It seems that the need to hark back to the past, using photographic images or indeed cinema posters, is now stronger than ever. Even with the recent global financial crisis, it seems that investors are happy to continue to purchase *aesthetically pleasing* products. Noshir Anklesaria of Vintage Image (www.vintageimage.co.uk) predicted that this would happen, and in 2011 he turned his 30-year hobby into a fully fledged business. He still collects but now also sells vintage original movie posters, enamel and illuminated signage and other original images. His differentiator is that they are all original and vintage. In the past two years the majority of business has been transacted at vintage and retro fairs held around the UK, and so ecommerce usage has been minimal.

As is common in these situations, this SME (small and medium-sized enterprise) went from

istock © Victorburnside

having a personal 'love and enthusiasm' for the product to actively having to *market* to a wider audience. During that transition period, Noshir was so caught up in trying to get the product out there, that the planning aspects related to the business (both strategic and tactical) were left by the wayside. To ensure that Vintage Image remains firmly on a growth **trajectory**, there needs to be some immediate changes. Recent changes have included careful analysis of the current customer base and proposed target audience, technology usage and ecommerce strategy, customer relationship marketing and reputation management.

However, these changes have only been brought to fruition as a result of careful marketing planning. Noshir wanted to use strategic marketing planning to validate the company's aims and objectives for the next five years. Three particular strands of the implementation plan were recognised. First, the marketing-planning process needed to provide information on the following areas: market trends, opportunities, competitive threats, internal capabilities, brand proposition, and target markets. Second, the ecommerce offering needed specialist knowledge and so a company recognized for its work in search engine optimization was brought in to cost the development and streamlining of the online offering. The third and final strand before the planning implementation phase was to allocate financial resources to the tasks which needed completing in order to achieve the goals the company had set out. A true example of the *objective and task method* (see Table 11.7) in motion!

Of course, the method with the tick clearly indicates that there is *only one* method (objective and task) that will give us the best chance of achieving our goals and objectives. Whilst the other methods are used by many organizations around the world, their effectiveness to be questioned has, and thus their success rate.

The second step is to decide the contents of the budget. A marketing manager, when compiling a budget of this nature, should include a variety of expenses that will cover the constituent parts of the plan. These are usually derived from two key areas of the mix:

- *Price*-related expenses: Anything that reduces the expected gross income by discounting – for instance, through bulk-buy/quantity discounts, trade promotional discounts, loyalty schemes, personal selling through sales commissions/expenses – should be included here
- *Promotion*-related expenses: Advertising, social media, sales promotions, public relations, events and experiential marketing, direct and digital marketing, personal selling

There is also the small issue of the timescales that are being budgeted for. Many organizations tend to use short-term, tactical, annual planning cycles, which forecast the coming year's sales, turnover and profits. However, those marketers who develop detailed *strategic* marketing plans will know that, by their very nature, strategic plans are steeped in the medium to long term, and thus the results of the short-term plans should be fed back continuously into the longer-term plans. This includes budgetary information. If there is a variance between forecast and actual, or perhaps a deviation from the expected results, the organization should determine the resultant effects and how quickly it should take **remedial** or corrective action.

STEP 7: IMPLEMENTATION AND CONTROL – MARKETING METRICS

Drucker (1986) makes a valid point. It is not just 'the thought that counts' here. The organization has to have the capabilities necessary to implement the plan. Otherwise, what we are left with is something that Nigel Piercy (1997) called SPOTS – 'Strategic Plan On The Shelf'. This intimates that whilst plans are formulated for reasons such as raising capital, they are usually shelved thereafter.

Implementing strategy is not without its problems and Owen (1982) identified four reasons for this:

'The best plan is only a plan, that is, good intentions, unless it degenerates into work'

(Peter Drucker)

- The strategy being devised needs to be matched with the structure currently in place so that they support each other. This, coupled with the fact that the product portfolio should also deliver what the organization's target market wants, means that there is undoubtedly going to be some conflict along the way
- With new strategies, there are new 'communications' problems. The organization may not have the systems in place to receive sufficient and timely feedback as to the progress of the new strategy and it is therefore troublesome to make any rectifications to operational plans
- Staff have to contend with the uncertainty and risk that are often associated with a change in strategy. Unless carefully managed, these risks will hinder the smooth progress of strategic change
- Organizational 'systems' that are currently in place (e.g. delivery, communications, pay structures, staff development, management levels/hierarchy) are often firmly embedded in the very fabric of the organization, and are therefore difficult to change quickly. The problem is that they may not work well with the new strategies that are being implemented and will therefore once again hinder successful implementation

11

By using a combination of what we now know about implementing marketing strategies and what Owen (1982) suggested about strategic change, it should be possible not to fall into the SPOTS trap. The following questions should help:

- Have you identified who is clearly responsible for each objective of the marketing plan?
- Do your marketing staff have the ability to deal with the areas identified in the plan?
- Is the number of new strategies and objectives limited to a few, rather than a lot?
- Have you identified the necessary actions required to implement the marketing strategy?
- Do you know who is responsible and for what, and over what time period?
- Have you pre-established 'milestones' (progress measurement points, which may be financial or time-bound) so that the organization can measure the results and take any remedial action if necessary?
- Which other monitoring and control systems have you put in place to measure performance?

Marketing metrics

That last point about measuring performance is one that is fast becoming a 'hot topic' for marketers. Historically, marketers have had a rough ride when it comes to marketing metrics – that is, measuring the impact of what they do. And things are getting worse. In a 2011 study conducted by IBM among 1,700 chief marketing officers (CMOs) from around the world, it was reported that: 'It's difficult to measure the ROI of […] marketing effort[s] because [marketers] don't have the right tools to provide [them] with the analysis' (IBM, 2011).

In order to identify the right metrics and use them accurately, many CMOs will need to work more closely with their colleagues in the finance function, starting with the chief finance officer. They will also need to provide financial training for their staff and recruit marketing people with strong financial acumen.

Table 11.8: Percentage of CMOs reporting unpreparedness for managing key market factors
Source: IBM, 2011

Data explosion	71%
Social media	68%
Growth of channel and device choices	65%
Shifting consumer demographics	63%
Financial constraints	59%
Decreasing brand loyalty	57%
Growth market opportunities	56%
ROI accountability	56%
Customer collaboration and influence	56%
Privacy considerations	55%
Global outsourcing	54%
Regulatory considerations	50%
Corporate transparency	47%

The IBM study highlighted how 'unprepared' board-level marketers really are, let alone those working further down the hierarchy. More than 50 per cent of respondents believed that they were 'unprepared to manage the impact of all but two out of 13 key market factors' (see Table 11.8).

This study is not unique in identifying the importance of marketing metrics. Here are some leading figures giving their take on the subject (Farris et al., 2009):

Measurement is critical to the health of any business (Kimberley B. Dedeker, Vice President Global Consumer & Market Knowledge, P&G).

Better metrics lead to better decisions, which lead to better outcomes (Erv Shames, former CEO, Kraft Foods).

Marketing is being challenged, as never before, to be accountable (David Aaker, author of Brand Portfolio Strategy).

So, as marketers, what are we to do? What metrics should we be using? What should we be measuring, and how often? The basic starting point is a list of marketing metrics in use in UK firms (see Table 11.9) created by Ambler et al. (2004).

Table 11.9: The use of marketing metrics in UK firms

Source: Ambler et al., 2004

Rank	Metric
1	Profit/profitability
2	Sales, value and/or volume
3	Gross margin
4	Awareness
5	Market share (value/volume)
6	Number of new products
7	Relative price
8	Customer dissatisfaction
9	Customer satisfaction
10	Distribution/availability

This was further expanded upon by Farris et al. (2009), who highlighted the key areas that should be measured and provided in-depth explanations of what the marketer needs to consider and also what purpose particular metrics serve. In my experience, marketing students at undergraduate level quite often struggle with developing a framework of potential measurement areas. This is through no fault of theirs! There is a lot to think about when it comes to measuring the effects of marketing for an organization and so, to help with this, I have highlighted in Table 11.10 some examples of important metrics, which will get you started when it comes to thinking about what should be measured. You will see that the table (partially adapted from Farris et al., 2009) has been sectioned according to the six steps of the marketing planning ladder used in this chapter. This will enable you to make the connections more easily. How you actually implement the measurement depends very much on the size, nature, structure and sector of the organization whose marketing you are measuring!

11

Table 11.10: Marketing metrics associated with the six steps of the marketing planning ladder

	Possible marketing metrics	Definitions How to derive metrics How they should be used
Step 1: Mission, aims, goals and objectives Will enable the formulation of pricing strategy which contributes to the overall plan (should be used in conjunction with pricing metrics from Step 5)	Unit margin Percentage margin	Unit price less the unit cost Unit margin as a percentage of unit price
	Target volume Target revenue	An overview of the break-even calculation and profit targets Conversion of target volume to target revenues by using average prices per unit
	Contribution per unit Contribution margin	Unit price less the variable costs involved Contribution per unit divided by the unit price
	Hierarchy of effects (see further breakdown of individual metrics in Steps 2 and 3 below)	Helps to measure awareness, importance, attitudes, beliefs, intentions to try, buy, repeat purchase
Steps 2 and 3: Situational analysis; SWOT and STP analysis	Market share	This can be viewed from a number of perspectives: • Revenue (sales revenue as a percentage of market sales revenue) • Unit (unit sales as a percentage of market unit sales) • Relative (brand market share divided by the total competitor market share)
	Market penetration	Measures the number of sales of a product or service as a percentage compared with the total theoretical market for that product or service
	Brand penetration	Measures the number of sales of a brand as a percentage compared with the total theoretical market for that brand
	Heavy usage index	Measures the relative usage of a particular product category by customers of a specific brand
	Awareness and top of mind (you should also consider the 'knowledge' that the market has about your product, service or brand and, more importantly, consider the 'beliefs' or perceptions that are held by individual customers)	Percentage of total target population that is aware of a brand and then a measure of the saliency of the brand (i.e. those that would consider your brand first)

(continued on next page)

	Purchase intentions Purchase habits	Anyone can say that they like your brand but can you measure the probability of intention to purchase? Furthermore, do you have statistics showing the frequency of purchase of your products or brands and can you therefore identify the heavy users?
	Loyalty (share of requirements and willingness to pay premium prices)	Are you able to predict future revenue streams by identifying the level of commitment existing customers have to a product or brand (this can be done by isolating the 'brand purchases' as a percentage of total category purchases by buyers of that brand)?
	Customer satisfaction	Not an exact science as there are many other variables that impact upon 'satisfaction'; nonetheless, it measures the likelihood of customers repurchasing – it also enables the organization to make adjustments to its service levels if customers show any dissatisfaction, hence enhancing customer loyalty as well
Step 4: Marketing strategies	Customers	Measures the number of individuals or households or online IDs that registered, ordered and/or bought from the organization
	Retention Average retention cost Recency	Retention measures the ratio of customers retained compared with the number lost or at risk Retention cost measures the spending on a per-customer basis Recency measures the length of time since a customer's last purchase When these are combined they enable the company to track and measure any changes in customer activity, and then take remedial action if necessary
	Customer profit	Customer profit is not often on an organization's radar, especially SMEs – it looks specifically at customer relationship management (CRM) in terms of the ratio between revenues earned and the associated costs of relationship development, and therefore measures which customers are profitable and which are actually costing the company money and therefore diminishing profits

11

(*continued on next page*)

	Customer lifetime value (CLV)	Measures a part of the customer relationship which shows the present value of the future cash flows that will be a direct consequence of the current relationship; therefore, an organization making decisions that pertain to CRM activity should do so on the basis of improving CLV
Step 5: Decisions about the marketing mix Here we take a look at marketing metrics that contribute to the measurement of the 4 Ps (product, price, place and promotion, including *media metrics*)	Trial Repeat volume Penetration	These three are linked from a 'customer product usage' perspective Trial focuses on the product usage by first-time users as a percentage of the target population Repeat buyers should be considered for the number of products they repeatedly purchase in any given period Penetration measures all the users in the previous period, multiplied by the repeat rate for the current period, as well as the new 'trials' in the current period Together, they provide a good picture of the population buying from the organization in the current period
	Year-on-year growth Compound annual growth rate (CAGR)	Measures the percentage change in growth from one year to the next To derive the most value, it should be used in conjunction with market share Whilst CAGR will not reflect the individual year-on-year growth, it is helpful in averaging growth rates over longer periods (which is especially useful for long-term marketing strategy planning)
	Cannibalization rate	As organizational product portfolios grow, and with new product development (NPD) rife within growing companies, the issue of 'cannibalization' becomes more and more apparent; here we measure the reduction in sales of existing products as a direct result of introducing new products, thus *cannibalizing* one's own product line
	Price elasticity of demand	Measures changes in quantity demanded in response to changes in price

(*continued on next page*)

Price premium	By analysing the percentage by which the price of a brand surpasses an industry 'average' price, we are able to measure how the price of a particular brand compares with that of its competition
Channel sales pipeline and its effectiveness	An analysis of where customers are in terms of the various stages of the sales cycle, thus enabling the organization to measure the current sales and forecast sales
Numeric distribution	This is the percentage of stores that a product is sold in; it enables the organization to determine the penetration it has accomplished within channels
Facings	Measures the current brand visibility *on the shelf* within participating outlets
Out-of-stock	Conversely to facings, measures the number of participating outlets that are showing they do not have any product for sale; this is a logistics problem and enables the organization to measure the differences between effective supply and demand
Channel margins	Evaluating the amount of 'channel value-add' within the selling price enables an organization to measure the channel profits as a percentage of channel selling price – a useful measure for comparing margins within the supply/value chain
Baseline sales **Incremental** sales (sometimes also known as 'promotional lift')	Helps an organization to ascertain the expected level of sales that would be achieved without any marketing activity Incremental sales refer to sales that, on the contrary, are attributed totally to the marketing activity carried out by the organization; the difficulty with this is that it is often problematic to ascertain all the other issues from the wider environment that may impact on sales, e.g. competitor behaviour
Coupon redemption rates	Measures the success of coupon 'lift', i.e. the number of people who actually used the coupons as a part of the transaction; it is calculated by totalling the coupons redeemed divided by the coupons distributed

11

(*continued on next page*)

	Impressions (also known as both opportunities-to-see and exposures)	Here we use the word *impressions* to understand literally how many times an online advertisement is loaded on a user's screen; however, it does not tell us the length of the 'view', i.e. whether it is merely a passing glimpse or a prolonged study – it is constructed by taking the *reach* (the number of people seeing it) and multiplying by the *frequency* (the number of times they see it), and is often presented as a cost per thousand impressions as this is easier to work with numerically than the cost per single impression
	Net reach	Net reach measures the estimated number of individuals in the audience for a promotional communications message that is reached at least once during a specific period of time
	Average frequency	Average freqency measures the strength of concentration of an advertisement on a particular population, i.e. the average number of times that an individual is exposed to and receives an advertisement
	Share of voice	This is the advertising *weight* of a brand and is expressed as a percentage of a defined total market or market segment in a given time period; the weight is usually defined in terms of expenditure, ratings, web presence, physical presence, etc
	Visits	The purpose here is to measure the audience traffic on a website Visits will measure the number of unique viewings a website has
	Page views	Page views measures the number of times a web page is opened
	Page hits	Page hits measures the retrieval of any item, such as a page or a graphic, from a web server – for example, when a visitor calls up a web page with nine graphics, that makes ten hits: one for the page and nine for the graphics; for this reason, hits are often not a good indication of web traffic

(*continued on next page*)

	Clickthrough rates	This is all about the effectiveness of web advertising Clickthrough rates count the number of customers who are suitably interested to click through the advertising shown
	Cost per click cost per order	The cost per click/order is calculated by taking the advertising cost and dividing it by either the number of clicks generated or the number of orders generated, respectively
Step 6: Marketing budget	Marketing spending	An analysis of costs that make up the total marketing spend
	Net profit	Measures the basic profit made and is calculated by deducting the total costs from the sales revenue
	Return on marketing investment (ROMI)	The purpose of ROMI is to measure the degree to which spending on marketing contributes to profits; as we have already seen in this chapter, marketers are under increasing pressure to 'show a return' on their activities – ROMI is the contribution attributable to marketing (net of marketing spending), divided by the marketing 'invested' or risked

CONCLUSION

One of the earliest examples of organized *marketing in action* is religion. Even though they will not consciously have called it '*marketing planning*', prophets of the world's religions used marketing activity in devising plans in order to attract customers to buy in to their products, services, beliefs and brands. For example, followers of the world's first **monotheistic** religion, Zoroastrianism, dating from approximately the 14th century BCE, believe in three core tenets: Humata, Hukhta, Hvarshta.

These three tenets, this philosophy of pragmatism based on a systematic approach, works very well as a foundation for *value-added* marketing planning:

'Good Thoughts, Good Words and Good Deeds'

(Three core tenets of Zoroastrianism)

- **Thoughts:** To solve problems in a complex business system and turn the workings to your advantage, you need to capture that complexity and seek to simplify it. Think about and examine the whole picture, not just the current marketing plan in isolation, because challenging issues rarely stem from a simple problem or have a simple 'magic bullet' solution. Understand how the whole system works – your organizational system and the competitive system that surrounds you
- **Words:** Learn from your experiences and from the organizations and industries that surround you. But remember that every individual, every business and every problem is unique. You should develop solutions that provide clear and transparent explanations to your organization – offering opportunities and choices that

11

match your organizational ambitions. View target markets from the outside in, placing the priority on your customer's perspective. Your approach should lead to conversations about continued change in the market, the aim being new and incremental growth opportunities and actionable market strategies that are bold yet pragmatic. These strategies should be accompanied by detailed road maps and tactical programmes so that you can realize tangible benefits now and in the future

- **Deeds:** Most of the expertise of an organization lies in the heads of those who work there, because expertise in marketing planning is not just about facts. It is about a perception of business patterns and 'gut feeling', about knowing how to react to circumstances, about knowing when something will work and when it will not. Your solutions and recommendations for action emerge from the commitment that your people personally dedicate to the problem

Believe in marketing planning; believe in keeping chaos at bay.

Case study
A taste of Malta

THE FIRST TASTE A TRAVELLER TO MALTA MAY have of Maltese wine is on an Air Malta flight. This context offers an opportunity to form an impression of Maltese wines and to stimulate interest in discovering them once in Malta. It therefore contributes to the awareness of Maltese wines amongst foreign travellers and to the recognition abroad of Malta as a country of origin for wines. The company that supplies wines sold on Air Malta flights, Delicata, has recognized the importance of having its wines on Air Malta flights as part of its marketing communications strategy, creating awareness of the brand name and signalling the importance of Delicata as the largest producer of wine in Malta.

istock © RadeLukovic

Air Malta, like other scheduled airlines, is under pressure to cut costs to compete with other (and particularly low-cost) airlines and this translates also to a squeeze on suppliers. These conditions lead the supplier to accept the supplier's role for the sake of prestige and brand exposure rather than for the profitability of the account.

Given this cost-cutting context, which is common to other scheduled airlines as well, the type of wine

in economy class on short- and medium-haul flights will be relatively basic. The traveller does not expect a wine of higher quality in such a context unless it is in business or first class. Served as it is in little plastic glasses, the red would not have the chance to breathe and a white is likely to reach the passenger underchilled. In sum, an entry-level wine is acceptable to the airline passenger. At a price to the traveller of £3/€4, it allows at least some margin of profitability for the airline.

Yet, does it seem that there is a missed opportunity? For a small country whose wines are largely unknown abroad, the flight offers an opportunity to expose the international traveller to Maltese wines – to quality wines produced in Malta, to literature explaining Maltese wine and to the promotion of wine tours as part of a growing wine tourism element in Malta.

The lack of a marketing communications strategy already in existence either on Air Malta flights or at Luqa International Airport is emblematic of the absence of a strategic plan to create awareness and promote the interests of the wine-producing sector in Malta, whether by the sector itself or by the government. Why this should be the case is explainable in large part by the structure of the sector in Malta in terms of the interests of the main producers and the international context in which the Maltese wineries are competing.

EU imports

With the opening of Maltese markets to EU imports, Maltese wineries sought to respond to the new competition in the Maltese markets by acting decisively on improving quality. To understand the reaction of Maltese companies to this competitive scenario, one has to consider how Maltese wine had a history of producing wine from imported grapes and juice that were in some cases mixed with locally produced wine. Faced with EU imports that were characterized by a superior price–quality ratio to Maltese ones, improving quality and establishing a *Maltese origin label* became a priority which led to the creation of the Maltese certification of origin (DOK), equivalent to the Italian DOC.

For the quality improvement programme to succeed, a necessary element was the expansion of vineyards in Malta and the control of the quality of production. As well as extending their own vineyards, the major wineries expanded their relations with local farmers. The two major Maltese wine producers (Delicata and Marsovin) adopted successful production models based on an organic expansion of production. Whilst they did in part expand their own estates, they also built a network of local producers, essentially buying in grapes from many small estates or even plots with comparatively low production. These suppliers were subjected to the same methods and quality control standards as their own estates, allowing uniformity in type and quality of grapes. As well as not necessitating the capital investment that would be necessary on expanding estates, this production model also had the advantage of flexibility compared with sourcing grapes solely from the company's own estates. The quantity of grapes purchased could be varied on the basis of projected sales and new relationships with farmer-suppliers forged if needed.

As Maltese grape production does not benefit from the lower costs associated with the economies of scale of larger foreign producers, the major Maltese wineries sought production models that would suit the particular Maltese conditions. The small farmer-suppliers benefited from having a stable buyer who would absorb their whole production and therefore avoid their having to be subject to the vagaries of the internal market. However, the competitive pressures placed on the wineries themselves have often transferred to the farmer-supplier, who has been squeezed on price.

The wineries and their offerings

Maltese wine producers, while varied in size, remain family-owned SMEs. There are five major independent producers of wine in the Malta region: Emmanuel Delicata, founded in 1907, Marsovin, founded in 1919, Meridiana, founded in 1985, Montekristo, founded *c*. 1995 and Camilleri Wines, established in 2000. All of the wineries offer some form of wine tasting or cellar tour.

Emmanuel Delicata

Customized tours can be arranged by appointment for groups of 12 people or more. Normally, these tours cover a historic overview of wine production at this wine producer, which has now been established for over a century. The cellar tour and wine tasting takes place in the historic tasting vaults, located underground at the site at Paola Waterfront. Over the past five years, a number of the Delicata wines have been entered into international wine competitions and many have started to win awards. This all started with the Grand Cavalier Chardonnay 2006, which won a Bronze Medal in the 'Chardonnay du Monde' competition in Burgundy. In addition to the wine tasting at the winery, Delicata offers another chance to taste its range of wines at a four-day wine festival, usually held in Valletta during August.

Marsovin

Again, tours also start off with a historic introduction but they also provide an in-depth explanation of the wine-making process. Visitors are then guided through to the cellars, where the red wines are maturing in over 200 French and American oak barrels. Guests are treated to a short film about the 'Cassar de Malte', the sparkling wine of Malta, which is made here using the same method as champagne – '*méthode champenoise*'. Marsovin wines are then served in the tasting area and accompanied by a variety of locally produced Maltese finger foods. Marsovin's wines can also be purchased in the well stocked retail outlet.

11

Meridiana

A short drive from Naxxar towards the national stadium in Ta' Qali is the Meridiana Wine Estate. The purpose-built limestone winery and administration building is surrounded by Meridiana's picturesque vineyards. Its expert and enthusiastic wine maker, Roger Aquilliera, is usually on hand to conduct wine tours and tutored tastings of a few of the hand-crafted wines. Given the sumptuous surroundings of the scenic 'inner court', visitors and guests can hire the venue for personalized wine tastings or other events. Meridiana's founder, Mark Miceli-Farrugia, has a real passion for Maltese wines. The company's mission is to produce 'world class wines of Maltese character'. This is perfectly reflected in the wines produced at this *boutique* winery.

Montekristo

In Hal Farrug, at the outer limits of an area called Siggiewi, and not too far from Luqa airport, is one of Malta's newest wineries – Montekristo Beverages and Vineyards. It is a 20-acre country estate which, at its heart, has a 'chateau' surrounded by a newly equipped winery and vineyards. Underground there are large, purpose-built vaults and the wine storage areas are temperature and humidity controlled. Although the site is still under construction and not fully open to the public, there are some banqueting, restaurant and conference facilities which are available to hire. This is very much a *full-service* offering.

Camilleri Wines

Further inland, in the town of Naxxar, is a young and dynamic winery called Camilleri Wines. The company started in 2000 and its first wine made wholly using Maltese grapes was launched in 2004. It now produces 21 wines under seven different labels. Camilleri also provides guests with an opportunity to indulge in a 'tutored wine tasting' where one can learn a lot more about the wine in a custom-made tasting area adjacent to the retail shop. If you come for a tasting here, perhaps you will get a chance to taste Malta's only *viognier* grape, from the Palatino range. In addition, visitors to Camilleri can visit one of the managed vineyards.

Wine tourism

Even with the rich **viticulture** and wine heritage in Malta, there is as yet no official 'wine route'. Visitors wishing to take a closer look at the Maltese wine industry will have to rely on their own organizational skills to make up a *wine-tasting tour*.

The Institute of Tourism Studies (ITS) had identified a need to provide information to the independent traveller in a project it calls '*relational tourism*'. It had hoped to have an area within the ITS website

where wine and viticulture could be identified as one of six areas of cultural interest. However, to date this project is still ongoing. All the Maltese wine producers had been involved and welcomed the project. When Mark Miceli-Farrugia, CEO of Meridiana Wine Estate, was recently asked whether there was any mileage in pursuing a strategy of wine tourism, he said: 'Whilst I was the Maltese ambassador to the US, everybody knew I was in the wine business, and I visited every large community of Maltese peoples, in amongst other communities. I didn't receive one enquiry about our wines except when they wanted it for free so I don't think we're there yet.' There are many models of wine tourism that exist around the world, and the Maltese government is keen to pursue a marketing strategy whereby wine tourism comes to the forefront of international marketing campaigns devised by the ITS. Of course, this is in addition to the more immediate and perhaps simpler issue of exporting Maltese wine.

Customer communications

The notion of these SMEs forging a direct relationship with customers in this relatively small community is somehow seen as redundant. The companies are already literally close to the community in the sense that the company premises, estates and vineyards are visible to a population that knows the island like the back of its hand. Even if people do not often go past the wine locations, knowing where things are and who they are owned by is part of small community and small island existence.

Promotional activities such as newspaper advertisements relating to fairs or promotions also achieve high visibility in a country with only three main newspapers. Similarly, promotional activities at the point of sale in supermarkets involve direct contact between people and the company in the form of its staff. These may involve printed material and the use of promotional staff in the supermarket aisle offering samples or special offers and discounts on purchase.

In the UK or other large nation states, creating a relationship with customers would take on a different connotation. The marketing methods typically used to establish a relationship – perhaps even a two-way relationship where the aim is to engage the customer actively with the company – may appear artificial to the consumer in a small community and seem a waste of resources to the company precisely because they appear artificial. This is not to say that such operations are not used in Malta and in fact they are used particularly by larger companies such as banks and main car importers, which deploy relationship marketing techniques. However, these family-owned SME wineries have invested their relationship marketing effort primarily at the B2B level in cementing the relationship with retailers, restaurants, bars, airlines and so on. At the customer level, the marketing effort was deployed on promotions, particularly price promotions such as multi-buy discounts or free bottles of wine with the next visit to certain restaurants. These elements were all forms of price promotion and also served to cement relationships with retailers which benefited from being able to offer a benefit to customers at no cost to them!

The retail environment

When investigating retail marketing practice, it was found that Maltese family-owned wineries adopted strategies that integrated a low-risk approach to product development. For example, the wine company with the largest variety of products, Delicata, put forward a diverse product offering so as to cover most mass-market price levels and some premium ones. Its marketing communications consisted of periodic promotional strategies operating at single store and restaurant level or through discounts and promotions in the print media. This approach seemed to be an expression of a low-risk mindset. The strategy of diverse product offering served to ensure different segments were targeted at different price points. This strategy was possible thanks to the availability of large shelf space in supermarkets, food and convenience stores, which exceeded anything available to a single producer in the UK. Instead of the prompt development or suppression of product lines, the retail stores allowed a strategy of displaying all product lines and responding to demand through gradually altering production in response to demand.

Summary

This is a complex situation yet holistic planning at every level seems underdeveloped. Do the wineries need a clearer B2C and B2B marketing strategy? Who is the target audience (internally within Malta, and externally outside Malta)? Who is ultimately responsible for the planning of such activity – the Maltese government, ITS and/or the wineries themselves? The necessity for an efficient strategic marketing plan in the region has been alluded to here, but needs to be agreed by local and central public authorities, wineries, viticulture specialists and societal representatives. Inputs into such planning activity will include the evaluation of existing markets and export markets, analysing Malta as a tourist destination using current promotional material, and establishing strategic goals (such as the volume of wine tourists, investment required, earnings from tourism activities and brand benefits). There undoubtedly seems to be a lack of bona fide communications strategies in place, and thus there is an opportunity to set in place a regional public–private partnership for the development of the wine sector. In order to answer such questions, it is necessary to frame a marketing plan using the seven steps of the marketing planning ladder shown in this chapter.

Sources

www.guidetomalta.net/articles/maltese-wine-malta-wine-tourism/ [(Accessed February 2012)
Braudel, F. (1996) *The Mediterranean and the Mediterranean World in the Age of Philip II*, University of California Press, Vol. 1, p. 150

11

Butler, L. (1966) 'The Maltese People and the Order of St John in the Sixteenth Century', *Annales de l'Ordre Souverain Militarie de Malte*, 24, p. 135

Ciappara, F. (2001) *Society and the Inquisition in Early Modern Malta*, PEG Publications, Malta, 2001, pp. 53–5

Sethna, Z. and Foxell, E. (2012) 'Exploring Maltese Entrepreneurial Marketing over a Glass of Wine', Academy of Marketing Conference 2012, University of Southampton

Questions

1 Critically assess the link between the Maltese wine industry and Air Malta. What are the likely marketing advantages and disadvantages that may result from such a relationship?

2 'For a small country whose wines are largely unknown abroad', develop an outline marketing plan aimed at taking on the established and well known market leaders.

Review questions

1 What are the seven steps on the marketing planning ladder? Identify and then discuss the importance of each step.

2 In order to compile a comprehensive plan, you will of course need a lot of detail. However, by applying the seven steps you have just identified to the outline case study (at the end of this chapter), you can start to put together a skeleton marketing plan for Maltese wine.

3 What are some of the marketing metrics that should be considered when making decisions about the marketing mix?

Group tasks

1 Through your period of marketing studies, you will have come to understand that marketing planning has never been the simple step-by-step approach described so enthusiastically in most prescriptive texts and courses, including this one! Back in 1992, Malcolm McDonald commented that 'the moment an organization embarks on the marketing planning path, it can expect to encounter a number of complex organizational, attitudinal, process and cognitive problems, which are likely to block progress'.

2 Using the seven-step planning ladder from this chapter, combined with your knowledge stemming from Macdonald's opinions above, create and compile a detailed marketing plan for a company of your choice (you may choose from any sector that you are familiar with). You should aim to identify and develop appropriate marketing metrics for that sector in order to measure the company outcomes.

Glossary/Key terms

Break-even point: The point where marginal revenue equals marginal cost. Upwards movements after this point indicate profits for a company.

Core competences: Unique skills and abilities that set a company apart from the competition.

Cost leadership: The ability to produce at lowest delivered cost in comparison with competitors.

Market share: Percentage of sales in a given market held by a company in relation to others competing in the same market.

Marketing plan: A document that assembles and summarizes marketplace conditions, and the strategies and specific actions to use to achieve stated objectives.

Marketing planning: The process of researching and analysing the market and situations and then developing marketing objectives, strategies and plans that are appropriate for the organization's resources, competences, mission and objectives, followed by implementation, evaluation and adjustments as needed to achieve the objectives (Wood, 2003, p. 3).

Mission: A statement of the main purpose of an organization, its focus and how it strives to position itself with stakeholders.

Niche market: A small segment of the market which may have a different set of needs.

Segmentation: A method of categorizing customers within a market according to similar needs, marketing habits or attitudes and which can be attended to using marketing techniques.

Vocab check list for ESL students

Detrimental	Mechanism	Plethora	Throttle
Endeavours	Misconstrued	Remedial	Trajectory
Incremental	Monotheistic	Strewn	Viticulture

Definitions for these terms can be found in the 'Vocab Zone' of the companion website, which provides free access to the Macmillan English Dictionary online at www.palgrave.com/business/Gbadamosi

Further reading

M. H. B. McDonald (1992) 'Ten Barriers to Marketing Planning', *Journal of Business and Industrial Marketing*, Vol. 7, No. 1, pp. 5–18

This paper provides a comprehensive insight into the problems usually encountered in the marketing planning process. It is seemingly outdated but most of the current publications appear to be regurgitating the same ideas, so it is better to get them from the original source.

F. Ekwulugo (2011) 'Marketing Planning in Small Businesses', in S. Nwankwo and A. Gbadamosi (eds) *Entrepreneurship Marketing: Principles and Practice of SME Marketing.* London: Routledge, pp. 356–66

This chapter may be attractive to marketing students as it relates the marketing planning process to small business contexts – an area that is ignored by many authors. This contribution therefore gives a different perspective of marketing planning because of its contextual focus.

M. Wood (2003) *The Marketing Plan: A Handbook.* New Jersey: Prentice Hall

This is a practical, action-oriented book. It guides readers on how to develop a marketing plan.

References

AMA (2007) 'Definition of Marketing' http://www.marketingpower.com/aboutama/pages/definitionofmarketing.aspx (Accessed on 23rd July, 2013)

Ambler, T., Kokkinaki, F., and Puntoni, S. (2004) 'Assessing Marketing Performance: Reasons for Metrics Selection', *Journal of Marketing Management*, 20, pp. 475–98

Blythe, J. and Megicks, P. (2010) *Marketing Planning: Strategy, Environment and Context.* Upper Saddle River, NJ: FT Prentice Hall

Burgess, J. (2012) 'The iPhone Moment, the Apple Brand and the Creative Consumer: From "Hackability and Usability" to Cultural Generativity', in L. Hjorth, I.

11

Richardson and J. Burgess (eds) *Studying Mobile Media: Cultural Technologies, Mobile Communication, and the iPhone*. London: Routledge

Campbell, A., Devine, M. and Yeung, D. (1990) *A Sense of Mission*. London: Hutchinson Business Books

CIM (2009) www.cim.co.uk/filestore/resources/10minguides/7ps.pdf (accessed on 10 June 2012)

Day, G. S. (1990) *Market-driven Strategy: Process for Creating Value*. New York, NY: The Free Press

Dibb, S., Simkin, L., Pride, W. and Ferrell, O. C. (2006) *Marketing: Concepts and Strategies* (5th edn). Boston, MA: Houghton Mifflin

Drucker, P. F. (1986) *Management Tasks, Responsibilities and Practices*. Truman Tulley, NY: E. P. Dutton

Farris, P. W., Bendle, N. T., Pfeifer, P. E. and Reibstein, D. J. (2009) *Key Marketing Metrics: The 50+ Metrics Every Manager Needs to Know*. Harlow: Pearson Education

Freytag, P. V. and Clarke, A. H. (2001) 'Business to Business Market Segmentation', *Industrial Marketing Management*, 30 (6) pp. 473–86

Henderson, B. D. (1979) *Henderson on Corporate Strategy*. Cambridge, MA: Abt Books

Hollensen, S. (2006) *Marketing Planning: A Global Perspective*. Maidenhead: McGraw-Hill

IBM (2011) *From Stretched to Strengthened: Insights from the IBM Global CMO Study*, www.ibm.com/cmostudy2011

Kohli, A. K. and Jaworski , B. J. (1990) 'Market Orientation: The Construct, Research Propositions, and Managerial Implications', *Journal of Marketing*, 54 (April), pp. 1–18

Kotler, P. and Keller, K. L. (2006) *Marketing Management* (12th edn). Englewood Cliffs, NJ: Prentice Hall

McDonald, M. (1984) *Marketing Plans*. London: Butterworth-Heinemann

McDonald, M. (2007) *Marketing Plans: How to Prepare Them, How to Use Them* (6th edn). London: Butterworth-Heinemann

Narver, J. C. and Slater, S. F. (1990) 'The Effect of a Market Orientation on Business Profitability', *Journal of Marketing*, 54 (October), pp. 20–35

Owen, A. A. (1982) 'How to Implement Strategy', *Management Today*, July

Oxford Minidictionary (1991) Oxford University Press

Piercy, N. (1997) *Market-led Strategic Change: Transforming the Process of Going to Market*. Oxford: Butterworth-Heinemann

Pook, S. (2001) 'Sex Shop is Fined because its Videos are "Too Tame"', *Daily Telegraph*, www.telegraph.co.uk/news/uknews/1318548/Sex-shop-is-fined-because-its-videos-are-too-tame.html (accessed 21 June 2012)

Porter, M. E. (1985) *Competitive Advantage*. New York, NY: The Free Press

Porter, M. E. (1990) 'How Competitive Forces Shape Strategy', *Harvard Business Review*, 57 (2), pp. 137–45

Sethna, Z. (2006) 'An Investigation into how Individual and Organizational Consumption is Affected when Dealing with SME Organizations from Emerging Economies', *Asia Pacific Journal of Marketing and Logistics*, 18 (4), pp. 266–82

Sethna, Z., Jones, R. and Harrigan, P. (2013) *Entrepreneurial Marketing: Global Perspectives*. Scarborough: Emerald Publishing

Treacy, M. and Wiersema, F. (1993) 'Customer Intimacy and Other Value Disciplines', *Harvard Business Review*, January–February, pp. 84–93

Wood, M. (2003) *The Marketing Plan: A Handbook*. Englewood Cliffs, NJ: Prentice Hall

12 MARKETING IN A GLOBAL CONTEXT

TAO CHANG & SHUYU LIN

MANCHESTER METROPOLITAN UNIVERSITY

CHAPTER CONTENTS

LEARNING OUTCOMES

The content of this chapter will help you to:

- Explain the importance of international marketing in the contemporary world of global business
- Understand the arguments for why firms go international
- Compare the differences between four main entry modes in relation to value delivery in a foreign market
- Apply knowledge of value delivery to planning and implementing international marketing strategy

Manchester United: A local club with global dominance

THE LONG AND CHEQUERED HISTORY OF Manchester United Football Club (fondly called *ManU* by the growing band of ardent supporters) brings to life one of the most popular clichés in contemporary marketing, which is, 'Think global, act local'. Anyone interested in the globalization of sports marketing need look no further than ManU.

ManU, formed in 1878, is probably one of the most popular football clubs in the world today and certainly the most successful in the UK. The club's triumphs in the field of football (20 times champions of England and 13 Premier League titles, in addition to European successes) simply exemplify its tenacity in continuing to reinvent itself through a strategic mindset as a global super star – promoting global networks of supporters and merchandising, and strengthening its market position through a continuous product development strategy (that is, acquiring world-class players). Masterminded by Sir Alex Ferguson in recent times, ManU is a club that is firmly rooted in its history and, importantly, uses this platform to gain global prominence.

The city of Manchester, where the Old Trafford hub of ManU is situated, is renowned in history as a pace setter in textile manufacturing during the

istock © creativedoxfoto

industrial revolution and, in fact, enjoys the accolade of being the 'world's first industrialised city' (Kid, 2006). From its local hub, ManU has literally achieved the status of an iconic brand. The club is one of the wealthiest and most supported in the world. After being floated on the London Stock Exchange in 1991, it took a pioneering position, and was the first football club in the world to be valued at more than $3 billion in January 2013. According to the popular press, ManU enjoys the highest average home attendance in Europe and also tops the list of 25 best supported clubs in Europe. Its fan base is truly worldwide, with 200 officially recognized supporters' clubs in at least 24 countries. In July 2010, the worldwide fan base was suggested to be around 333 million. This is largely the result of a skilful strategy in marketing itself globally (netting around £412 million from merchandising and a sponsorship deal that is said to be worth around £80 million).

For many football clubs in the first tier, the questions often asked are: how did ManU 'conquer' the world? Could that success be replicated? If so, how? Obviously, these are very open questions, leaving international marketing students scratching their heads for answers.

INTRODUCTION

The reason companies expand internationally and the value they derive or deliver by doing so have continued to engage the attention of both marketing scholars and practitioners. It is still not settled whether the 'dash for profit' or the 'drive for differentiation' (or both) is the primary motivator for globalization. Firms are interested in seeking to reduce the cost of doing business (for example, through low taxes, low production costs, nearness to raw material, closeness to new and emerging markets), which might make global expansion attractive. It is also possible that the underlying reason has to do with seeking to achieve stronger market differentiation by exploiting networks that extend the firm's customer value position in the market. Quite likely, both reasons (profit and customer value orientations) combine in some ways to explain why firms are interested in foreign markets because, fundamentally, both offer different perspectives of 'value'.

However, what is incontrovertible is that the world we live in today is increasingly interconnected and interdependent. Consumer values and types found in London may not be remarkably different from what may be observed in Mogadishu (Somalia). Consumer tastes and preferences are acquiring a global underpinning probably because of the effects of improving information technology across the world. At a macro level, the world economy is becoming more connected so that what happens in one part of the world quickly affects trends in other parts. A clear example was the recent banking crisis that started in the USA but led to recession in major economies across the world. Yet, there are some fundamental differences between markets and cultures across the world. These differences make international marketing a hazardous undertaking. Therefore, careful planning is necessary if success is to be achieved. The point has to be made that going abroad is not always profitable for companies.

Essentially, marketers are perpetually watching global trends to be able to figure out where new markets are springing up and where better economies of scale and scope may be obtained. This 'globalizing trend' necessitates a greater level of agility in marketing strategies designed to take advantage of global markets and consumer value opportunities. In this chapter, we will consider some of the basic arguments around internationalization of marketing in order to provide the foundation knowledge necessary for a deeper treatment of the subject at a later stage in the study of international marketing.

PERSPECTIVES ON GLOBAL MARKETING

Think and discuss

Select an international company. What features do you think make this company an 'international company'? In what ways might an international company differ from a local company?

The past 50 years have seen a rapid growth in international business activities as companies seek to expand their value-adding operations. For many, it has meant expanding their manufacturing infrastructure in 'low-cost' countries in order to bring down the price paid by the consumer and also afford better profitability prospects for the company. In other instances, firms seek new markets in order to satisfy consumer values which are increasingly becoming interconnected (sometimes referred to as the 'global consumer culture'). Thus, in expanding globally, firms have been presented with both opportunities and threats in highly competitive business environments. For an international company, it is imperative to develop marketing strategies in order to deal with constant changes in global contexts. In this regard, companies would also have to bear in mind the need to provide exceptional value to their customers while devising appropriate marketing strategies.

The international marketing phenomenon could be related to the English Premier League football clubs that are regularly seen in the summer months playing exhibition and friendly matches in Africa, Asia and in some cases South America. Whilst they should all be applauded in their attempt to export sporting excellence, gamesmanship and fair play, a deeper motivation might be that of the economic spend

12

generated by a growing fan base, international presence and brand development. The same can possibly be said regarding Tesco and its foray into the Chinese market – indeed, there are rich pickings to be had by those enterprises that successfully develop and maintain a presence in a new or emerging market. Examples include Walmart, which has successfully entered the UK market under the Asda chain of stores, which it now owns.

GLOBALIZATION DRIVERS

The standardization versus differentiation arguments seem to form the basis of international marketing strategies. Levitt (1983) proposed the idea of a *global village* and converging commonality resulting in homogenized tastes and a unified global market. Global organizations need to pursue global strategies and produce globally standardized products to achieve economies of scale. However, Levitt's globalization hypothesis has been challenged by scholars because many barriers exist to the standardization of products and strategies across different cultures and markets. Therefore, there is a growing argument that business needs to adapt products, production and marketing strategies to specific markets.

Many uncertainties are presented as firms go international. Nevertheless, some factors trigger companies to globalize their activities. For example, companies may globalize partly because:

- They are in search of growth and new markets
- They want to get closer access to sources of raw materials (closer to the source of raw materials means lower costs)
- They are motivated by the profit potential to be gained from international expansion
- They want to achieve cost minimization (for example, by locating and using cheaper labour)
- They are driven by prestige
- There may be more competition in their home country and less in foreign markets

Apart from the gains they may desire, it is important that companies take into account other factors when making internationalization decisions. The factors include:

- Knowledge of the market
- Availability of resources
- Entry strategies to be used
- The market environment

Think and discuss

To what extent do you think that 'culture' is an issue in international marketing? Use examples to illustrate your answer.

Obviously, this points to a range of challenges that are likely to confront an internationalizing firm. The challenges could be linked to cultural aspects because culture could profoundly influence consumer behaviour and business interactions. Culture could also impact the marketing mix (such as design perceptions or pricing perceptions). In many cases, international firms need to adapt to the way deals are negotiated; they need to be careful with names of products; they need to respect the culture of the host country. In addition, international firms are encouraged to guard against ethnocentric behaviour. Other challenges could include a broad range of risks (such as political risks). Each country has the right to allow foreign businesses to operate in its country or withhold permission for them to do business. They can encourage or discourage firms by offering specific support or incentives. It is also possible for

The rage against Nike over sweatshops

Nike is a well known global brand. Its 'swoosh' logo enjoys a mass appeal across different segments of the global market. This multinational, which adapted its name from the Greek goddess of victory, has certainly achieved victory in being a market leader in the sale of sports footwear, apparel, equipment and accessories. It is one of the world's largest suppliers of athletics shoes. Whilst the company is undoubtedly successful in the global marketplace, its iconic brand image has taken a battering over allegations about running sweatshops and using child labour in its production facilities in South–east Asia. It is accepted that the company did not directly operate the sweatshops but it has an implied obligation to ensure that its suppliers in foreign markets conform to accepted employment standards in its home countries. Thus, the highly publicized case of 'Nike sweatshops' (which seems never to end) demonstrates how vulnerable multinationals can be to what happens across the broad range of their value chain. There are many instances of multinationals that are metaphorically in Nike's shoes.

them to ban foreign companies or they can control the business environments by pursuing policies that may not be in favour of foreign companies.

International marketing activities are affected by the policies of both home and host country. However, one of the most profound concerns of international firms is the level of political stability in a foreign country. But each internationalizing firm must find a way to navigate and cope with the changing environment. Another crucial issue confronting international firms (and the general public) is how to adapt to the culture in foreign countries, especially how they deal with local labour forces, the environment and the manipulation of the marketing mix. Therefore, it is expected that each company seriously thinking of entering markets and wanting to achieve success there should practise good corporate citizenship and be responsive to various publics. This also includes pursuing the social and economic goals of the host country.

VALUE CREATION IN PRODUCTS AND SERVICES

Some scientists have claimed that the world is flat – and so it is in the international business context. For some companies, international expansion and globalization have become a vital aspect of strategy development and implementation. They proactively explore new opportunities to generate extra value appears worth pursuing. However, global expansion may at the same time increase competitive risks. That is, a company is more likely to expose itself to new competitors and a significantly sophisticated, entirely unknown market. Country economies differ substantially and each country contributes to the world economy as a whole with its distinct features. The main concern for international businesses about adding value is to balance the gains and the cost of trade. Companies will find the market very different across countries with regard to variations in pricing, wages, production costs, standard of living and business policies. Those differences create inequalities at the same time as significant business opportunities to add value. Companies can benefit from reducing

12

manufacturing costs by outsourcing to offshore factories. They can also gain advantages by hiring an overseas agent who has expertise in marketing and sales in the expanding region. In addition to the aforementioned benefits, the costs of entering international markets should be taken into consideration very carefully. Additional costs may arise from transaction costs, resource acquisition, transportation costs and overtime. For example, businesses need to pay the costs of searching for information about suitable manufacturers and negotiating with overseas agents, as well as dealing with contractual hazards when they occur. Also, products may take weeks to arrive from the exporting country, along with the rising cost of transportation. To maximize value, firms should analyse carefully all the aspects of the business operations internally, as well as external factors including suppliers, partners, competitors and, most importantly, customers, in a comprehensive and holistic manner. The reason for undertaking such analysis is that value can only be captured when the linkages of all the value-adding activities are well connected in an integrated manner. Any gaps that are found will lead to a failure of the business in the complicated global marketplace.

It is worth noting that the nature of value is dynamic, as it varies according to the different perspectives taken by providers and receivers. In the business context, these are organizations and customers. Judgements of value, from the customer perspective, are based on assessments of fit between quality and price. In other words, the fit is reached when the price the customer is willing to pay is equal to the level of need that is fulfilled. In most cases, customers expect the 'value' to exceed the price. If it turns out the other way (that is, cases where price exceeds value), then 'consumer dissatisfaction' sets in. As most marketers appreciate, consumer dissatisfaction will lead to high rates of consumer complaint behaviour and brand switching. It is often assumed that dissatisfied customers communicate their dissatisfaction with higher levels of frequency than they do when they are satisfied. That is, at individual consumer level, a customer who is dissatisfied tells at least four other people, whereas they will tell only two people when they have made a favourable purchase decision. This is a case of 'negative word of mouth' versus 'positive word of mouth' – the intensity of each scenario is determined by consumer value rating.

The way that a firm goes about creating the value that it intends to deliver to customers in the foreign country shapes the international marketing strategies of the firm (Rindova and Petkova, 2007). That is to say, value creation is an innovation-oriented activity and is one of the most important functions of a firm in that it leads to profit making (Priem, 2007). Moreover, a customer may be willing to pay extra for the added value which they perceive to be valuable and feel is worthwhile. This perceived value is judged according to the perception regarding the product or service prior to its actual use (Rindova and Petkova, 2007). Value capture, in contrast, is defined as 'the appropriation and retention by the firm of payments made by consumers in expectation of future value from consumption' (Priem, 2007, p. 220). In other words, this refers to the need to ensure that a firm's products or services meet customers' wants and expectations. Value can only be captured through an economic exchange of firms receiving payments from customers and customers taking products and services from firms. Further, the price represents the point where there is agreement on the value by the customer and the organization. In the international marketing context, the value delivery mechanism can be much more complex, subject to the level of commitment a firm considers making in the foreign market. This, as a result, shapes the international marketing strategy of a firm. Before explaining further the market entry modes in relation to value delivery, there is a need to clarify how a firm delivers value in general terms.

THE VALUE CHAIN

Firms based in the same sector may differ in the scope and type of their value chain activities in order to differentiate themselves from their competitors and satisfy the customer needs (Porter, 1985). This is because every organization has a set of firm-specific core competences and resources which are difficult for its competitors to imitate. There is no exception when it comes to developing and implementing international marketing strategy. In practice, firms first make choices about which internal functions to emphasize, de-emphasize and outsource to a third party. Decisions are made according to a company's strategic vision with regard to the market position which it pursues internationally. For example, a manufacturing company tends to prioritize production activities in an attempt to provide the best possible quality product to satisfy customer needs. In contrast, a distribution company is more likely to invest in enhancing reliability and efficiency of delivery infrastructure.

Developing firm-specific criteria for decision making is crucial to a firm's success. According to the notion of the value chain, the combination of business activities, both primary and support, creates a critical path to reap competitive advantage. It has been recognized as a systematic approach to effectively examining the development of competitive advantages in the marketplace. A company's value chain consists of the interrelated set of value-creating activities the company performs internally. Primary activities include inbound logistics, operations, outbound logistics, marketing and sales, and service. Support activities involve human resources, accounting and finance, technology and procurement. It is important to note that the primary activities and the related support activities together create value to the end-customers. They both certainly need each other in order to culminate in the total value delivered by an organization. To make the value chain function fully, the primary activities must first and foremost create and build value for customers and there is a need for support activities to facilitate and enhance the performance of the primary activities. The value chain is also a useful tool for companies to evaluate their marketing strategies in greater depth. They can gain a holistic view of a total package or a collection of primary and support value-adding activities undertaken in the course of designing, producing, marketing, delivering and supporting products or services launched.

Developing competitive advantage linkages between the value chain and the firm-specific core competence will provide information about which value-added businesses the company should invest in further. Such possible linkages are strategically important developments in the international expansion context since the linkages are often unique to the organization and difficult for competitors to imitate.

12

EasyJet powers global marketing strategy on customer value

Established in 1995 by UK businessman Sir Stelios Haji-Ioannou, of Cypriot origin, EasyJet set out to revolutionize the airline industry through its 'no frills' service orientation. With a fleet of around 200 aircraft and 8,000 employees across Europe, EasyJet aims to make 'flights as affordable as a pair of jeans'. However, internal rancour saw the company going adrift until three years ago, when a new marketing director was appointed. By 2010, the once well loved low-cost airline had been recording the worst punctuality record in Europe, profits were low and customer satisfaction levels had taken a nose-dive. The newly appointed marketing director latched on to innovative technological devices which put customer value at the centre of the recovery process. These, in turn, have fundamentally helped to bring the airline back to profitability.

Using a mobile platform and apps, and supported by excellent customer relationship management (CRM) systems, the company de-cluttered the process of travelling and improved the customer experience of flying. Remarkable improvements have been evident in the process of booking flights, making changes to booked flights and ticketing (the company intends to achieve completely paperless ticketing before the end of 2013). Also, real-time customer information is provided seamlessly in different languages. These innovations have de-stressed the boarding process and improved the overall process of airline travel. Customers have responded positively. EasyJet's Luton and Gatwick hubs are once again buzzing; annual profits increased by 28 per cent in 2012 despite the difficult time most airlines faced during the year, and the share price rose 150 per cent. The company moved from being the worst in punctuality to being the best at Luton and Stansted airports, adding more planes and more routes and outperforming rivals – for example, on the lucrative London to Moscow route.

istock © BrianAJackson

WHY COMPANIES INTERNATIONALIZE

As we have said, the reasons or factors driving a firm to internationalize are many and varied. Different situations may trigger internationalization and these may differ from company to company and from sector to sector.

TRIGGERS FOR MARKET INTERNATIONALIZATION

Straightforward treatments of this topic are provided by Lowe et al. (2011) and by Ibeh and Analogbei (2011). From their discussions, it appears that two principal factors account for why firms may seek to go international: adverse conditions in the home market and opportunities in the foreign market.

According to Lowe et al. (2011, p. 292), adverse home market conditions could include factors such as:

- The high cost of doing business or overregulation
- Downturn in the local economy or poor economic growth
- Increased competition from international suppliers
- Rising costs of moving inventories to foreign markets
- Large volumes of stock which cannot be sold, probably due to weak demand
- Underutilization of managements talents and skills
- Underutilization of production capabilities
- Need to spread risk across several markets

Foreign market opportunities may include:

- Identification of specific and attractive profit and growth potentials
- Identification of potential for competitive advantage in foreign markets that may be gained by repositioning current products or services
- Public policy support for export promotion, such as tax incentives given to companies that export their products
- Public policy incentives in foreign market environments – for example, many developing countries are giving all sorts of incentives such as tax holidays, free access to land or subsidized infrastructure support to foreign companies wishing to invest in their countries

In their work, Ibeh and Analogbei (2011) suggest three interrelated factors:

- Person-specific factors (decision-maker variables): These are instances where a new chief executive officer (CEO) decides to change strategic direction by focusing on foreign markets. The emphasis is on personal factors that drive the internationalization process. These include the CEO possessing certain characteristics, such as:
  - Having a global vision
  - Having international experience
  - Being internationally proactive
  - Being highly networked
- Firm-specific factors within a company that may include:
  - Possession of knowledge-intensive assets, such as specialized skills or resources, or innovative products that could be uniquely marketed in foreign markets
  - Possession of high-quality differentiated products – for example, if a company produces the sort of product that only it or a very few others know how to produce
  - Provision of a superior level of service which is valued and demanded in foreign markets
  - Pursuit by the company of an aggressive growth strategy
  - Identification of a market niche and the firm positively pursues a niche marketing strategy
- Firm's environmental factors: These are the wider environmental factors and incentives to which a firm may be drawn. They might include:
  - The firm is offered helpful support programmes
  - The firm is offered quality supporting infrastructure

12

BARRIERS TO MARKET INTERNATIONALIZATION

International market spaces are dynamic and changing at such a fast pace that firms are increasingly having difficulties in coping. Your knowledge of the marketing environment will readily bring to mind the wide variety of influences likely to impact an international marketing operation. Put simply, some of the barriers to international marketing are likely to arise from (Lowe et al., 2011):

- Language and cultural barriers
- Currency compatibility and transfer of capital
- Navigating the maze of rules and regulations, which may be unfamiliar to the international marketer
- Lack of trained manpower in foreign countries, especially in less developed countries where there is an acute shortage of well trained workers
- Lack of transparency in market dealings, especially corruption and other forms of unethical practices – much of which may be unlawful in the home markets but lawful in foreign markets
- Instability of governments, especially in many developing countries with weak public administration systems. Many of these developing countries are where newer markets are emerging and are therefore attractive to international marketers

Think and discuss

To what extent do you think that 'culture' is an issue in international marketing? Use examples to illustrate your answer.

Example 12.3:
Turkish Airlines: A carrier with global ambition

Turkish Airlines has a much broader global reach and network than most people realize, but the company, which previously played shy, is now taking steps to assert its competitive power as a global carrier. In fact, the company flies to more countries than any other airline in the world. It is one of the fastest growing in Europe, and has the third largest and youngest fleet (meaning that it has a collection of newer aircraft relative to the competition). It also has a strong global niche marketing strategy – noted for some of the places (e.g. Somalia) that only it and a few other airlines serve, and it offers the best coverage throughout Africa of any major airline.

Reproduced with permission of Turkish Airlines

Underpinning the company's growth ambition is its customer value orientation. For example, 'most airlines offer a better standard in economy class for a higher fare but Turkish offers a standard that is effectively Business Class "elite" and normal Business Class is closer to what counts as First Class in many airlines' (Business Plus Magazine, April 2013). Other ways of stretching customer value are a strong focus on food, providing an inflight chef for Business Class passengers on long-haul flights. Relentlessly, Turkish Airlines is not only challenging for a top spot as a global carrier but also consistently reinforcing value-adding services to strengthen its competitive base.

- Unfavourable operating conditions in foreign markets, such as the state of the infrastructure

MARKET ENTRY MODES

The process through which firms enter foreign markets (entry mode) is an important element of a firm's market entry strategy. Very often, firms have concerns about the level of control they are able to exercise over critical resources in foreign markets (see Figure 12.2). Anderson and Gatignon (1986) indicated that full control modes are based on sole ownership while shared control modes are based on collaboration. To investing firms, different entry modes represent varying levels of control, commitment and risk (Dunning, 1988; Shenkar, 1990). There are four entry modes that are generally considered when entering foreign markets. These are exporting, licensing, joint venture and manufacturing. Each has particular advantages and shortcomings, depending on company strengths and weaknesses, the degree of commitment the company is willing or able to make and market characteristics (Ghauri and Cateora, 2010).

Figure 12.1: Critical resources

R&D | Production | Logistics | Marketing | Sales | Service

EXPORTING

Exporting refers to situations where a firm manufactures products in one country and transfers them to markets in another country. This is probably the easiest way to gain a presence in international markets. However, there may be problems in the form of tariffs and barriers, as well as the cost of transport, which may increase the price of the product. On the positive side, this mode reduces the potential risks of operating overseas, especially when a firm knows little about the market. This method also gives firms an opportunity to familiarize themselves with a foreign country before deciding to relocate manufacturing overseas.

If a company attempts to minimize the costs associated with expanding overseas, it could choose to export goods from its home market to foreign countries. Exporting can help the company to save the costs associated with setting up wholly owned operations abroad. Many companies take exporting as the easiest approach to start their entry into foreign markets. Through this method, firms may not have many liabilities compared with other modes of entry. However, producing goods in a foreign country could sometimes prove much cheaper. There are usually high transportation costs associated with exporting. In addition, tariff barriers can hinder exporting.

When it comes to value delivery, exporters must work closely with other business partners that have expertise in importing, logistics and distribution. In other words, partnership relationships are crucial so as to have products and services available to end-consumers. Without partnering with other businesses based in the foreign country, the company is unlikely to deliver value through exporting goods to the customers across borders. For example, any organizations engaged in exports

12

require the services of a customs clearing agent and freight forwarder. These partners offer a series of services for managing customs clearance for imports and exports through the ports and airports to ensure a smooth process of exporting goods to another country. Logistics procedures, including booking air or shipping space and arranging documentation, are handed over to a trusted local company based in the foreign country rather than being handled by the exporter. The host company mainly has the responsibility for product development and production but relies on the contracted firms to complete the rest of the value-added activities based on their expertise. The advantages and disadvantages of exporting are summarized in Table 12.1.

Table 12.1: Advantages and disadvantages of exporting

Advantages	Disadvantages
• Realize economies of scale • Avoid the manufacturing set-up cost • Higher domestic employment • Foreign exchange generated	• High transportation cost • Trade barriers and tariffs for imports • Problems with foreign marketing agents

LICENSING

A licensor grants the right to a licensee for the use of a trade name – for the distribution of imported products or for the use of production processes – for a specific period. In return, the licensee needs to pay a royalty fee to the licensor. By adopting this mode of entry, firms do not need to invest significant capital to establish a presence overseas. This allows another firm in an overseas market to offer a service or manufacture a product for a fee paid to the originator. Firms can also avoid the risks and costs of establishing a wholly owned subsidiary. At the same time, firms

It is not only SMEs that embrace the licensing approach. Large organizations in the luxury sector also adopt this entry mode to penetrate foreign markets. Burberry is a perfect example of an organization granting licences to break into the Japanese market. In Japan, Sanyo Shokai and Mitsui & Co. are granted the licence agreements to design, produce and market exclusive ranges which are only available in Japan and other Asian countries. Apart from royalties paid to Burberry on a monthly basis, both licensees must achieve minimum monthly advertising and marketing targets. And despite Burberry not being able to fully control the licensees, they are still able to put control mechanisms in place subject to contract.

For example, in 2009 Burberry amended the apparel licence with Sanyo Shokai and Mitsui & Co. with the aim of increasing profits. It raised royalty payments and operating profit increased by approximately £4 million. In addition, enhanced performance criteria based on higher levels of production were introduced. Finally, it was specified that the licence agreement would expire five years earlier than planned (Burberry, 2009).

Near-to-market capabilities benefit the company by eliminating the challenges of managing a foreign market from a distant host country with limited local market intelligence. Also, such exclusive use of licensed third parties in Japan allows Burberry to deliver customer value to a defined market by integrating the local expertise, knowledge and commitment of established and reputable regional organizations.

Starbucks open in India

Starbucks brought its coffee shops to India through an $80 million Indian joint venture with Tata Global Beverages (Financial Times, 2012). The plan was to expand rapidly by having Starbucks coffee shops available to the public in all the major cities and second-tier towns

istock © davincidig

in a year. The 50/50 joint venture was formed as Starbucks recognized the challenges and risks that would be involved in seeking to enter India's $450 billion retail market without a local partner. In addition, not only the coffee shops but also Starbucks' products are available to the Indian market through Taj Hotels and the TajSATS airline catering business. These two businesses are both part of the Tata group, one of the most recognizable conglomerates in India.

can avoid the hidden cost of import tariffs and documentation. Many small and medium-sized enterprises (SMEs) favour this mode of entry. It could be used as a supplement to exporting or manufacturing. It will also help firms to deal with political uncertainty. However, adopting this mode will not allow firms to have 100 per cent control on licensees. It would appear that this mode could be the least profitable way of having an overseas presence. In addition, it can be difficult to get adequate licensees and supervise them. See Table 12.2 for a summary of advantages and disadvantages.

Table 12.2: Advantages and disadvantages of licensing

Advantages	Disadvantages
• Control over operational and strategic decision making in foreign countries • Low resource commitment • Low capital risk • Protection of trademarks	• Lower profit potential • Passive interactions with the market • Creates possible future competition • Disclosure of critical knowledge in innovation

JOINT VENTURES

Joint venture refers to firms from one or more countries establishing a brand new firm in the expanding market. A joint venture is usually owned by two or more firms in different countries. Compared with exporting and licensing, a joint venture would require larger investments and more commitment from an investing firm. However, it is better positioned in the local market with help from a local partner. There will be fewer problems understanding the local culture and language than with wholly owned subsidiaries. As it is a joint effort and entity, different risks and costs will be shared as well. In particular, economic risks and political risks would be shared. However, it can be difficult to maintain sole control of core technologies when there is a partner. The two parties may have different views with regard to implementing policies and ideas and gaining control of internal and external affairs. This market

12

entry mode will lead to better supply chain integration. Also, such a high-involve-ment entry strategy will allow the firm to have stronger control over the situation and, at the same time, to have opportunities to create a tailored approach that suits the local situation.

Organizations can benefit from rapid expansion as well as increased productivity and capacity by adopting the joint venture approach. Added value is created through sharing resources with the selected partners. Joining forces enables a company to access distribution networks, reduce risks and costs through sharing, and access greater resources and expertise in the local context. The resources and expertise are found in the area of the main business functions along the value chain. In other words, forming a joint venture is a strategic endeavour for acquiring critical resources and bridging the gaps that may in fact be linkages in the value chain. For instance, using the partner's customer database for marketing purposes may be effective when trying to take a product to a specifically defined market where a foreign firm may have limited experience and have to depend on the local partners' knowledge. Table 12.3 summarizes the advantages and disadvantages.

Table 12.3: Advantages and disadvantages of joint ventures

Advantages	Disadvantages
• Partners bring complementary resources and expertise to the new firm • All parties supply financial capital • Better relationship with local organizations • Better adaptation to the local market	• Culture differences among joint-force parties • Conflicts over how the business should be operated • Disclosure of critical information based on knowledge sharing and exchange • Less control over operational and strategic decision making

MANUFACTURING

In contrast to the joint venture entry mode, manufacturing will allow firms to have 100 per cent ownership. This entry mode is sometimes referred to as creating a wholly owned subsidiary.

There are two main ways of establishing a wholly owned subsidiary. A firm could set up a completely new operation or it could acquire an existing firm in a foreign country. In other words, firms can either adopt a greenfield strategy by establishing a subsidiary from the ground up, or acquire an existing enterprise in the target market. By so doing, the investing firm will be able to have full control of the entire opera-tion. This gives the organization the great opportunity to engage completely in global strategic coordination and at the same time experience local economies. Example 12.6 is a good illustration of the notion: *think global, act local*.

Data protection is another consideration in relation to establishing a wholly owned subsidiary. This is because firms are likely to be better able to integrate and manage the information system without exposing sensitive data through a wholly owned subsidiary than through other approaches such as joint ventures and partnerships. In addition, businesses can take advantage of cheap local labour and reduced transportation, and can explore suitable raw materials. This is particularly the case in less developed countries. The company will not lose its core competence, in particular its core technology. However, as the result of full commitment and

Tesco enters the Hungarian market

In 1995, Tesco entered the Hungarian market by acquiring an existing retailer, S-Market. This was Tesco's first attempt at operating an international business. Since then, it has expanded and become the fourth largest employer in Hungary, with 115 hypermarkets and 90 smaller stores across the country. Tesco then sought international growth by replicating its successful business model in other foreign markets. Today, Tesco operates in 14 markets across Europe, Asia, and North America.

Tesco believes that the key word for success is 'local'. That is, all retailing operations are local. More importantly, the company effectively applied its key knowledge and business value in the global context to benefit performance and sharpen its competitive edge around the world. By so doing, Tesco delivers incredible value to its diverse customer base through exercising its worldwide universal corporate strategy of understanding customers and aiming to be the first to meet their needs in each of the local markets.

high involvement in operating in the foreign country, this entry method could be risky and the most expensive mode. The advantages and disadvantages are summarized in Table 12.4.

Table 12.4: Advantages and disadvantages of manufacturing

Advantages	Disadvantages
• Lower transportation costs • Quick response to local demand • Access to local market intelligence	• Higher-level resource commitment • High country risks

THE INTERNATIONAL MARKETING ENVIRONMENT

Over the past four decades, fundamental shifts have been occurring in the world and these are having an impact on the international marketing environment. Examples are the emergence of Brazil, Russia, India and China (the BRIC economies) as dominant economies in the world. The rising economic power of China, for example, has remarkably altered patterns of world trade and global investment flows. Another interesting development has been the growing role of regional economic blocs such as the European Union (EU), North American Free Trade Agreement (NAFTA), Central American Common Market (CACM), Association of Southeast Asian Nations (ASEAN) and Economic Community of West African States (ECOWAS). These economic unions may influence the cost of doing business internationally through restrictive practices (such as the imposition of tariffs/trade barriers and all sorts of regulations relating to mergers, acquisitions, investments, production practices, capital remittances and quality standards).

In general, the environment of international marketing is not fundamentally different from the environment discussed in Chapter 2. In summary, key elements include:

● International economic environment. This may include consideration of factors such as:

12

Example 12.7:
Lessons from the launch of Ford B-Max

Marketers, both practitioners and theorists, have had to learn important lessons from Ford. The company's founder, Henry Ford, provided marketers with the cliché, in relation to its Model T car in 1930, 'you can have any colour so long as it's black'. Marketers have used this statement to capture the thrusts and problems of mass production (production orientation, discussed in Chapter 1). Marketing lessons from Ford did not stop with the Model T.

In order to turn around declining European sales, the B-Max, with which yet again Ford has redrawn the boundaries in marketing strategy, was launched in 2012. The conventional industry practice has always been to be secretive and keep the market guessing about new product development. In the case of the B-Max, its launch was preceded by about nine months of promotions – the longest ever for Ford prior to introduction of a new product to the market. The market reacted positively to this new idea – with pre-orders going above 1,000 (equivalent of £20 million in sales for the model).

The new approach saw Ford overhauling its marketing communications strategy by being more selective in the choice of channels to use. The company chose a few channels which it felt could deliver desired business objectives more effectively rather than use all available channels as had previously been the case. For example, it teamed up with the *Daily Telegraph* and Global Radio as part of the B-Max campaign, offering readers and listeners access to exclusive events. Based on the successful pre-launch campaign for B-Max, the company is eager to replicate the approach for future models. To underline the shift in strategy, Ford's UK Marketing Director had this to say: 'Previously marketing was slightly condescending to customers by not talking about new models until about two weeks before launch. It was often regarded as negative, but now we take the front-footed approach. Because people want to talk about it, we may as well embrace it' (*Marketing Week*, 11 October 2012, p. 4). Simply, this is a classic customer value management approach.

- Stage of economic development (usually classified as developed, developing or subsistence economy). The stage of economic development may impact the prospects of international marketing. For example, the TRIAD (EU, North America and Southeast Asia) controls about 90 per cent of world trade in manufactured goods
- Income per capita: High income per capita economies signify rich markets and a high level of international activities
- Exchange rate fluctuations: Fluctuations in exchange rate which affect the value of a nation's currency could positively or negatively influence international marketing activities
- International social and cultural environment:
  - Culture: Differences in culture are probably one of the most formidable factors impacting international marketing. However, with increasing globalization, the impact of culture is no longer as severe as it used to be. Nevertheless, the international marketer must be sensitive to cultural issues relating to specific norms and

values, attitudes, religion, modes of dressing and etiquette. For example, it would be 'marketing suicide' to attempt to export pork to Saudi Arabia or Kuwait

- Language is also an important factor in international marketing, not so much by way of personal conversations but in marketing communication. It is quite easy for international advertising targeting a local audience to use phrases, slang or abbreviations that may be repugnant in the local market or put the company in a poor light

- International technological environment:
  - Ease and depth of use of internet technology
  - Access to telephone services
  - Extent of development of general technology infrastructure: This has an impact on manufacturing capabilities, product distribution and supply chain management. A poor state of technology adversely affects international marketing operations

- International political-legal environment:
  - Political risk assessment: Political conditions are an important consideration. It does not make sense to invest in politically unstable places where violence may put the firm and its resources in jeopardy
  - Labour conditions: Labour conditions are internationally different (see Example 12.1) and need to be monitored
  - Legal instruments: Tax laws, import/export requirements and other regulations may affect international marketing
  - Rule of law: It is important to assess the credibility of the judiciary in order to assess whether the rule of law effectively applies in a specific market environment. This has implications regarding legal protection of investments, lives and properties

INTERNATIONAL MARKETING STRATEGY

International marketers are frequently faced with a range of decisions that they have to make to be able to compete effectively. Making a decision to 'go international' and the mode of entry are only a part of the decision. They will also have to decide which products to market internationally and how to price, distribute, promote and segment the market in ways that help to deliver value to the consumer and, in return, achieve competitive advantage.

International marketing strategy is simply about putting all the building blocks together – making both short-term and long-term decisions that lead a firm to achieve its international marketing goals. By and large, these decisions revolve around the controllable elements of the marketing environment, largely the marketing mix.

In summary, elements of international marketing strategy comprise:

- Product strategy: Decisions about which product (tangible or intangible) to offer to the market in order to satisfy the customer
- Pricing strategy: Decisions about how to set a profitable and justifiable process
- Distribution strategy: Decisions about how to get products to reach the consumers who need those products, where and when they want them
- Promotional strategy: Decisions about promotional tools to connect customers

12

Example 12.8:
Westfield: Redesigning the future of spaces

Shopping used to be a boring and unexciting activity … well, for many. However, with the emergence of mega shopping plazas such as Westfield, the landscape of shopping is changing dramatically. These mega shopping arenas are not simply providing spaces for buyers and sellers to exchange goods, services and monies. They

istock © Declofenak

are also seeking to improve the enjoyment of shopping so that shoppers will keep coming back.

Westfield's iconic centres in both west and east London are a glimpse into the future of the shopping experience. The centres could pass as a hub for all sorts of networking activities, with a place to meet, shop and eat, and a full calendar of arts and educational activities. To ensure that it remains a 'premier league player' in the provision of unique shopping experience as well as a leisure destination, Westfield is adopting all-embracing digital technology channels aimed at reaching shoppers directly through their mobile devices. Through a range of interactive technology (such as mobile apps, emails and SMS), targeted information about marketing events and promotions is sent directly to those with relevant interests. For example, shoppers with children might be sent information about kids' TV characters appearing at Westfield. The overarching goal in the marketing planning approach is to deliver value to shoppers seamlessly.

effectively with the company and its products

- Segmentation and targeting strategy: Customer-oriented marketing begins with a clear understanding of the customer group(s) to serve, their unique needs and values

STANDARDIZATION AND DIFFERENTIATION

Think and discuss

Research Starbucks and McDonald's. What do you think of their international marketing strategies? Try to establish whether they pursue standardization or differentiation strategies.

The controversy over whether firms should standardize their products for international marketing purposes or customize for specific markets has been ongoing for some time. There are advantages and disadvantages in each approach and it seems the only agreement is that firms should standardize as much as possible to achieve scale economies and increased factor efficiency whilst providing as much differentiation as the foreign market needs (Maktoba and Nwankwo, 2009).

Highly competitive international firms guard their supply chain jealously and often source factor inputs from fewer suppliers that are integrated with their control processes. The quest for international competitiveness in many cases instigates a strategy of standardization. Highly standardized products have easier access to the international market than customized products because of the tendency to achieve wider market penetration based on price competitiveness. This strategy could lead to the achievement of greater efficiencies and to gaining economies of scale. It has also been pointed out that the degree of marketing standardization is significantly higher in a wholly owned subsidiary than in joint ventures. Therefore, adopting the standardization approach to serve the international market may be desirable in so far as developing identical products across national markets can increase the company's trade. However, the standardization approach may lead to some difficulties which may undermine the international operation. A recurrent criticism of standardization is the tendency towards ethnocentrism – that is, treating foreign markets as if they were mirror images of the company's home market.

CONCLUSION

International marketing has been practised for centuries – as far back as people started exchanging goods and services across national boundaries. However, the field is constantly changing. This is as expected because the world we live in is in a perpetual state of flux. Some areas are economically growing and offering new opportunities while others are declining and becoming risky for business. At the same time, capital movements, transportation and communications across global frontiers have become much easier and more transparent. An increasing wave of migration and population movements is also shifting market bases and segments as never before. The wave of change affecting all facets of international marketing seems far reaching. This calls for careful planning in how firms approach international marketing.

Additionally, international marketing is no longer the exclusive preserve of multinationals and large companies. Small companies have become increasingly agile. Interconnectedness in the global supply chain might result in an individual-owned small company in a remote part of Africa supplying raw materials to a manufacturing company in Hong Kong. Therefore, for small, medium and large businesses, developing an international marketing mindset is not an option but a necessity.

Case study
The UK designer fashion industry

IN CREATIVE INDUSTRIES SUCH AS FASHION, availability and accessibility of required resources have a huge positive influence on innovation success. Given the naturally lean resources, designer SMEs (small and medium-sized enterprises) tend to enter the foreign market by adopting methods that require less involvement since they do not have sufficient resource base to support heavy investment with high risks of failure. Exporting is the perfect example here. Attending trade shows to exhibit their new collections is considered the most effective approach for exploring exporting opportunities by connecting with international buyers. This is because trade shows create a group selling environment by bringing hundreds of buyers to meet designers at one specific venue within a defined date range. The designers then are more likely to benefit from maximizing foreign sales accounts through showing their collections to numerous buyers from all over the world whom they would not be able to see during the off-selling period. The ready-to-wear trade shows are part of the Paris, Milan, London and New York Fashion Weeks. The UK-based fashion designer Michelle Lowe-Holder attends regularly to showcase her collections to potential buyers.

The increasing importance of selecting the best-suited trade fairs for the product relies on thorough research about the different events. In other words,

12

attending trade shows is a strategic conduct that should be in line with the overall corporate strategy in relation to international marketing policy. In practice, designers state that showing at the same place for a few seasons is crucial for the label to be recognized. This not only encourages the press and buyers to reinforce their recollection of the label but also shows how much commitment and determination the designer is devoting to the business. This is consistent with the theory stating that exporting should be the first step for businesses seeking international expansion opportunities.

Designers, generally speaking, start their first exhibition in the country where they work and were educated. This is because they are much more familiar with the marketplace and it is relatively

istock © illustrart

less expensive than showing abroad. As the business grows, they may start to attend more than one trade show globally with the aim of tackling a wider range of markets. The decision therefore has to be made about which tradeshows have the potential to accomplish the set objectives of brand awareness and boosting sales. The results can be very positive as the business is able to gain exposure to buyers worldwide. The London-based fashion designer Karl Donoghue considers that using sales agents in foreign countries can also be viewed as an effective approach to expanding horizontally into international markets. Since financial constraints have become less active, hiring sales agents to deal with orders and set up

showrooms across countries is more feasible. This is another form of knowledge sharing. The advice from the contracted agent is valuable with regard to gaining an understanding of consumer preferences when entering a foreign market. Knowledge sharing and acquisition become increasingly intensive alongside business growth. More possibilities for accessing external knowledge are found by developing professional networks. Networking then has been proven to be beneficial since it enables designers to improve continuously with regard to providing excellent product-based creativity or to enhancing the innovation processes associated with production and commercialization in particular.

With business growth, designer SMEs start to consider additional involvement in a selected foreign market. At the same time, they are also aware of the risks. Thus, collaborations with existing clients based in the foreign country become a less costly and risky choice. Karl Donoghue explained that developing an exclusive range with the local boutiques or department stores allows designer SMEs to extend their control mechanisms from design to marketing and retailing. Also, this gives designer SMEs opportunities to connect themselves better with the local consumers without investing in their own retail outlet. The idea of collaboration enables them to test the market through delivering a relatively experimental range made of new fabrics and designs, price points. It could also be beneficial to use collaborations as an opportunity to present the range as a completed concept via visual merchandising that would be seen later in the store. The result has reflected a possible way for designers to expand into a new market before they are fully committed to the decision. Sometimes designers deliberately use collaborations as stimuli to refresh their ideas of market expansion. It is therefore easy to understand the reason why designers evaluate and select the collaborative partners very carefully since the decisions must reflect the designer SME's brand image. Given this, they tend to work on an exclusive range with their long-term clients or companies in a similar high-end fashion segment.

Questions

1 Given the challenges for designer SMEs to enter international markets, what do you believe should be a business's priorities for planning and implementing an international marketing strategy?

2 Why did designer SMEs choose to collaborate with the existing clients of local retailers such as boutiques and department stores, and with what benefits?

3 To what extent should designer SMEs balance their international marketing strategy to exploit existing market intelligence? To what extent should they continue to explore foreign market opportunities as the company grows?

Review questions

1 How would you define international marketing?
2 What are the main foreign market entry modes in the global market context?
3 Describe different types of market entry strategies that an enterprise can adopt.
4 Compare and contrast the market entry strategies in terms of involvement, risks and value delivery.

Group tasks

1 Identify 25 of the world's leading global marketers, judged by sales volume. There are databases to help you, such as Global 100, which may be accessed through www.forbes.com or Google. From this list, choose a particular company that you are interested in following on online platforms. Explain why you have chosen this particular company. Then answer these questions:

  ● What makes the company unique?
  ● To what would you attribute its success (if successful) or failure (if a failing company)?
  ● What potential weaknesses do you see in this company?

2 Suggest what you think could be done for the company to keep or improve its ranking position in the future.

Glossary/Key terms

CRM (customer relationship management): Strategies and tools that a company uses to drive relationship programmes intended to bring the company closer to its customers.

Differentiation: The process of establishing distinctions between competing firms and products.

Economies of scale: Cost advantages that a firm may gain through increased production.

Exchange rate: The price of a nation's currency in terms of how it can be exchanged with another country's currency.

Factors of production: Land, labour and capital.

Global village: The notion that the world is so interconnected that national boundaries are not severely deterrent to international business transactions and consumption.

Globalization of market: The breaking down of national market frontiers and emergence of a huge world market.

12

International business: Business conducted across national boundaries.

Standardization strategy: This happens when a firm engages different markets with the same products, without much attention to the need to adapt the product for specific markets.

Strategy: A course of action followed by a company to achieve its goals and objectives.

Supply chain: Total sequence of suppliers and activities that contribute to the creation and delivery of products.

Value chain: Different components and activities through which value could be created in the production and marketing of products.

Vocab check list for ESL students

Applauded	Ethnocentrism	Liabilities
Commonality	Imperative	Niche
Conglomerates	Judiciary	Subsidiaries

Definitions for these terms can be found in the 'Vocab Zone' of the companion website, which provides free access to the Macmillan English Dictionary online at www.palgrave.com/business/Gbadamosi

Further reading

I. Doole and R. Lowe (2008) *International Marketing Strategy: Analysis, Development and Implementation* (5th edn). Cengage.

This is probably one of the best textbooks on international marketing, clearly written and with good examples based on a European/UK perspective.

K. Ibeh and M. Analogbei (2011) 'International Entrepreneurship and SME', in S. Nwankwo and A. Gbadamosi (eds), *Entrepreneurship Marketing: Principles and Practice of SME Marketing*, pp. 273–84.

In many cases, international marketing is associated with large business. But small businesess can also engage in international marketing, made much easier by advances in information technology. This chapter brings into focus the SME contexts of international marketing.

References

Anderson, E. and Gatignon, H. (1986) 'Modes of Entry: A Transactions Cost Analysis and Propositions', *Journal of International Business Studies*, Fall, pp. 1–26

Burberry plc (2009) 'Amendment of Licence Agreement in Japan', www.burberryplc. com/media_centre/press_releases/2009/2009-10-02 (accessed 3 July 2012)

Dunning, J. H. (1988) 'The Eclectic Paradigm of International Production: A Restatement and Some Possible Extensions', *Journal of International Business Studies*, 19 (1), pp. 1–31

Financial Times (2012) 'Starbucks Plans $80m Indian Joint Venture', www.ft.com/cms/s/0/901708e0-4b55-11e1-88a3-00144feabdc0.html#axzz1zfw2Ypie (accessed 3 July 2012)

Ghauri, P. and Cateora, P. (2010) *International Marketing* (3rd edn). New York, NY: McGraw-Hill Higher Education

Ibeh, K. and Analogbei, M. (2011) 'International Entrepreneurship and SME', in S. Nwankwo and A. Gbadamosi (eds), *Entrepreneurship Marketing: Principles and Practice of SME Marketing*. London: Routledge, pp. 273–84

Kid, A. (2006) *Manchester: A History*. Lancaster: Carnegie Publications

Levitt, T. (1983) 'The Globalisation of Markets', *Harvard Business Review*, May–June, pp. 92–102

Lowe, R., Doole I. and Mendoza, F. (2011) 'Cross-cultural Marketing Strategies', in Nwankwo, S. And Gbadamosi, A. *Entrepreneurship Marketing: Principles and Practice of SME Marketing*, London: Routledge, pp. 285–308

Maktoba, O. and Nwankwo, S. (2009) 'Influences of Firm Characteristics and Host Country Environment on Foreign Market Involvement', *Journal of Global Academy of Marketing Science*, 19 (2), pp. 7–18

Porter. M. E. (1985) *Competitive Advantage*. New York: Free Press

Priem, R. L. (2007) 'A Consumer Perspective on Value Creation', *Academy of Management Review*, 32 (1), pp. 219–35

Rindova, V. P. and Petkova, A. P. (2007) 'When is a New Thing a Good Thing? Technological Change, Product Form Design, and Perceptions of Value for Product Innovations', *Organization Science*, 18 (2), pp. 217–32

Shenkar, O. (1990) 'International Joint Ventures. Problems in China: Risks and Remedies', *Long Range Planning*, 23 (3), pp. 82–90

12

13 SOCIAL MEDIA MARKETING

CHRIS IMAFIDON

UNIVERSITY OF EAST LONDON

CHAPTER CONTENTS

LEARNING OUTCOMES

The content of this chapter will help you to:

- Understand the impact of social media on marketing
- Explain the major components and tools of social media
- Evaluate the effectiveness of social media tools
- Outline and discuss the advantages and disadvantages of social media in marketing
- Explain how social media enhances value for consumers and businesses

Marketing in action
US presidential elections: Marketing Obama

IN 2008, SOCIAL MEDIA WERE JUST GAINING popularity all over the world, which coincided with Barack Obama's first campaign. John McCain of the Republican Party stood no chance – he had fewer Twitter and Facebook fans. According to statistics regarding use of social media, Obama had more than 2 million friends on Facebook while McCain had only 600,000. The video broadcasting site, YouTube, played a significant part in the campaign. More than 1,800 videos were published to the channel by Obama's supporters, which received about 115,000 subscribers compared with John McCain's YouTube channel with only 28,000 subscribers during his first-term election in 2008. Also, SM played a phenomenal role in Obama's re-election in

2012 – leading some to suggest that Obama's presidency is partly a creation of social media.

In 2012, according to a research by Pew Internet, 22 per cent of registered voters informed others of how they voted through social networking sites such as Facebook and Twitter. In addition, about 25 per cent of Barack Obama's supporters posted their presidential preferences compared with 20 per cent of Mitt Romney's followers. Furthermore, 30 per cent of registered voters were encouraged to vote by friends and family through various posts and tweets on social media platforms. '*Four more years*' was the phrase that President Barack Obama used to announce his re-election on Twitter. Eventually, it became the most popular tweet ever with over half a million 'retweets'.

INTRODUCTION

Web-based social media (SM) are today the most used application tool connecting businesses and customers and markets. The effect of SM on product, service, place, idea, and social and 'personality' marketing is widespread. In fact, its effective deployment for marketing purposes is proving to be a major source of advantage. The growing usage of SM indicates a huge platform for individuals and organizations to connect with the outside world and advertise their products and services free online. With the world's most popular social networking site, Facebook, having over 1 billion daily logged-in users, it has become an indispensable marketing asset for branding and general marketing.

In modern times, firms operate in highly complex and competitive environments in which more and more customers are demanding the creation of value. Increasingly, companies are also regarding customer value as a major avenue for seeking

Example 13.1:
Product branding using Twitter

There are over 10 million people in the UK who use Twitter. Today, nobody thinks that social networking is only for young people and techie geeks. Any individual or organization that is not utilizing social media would be missing out on opportunities to promote its skills, services or products or, at the very least, a chance to raise its profile within its sector and globally.

Source: https://twitter.com/ChrisImafidon

Image: The Twitter page of the author Chris Imafidon (@ ChrisImafidon)

Think and discuss

Use any internet search engine to identify a company that is presently 'trending'. Outline the reasons why the company is trending and the role of SM in the process.

competitive advantage. Against the backdrop of growing interest among firms in creating and delivering superior value to customers, SM tools have become very important for relationship building, networking and bonding.

The term 'social media' is not totally new. As individuals, we have constantly kept social connections with family, friends and colleagues at work. However, the world wide web Version 2.0's technological advances have radically changed almost everything. It simply made our networks visible, accessible, virtual and flexible with enormous speed. As of 2 March 2013, over 1 billion people are registered on Facebook (Checkfacebook, 2013) and over 500 million registered active users are on (Smith, 2013).

SM, commonly referred to as Web 2.0, is the means through which people interact and share information in a community. Web-based SM is the electronic interaction between two or more persons via a web application or social networking site (SNS) (Paula, 2010). The web has now become a primary source of knowledge, SM being the focal point as it accounts for one in every six minutes spent online. Furthermore, when it comes to data sharing, the volume of content circulated in SNSs is quite staggering. Every minute, 60 hours of video is uploaded to YouTube, 3,000 images go up on Flickr and more than 700 YouTube links are tweeted (CIPR, 2012).

SOCIAL MEDIA OVERVIEW

DEFINITION OF SOCIAL MEDIA

SM has many definitions based on the background, context and perceptions and usage of the individual or institution. It is commonly defined as interactive tools that allow users to generate and publish dynamic contents while communicating and building communities around the world (Magda and Hana, 2012).

SM can be described as an online social experience driven by the sharing of digital **artefacts** such as posts, images and videos. It is a flexible system that allows users to edit their contents through access control settings. Clearly, this is a great development with positive implications for marketing.

13

CONCEPTUAL DESCRIPTION OF SOCIAL MEDIA

From the mid-1990s, attention has been dedicated to understanding the interactive functions of the internet. Early scholars observed that the internet was used mostly for interpersonal communications. The evolution of SM (for example, Facebook, MySpace, Twitter) has significantly increased online platforms for social interaction, and as the trend continues to grow, a study revealed that more than 50 per cent of SM users regularly maintained profiles and interacted on multiple social networking platforms (Hampton et al., 2011).

Most SNSs provide free services such as allowing users to:

- Create a public or semi-public profile within the system
- Express and maintain a list of other users with whom they share a connection, commonly referred to as 'friends' or 'followers'
- Blog about any issue of interest, such as their moods, current affairs, business
- Traverse their list of 'friends' and those made by others within the system

A recent development by Facebook is the functionality for users to perform specific graph searches on places and events which their 'friends' have been to, and so much more. Globally, Facebook still leads with over 901 million 'monthly active' users worldwide with a total revenue of $5.1 billion in 2012. The rise of SM in 2012 gives no indication that the technology will fade out any time soon. If we look at it more critically, it will become clear that the usefulness of SM relates to many segments of society such as job seekers, fun-lovers, and marketers who are interested in communicating value to their target markets.

STATISTICS AND USAGE OF SOCIAL MEDIA

As a specific example, a recent US survey by the Pew Research Center (2012) shows that young adults use major social networks more often than others. Some 67 per cent of internet users utilize the services of Facebook, while 16, 15, 13 and 6 per cent of internet users use Twitter, Pinterest, Instagram and Tumblr respectively (Pew Internet, 2012).

People under the age of 50 regularly surf SNSs of all kinds and users between the ages of 18 and 29 are the most likely of any demographic group to do so. Moreover, women are more likely to use SM services than men, with urban more dominant than rural users.

Nevertheless, something that is becoming very clear now is that the use of social media is on the increase and the popularity is spreading across different consumer groups. This informs us of the huge potential it has for the marketing of products and services.

PREVIOUS TRENDS IN SOCIAL MEDIA

The swift expansion of information technology has made SNSs gain huge attention from the masses. The concept of social networking simply evolved from varying social needs, such as creating or strengthening relationships and searching for people with like minds and interests, as well as information and knowledge sharing.

In 1995, the creation of classmates.com introduced a new trend in the world of information and communications technology which changed the way people used the web. It was the dawn of Web 2.0. The site, created by Randy Conrad, allowed users to find and connect with old friends from the same school. Currently, Classmates has more than 40 million active users in the United States and Canada.

The Classmates SNS was the best way to meet old classmates just before the boom of SM in 2003/04. Ironically, today, it is seen as a dinosaur that extorts users for features that most SNSs provide without a cost. One of the pros of the site is the huge registration rates and integrated events that make finding old classmates and planning reunions quite fast. However, these pros comes with a few cons such as a cluttered user interface, which makes it tiring to use, and charging for the use of features that must compete with new, innovative features that other SM sites provide for free (Davies, 2010).

Later, in 1997, sixdegrees.com was developed with a different concept that allowed members to list friends, acquaintances and family members with the aim of seeing connections with other social networks. The site, which was founded by Andrew Weinreich, an entrepreneur-cum-internet executive, was simply based on a contacts-style type of SM. The founder drew his inspiration from the myth that every person is connected to every other person by no more than six steps, popularly known as 'the six degrees of separation', combining features that are found in modern contemporary social networks which enhance online dating.

Unfortunately, Sixdegrees faded into obscurity after a decade of prominence during which it leveraged the support that SNSs such as Facebook enjoy today. Some analysts have suggested reasons why Sixdegrees did not last long, such as the under-development of web technology, which was unable to support features needed to enhance the utilities of the application. Moreover, inadequate finance limited the site to engaging its audience through the development of programme-driven features. Other factors include its inability to make a profit from online advertising, caused by the post-April 2000 recession as well as the tragic incidence of 9/11. A major cause of this was the fact that the online advertising industry was not mature enough at that time to support the business model of sixdegrees.com. Although the website closed its services in 2007 with a million users, it has since reopened for old members to use but does not permit registration by new users (Sixdegrees, 2013).

Other social networking websites started adopting the system introduced by Class-mates and Sixdegrees. In 1999, cyworld.com, a South Korean SNS, was launched with the functionality that allowed users to have spaces that were 'apartment like', relating to a 'sim-world' type of experience. In 2005, a survey revealed that 25 per cent of South Koreans were active users of the site. The 'cy' in Cyworld stood for cyber for many people, but it plays on the Korean word for 'relationship'.

Cyworld is an innovative SNS that comprises various services including profile pages, online fans' music, regional communities such as 'Ou Yu', 3D virtual space and 'Mini Life'. In the site, users can express their individual identities and meet old and new friends.

As technology began to skyrocket, 21st-century SM users witnessed a dramatic twist as the innovative trend of Web 2.0 continued to blossom. In 2002, friendster. com was born, the website that currently has 90 per cent of its traffic from Asia and is used for dating and finding new events, groups and hobbies. The site has over 115

Think and discuss

Do you think that SM is becoming increasingly disruptive to people and business or is a great marketing tool? Set up and justify your argument.

13

million registered users, attracting 61 million visitors every month.

Similar to most SNSs, the features of Friendster allowed users to communicate with other users, share online content, brands and hobbies, and discover current trends and events. At its prime, the site reached tens of millions of registered users, but it lost its popularity and was bought by MOL Global in December 2009 for $26.4 million (Davies, 2010).

In February 2013, researchers at the Swiss Federal Institute of Technology (SFIT) investigated Friendster, Live Journal, Facebook, Orkut and MySpace with the aim of identifying the survival factors of SNSs as well as their ability to withstand the ever changing environmental and user demands. In 2009, Friendster suffered some technical problems due to a comprehensive redesign and users started seeping away. It closed down in 2011 but later reopened services as an online gaming and dating platform. Findings from the SFIT research, led by David Garcia and co-authored by Pavlin Mavrodiev and Frank Schweitzer, explained social pliability as the 'ability of an online community to deal with certain environmental changes', particularly the graphical user interface (GUI) of an SNS. In addition, if the costs involved with being a member of an SNS far exceed the perceived benefits, then users are likely to leave, along with their collective connections. All these problems may lead to the alienation of the social site (Garcia et al. 2013).

Before the demise of Friendster, the cost-to-benefit ratio dramatically increased as a result of comprehensive user interface and technical malfunctioning. This surely proves that the environmental structure (design) of an SM impacts significantly on its success.

The year 2003 saw the meteoric rise of myspace.com, which became the most popular SNS in the US in 2006, with its hundredth million account created. The **empirical** advancement of the MySpace site has been credited to the staff of eUniverse, who were working with Friendster, saw the huge potential of online social networking and then mimicked the popular features of the SNS (Friendster, 2003).

MySpace, which has its headquarters California, United States, is currently ranked the 255th website in the world according to Alexa Internet (April 2013). The social network offers functionalities for creating networks of friends, personal profiles and groups, and uploading media contents such as photos, videos and music (Mashable, 2013).

One of the likely questions that will come to our mind while reading these previous tends in social media is 'how do these relate to the marketing of today?'. One notable relevance of these trends lies in the area of word-of-mouth (WOM) communications between consumers. When consumers have an opportunity to relate with one another freely, there is a high probability that they will share information about the goods and services that they use and even advise others on consumption decisions.

THE EVOLUTION OF WEB 3.0

Let us now look at another important area of social media and marketing communications – Web 3.0. The world wide web (commonly known as 'the web') is a techno-social digital artefact that enhances human cognition, cooperation and communication (Aghaei et al., 2012). Web-based communication has taken over from phone-based and face-to-face communication with fewer limitations in local communities. The mobile structure of the internet has enabled the convenience of global communication (Helm et al., 2013). The increase in fixed and mobile broadband has provided an architecture for a richer multimedia communication environment. The outcome has been a swift diversion from a **polarized** communication system to a multi-content style of communicating.

Web 1.0 represents the first implementation of the web, which is widely considered as 'read only' web (Aghaei et al., 2012). In other words, the early evolution of the web allowed users to surf for information with little user interaction. Web 1.0 is a simple mono-directional system which businesses used to present products and services online for visitors to 'read only' and then contact them if interested. The initial goal of website owners was to establish an online presence as well as making information available at any time to anyone. The functionality for a user to contribute to web contents and interact with other web users has changed the structure of the web (Aggarwal et al., 2012). For instance, SNSs such as Facebook and Twitter totally depend on user data upon registration and daily updates to operate successfully.

In the last two decades, technological advances have brought more social interaction, profile creation and communication than ever before and of course many implications for marketing. Some postulations have pointed to one of the main causes as the spread of broadband internet, although advances in web applications have greatly impacted this development. Web 2.0 plays a significant role not only for societies and communities but also for established enterprises.

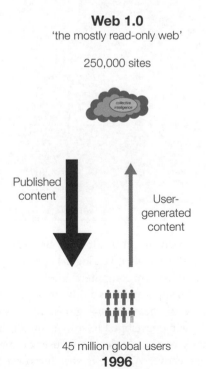

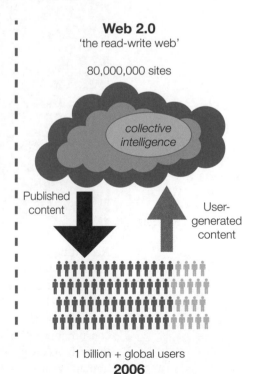

Figure 13.1:
Comparing the impact of structural changes to the web
Source: Aggarwal et al., 2012

Web 2.0 was defined as a combination of economic, technological and social trends that forms the foundation for 'future' internet (Spivack, 2011). The authoring of web content has been shifted from platform providers to the end-users, making the web an attractive and active environment (see Figure 13.2). End-user contributions to web authoring actually began when various platforms provided flexible functionalities for sharing individual contents without the ability to change them, using tools included in these platforms. Some examples of these services are youtube.com and wikipedia.org.

The next phase of Web 2.0 began when users were able to customize parts of the media platforms using software plugins and widgets to change the core patterns of the platform according to individual preferences.

A trending innovation driven by Facebook is the enabling of application programming interface (API), which allows users to add applications to individual accounts and share contents with added applications. Embedding rich applications with the extensive use of opened APIs adds additional functionalities to profiles in the form of video uploads and image slide shows. This expands the diverse potential for user interaction, making Web 2.0 the de facto standard for modern web design frameworks (Aghaei et al., 2012).

Web 1.0	Web 2.0
Reading	Reading/writing
Companies	Communities
Client-server	Peer to peer
HTML, portals	XML, RSS
Taxonomy	Tags
Owning	Sharing
IPOs	Trade sales
Netscape	Google
Web forms	Web applications
Screen scraping	APIs
Dial-up	Broadband
Hardware costs	Bandwidth costs
Lectures	Conversation
Advertising	Word of mouth
Services sold over the web	Web services
Information portals	Platforms

Figure 13.2: Comparing Web 1.0 and Web 2.0
Source: Aghaei et al., 2012

According to world wide web inventor, Sir Tim Berners-Lee, Web 3.0 could be defined as **semantic** web. This means it is a logical approach in the art of web technology which can be understood by computers. The ability to enable websites to be deciphered by machines and applications is a milestone dealt with by Web 3.0.

Currently, the structure of the web is a global file system designed for user consumption. Web 3.0 is being developed to solve some of the existing problems of the web. As a web of data sets, a semantic web focuses on machines first and brings humans as a second perspective. Web 2.0 is structured on building communities, content sharing, blogs and tagging, such as through Wikipedia, Google and Facebook. Web 3.0 is structured around individuals, lifestreams and user engagement and, most especially, around consolidating dynamically created contents, such as through Dbpedia and iGoogle (Aghaei et al., 2012).

Still in conception among web technological advances is Web 4.0. Although this stage in web development has not been thoroughly **elucidated** in simplistic form, machines would be intelligent in understanding web contents and would execute them using the dynamics of artificial intelligence to make fast decisions on websites to load first with quality performance and commanding interfaces (Spivack, 2011).

Web 4.0 can be categorized under the read-write-execution concurrency of the web, which may function in a manner similar to an operating system to achieve a huge mass of online participation, providing global distribution and collaboration between vital communities such as social, business and politics. Technocrats have predicted that Web 4.0 will be parallel to the human brain, which means a robust web of intelligent interactions such as the Siri application developed by Apple.

Blogging and micro-blogging

The term 'blog' was coined from the word 'weblog'. It is simply an unlimited web-based content-sharing framework proposed by Jorn Barger in 1997. Blogs are included in web pages called 'posts' and are published chronologically. Most blogs are text-based, but recent developments in web-craft have seen instances of photo blogs, video blogs and podcasts. The most popular blogging platform is Wordpress, which is a free open source tool as well as a content management system driven by PHP and MYSQL. Wordpress has the functionality to nest multiple categories of posted articles as well as providing the user with autonomous control of all blogs from a dashboard. This approach is now being used by many organisations in various sectors of the marketplace to interact more closely with their customers.

A recent development in the blogosphere is the introduction of the SNS called Tumblr, which allows registered users to effortlessly blog about anything of interest. Users can post large volumes of text, photos, quotes, links, music and videos from sources such as browsers, smartphones, personal computers and emails, irrespective of the physical location of the user. As with Wordpress, users can control the contents created on the site from the dashboard (Tumblr, 2013).

Micro-blogging is a new technological advancement in Web 2.0 as a medium for communication. Unlike other social network services, the relationship between users can exhibit a multidirectional flow in connection and communication. In micro-blogging websites such as Twitter, the number of content authors can easily attain the order of hundreds of thousands, with users participating in various topics of interest popularly identified by hash tags (such as #topic). A frequently used feature of Twitter is the 'retweet' button, which gives a user the ability to share a tweet of interest irrespective of the content (Child et al., 2012).

The professional rewards of blogging: How Twitter explores this goldmine

As discussed above, the important characteristics of Web 2.0 include community and collaboration, employing the services of modern SNSs such as Twitter, Facebook, Yokos and YouTube.

13

Online marketing through user-to-user interaction (word of mouth) is highly multifaceted and difficult to influence. A tremendous SM technological tool, used in propagating this trend of user-to-user marketing, is micro-blogging – a communication service embedded in the Twitter social network. Within the Twitter application, micro-blogs are short comments that users write publicly to 'followers' in no more than 140 characters. This micro-blog is commonly referred to as a tweet and the process of micro-sharing or micro-updating is popularly referred to as tweeting. The paradigm of micro-blogging allows SM users to share sentiments about various brands with other people in a pattern that supersedes previous methods of online marketing (Su et al., 2010).

Reproduced with permission of Twitter

Most tweets are premeditated and targeted for effective marketing and can assert, promise, warn or inform users. Although micro-blogging is gradually taking over mass communication, it may be detrimental to the users concerned if sensitive micro-blogs get to the wrong people with malicious intentions (Child et al., 2012).

Micro-blogging affects brand knowledge, which may lead to determining the outcomes of consumer behaviour. Typical consumer-to-consumer (user-to-user) and business-to-consumer (company-to-individual) interactions can easily be traced to brand satisfaction. Therefore, a company's tweets and replies to tweets or retweets on its micro-blogging accounts affect brand acceptance and, most especially, trust, which they work tirelessly to promote.

Macro-blogging is a term used to describe the interconnections of all weblogs. A macro-blog is a website dynamically controlled and maintained by a user who publishes current trends or personal opinion on issues, and keeps story dairies and journal articles, without any content limits. Related contents of macro-blogs may contain photos, videos and podcasts as seen on the macro-blogging website Tumblr.

Macro-blogs are good platforms for businesses to establish and grow their brands. Some bloggers create rich contents that enhance a multidimensional flow of information through the traffic they generate. Studies have demonstrated that more than 80 per cent of internet users are keen on receiving personalized information from the sites they visit. This means adverts should mainly be based on the page contents of the website and not necessarily the demographics of the visitor (Child et al., 2012).

Macro-blogging allows users to express their interests to any capacity. During blogging, active comments reflecting sentiments about a business organization or product may be made. Macro- and micro-blogging have created dynamic marketing strategies for many businesses to promote their products, brands and services with minimal cost compared with traditional advertising media (newspapers, TV and radio). Considering Twitter's prospects, there are paid and free services that allow users to operate successful accounts. These services strategically suggest potential followers for subscribers' accounts – that is, people who could be receptive to their marketing.

The goal of SM marketing is not just to inform consumers about products, but to understand the core needs of customers. For example, web applications such as 'Tweepi' and 'Twellow' help users to find people with the most followers (Twellow, 2013). The blogging functionality of social networks is one of the greatest techniques for building discussions around trending events. For example, the Twitter hashtag (#) placed before any word enhances the visibility of that particular topic. This lets users navigate easily to issues that captivate their interests.

One of the biggest questions relating to the issue of micro-blogging is: how does Twitter generate revenue as the platform provider?

Twitter made a public announcement in April 2010 about a new alternative to online advertising (Jansen et al., 2009). The idea was to offer various businesses the opportunity to purchase promoted tweets that would appear in search outputs made on the site. Interestingly, this became a landmark in the income-generating capacity of Twitter as companies such as Red Bull, Sony and Starbucks subscribed immediately. Studying the 'who to follow' section on Twitter's sidebar, one almost always notices that the top account listed has a 'promoted' icon attached to it.

A brilliant cash flow idea by Twitter is the functionality added for businesses to upgrade their profile pages to enhance brand awareness. Although this comes with monetary costs, the functionality allows subscribed users to add their personal logos or use any other form of visual branding on their profiles such as images and video links, which are highly engaging.

TYPES OF SOCIAL MEDIA

We have already discussed a range of SM tools. An account of these cannot be exhaustive because newer tools and applications are being introduced frequently. However, here some of the most dominant platforms (at least, for now). Later in the section, LinkedIn will be used for deeper illustration.

- **Twitter:** This is a fast-growing platform, with 16 per cent of internet users making use of it. A demographic profile of users shows that the majority are under 50 years of age, with the largest proportion in the 18–29 age bracket
- **Pinterest:** Launched in 2010, this online pinboard has attracted 15 per cent of internet users to its virtual scrapbooking. The majority of users are upwardly mobile, with women dominating
- **Facebook:** This SM giant remains the most used social networking platform in the world (see Figure 13.3). Two-thirds of world internet users claim to have active Facebook accounts. Women are more likely to use Facebook than men, most especially adults between the ages of 18 and 19.

13

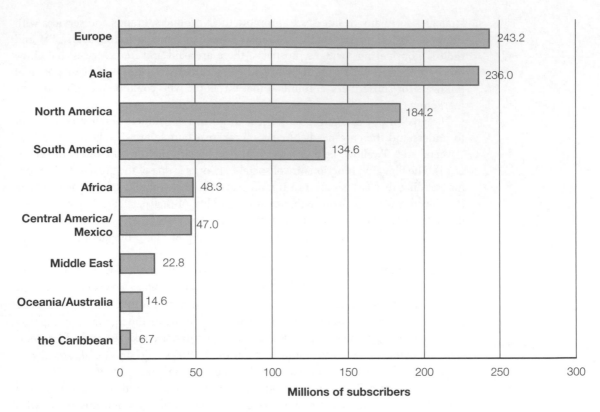

Figure 13.3: Worldwide Facebook usage, September 2012
Source: Internetworldstats, 2012

LINKEDIN: THE MOST TRUSTED SOCIAL MEDIA SITE

LinkedIn is regarded as the world's largest professional SNS with over 200 million users (LinkedIn, 2013). According to a survey in May 2012 of 1,900 LinkedIn users, 87 per cent trust the SNS as a source of information affecting decision-making. The mission of LinkedIn is simply connecting professionals in the world, making them more successful and productive. The site grants its users access to people, jobs, news, updates and insights that help career and professional development (Auradkar et al., 2012).

LinkedIn is the number one SNS for business professionals searching for bigger opportunities. Members of the site are widely considered to be influential regarding decision making, and there is more confidence in the information content of the site than for other SNSs. Trust is a necessity when it comes to being active in a web-based SNS. An SM void of trust may lose its integrity and gradually depreciate (Sorensen, 2009).

Since May 2003, when LinkedIn was launched, many SNSs have evolved and most have adopted the profile-centric structure approach A few SM sites such as LinkedIn are focused on developing professional social networks for their users. The company, founded in 2003 by CEO Reid Hoffman, is funded by Greylock, Sequoia Capital, Bain Capital Ventures, Bessemer Venture Partners and the European Founders Fund (Jennifer, 2009).

When LinkedIn was launched, the five founders (Reid Hoffman, Allen Blue, Konstantin Guericke, Eric Ly and Jean-Luc Vaillant) invited 300 people to join and within a month it had registered 4,500 members. By the end of 2003, membership had grown to 81,000. Then, within a year of its launch, the site increased to 500,000 members worldwide (Rameshbhai, 2011). LinkedIn is a free online SM, but its premium services (such as LinkedIn jobs), which began in May 2005, are for a fee. We will now look at the benefits of LinkedIn to users including businesses.

Benefits of LinkedIn

Information integrity

The quality of professional content created in LinkedIn provides immense opportunities for users. LinkedIn increases the efficiency of building references that may be useful at strategic times, especially in relation to job openings, interviews and contract negotiations. Due to the strict adherence at the core of the site, many human resource (HR) professionals and CEOs of multinationals utilize the professional profile information created by users as a base for accessing potential employment seekers (Barrigar, 2009).

Quality connections

An important feature in LinkedIn is the 'LinkedIn Today' news section, which gives users the opportunity to qualify the connections they make by following relevant industry news and using the information as the context with which they build quality. LinkedIn is also very efficient when it comes to business-to-business (B2B) networking. In March 2011, a study surveyed 600 professionals who were knowledgeable about their company's marketing strategy. The results showed that Facebook is more effective for business-to-customer marketing but LinkedIn is still the best platform for B2B networking (Kaplan and Haenlein, 2010).

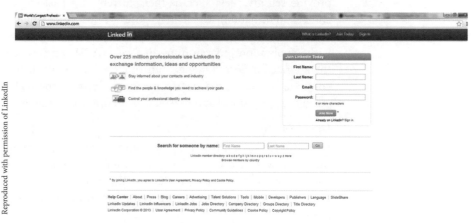

Reproduced with permission of LinkedIn

Reliable referrals

The chances of connecting with relevant professionals in building a strong and reliable referral base are relatively high in LinkedIn, due to the professionally structured orientation of the site.

Company tracking

LinkedIn provides the opportunity for users to track companies related to their job interests. For instance, a user can get first-hand information about openings in the sales department of XYZ Company from a LinkedIn connection before the offer is publicly posted. The career benefits of LinkedIn in this regard cannot be over-emphasized. Users can be professionally profiled, which will allow other professionals looking for related skills to connect with them.

Employers' search optimization

The traditional method of recruitment includes processes such as:

- Asking candidates to submit their qualifications
- Asking a candidate to sit a workbench exercise to verify the claims on their CV
- Requesting references from third persons to verify the impressions they have about the candidate
- Forming a panel that sits before the candidate to conduct a formal interview

This comes with quite a number of limitations, such as the time spent in scheduling series of interviews and the cost of advertising an opening in the mass media (for example, TV, radio and newspapers).

To a substantial extent, the evolution of LinkedIn has helped recruiters and potential employees save time and money in connecting with the right candidates and companies respectively. Critically examining the data set of a typical LinkedIn profile page, candidates can now easily be shortlisted for interviews based on the content of their profile and the references of their connections on site (Capiluppi et al., 2013).

Disadvantages of LinkedIn

Identity theft risk

In order to optimize the full utilities that LinkedIn provides, a typical user must provide sensitive data such as their current and past employers, as well as current contact information, which may pose a huge vulnerability in the area of identity theft if a breach in LinkedIn security settings occurs. Making use of this vulnerability is the application programming interface (API), which allows users to synchronize their LinkedIn post contents with other SNSs to which they belong. Pundits have continuously argued that a strict measure of privacy should be implemented to distinguish the professional and personal life of SM users (Anderson and Stajano, 2012).

Operation costs

LinkedIn runs a multi-tier membership system for premium users to gain access to the more advanced features – such as reference searches, contacting any LinkedIn connection directly via e-mail and the instant messaging system that the site provides. The user must pay an executive monthly fee of £48.95 or a business plus fee of £29.95.

This fee may not be financially feasible for the average qualified college graduate still living with his/her parent, thus hindering the chances of quality potential employees creating a connection with the right companies and vice versa.

Too much information

One of the greatest security vulnerabilities of modern SNSs is the dissemination of too much information. LinkedIn is the leading site that requires too much information from users that could be exploited by competitors of an organization, a former employee gone rogue or cyber criminals with malicious intentions. For example, people who work as IT professionals in companies providing services such as firewall vendors, hardware vendors and penetration testers may include the items shown in Figure 13.4 in their list of work experience on their LinkedIn profiles.

Currently working with IT security	Management, Office & QA support software
Firewalls Proxy servers Mail gateways AntiVirus Spam Encryption PKI OS • Windows 2000, Windows 2003 • Windows XP • Linux Red Hat, SUSE SLES Product experience • Checkpoint • Cisco • BlueCoat • RSA Security • Symantec • Trend Micro • F-Secure • Exim • Spamassassin Linux security baselines Windows security baselines Disaster recovery guidelines Service level agreements	Microsoft Office (Excel, Word, Access) Operating systems/system tools • FreeBSD (3 years experience) • Windows 2000/03 (8 years experience) • Windows XP (5 years experience) • SMTP (Postfix) (2 years experience) • imap (2 years experience) • pop3 (2 years experience) • spamassassin (1 year experience) • cyrus-sasl2 (1 year experience) • clamav (2 years experience) • apache (2 years experience) • mysql (2 years experience) • postgresql (2 months experience) • rrdtool (1 year experience) • nagios (1 year experience) • snmp (2 years experience) • snort (1 year experience) • nessus (1 year experience) • radius (1 year experience) • squid (2 years experience) • pppd (2 years experience) • bind (2 years experience) • jail (1 year experience) • ftpd (2 years experience)

Figure 13.4: Typical profile information of an IT security professional

From the information given, an attacker would have access to the degree of security measures the target company uses to protect itself as well as the type of operating system and how long it has been used. For a highly experienced malware attacker, this is enough information to launch a devastating attack on the victim company and, in the long run, impact negative financial consequences on the business (Lenkart, 2011).

13

THE IMPACTS AND BENEFITS OF SOCIAL MEDIA

The usefulness of the internet has grown from initial services such as emails and basic graphical-based websites into a mainstream phenomenon. In today's technological era, there is unlimited access to the internet from various locations such as cybercafés, offices and homes through the rapid development of computing tools such as desktop computers, laptops, tablets, smartphones and notebooks, which are readily obtainable and quite affordable.

Think and discuss

Develop a proposal outlining which social media platform(s) O2 might use to reach and deliver value to customers more effectively; recommend (with justification) the most viable option for the company in your opinion.

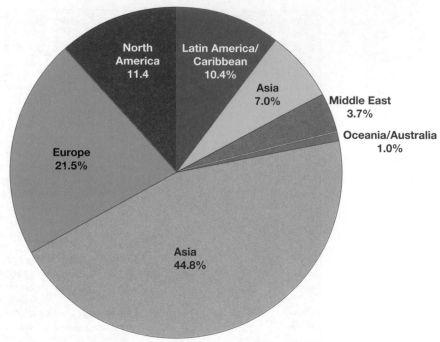

Figure 13.5: World statistics of internet users, 2012
Source: Internetworldstats, 2012

Evolving from a phase of mere popularity to an absolute necessity over the last ten years, the internet has increased **exponentially** with the development of creative web-based applications such as SNSs (Facebook, LinkedIn, Instagram), real-time blogs, micro-blogs (Tumblr, Twitter), instant messaging, e-commerce, social-commerce, live video streaming, podcasting, webinars and cloud storage applications such as Google drive and Dropbox (Narendran, 2010).

Information technologists have associated the sudden rise of the internet with the proliferation of tablets, mobile phones and other smartwares, as well as machine-to-machine connections, thus increasing the demand for internet connectivity. Projections for 2016 are that 18.9 billion network connections will have been created, which is equivalent to an average 2.5 connections for each person. Forecasts also reveal that by 2016 there are expected to be 3.4 billion internet users, which represents 45 per cent of the world's projected population from the United Nations report. Broadband speed is also expected to increase from nine megabits per second (Mbps) in 2011 to 34 megabits per second in 2016 (Cisco, 2013).

Analysts have also predicted that 1.2 million video minutes travel the internet every second by 2016, with more than half of the world's internet traffic coming from wi-fi connections (business-technology-roundtable, 2013).

MOTIVATION FOR SOCIAL MEDIA USAGE

Social networks such as Facebook, LinkedIn, Instagram and Twitter have now become a daily routine for many people, who regularly update individual text and image statuses and also check what 'friends', 'connections' or 'followers' are doing in real time. The rapid growth of user registrations, dissemination of sensitive information and networks on SNSs makes it a huge tool for marketing and advertising for most companies seeking to improve brand quality and internet significance.

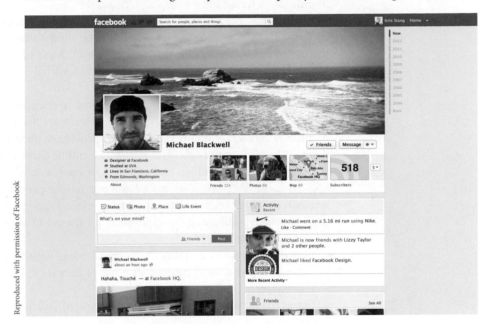

Reproduced with permission of Facebook

Therefore, the study of users' motivation for social media usage is an important resource for the improvement of service by social media providers, which of course includes security and functionality in order to optimize users' experience.

To explain this sub-topic, we will now explore the findings from other related work concerning the main motivations behind the use of SM.

- **A source of pleasure and enjoyment:** According to recent research, the most influential factor behind the continued use of SNSs is the following by a high number of 'friends'. Moreover, perceived compliments that users receive on posts have a greater influence than the number of 'friends'. The findings also revealed a notable difference in SM usage between men and women. The number of 'friends' is a determinant factor affecting their use for women but this is not the case for men. Sledgianowski and Kulviwat (2009) argued that an SNS is a pleasure-oriented information system that the individual becomes more willing to use as more friends or peers join. In 2010, Baker and White supported this argument. Based on these considerations, this study posits that in the context of a pleasure-oriented information system, pleasure and enjoyment are principal motivations for its continued use (Baker and White, 2010).
- **Variation in personality behaviours:** Investigating the role of personality behaviours as one of the factors in the use of SM has often involved a descriptive analysis

13

of five broad personality traits. These are **neuroticism**, extraversion, openness, agreeableness and conscientiousness. Neuroticism is a personality dimension that is described by adjectives such as tense (vs. relaxed), nervous (vs. at ease) and moody (vs. steady) and its inverse is labelled emotional stability (Denissen and Penne, 2008).

Extroverts are typically adventurous, sociable and talkative, whereas introverts are typically quiet and shy. Extraversion has been shown to correspond with the use of the instant messaging system that some SM sites provide, such as Facebook. Within Facebook, extraverts have been shown to be members of more 'groups' and in most cases have a huge number of 'friends'.

People with openness to experience have **scalable** interests, preferring familiarity and common practice. Openness has been demonstrated to correspond with the use of instant messaging services and with the use of a wider variety of Facebook's features such as 'poking' and 'tagging' (Amichai-Hamburger and Vinitzky, 2010).

Agreeableness can be defined as the measure of friendliness of a person. Ironically, it is believed that individuals who agree less have the tendency to have a huge number of contacts online as the use of SM provides a means to build relationships that may be difficult to establish and maintain offline (Ross et al., 2009).

Conscientious individuals are believed to have a strong inclination to avoid SNSs because they see it as a tool for promoting procrastination and mental laziness, and it serves as a distraction from more necessary tasks. Based on these analyses, six hypotheses on the motivation for the use of SM relative to personality traits are derived:

– Neuroticism may be correlated with social use of both Facebook and Twitter
– Extraversion may be correlated with use of Facebook, Instagram, Pinterest and
– Foursquare
– Extraversion may be negatively related to use of Twitter and LinkedIn
– Openness may be correlated with both social and informational use of Facebook, Twitter, LinkedIn and Tumblr
– Agreeableness may be unrelated to social network use
– Conscientiousness may be negatively correlated with Facebook, Twitter, Instagram, Pinterest, Orkut, Foursquare and Bebo

- **A tool for connecting with family and friends:** According to a report by Pew Research Center (2011), internet users say that connections with members of family and friends are the main reasons for using SM platforms such as Facebook, Twitter and Instagram.

However, some revealed that reconnecting with old classmates is the main consideration for the use of Facebook.

The figure shows that female SM users are more numerous than male users (72 per cent vs. 55 per cent). Seven in 10 users under the age of 50 say that staying in touch with current friends is a main reason they use SM platforms, and over half claim that connecting with old friends they have lost contact with is just as important. In addition, users of Twitter are more interested in connecting with celebrities than users of other SM (Kumar et al., 2013). One in 10 Twitter users revealed that reading tweets created by celebrities is a main reason they use online social networks (Jansen et al., 2009).

- **Usefulness:** Academic scholars have discovered that the usefulness of a system has a positive significant influence on the adoption of it. A user is concerned with whether the SNS has the functionality that allows the creation and maintenance of relationships and also builds profiles that give room for self-expression and promotion.

Big multinationals now routinely exploit the power of SM. Coca-Cola is a case in point. The company proactively exploits the marketing power of Facebook to engage directly with customers. Thus, the company is able to gauge customers' sentiments and reactions to its marketing as well as their changing values and preferences.

THE VIRAL PROPENSITY OF SOCIAL MEDIA

Most SM platforms provide users with modern, user-friendly functionalities to share news, opinions and information. Ironically, some online user-generated contents have been proven to be more viral. That is, a message or file self-propagates to everyone, even those who have not requested the message. Therefore, in this section of this work, the key elements affecting the viral **propensity** of some SM contents are reviewed, using a comparative analysis of the traditional mass media (TV, radio, newspapers) versus modern mass media (mobile devices, SNSs, internet), with a combination of well known case studies that aim to demystify proven hypotheses concerning some viral catalysts of a few online SM contents.

The effect of information and communications technology remains a subject of debate in the field of political science. Some early political analysts argued that the traditional media were changing election campaigns although other political observers have downplayed these hypotheses. However, 21st-century politicians have totally embraced the contemporary media (Facebook, Twitter) because they are seen as a more effective tool that **circumvents** the structured and one-way contact available to them through traditional media (Posetti, 2010; Westling, 2007).

To expand on this topic further, a brief overview on 'political candidate **salience**' is examined using Twitter. Candidate salience can be defined as the extent to which political candidates are discussed by the masses in an online SNS. According to an empirical framework, the number of discussions about a politician is equivalent to the total number of tweets about that politician (Sounman and Nadler, 2012). When a politician tweets, his followers receive the messages and a discussion is generated in the Twitter social community. This may take the form of a retweet or a comment. The higher the number of tweets made by a political candidate the greater the chance that such a candidate will be discussed in the tweeting community (Posetti, 2010). For instance, as we saw at the beginning of this chapter, the major SNS used in the political campaign of President Barack Obama was Facebook. His Facebook page relayed information about his whereabouts and relevant news from the White House. Moreover, the page listed Obama's favourite movies, television shows, books and hobbies, as seen on the average Facebook user's page. Obama's campaign team maintained Facebook pages specific to certain demographics, such as Latinos, Asian Americans and Pacific Islanders; the pages consisted of posts with relevant videos and links that related to the aforementioned demographics.

13

Example 13.2:
Viral tendencies of the world wide web

Internet reporter Matt Drudge, with only 85,000 subscribers on his maverick-styled news collation website (Drudgereport, 1998), published a story on a Saturday night to some of the audience of the world wide web. On Sunday morning the next day, the scandalous news had become a big hit on internet news groups and then it gradually flowed to the mainstream of political discussions.

Consequently, on Wednesday, the newspapers (traditional media) ran the story, which was more than three days after it had gone viral on social media websites at that time. Social media have now become part of the human race, both in personal and professional lives. Social media have a huge impact in the world of journalism, marketing, politics and product branding. Users around the world are now taking advantage of the enormous benefits associated with its persistent and targeted use.

ADVERSE IMPLICATIONS OF SOCIAL MEDIA ON EMPLOYMENT

There are many online resources on the positive impact of SM concerning employability and job opportunities. However, this section of the research examines the negative effects associated with the misuse of SM and their adverse effects on the employability of the personalities involved.

As the level of seriousness of online contents increases, the recruitment routines and protocols of most companies are changing proportionately. According to a survey of 2,667 HR professionals in Chicago, America, about 45 per cent examine the profile contents of applicants' SNSs before consideration for employment, while 11 per cent do so a year or more after the job has been granted. In the Chicago report, the industries usually interested in screening applicants through web-based SM or search engines include those specialized in business services (53 per cent), information technology (63 per cent) and public and private security industries. Some potential employers are active users of various social networks. According to the report, 29 per cent use Facebook, 26 per cent use LinkedIn, 21 per cent use MySpace, 11 per cent make good use of blogs and search engines while about 7 per cent ardently follow potential applicants on Twitter.

SM recruiting is fast becoming a de facto standard and an essential tool for HR practices. Jobvite, a recruitment software provider, published a report in 2012 that revealed that 92 per cent of US companies are using SNSs, with LinkedIn taking the lead as the first preference for potential employers.

Unfortunately, the Jobvite report showed that almost three out of four potential employers and HR professionals still check candidates' SM profiles, with nearly 48 per cent claiming they do so even if the profile names of prospective applicants are not provided. Potential candidates are denied job placements when unethical and immoral contents are found on their page.

At the time of preparing this work, a real-life scenario, which occurred on 9 April 2013, showed all to clearly the potential effects of the misuse of SM on the employability and reputation of a user. A controversial story that was published online reported that the first Kent youth police and crime commissioner, Paris Brown, had quit her job after investigations into racist and homophobic tweets she had made on Twitter about three years earlier. The offensive tweets boasted about her sex life, violence, drinking, drugs and binges, which eventually cost her the £15,000-a-year taxpayer-funded position and a dented reputation.

CONCLUSION

The reviews contained in this chapter show that the growth of the Internet is the driving force behind the sudden rise of its relevance to daily activity and its ease of use. As a result, many have predicted a phenomenal growth of the web by 2016, as the internet grows exponentially. Then the importance of SM will continue to increase and marketers will need to understand and employ the evolving power of SM. The chapter went on to report on the concept of macro-blogging and micro-blogging and how product owners are benefiting from these solutions.

In addition, there was a historical review of the earliest social networks, which showed that many social networks did not last because there were very few user-engaging apps and widgets to embed in such sites. The viral propensity of social networks was explored through real-life case studies to demonstrate the sheer power and reach of SM.

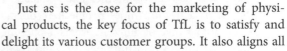

Case study
Social media marketing at TfL

Transport for London (TfL), which was created in the year 2000, essentially to implement the Mayor's transport strategy for London, is widely known for its role in the city of London. As a city that attracts tourists from all over the world and serves as home to many professionals, it is imperative to have an efficient transportation system – this is the responsibility of TfL. To create value for its various customer groups, the organization manages several transportation-related activities, which include London's buses, London's river services, Docklands Light Railway (DLR), London Underground, and London Overground.

Reproduced with permission of TfL

Just as is the case for the marketing of physical products, the key focus of TfL is to satisfy and delight its various customer groups. It also aligns all its marketing mix elements to be geared towards creating and delivering value to these customers, who are of different age groups and various lifestyles. One of the elements that has experienced dramatic and unprecedented change in recent times is marketing communications. Like most other customer-oriented companies, the tools in TfL's integrated marketing communications system have been significantly widened to include SM tools such as Facebook, Twitter and YouTube to deliver and communicate value to its

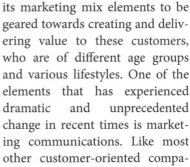

13

various customer segments. TfL customers now use SM tools to check updates about travelling around the city.

The role of SM in TfL's marketing communication strategy became more appreciated during the London 2012 Olympics. The company used this avenue as an opportunity to warn its customers about busy routes, and advised them of alternatives that could save them the stress or the complexities that may have arisen if extremely busy routes were used. Since marketing is about identifying the needs and wants of the target markets and providing appropriate offerings to satisfy them, at a profit to the organization, TfL was not ready to sacrifice its customers' satisfaction for anything else, especially during this historic moment. So, apart from making transportation provision for customers to move freely to various Games centres and other places of interest, the company extended its use of SM during the London 2012 Games as part of its 'Get Ahead of the Games' campaign. For example, there were individual Twitter accounts for each of London Underground's Tube lines. This meant that commuters who would be travelling on the Bakerloo line could be well informed about how their journey might be affected by the planned travelling schedules on the Northern, Jubilee, Victoria and other lines. As a sign of its deep commitment to creating value for its customers, TfL ensured that these Twitter accounts were linked to its main SM channels on YouTube and Facebook. In the words of Vernon Everitt, the TfL Marketing and Communications Managing Director, 'With a million more people here during the Games and a range of different events happening every day, our public transport network and roads will be exceptionally busy ... our SM tools ... are an increasingly important way of offering people advice and support'. This anticipatory comment from Everitt indicates that, like other marketing communication tools, SM also involves planning to be sure the information being disseminated is reaching the receiver.

In most cases, effective use of SM is closely linked to the activities of other businesses. This is evident in the case of TfL. Its use of SM involves working closely with other strategic partners such as O2 and Virgin Media. As Londoners now have access to the internet on more than 120 stations, the use of SM by TfL customers is on the increase. As London Underground celebrated its 150th anniversary in January 2013, it became very clear to customers that the transport company has changed significantly over the years by using modern technology to improve customer service, including the use of SM. So customer-focused companies like TfL have realized that, to create value for customers, the use of SM as a marketing communication tool is becoming increasingly relevant.

**By Dr Ayantunji Gbadamosi,
University of East London, UK**

Sources

Ingram, K. (2013) 'Facebook Case Study: Marketing with Coca-Cola'. Available at: http://www.cmswire.com/cms/customer-experience/facebook-case-study-marketing-with-cocacola-020927.php. Accessed 1 June 2013.

Moth, D. (2013) 'How Coca-Cola uses Facebook, Twitter, Pinterest, and Google'. Available at: http://econsultancy.com/uk/blog/62548-how-coca-cola-uses-facebook-twitter-pinterest-and-google. Accessed 1 June 2013.

Questions

1 Using TfL as an example, explain how a transportation firm can use SM to create value for its customers.

2 Assume you have been invited to give a talk on the benefits of the use of SM tools to a service-oriented firm like TfL. What will be the basic points that you will discuss at this event?

3 Explain how TfL can use Facebook and Twitter to introduce new products or processes.

4 Which of the SM tools including those being used by TfL would you recommend to a friend who is about to open a new restaurant in London? Give reasons to support your choice.

Review questions

1 What is the best definition of social media?
2 Why are there many definitions of SM?
3 Is there a gender difference in the usage of each type of SM in marketing?
4 Is economic class a factor in the usage of SM?
5 How are multinationals such as Coca-Cola using the marketing power of SM?

Group tasks

1 Each member of the group should open a new Twitter account and explore the interaction in sharing viral videos on YouTube. Then every member should visit the Excellence in Education programme's Facebook page and record the number of likes and comments on the most recent postings. This should be compared with the BBC and CNN pages.
2 Using Google as a search engine, identify other multinationals similar to Coca-Cola that have used SM for their marketing campaigns in the last six months. Find out the advantages of less popular SM sites such as yookos.com or sleeky.net.

Glossary/Key terms

Avatar: An image or username that represents a person online within forums and social networks.

Blog: A word that was created from 'weblog'. Blogs are usually maintained by an individual or a business, with regular entries of commentary, descriptions of events or other material such as graphics or video. Entries are commonly displayed in reverse-chronological order. 'Blog' can also be used as a verb, meaning to *maintain or add content to a blog.*

Blogger: A free blogging platform owned by Google that allows individuals and companies to host and publish a blog, typically on a subdomain – example: your blogname.blogspot.com; a person who blogs.

Bookmarking: Online bookmarking follows the same idea as placing a bookmark in a physical publication – you are simply marking something you found important or enjoyed, or noting where you left off to continue reading later. The only difference online is that it is happening through websites, using one of the various bookmarking services available such as Delicious.

Connections: The LinkedIn equivalent of a Facebook 'friend' is a 'connection'. Because LinkedIn is a social networking site, the people you are *connecting* with are not necessarily people you are friends with, but rather have met in brief, heard speak or know through another connection.

Facebook: A social utility that connects people with friends and others who work, study or live around them. Facebook is the largest social network in the world with more than 800 million users.

Flickr: A social network based around online picture sharing. The service allows users to store photos online and then share them with others through profiles, groups, sets and other methods.

Forum: Also known as a message board, a forum is an online discussion site. It originated as the modern equivalent of a traditional bulletin board, and a technological evolution of the dial-up bulletin board system.

13

Google+: Google's new social network. It differs in that it promotes social sharing that is more similar to how people share in real life by providing features such as the ability to limit who you are talking to, creating one-to-one conversation.

hi5: A social network focused on the youth market. It is a social entertainment destination, with a focus on delivering a fun and entertainment-driven social experience online to users around the world.

Inbound marketing: A style of marketing that essentially focused on permission-based marketing techniques that businesses can use to get found by potential customers. They convert those prospects into leads and customers, and analyse the process along the way. Inbound marketing leverages tactics such as search engine optimization, blogging, SM, lead generation, email marketing, lead nurturing and analytics. It is in direct contrast to outbound marketing, which utilizes traditional interruptive marketing tactics such as direct mail, trade shows, print and TV advertising, and cold calling.

Instant messaging: A form of real-time, direct text-based communication between two or more people. More advanced instant messaging software allow clients enhanced modes of communication, such as live voice or video calling.

LinkedIn: A business-oriented SNS. Founded in December 2002 and launched in May 2003, it is mainly used for professional networking. As of June 2010, LinkedIn had more than 70 million registered users, spanning more than 200 countries and territories worldwide.

LinkedIn Today: LinkedIn's own version of a social news service. Every industry on LinkedIn (marketing, journalism, technology, etc.) has its own LinkedIn Today. Stories are selected based on which ones are posted and shared the most by users of LinkedIn.

MySpace: An SNS owned by News Corporation, MySpace became the most popular SNS in the US in June 2006 and was overtaken internationally by its main competitor, Facebook, in April 2008.

News feed: Literally, a feed full of news. On Facebook, the news feed is the homepage of users' accounts where they can see all the latest updates from their friends. The news feed on Twitter is called Timeline (not to be confused with Facebook's new look, also called Timeline).

Podcast: A non-streamed webcast that is a series of digital media files, either audio or video, released episodically and often downloaded through an RSS feed.

Retweet: When someone on Twitter sees your message and decides to share it with his/her followers. A retweet button allows them to resend the message quickly with attribution to the original tweeter.

Social media: Media designed to be disseminated through social interaction, created using highly accessible and scalable publishing techniques.

Social media monitoring: A process of checking and responding to mentions related to a business that occur in SM.

Trending: The most popular term searched by users of a search engine within a period.

Vocab check list for ESL students

Artefact	Empirical	Polarized	Scalable
Circumvents	Exponentially	Propensity	Semantic
Elucidated	Neuroticism	Salience	

Definitions for these terms can be found in the 'Vocab Zone' of the companion website, which provides free access to the Macmillan English Dictionary online at www.palgrave.com/business/Gbadamosi

Further reading

J. Akunuri (2011) 'Internet Marketing' in S. Nwankwo and A. Gbadamosi (eds) *Entrepreneurship Marketing: Principles and Practice of SME Marketing*. Oxford: Routledge, pp. 171–95

This book chapter looks at how the use of social media is increasingly being embraced by small and medium-sized enterprises (SMEs) and discusses various approaches these businesses adopt to the use of this marketing communication mode to create and deliver value to their customers.

M. Bruhn, V. Schoenmueller and D. B. Schäfer (2012) 'Are Social Media Replacing Traditional Media in Terms of Brand Equity Creation?', *Management Research Review*, Vol. 35, No. 9, pp. 770–90

Essentially, this paper investigates the relative impact of brand communication on brand equity through social media as compared with traditional media.

L. Hansson, A. Wrangmo and K. S. Søilen (2013) 'Optimal Ways for Companies to use Facebook as a Marketing Channel', *Journal of Information, Communication and Ethics in Society*, Vol. 11, No. 2, pp. 112–26

Even though a good number of users are familiar with business and marketing activities on Facebook, they use it basically for fun and personal purposes. The aim of this paper is to discover how companies can optimize their use of Facebook as a marketing channel.

M. Mitic and A. Kapoulas (2012) 'Understanding the Role of Social Media in Bank Marketing', *Marketing Intelligence and Planning*, Vol. 30, No. 7, pp. 668–86

This paper investigates the role of Web 2.0 and social media in relationship marketing (RM) in the banking sector. It is positioned to address why some banks resist the Web 2.0 trend, how this is aligned with their RM approaches and what the alternative paths for advancing customer relations could be.

References

Aggarwal, A., Singan, A. R., Kumaraguru, P. (2012) 'PhishAri: Automatic Realtime Phishing Detection on Twitters'. *IEEE*, 1 (1), pp. 1–12

Aghaei, S., Nematbakhsh, M.A., Farsani, H.K. (2012) 'Evolution Of The World Wide Web: From Web 1.0 to Web 4.0'. *International Journal of Web & Semantic Technology*, 3 (1), pp. 1–10

Aleksandrovna, M. Y. (2012) *Sentiment Analysis Within and Across Social Media Streams*. PhD Thesis. University of Iowa: USA

Amichai-Hamburger, Y., & Vinitzky, G. (2010) 'Social Network Use and Personality'. *Computers in Human Behaviour (ScienceDirect)*, 26, pp. 1289–95

Anderson, J. and Stajano, F. (2012) 'Not That Kind of Friend: Misleading Divergences between Online Social Networks and Real-World Social Protocols'. *University of Cambridge Computer Laboratory*, 1 (1), pp. 1–6

Auradkar, A., Botev, C., Das, S. et al. (2012) 'Data Infrastructure at LinkedIn' *2012 IEEE 28th Inernational Conference on Data Engineering*, 1–5 April 2012, Washington DC, pp. 1370–81

13

Baker, R. K. and White, K. M. (2010) 'Predicting aAdolescents' Use of Social Networking Sites from an Extended Theory of Planned Behaviour Perspective'. *Computers in Human Behaviour*, 26, pp. 1591–97

Barrigar, J. (2009) 'Social Network Site Privacy; A Comparative Analysis of Six Sites'. *Office of the Privacy Commissioner of Canada*, 1 (1), pp. 1–52

BBC News (1998) 'Scandalous Scoop Breaks Online'. Available at: http://news.bbc.co.uk/1/hi/special_report/1998/clinton_scandal/50031.stm. (Accessed 3 April 2013)

Bernstein, M. S., Bakshy, E., Burke, M., Karrer, B. (2013) 'Quantifying the Invisible Audience in Social Networks. *Stanford University HCI Group*', 1 (1), pp. 1–5

Brewster, T. (2013) 'Privacy Regulator Keeps an Eye on Facebook Graph Search'. Available at: www.techweekeurope.co.uk/news/irish-privacy-regulator-facebook-graph-search-104507. (Accessed 16 March 2013)

Business-technology-roundtable (2013) 'Five Key Factors Drive the Internet Growth Trajectory'. Available at: http://business-technology-roundtable.blogspot.co.uk/2012/05/five-key-factors-drive-Internet-growth.html. (Accessed 3 April 2013)

Butt, S. and Phillips, J. G. (2008) 'Personality and Self-Reported Mobile Phone Use'. *Computers in Human Behaviour*, 24 (2), pp. 346–60

Capiluppi, A., Serebrenik, A. and Singer, L. (2013) 'Assessing Technical Candidates on the Social Web'. *IEEE Software*. 1 (13), pp. 45–51

Career Builder (2009) 'Forty-five Percent of Employers Use Social Networking Sites to Research Job Candidates, CareerBuilder Survey Finds'. Available at: www.careerbuilder.com/share/aboutus/pressreleasesdetail.aspx?id=pr519&sd=8/19/2009&ed=12/31/2009. (Accessed 3 March 2013)

Checkfacebook (2013) Checkfacebook. Available at: www.checkfacebook.com/. (Accessed 16 March 2013)

Chen, R. (2013) 'Member Use of Social Networking Sites — An Empirical Examination'. *Decision Support Systems (Science Direct)*, 11 (54), pp. 1219–27

Child, J. T., Haridakis, Paul M., Petronio, Sandra (2012) 'Blogging Privacy Rule Orientations, Privacy Management, and Content Deletion Practices: The Variability of Online Privacy Management Activity at Different Stages of Social Media Use'. *Computers in Human Behaviour (Science Direct)*, 1 (28), pp. 1859–72

Child, J. T., Petronio, S., Esther A., Budu, A. and Westermann, D. A. (2011) 'Blog Scrubbing: Exploring Triggers That Change Privacy Rules'. *Computers in Human Behavior (ScienceDirect)*, 27 (5), pp. 2017–27

Christofides, E., Muise, A. and Desmarais, S. (2012) 'Hey Mom, What's on Your Facebook? Comparing Facebook Disclosure and Privacy in Adolescents and Adults'. *Social Psychological and Personality Science*, 1 (2), pp. 1–8

Christopher, M. H., Heng, X., Joey, J. L. and Mary, B. R. (2009) 'Privacy as Information Access and Illusory Control: The Case of the Facebook News Feed Privacy Outcry'. *Electronic Commerce Research and Applications*, 9 (1), pp. 50–60

CIPR, The Chartered Institute of Public Relations (2012) *Share This: The Social Media Handbook for PR Professionals*. UK: Wiley

Cisco (2013) 'Cisco Visual Networking Index: Global Mobile Data Traffic Forecast Update', 2012–2017. Available at: www.cisco.com/en/US/solutions/collateral/ns341/ns525/ns537/ns705/ns827/white_paper_c11-520862.html. (Accessed 12 March 2013)

Correa, T., Willard, A. and Gil de Zúñiga, H. (2010) 'Who Interacts on the Web? The Intersection of Users' Personality and Social Media Use'. *Computers in Human Behaviour,* 26, pp. 247–53

Davies, L. (2010) 'Timeline: a History of Social Networking Sites'. Available at: http://lauramdavies.wordpress.com/2010/02/11/timeline-a-history-of-social-networking-sites/. (Accessed 3 April 2013)

Denissen, J. A. and Penne, L. (2008) 'Neuroticism Predicts Reactions to Cues of Social Inclusion'. *European Journal of Personality*, 22 (3), pp. 497–517

Diffen (2012) 'Facebook vs. Twitter'. Available at: www.diffen.com/difference/Facebook_vs_Twitter. (Accessed 18 March 2012)

Drudgereport (1998) 'Newsweek Kills Story On White House Intern'. Available at: www.drudgereportarchives.com/data/2002/01/17/20020117_175502_ml.htm. (Accessed 3 March 2013)

Dubai School of Government (2012) 'Social Media in the Arab World: Influencing Societal and Cultural Change'? *Arab Social Media Report,* 2 (1), pp. 1–29

Fan, T. and Chang, C. (2011) 'Blogger-Centric Contextual Advertising'. *Expert Systems with Applications*, 38 (1), pp. 1777–88

Friendster (2003) 'Friendster'. Available at: www.friendster.com/. (Accessed 10 March 2013)

Guadagno, R. E., Okdie, B. M. and Eno, C. A. (2008) 'Who Blogs? Personality Predictors of Blogging'. *Computers in Human Behaviour*, 24 (5), pp. 1993–2004

Gupta, M., Jha, S. C., Koc, A. T. and Vannithamby, R. (2013) 'Energy Impact of Emerging Mobile Internet Applications on LTE Networks: Issues and Solutions'. *IEEE Journals & Magazines*, 51 (2), pp. 90–7

Gracia, D., Mavrodiev, P. and Frank Schweitzer, F. (2013) *Social Resilience in Online Communities: The Autopsy of Friendster.* Available at: www.sg.ethz.ch/research/publications/. (Accessed 1 June 2013)

Hagar, C. (2013) 'Crisis Informatics: Perspectives of Trust – Is Social Media a Mixed Blessing?' *SLIS Student Research Journal,* 2 (2), pp. 1–6

Hampton, K. N., Goulet, L. S., Rainie, L. and Purcell, K. (2011) 'Social Networking Sites and Our Lives'. *Pew Research Center*, 1 (1), pp. 1–84

Helm, R., Moller, M., Mauroner, O. and Conrad, D. (2013) 'The Effects of a Lack of Social Recognition on Online Communication Behaviour'. *Computers in Human Behaviour (ScienceDirect)*, 29 (3), pp. 1065–77

HubSpot (2011) 'Study: LinkedIn Is More Effective for B2B Companies'. Available at: http://blog.hubspot.com/blog/tabid/6307/bid/10437/Study-LinkedIn-Is-More-Effective-for-B2B-Companies.aspx. (Accessed 8 March 2013)

Internetworldstats (2012) 'Internet Usage Statistics: the Internet Big Picture'. Available at: www.Internetworldstats.com/stats.htm. (Accessed 5 March 2013)

Jansen, B. J., Zhang, M., Sobel, K. and Chowdury, A. (2009) 'Twitter Power: Tweets as Electronic Word of Mouth'. *Journal of the American Society for Information Science and Technology*, 60 (11), pp. 2169–88

Jennifer, B. (2009) 'Social Networking Site Privacy; A Comparative Analysis of Six Sites'. *The office of the privacy commissioner of Canada*, 1 (1), pp. 1–52

Kaplan, A. M. and Haenlein, M. (2010) 'Users of the World, Unite! The Challenges and Opportunities of Social Media'. *Business Horizons,* 53 (1), pp. 59–68

Kietzmann, J. H., Hermkens, K., McCarthy, I. P. and Silvestre, B. S. (2011) 'Social

13

Media? Get Serious! Understanding the Functional Building Blocks of Social Media'. *Business Horizons*, 54 (3), pp. 241–51

Kumar, S., Morstatter, F., Zafarani, R., Liu, H. (2013) 'Whom Should I Follow? Identifying Relevant Users during Crises'. ACM Conference on Hypertext and Social Media, 1 (1), pp. 1–9

Lee, P. J. (2010) 'A Qualitative Study of the Facebook Social Network: The Desire to Influence, Associate, and Construct a Representative and Ideal Identity'. MA Thesis. Long Beach, CA 90840: California State University.

Lenkart, J. J. (2011) 'The Vulnerability of Social Networking Media and the Insider Threat: New Eyes for Bad Guys'. MA Thesis. Monterey, California: Naval Postgraduate School.

Lenney, J. (2012) 'Use Social Media Marketing to Grow Your Business'. Available at: www.empowernetwork.com/empowerftw/use-social-media-marketing-togrow-your-business/?id=empowerftw. (Accessed 9 April 2013)

Lin, K. Y., Lu, H. P. (2010) 'Why People Use Social Networking Sites: An Empirical Study Integrating Network Externalities and Motivation Theory'. *Computers in Human Behaviour (ScienceDirect)*, 27 (3), pp. 1152–61

LinkedIn (2013) *About LinkedIn*. Available at: www.linkedin.com/about-us. (Accessed 26 March 2013)

Magda, C. and Hana, M. (2012) 'Social Media and Home Education'. *Social Media and the Impact on Education,* 12, pp. 236–39

Mashable (2013) 'MySpace' Available at: http://mashable.com/category/myspace/. (Accessed 5 April 2013)

MySpace (2013) 'This is MySpace'. Available at: https://new.myspace.com/. (Accessed 9 March 2013)

Narendran, C. R. (2010) 'Exploitation of Vulnerabilities in Cloud Storage'. MSc Thesis. London UK: University of East London.

Onishia, H. and Manchanda, P. (2012) 'Marketing Activity, Blogging and Sales'. *International Journal of Research in Marketing*, 29 (3), pp. 221–34

Pai, P. and Arnott, C. (2013) 'User Adoption of Social Networking Sites: Eliciting Uses and Gratifications Through a Means–End Approach'. *Computers in Human Behaviour (ScienceDirect)*, 29 (3), pp. 1039–53

Paul, J. A., Baker, Hope M. and Cochran, Justin Daniel (2012) 'Effect of Online Social Networking on Student Academic Performance'. *Computers in Human Behaviour (ScienceDirect)*, 1 (28), pp. 2117–27

Paula, A. M. G. D. (2010) 'Security Aspects and Future Trends of Social Networks', *The International Journal of Forensic Computer Science*, 1 (1), pp. 60–79

Pew Research Centre (2012) *The Demographics of Social Media Users – 2012.* Available at: www.pewinternet.org/Reports/2013/Social-media-users.aspx. (Accessed 18 March 2013)

Pontiggia, A. and Virili, F. (2010). 'Network Effects in Technology Acceptance: Laboratory Experimental Evidence'. *International Journal of Information Management*, 30, pp. 68–7

Posetti, J. (2010) 'The #Spill Effect: Twitter Hashtag Upends Australian Political Journalism'. Available at: www.pbs.org/mediashift/2010/03/the-spill-effect-twitter-hashtag-upends-australian-political-journalism061.html. (Accessed 4 March 2013)

Rameshbhai, P. A. (2011) 'Comparative Study and Analysis of Social Networking Sites'. MSc Thesis. San Diego, CA: San Diego State University

Ross, C., Orr, E. S., Sisic, M., Arseneault, J. M., Simmering, M. G. and Orr, R. R. (2009) 'Personality and Motivations Associated with Facebook Use'. *Computers in Human Behaviour*, 25 (2), pp. 578–86.

Sadaf, A., Newby, T. J. and Ertmer, P. A. (2012) 'Exploring Pre-service Teachers' Beliefs about Using Web 2.0 Technologies in K-12 Classroom'. *Computers & Education*, 59 (3), pp. 937–45.

Safaran, C. (2010) 'Social Media in Education'. PhD Thesis. 8010 Graz, Austria: Graz University of Technology.

Shadbolt, N., Hall, W., Hendler, J. and Dutton, W. (2013) 'Web Science: a New Frontier', The Royal Society (Mathematical, Physical and Engineering Sciences), 371 (1987), pp. 1–6

Sixdegrees (2013) 'sixdegrees'. Available at: www.sixdegrees.com. (Accessed 9 March 2013)

Sledgianowski, D. and Kulviwat, S. (2009) 'Using Social Network Sites: The Effects of Playfulness, Critical Mass and Trust in a Hedonic Context'. *Journal of Computer Information Systems*, 1 (1), pp. 74–83

Slideshare (2013) 'The World's Largest Professional Networking Site has Over 200 Million Users in 200 Countries'. Available at: www.slideshare.net/punchmedia/linkedin-statistics-2013. (Accessed 26 March 2013)

Smith, C. (2013) How Many People Use the Top Social Media, Apps & Services? Available at: http://expandedramblings.com/index.php/resource-how-many-people-use-the-top-social-media/. (Accessed 16 March 2013)

Sorensen, L. (2009) 'User Managed Trust in Social Networking – Comparing Facebook, MySpace and LinkedIn'. *IEEE*, 1 (1), pp. 427–31

Sounman, H. and Nadler, D. (2012) 'Does the Early Bird Move the Polls? The Use of the Social Media Tool "Twitter" by U.S. Politicians and its Impact on Public Opinion', *Proceedings of the 12th Annual Interntional Digital Government Research Conference*, 12–15 June 2012, College Park, MD, pp. 182–6

Spivack, N. (2011) 'Web 3.0: The Third Generation Web is Coming'. Available at: http://lifeboat.com/ex/web.3.0. (Accessed 8 April 2013)

Su, C. L., Liu, C. C., and Lee, Y. D. (2010) 'Effect of Commitment and Trust Towards Micro-Blogs on Consumer Behavioural Intention: A Relationship Marketing Perspective'. *International Journal of Electronic Business Management*, 8 (4), pp. 292–303

Thackeray, R., Neiger, Brad L., Hanson, Carl L. and McKenzie, James F. (2008) 'Enhancing Promotional Strategies within Social Marketing Programs: Use of Web 2.0 Social Media'. *SAGE*, 9 (4), pp. 338–43

Thomas, K. and Nicol, D. M. (2010) 'The Koobface Botnet and the Rise of Social Malware'. *IEEE*, 1 (1), pp. 63–70

Tumasjan, A., Sprenger, T. O., Sandner, P. G. and Welpe, I. M. (2010) 'Predicting Elections with Twitter: What 140 Characters Reveal about Political Sentiment'. *Proceedings of the Fourth International AAAI Conference on Weblogs and Social Media*, 1 (1), pp. 178–85

Tumblr (2013) 'Follow the Blogs You've Been Hearing About. Share The Things That You Love'. Available at: https://www.tumblr.com/. (Accessed 10 March 2013)

13

Twellow (2013) 'Get Twitter Followers'. Available at: www.twellow.com/. (Accessed 10 March 2013)

Urch, B. (2013) *How Raytheon Software Tracks you Online* [Video]. Available at: www.guardian.co.uk/world/video/2013/feb/10/raytheon-software-tracks-online-video. (Accessed 28 February 2013)

Westling, M. (2007) 'Expanding the Public Sphere: The Impact of Facebook on Political Communication [Project]'. Madison: University of Wisconsin. Available at: www.thenewvernacular.com/projects/facebook_and_political_communication.pdf. (Accessed 4 March 2013)

WonKim, A., Ok-RanJeong, A. and Sang-WonLee (2010) 'On Social Websites'. *Information Systems (ScienceDirect),* 2 (35), pp. 215–36

Yuchi, X., Lee, X., Jin, J. and Yan, B. (2009) 'Measuring Internet Growth from DNS Observations'. Second International Conference on Future Information Technology and Management Engineering, 1 (1), pp. 420–3

Zhaoyun, D., Yan, J., Bin, Z. and Yi, H. (2013) 'Mining Topical Influencers Based on the Multi-Relational Network in Micro-Blogging Sites'. *School of Computer, National University of Defence Technology*, Changsha, China, 10 (1), pp. 93–104

Zuckerberg, M. (2012). Facebook Has 1 Billion Users, Mark Zuckerberg Announces In A Status Update. Available at: www.huffingtonpost.com/2012/10/04/facebook-1-billion-users_n_1938675.html. (Accessed 5 March 2013)

Acknowledgements

I would like to thank my previous students and colleagues who have worked with me on this fast-moving area of research. They include: Shaikh Mohmed Sajid, MSc (Internet Systems Engineering) and Ehinome J. Ikhalia, MSc (Information Technology). I salute the energy and enthusiasm of Anne-Marie Imafidon of Keble College, University of Oxford, and colleagues at the University of Cambridge (Security Seminar Series at the William Gates Computer Laboratory). I thank friends at the University of Oxford (Bodleian Libraries) and at the Research Division of the Excellence in Education Program (www.excellenceineducation.org.uk). I am grateful to staff at the Directorate of Research and Clinical Informatics section of Boots Healthcare PLC in London.

INDEX

Printed in China